THE PUBLICATION OF THIS BOOK IS DUE IN PART TO A GENEROUS GIFT BY THE WATSON-BROWN FOUNDATION.

The Spirit Divided

Memoirs of Civil War Chaplains

THE CONFEDERACY

Compiled & Edited by

John Wesley Brinsfield, Jr.

Mercer University Press, 2006

ISBN 0-86554-964-8
MUP/ H687

© 2005 Mercer University Press
1400 Coleman Avenue
Macon, Georgia 31207
All rights reserved

First Edition.
Second Printing

Library of Congress Cataloging-in-Publication Data

The spirit divided: memoirs of Civil War chaplains : the Confederacy /
compiled and edited by John W. Brinsfield.-- 1st ed.
p. cm.
Includes bibliographical references and index.
ISBN-13: 978-0-86554-964-7 (hardback : alk. paper)
ISBN-10: 0-86554-964-8 (hardback : alk. paper)
1. United States—History—Civil War, 1861-1865—Chaplains. 2. Chaplains,
Military—Confederate States of America—Biography. 3. United States—History—Civil
War, 1861-1865—Personal narratives, Confederate. 4. Confederate States of America.
Army—Chaplains—Biography. 5. Confederate States of America.
Army—Chaplains—History. 6. United States—History—Civil War, 1861-
1865—Religious aspects. 7. United States—History—Civil War, 1861-1865—Social
aspects. I. Brinsfield, John Wesley.
E635.S7 2006
973.7'78092275—dc22

2006001475

To Marietta Strout Branson (1918–2005),
daughter and mother of U. S. Army Chaplains,
whose encouragement and faith illumined the lives
of all those who knew her.

Contents

Preface

In 1887 the Reverend Dr. J. William Jones wrote of the Army of Northern Virginia, "any history of that army which omits an account of the wonderful influence of religion upon it—which fails to tell how the courage, discipline and morale of the whole was influenced by the humble piety and evangelical zeal of many of its officers and men—would be incomplete and unsatisfactory."[1] Since that time more than a century ago, thousands of books, articles, and websites have appeared, addressing not only religion in the Civil War armies, but also religion in American culture throughout the nineteenth century.[2] Comparatively few of these recent studies, however, have focused on the personal memoirs of Civil War chaplains and the spiritual leadership they provided both during and after the war.

Dr. Jones's warning about omitting the spiritual aspects of warfare from history is incisive. No one has ever seen an entire war, not in all of its military, political, economic, and psychological dimensions. Each participant sees only the part of the conflict in which he or she is involved. Memoirs of events from the American Civil War, or from any war for that matter, are therefore like pieces of a mosaic. When they are assembled, they form a collective impression of the innumerable dramas that took place within the minds and hearts of those who were there.

In this anthology of Civil War memoirs I have attempted to focus on a variety of primary source materials, many of them previously unpublished, to get a clearer impression of the ministries of the chaplains who served during that great conflict and of the environment in which they worked. Chaplains were among the most omnipresent observers on the battlefield, and some wrote extensively about their experiences. Eighty-seven of the 3,695 chaplains who served in both armies wrote regimental histories or

---

[1] J. William Jones, *Christ in the Camp, or Religion in the Confederate Army* (Harrisonburg VA: Sprinkle Publications, 1986) 5–6.

[2] There are currently more than 26,000 items on Web sites referencing religion and the Confederate Army as just one subset of this entire field.

published personal memoirs, not counting a multitude of letters and more than 300 official reports. Yet as far as I know, there has never been an extensive collection of memoirs from chaplains of both the Confederate and Union armies presented together.

Even as I was compiling and editing these records, new insights began to emerge. Many of the Confederate chaplains wrote that they opposed secession and submitted to it only when war was inevitable. At least two of these memoirs date from 1861 and 1864, before the war ended. Moreover, some of the ministers who became chaplains were active in ministry to slaves. They spoke out both before and during the war against the neglect and abuse of those held in bondage. For example, Rev. John L. Girardeau formed a large mission church for slaves in Charleston, South Carolina, before the war; Rev. Isaac Tichenor criticized the abuses of the slave system before the Alabama Legislature in 1863, and Chaplain Charles Oliver preached to black laborers in the Army of Northern Virginia in 1864 and believed that more needed to be done for them. While these efforts may appear trivial in the face of the enormity of the entire slave system, they do reflect that a social conscience was not completely lacking among the Southern chaplains.

Among the Union chaplains, I found numerous examples of ministering to the wounded of both sides, without discrimination, and a strong interest in helping freedmen and women gain an education for a place in a reunited country. Chaplain John McCulloch, for example, became the president of one of the first black colleges in Tennessee, and Chaplain Henry M. Turner worked for the Freedmen's Bureau before becoming chancellor of Morris Brown College in Atlanta and eventually an AME bishop.

One of the most common theological questions asked on both sides was, "Whose side is God on?" President Jefferson Davis declared the cause of Southern Independence to be a holy endeavor; President Abraham Lincoln wondered if the entire war was not an atonement for the national sin of slavery.[3] Chaplain Thomas Caskey of Mississippi warned that the war would be decided by "the heaviest guns best handled,"[4] while Chaplain Isaac Tichenor of Alabama insisted that God governs the world and "His hand is

---

[3] In Davis's first inaugural address and in Lincoln's second inaugural address.

[4] G. G. Mullins, ed., *Caskey's Book: Lectures on Great Subjects* (St. Louis: John Burns Publishing Co., 1884) 338.

in this war."[5] Chaplain J. William Jones found evidence of God's Spirit in the Great Revivals in the Army of Northern Virginia. Chaplain Amos Billingsley of Pennsylvania found the same Holy Spirit in the US Hospital at Hampton Roads. Chaplain Charles McCabe of Ohio encountered God's presence in Libby Prison. Was the Spirit divided? Was God on both sides or on neither?

The Civil War chaplains would never resolve the issue, although they proclaimed after the war, with full conviction, that the Holy Spirit was present in their experiences in both the Union and Confederate armies during the conflict—and in their lives thereafter.

The contributions of these chaplains continued through the greatest war ever fought on the American continent. They performed heroic service for soldiers and for their country even when they were underpaid, underfed, and unappreciated outside of the army. They conducted the only real evangelistic and pastoral work available for more than 2.5 million soldiers on both sides, efforts which resulted in the rebuilding of hundreds of churches and missionary enterprises after the war. They also became church and community leaders in the latter half of the century with influence far in excess of their numbers. These contributions become clearer as they are illustrated throughout the sections of the anthology: ministry in camp, on campaign, in prisons and hospitals, in evangelistic work, and in the post-war period.

In spite of their early service in an ecumenical army environment, Southern churches and their Northern counterparts clashed during the war. Ministers were driven from their churches by both armies. Churches were sometimes burned just because they were in the path of soldiers eager for victory and some measure of revenge. In more than two dozen cases, the Union army took possession of Southern churches and placed Northern missionaries in the pulpits. Therefore, after the war, despite common history, polity, liturgy, and even theology, the "war between the churches" resulted in a toughening of denominational lines and, not incidentally, the exodus of thousands of Southern black members into their own churches. The Union was restored, but the larger national denominations that split before and during the war—Methodists, Baptists, Presbyterians, and Lutherans—were not reunited during the nineteenth century. The implications of those events for some churches continue to this day.

---

[5] I. T. Tichenor, "Fast Day Sermon," unpublished manuscript, MF #0336, p. 7, Southern Baptist Historical Library and Archives, Nashville TN.

It has been a privilege to compile and edit these memoirs as some of the best written by eyewitnesses during or after the war. The chaplains who wrote them deserve to be remembered. They should be counted among the finest clergy America has produced, for they were not only heroes on the battlefield, but also heroes of the faith. That is why their biographies and their memoirs are included in these pages.

John Wesley Brinsfield, Ph.D.

Acknowledgments

Collecting an anthology of Civil War memoirs necessarily involves a small army of researchers, archivists, and librarians. At the risk of overlooking some, I would like to offer a word of thanks to the organizations and individuals that assisted in this research.

The Georgia State Department of History and Archives for providing documentation necessary to publish the Francis M. Kennedy Diary and the James M. Campbell Letters.

The South Carolina Department of History and Archives for supporting research related to John L. Girardeau's service record.

The Special Collections Department, Robert W. Woodruff Library, Emory University, for granting permission to publish the Charles J. Oliver journal and the George G. Smith memoir.

The Pitts Theological Library, Candler School of Theology, Emory University, for assistance in researching the Thomas Deavenport records in the Annual Conference Minutes of the Methodist Episcopal Church, South.

The South Caroliniana Library, University of South Carolina, Columbia, for help in locating the 1871 Memorial Day Address by John L. Girardeau at the Magnolia Cemetery in Charleston, and the biography of James P. Boyce.

The Military History Institute, Carlisle, Pennsylvania, for making their impressive collection of Civil War manuscripts and photographic archives available and for allowing the purchase of Civil War photographs for publication.

Ms. Annie Armour, archivist at the Sewanee Archives for permission to quote from the diary of Charles T. Quintard, Quintard Collection, Sewannee, Tennesee.

The National Archives, Washington, DC, for assisting in locating Civil War service records and reports by chaplains.

The Ohio Historical Society for advice on materials and photographs in the public domain.

The Southern Baptist Historical Library and Archives, Nashville, Tennessee, for allowing the purchase of the Tichenor diary for publication.

The Tennessee State Library and Archives for locating the Deavenport papers and making them available for publication from the public domain.

The Alabama State Department of Archives and History for help in researching the Battle of Shiloh.

The US Army Chaplain Archives, Fort Jackson, South Carolina, for furnishing the Herman Norton papers containing the reminiscences of Charles Holt Dobbs as well as the papers of many other Civil War chaplains.

The Tennessee Conference Archives, United Methodist Church, Nashville, Tennessee, for helping to locate the Thomas Deavenport records of service in the Methodist Episcopal Church, South.

The United States Copyright Office of the Library of Congress for helping ascertain that no copyrights were currently held on any books older than seventy-five years as used in this compilation and to Ms. Marybeth Peters of the US Copyright Office for recording the 2001 copyright on the Brinsfield collection of unpublished works by Chaplains Oliver, Smith, and Kennedy.

I would also like to thank Chaplain (Colonel) Douglas McCullough, US Army Reserve, Jackson, Mississippi, for drawing my attention to *Caskey's Book*; Chaplain (Colonel) William Nesbit, U.S. Army Forces Command, for stories about his ancestor, Charles T. Quintard; William Smedlund, for help in researching the journal of Charles J. Oliver; Dr. James I. Robertson, Jr., Distinguished Alumni Professor at Virginia Tech, for his interest and response; Ms. Ginger Cain, University Archivist at Emory University, for granting permission to publish the 1880 Thanksgiving sermon of Dr. Atticus G. Haygood; Ms. Debbie Yuhas, Ms. Gayle Levine, Ms. Vickie Orr, Ms. Stephanie Birch, and others who typed the manuscript at different times; and for my wife Patricia's forbearance while I indulged a dream of being in the presence of heroes.

Illustrations & Photographs

*Special Thanks to: Special Collections Department,
Robert Woodruff Library, Emory University;
South Carolina Baptists Convention; South Carolina
State Archives; Georgia State Archives*

*The Rev. James Anthony
Sandersonville, Georgia, pastor during
Sherman's March*

*Chaplain A. D. Betts
30th North Carolina Infantry, CSA*

*Chaplain James P. Boyce
16th South Carolina Infantry, CSA*

*William F. F. Broaddus
Post Chaplain
Charlottesville, Virginia, CSA*

Chaplain James M. Campbell
1st Georgia Infantry, CSA

Chaplain Thomas W. Caskey
16th Mississippi Cavalry, CSA

Chaplain John L. Girardeau
23 South Carolina Infantry, CSA

Lt. Gen. T. J. "Stonewall" Jackson, CSA

Chaplain J. C. Granbery
11th Virginia Infantry, CSA

Chaplain A. G. Haygood
15th Georgia Infantry, CSA

Chaplain J. J. Hyman
49th Georgia Infantry, CSA

Chaplain J. William Jones
13th Virginia Infantry, CSA

Chaplain F. M. Kennedy
28th North Carolina Infantry, CSA

Chaplain Asa M. Marshall
12th Georgia Infantry, CSA

Chaplain Charles J. Oliver
Troup Artillery, Georgia, CSA

Farm house near Raccoon Ford, Virginia. Sketch by Chaplain C. J. Oliver, CSA

Winter cabin, Army of North Virginia as sketched by Chaplain C. J. Oliver, CSA

Page from Chaplain C. J. Oliver's journal with his sketch of his winter cabin near Raccoon Ford, Virginia, 1864

The Army of Northern Virginia crossing the Potomac River in 1863 as sketched by Chaplain C. J. Oliver, CSA (Rider in foreground appears to be a black teamster.)

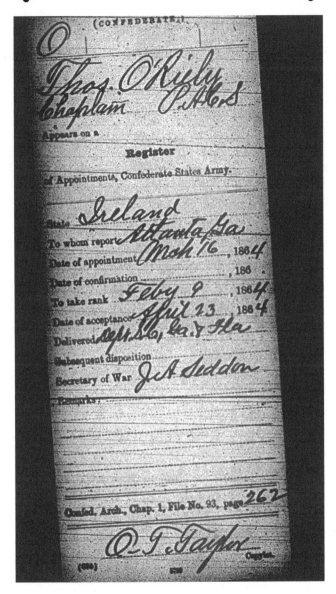

Father Thomas O'Reilly's register of appointment. He saved five churches in Atlanta from Sherman's torch.

Father Thomas O'Reilly
Atlanta Hospital Chaplain, CSA

Chaplain Charles T. Quintard
1st Tennessee Infantry, CSA

Father James B. Sheeran
Chaplain, 14th Louisiana Infantry, CSA

Chaplain George Smith
Phillips' Georgia Legion, CSA

Chaplain Isaac Tichenor
17th Alabama Infantry, CSA

Chaplain J. J. Ungerer
3rd Kentucky Mounted Infantry, CSA

Chaplain distributing religious tracts in the Confederate trenches

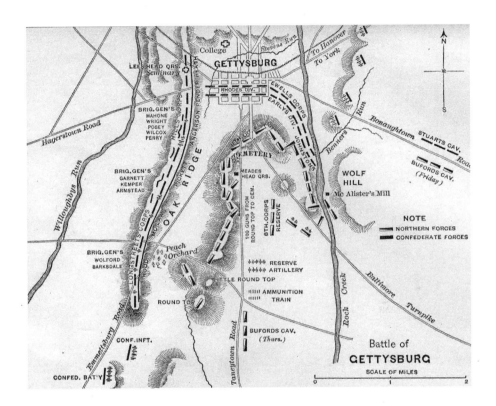

Map of Gettysburg Battlefield, July 1863

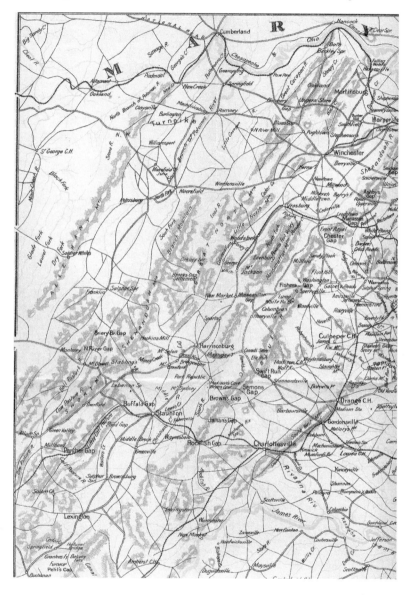

Civil War map showing passes in the Shenandoah Valley of Virginia

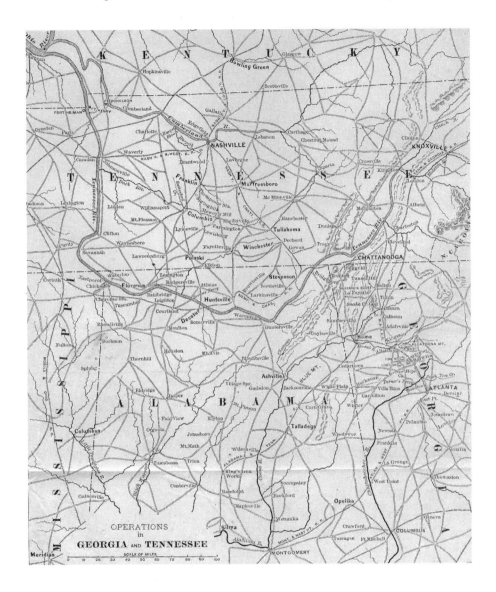

Map of Railroads and Roads used in Operations in Tennessee and Georgia, 1862–1864

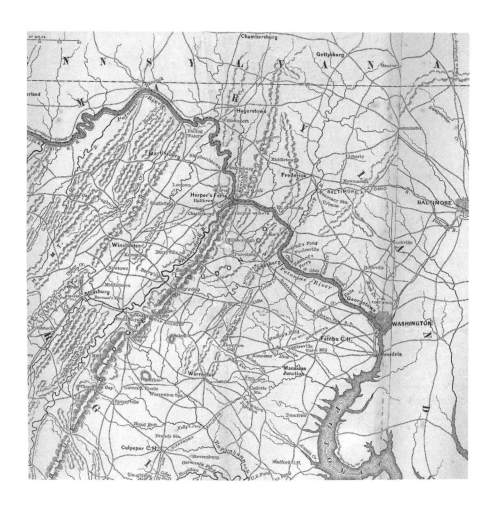

Civil War map of Northern Virginia showing roads and railroad lines west of Washington, DC

The Spirit Divided

Introduction

A Troubling Summons

Shall we go to battle...or shall we refrain?
1 Kings 22

The election of Abraham Lincoln as the sixteenth President of the United States on 6 November 1860 was a signal for South Carolina and six other states to secede from the Union. This was not the first call for secession in South Carolina; others had occurred in 1852 following the admission of California as a free state, and in 1859, after John Brown's raid at Harper's Ferry. This time, however, most Southern congressmen and senators in Washington agreed with the South Carolina delegation that Lincoln's policy of prohibiting unlimited expansion of slavery into the West would make it impossible for their states to remain in the Union.[1] As a minimum, the Republican platform was a threat to the fundamental principle that slaves were property and could be taken anywhere.

Accordingly, the legislature of South Carolina called for the election of a statewide convention to consider the future sovereignty of the state. This convention met in the First Baptist Church in Columbia on 17 December 1860 and then adjourned to Charleston, where the delegates unanimously adopted an Ordinance of Secession a few days later. The document itself, dated 24 December, charged that the federal government had departed from the original purposes and guarantees of the Constitution of the United States:

---

[1] Edward McPherson, *The Political History of the United States of America during the Great Rebellion* (Washington DC: Philp and Solomons, 1865) 37. Senator Andrew Johnson of Tennessee dissented and remained in his seat in the Senate when his Southern colleagues departed.

We affirm that these ends for which this Government was instituted have been defeated; and the Government itself has been made destructive of them by the action of the non-slaveholding States. Those States have assumed the right of deciding upon the propriety of our domestic institutions; and have denied the rights of property established in fifteen of the States and recognized by the Constitution; they have denounced as sinful the institution of slavery; they have permitted open establishment among them of societies, whose avowed object is to disturb the peace and to eloign the property of the citizens of other States. They have encouraged and assisted thousands of our slaves to leave their homes; and those who remain, have been incited by emissaries, books and pictures to servile insurrection.[2]

Moreover, the South Carolina delegates urged that seceding states band together as soon as possible into a new union. Robert Barnwell Rhett supported Montgomery as a meeting place, in part because there he would have the backing of William L. Yancey of Alabama for the purpose of erecting a permanent government. Delegates from five other states and twelve US Senators from the South, meeting in Washington, DC, on 5 January 1861, agreed to meet in Montgomery not later than 5 February.

Senator Jefferson Davis of Mississippi, one of those whose support was sought for the Montgomery meeting, initially had discouraged secession in 1860. The vital issue of the moment for Davis was whether the South was to continue to have an open frontier in the West. Lincoln settled this question declaring that while he would concede almost every other point at issue between the Northern and Southern sections, there should be no additional slave states. Thereafter Davis's course was predestined. When Mississippi seceded, he formally withdrew from the United States Senate on 21 January 1861.[3]

The meeting of the Montgomery Convention was moved forward to 4 February because Southern leaders including Alexander Stephens, Howell Cobb, Benjamin H. Hill, and Robert Toombs of Georgia; William L. Yancey of Alabama; Robert B. Rhett of South Carolina; and Lucius Q. C.

---

[2] J. A. May and J. R. Faunt, *South Carolina Secedes* (Columbia: University of South Carolina Press, 1960) 76–81.
[3] Dumas Malone, ed., *Dictionary of American Biography*, vol. 5 (New York: Charles Scribner's Sons, 1946) 127.

Lamar of Mississippi, felt that it would be easier to meet a month before Lincoln's inauguration on 4 March. Howell Cobb was elected president of the convention by acclamation, and the fifty delegates, including observers, drew up a provisional constitution for the Confederate States of America, reported out of committee on 7 February. Two days later, after Yancey withdrew his name from contention, former Secretary of War and ex-US Senator Jefferson Davis was elected president of the Confederate States.

One of the problems on President-elect Davis's agenda was South Carolina's ongoing dispute with President Buchanan over the status of Forts Sumter and Moultrie in Charleston Harbor. In December 1860, South Carolina Governor Francis Pickens had sent Commissioners R. W. Barnwell, J. H. Adams, and James L. Orr to meet with President Buchanan to secure the forts for the state. They thought Buchanan promised to do nothing to change the situation, but on 26 December, Major Robert Anderson moved his small command of eighty-one US artillerymen and engineers from Fort Moultrie to Fort Sumter, thereby strengthening the US presence in the harbor. When Buchanan sent a merchant ship, *The Star of the West* with supplies and 250 additional soldiers for the fort on 5 January, South Carolina batteries drove the ship outside cannon range and away from the harbor.[4]

In response to this developing crisis, on 15 February 1861, the Provisional Congress of the Confederate States at Montgomery resolved that Fort Sumter, South Carolina, and Fort Pickens, Florida, should be occupied as soon as possible, "either by negotiation or by force."[5] Military installations, and especially forts and arsenals belonging to the United States government, could not be allowed to exist on territory that belonged to the six sovereign states then in the Confederacy.[6] Jefferson Davis had not yet been inaugurated as president, nor had a cabinet been formed, but these matters did not interfere with what amounted to a resolution to go to war if necessary. The United States was now a foreign power and had no recognized legal authority in the Confederate States of America.

---

[4] Abner Doubleday, *Reminiscences of Forts Sumter and Moultrie in 1860–61* (Spartanburg SC: The Reprint Company, 1976) 93.

[5] E. Merton Coulter, *The Confederate States of America, 1861–1865* (Baton Rouge: Louisiana State University Press, 1950) 34.

[6] Ibid. Texas, Arkansas, North Carolina, Tennessee, and Virginia had not yet seceded when Jefferson Davis took office on 18 February. The citizens of Texas voted for secession on 23 February over the objections of Gov. Sam Houston.

When Davis was inaugurated on 18 February, he tried to assure the people of the South that these events did not mark a revolution, but a continuity of the old Constitution under new ownership. He hoped for peace, but was committed to independence for the South.

Religious leaders in the South, for the most part, reacted to these developments cautiously. Bishop James O. Andrew of the Methodist Episcopal Church, South, advised ministers in Alabama and Georgia to "avoid the topic of secession."[7] The Presbyterian General Assembly, in November 1860, had condemned "political intermeddling by professed Ministers of the Gospel," and sought to keep the churches focused on purely spiritual matters.[8] The Protestant Episcopal Church's bishops in the South, William Meade of Virginia and James Otey of Tennessee in particular, urged moderation with regard to supporting secession and requested all clergymen to pray for national healing. Most of the eleven Roman Catholic bishops in the South, including Bishop James Whelan of Nashville, viewed secession as something to be endured rather than embraced.[9] The Disciples of Christ left political issues to individual conscience.

In some parts of the South, especially in western Virginia and eastern Tennessee, many people were opposed to secession if it were justified merely because Lincoln had been elected. At the time of Lincoln's election, the Republican Party did not have a majority in the US House of Representatives or in the Senate. Withdrawal of senators and congressmen from the South would give the Republicans a majority in both houses and further imperil the balance of views that had produced national compromises for forty years. Since approximately two-thirds of white Southern males did not own slaves, secession was a peripheral issue for many small farmers, laborers, and mechanics who were more interested in earning a living for themselves and their families than in sectional politics.

These sentiments were soon overcome by the determination of President Davis and Governor Pickens to force the evacuation of Fort Sumter in April 1861. Even though Major Anderson reported to Brigadier General P. G. T. Beauregard, who had taken command of the Confederate defenses at Charleston, that he must run out of provisions and evacuate by

---

[7] Frank L. Hieronymus, "For Now and Forever: The Chaplains of the Confederate States Army" (PhD diss., University of California at Los Angeles, 1964) 12.

[8] Ibid., 38.

[9] Ibid.

15 April, Beauregard warned him on 12 April that the bombardment of the fort would proceed unless he surrendered immediately.[10]

At 4:30 A.M. on 12 April, sixteen Confederate batteries around Charleston Harbor began firing on Fort Sumter. Captain Abner Doubleday of the First United States Artillery, who was in the fort, wrote that about 1,800 shots hit the fort, setting one-fifth of it on fire. Major Anderson surrendered the fort when it was clear that no reinforcements from the Federal fleet off the coast would arrive. He evacuated Fort Sumter on Sunday, 14 April, with the loss of but one soldier, Private Daniel Hough, who was killed firing a final salute to the national colors.[11]

The next day, 15 April, President Lincoln called on the governors of states in the Union to furnish 75,000 volunteers to crush the rebellion. These volunteer militiamen were to be provided by the states on a quota basis. North Carolina, Tennessee, and Virginia were included in the quota call.

Governor Isham G. Harris of Tennessee, who had strongly favored secession, stated, "Tennessee will not furnish a single man for coercion, but 50,000 if necessary, for the defense of our rights and those of our southern brothers."[12] The other border states had heard Sumter's guns as well and reacted even more strongly against Lincoln's call for troops to suppress what Governor John W. Ellis of North Carolina called "the liberties of a free people."[13]

No one living in the South in 1861 could remember a country that did not recognize slavery as a legal institution. Southern political, educational, and religious leaders had defended the system for decades as sanctioned by the New Testament and the Constitution of the United States. The question in 1861, for most Southerners, was not whether slavery should be abolished or even contained, but whether the President of the United States had the authority to compel states to remain in the Union by force. Governor John Letcher of Virginia bluntly accused President Lincoln of inaugurating a civil war.

---

[10] Maj. Robert Anderson, USA, was Beauregard's artillery instructor at West Point from 1836–1838 and taught Sunday school for the cadets. Beauregard warned him an hour before the shelling began.

[11] Doubleday, *Reminiscences of Forts Sumter and Moultrie in 1860–61*, 144, 171, 181.

[12] John T. Moore and Austin P. Foster, *Tennessee: The Volunteer State 1769–1923*, vol. 1 (Nashville: S. J. Clarke Publishing Co., 1923) 470.

[13] Coulter, *The Confederate States of America, 1861–1865*, 42.

Accordingly, Arkansas passed an ordinance of secession on 6 May, and Tennessee declared itself independent on the same day. Virginia ratified the Confederate Constitution on 25 April and was admitted into the Confederacy on 8 May. North Carolina followed suit on 20 May.[14] Governor William Burton of Delaware replied that Delaware had no militia and thus could not comply with Lincoln's call. Governor Thomas Hicks of Maryland refused to send troops except to defend Washington. Governor Beriah Magoffin of Kentucky wrote, "I say, emphatically, Kentucky will furnish no troops for the wicked purpose of subduing her sister Southern states."[15]

Lincoln's summons for volunteers galvanized many of the uncommitted people of the South, in all classes and occupations, to support the Confederacy. The citizens of Tennessee, for example, who had voted against secession on 9 February 1861 by a margin of 64,000 votes, reversed their stand and began volunteering to serve in the state militia to defeat Northern aggression. In the next four years, 115,000 Tennessee soldiers would fight for the Confederacy.[16] Slaveholders and non-slaveholders alike united in their determination to defend their homes from invasion.

Many Southern churchmen also lined up to endorse the Confederate government. On 29 April the Georgia Baptist Convention, meeting in Athens, resolved that because "Abraham Lincoln is attempting, by force of arms, to subjugate these states…we consider it at once to be a pleasure and a duty to avow that both in feeling and in principle, we approve, endorse, and support the Government of the Confederate States of America."[17] In May the Southern Baptist Convention, meeting in Savannah, Georgia, and representing Baptist associations in ten Southern states, declared as "The Union constituted by our forefathers was one of coequal sovereign states we most cordially approve of the formation of the government of the Confederate States of America."[18]

The other Southern Protestant denominations soon drafted their own supporting statements. The Methodist Episcopal Church, South, was between General Conferences, but the Methodist ministers in the

---

[14] Ibid.

[15] Ibid., 46.

[16] Moore and Foster, *Tennessee: The Volunteer State 1769–1923*, 470.

[17] McPherson, *The Political History of the United States of America during the Great Rebellion*, 513.

[18] Ibid.

Tennessee Conference passed resolutions in November 1861, supporting the Confederate government and requesting Bishop Joshua Soule to "appoint as many preachers of this conference as he may deep proper to the chaplaincy of our army."[19] In the same month, Bishop Leonidas Polk, Episcopal bishop of the Diocese of Louisiana, directed Episcopal priests to substitute, in the prayer for those in civil authority, the words "the President of the Confederate States" for the previous "President of the United States." In December, Southern Presbyterians formed the General Assembly of the Presbyterian Church in the Confederate States at their meeting in Augusta, Georgia, and declared themselves "separate and independent" of the General Assembly of the Presbyterian Church in the United States of America.[20]

The action of these church bodies did not allay the alarm that many Southern preachers felt in their local communities. The Reverend Alexander D. Betts of Smithville, North Carolina, recorded his feelings,

> One day in April, 1861, I heard that President Lincoln had called on the State troops to force the seceding States back into the Union. That was one of the saddest days of my life. I had prayed and hoped that war might be averted. I had loved the Union, and clung to it. That day I saw war was inevitable. The inevitable must be met. That day I walked up and down my porch in Smithville and wept and suffered and prayed for the South.[21]

In South Carolina the Reverend James P. Boyce warned his sister Nancy that if war came, it would be the end of slavery. At his home near Macon, Georgia, the Reverend George G. Smith thought there "seemed to be now no choice between the Abolition of slavery and Secession;" and in Mississippi the Reverend Thomas Caskey wrote, "I didn't know exactly what position God would take in that fight. The issue was a personal one between us and the Yankees, and we must settle it, as best we could, among

---

[19] By 1862, one-fifth of the clergymen in the Tennessee conference were appointed to the Confederate Army as chaplains, soldiers, or missionaries. Hieronymus, "For Now and Forever," 12, 51.

[20] McPherson, *The Political History of the United States of America during the Great Rebellion*, 509, 515.

[21] William A. Betts, ed., *Experience of a Confederate Chaplain 1861–1864* (Greenville SC: privately printed, 1904) 6. There is a copy at the Pitts Theological Library, Emory University, Atlanta GA.

ourselves."[22] Within twelve months of the surrender of Fort Sumter, all four ministers, Betts, Boyce, Smith, and Caskey, would have served or be serving as chaplains in the Confederate Army.

[22] John A. Broadus, *Memoir of James Petigru Boyce* (New York: A. C. Armstrong and Sons, 1893) 184–85; George G. Smith diary, 13 July 1864, Special Collections Department, Robert W. Woodruff Library, Emory University, Atlanta GA; John K. Bettersworth, ed., *Mississippi in the Confederacy: As They Saw It* (Baton Rouge: Louisiana State University Press, 1961) 233.

Chapter 1

Reporting for Duty

Behold, God is with us…and his priests…
2 Chronicles 13

Before anyone could report for duty as a commissioned Confederate chaplain, there had to be a legal authorization for chaplains to serve in the army. Even though the Provisional Congress of the Confederate States had passed legislation establishing a War Department in February of 1861, it had not addressed the subject of the spiritual welfare of soldiers. Clearly thousands of young men leaving home to face the hardships of war would need some religious and morale support.

Church membership in the eleven Confederate states was estimated at twenty-five percent of the population, but the worshipping numbers were much higher, possibly as high as sixty-four percent of the eleven million people in the seceded states. Churches, mothers, and local politicians were already petitioning for the establishment of chaplains in the military forces. Accordingly, on 2 May Congressman Francis S. Bartow of Georgia reported a bill to provide for chaplains in the Confederate Army. After the required three readings, the bill passed and a commissioning process was set up for the president of the Confederate States to appoint chaplains for the duration of the war.[1]

The new law empowered the president to appoint chaplains to as many regiments, brigades, and posts as he "deemed expedient," and provided a

---

[1] Herman A. Norton, *Struggling for Recognition: The United States Army Chaplaincy, 1791–1865* (Washington DC: Office of the Chief of Chaplains, Department of the Army, 1977) 132. There was a provision for chaplains to serve in the Confederate Navy, but no naval chaplains were ever commissioned.

monthly pay of $85, which was midway between the pay of a second lieutenant and a first lieutenant. At a time when many state militia chaplains were paid $150 a month, the pay of a Confederate chaplain was barely enough to buy rations and forage for a horse—if the chaplain could procure one.[2]

The legislation contained no stipulations regarding age, physical condition, education, or ecclesiastical status. Neither did it include a description of required duties, which were left to the chaplain and his regimental commander to work out. There was no provision for uniforms, insignia of rank or function, or even any required military training. In the main, chaplains had to depend on their families and churches for ecclesiastical supplies for themselves and their soldiers.

Ministers, priests, lay preachers, or even pious soldiers who wished to be commissioned as chaplains, whether they were ordained or not, had to have the approval and written recommendation of a regimental commander. This could be secured by recommendation from third parties, by direct application, by transfer of a state commission, or by simply demonstrating the ability to preach, lead Bible studies, or conduct burial services in the absence of a regimental chaplain.

Regimental commanders frequently consulted the company grade officers and sometimes the noncommissioned officers and enlisted soldiers regarding the suitability of candidates. Once a candidate was recommended through the senior command to Richmond, a commission would be returned from the secretary of war on behalf of President Davis.

Of the 1,308 Confederate chaplains who served with commissions at sometime during the war, and whose names are known, it is estimated that forty-two percent were ordained ministers or priests, and fifty-eight percent deacons, local preachers, or laymen without full ordination. Of the 938 Confederate chaplains whose denomination is known, forty-seven percent were Methodist, eighteen percent Presbyterian, sixteen percent Baptist, ten percent Episcopalian, three percent Roman Catholic, and less than one percent for five other denominations.[3]

---

[2] Two weeks after the initial legislation passed, an amendment lowered chaplains' pay to $50 a month since they supposedly worked only one day a week. In April 1862, after many protests, their pay was raised to $80 a month.

[3] Frank L. Hieronymus, "For Now and Forever: The Chaplains of the Confederate States Army" (PhD diss., University of California at Los Angeles, 1964) 3, 341; Southern Baptist Convention, *Annual Report, 1866*, Southern Baptist

Although the pay was poor, there was some glamour for chaplains in being commissioned officers with the prospect of wearing a military uniform. With regard to chaplain uniforms, however, there was a freedom in individual dress that ran the gamut from plain civilian attire to outrageous combinations of military accoutrements. Soldiers told of a chaplain who reported for duty in deep blue clothing that made him look like a Yankee; of chaplains "who dressed like women" wearing clerical robes, and of one backwoods chaplain who reported in bearskin leggings, the only pair of their kind anyone had ever seen in a military unit.[4]

Many chaplains dressed in a plain gray uniform coat with gray trousers and such hats, belts, buckles, and pouches as they could find. At the beginning of the war, Chaplain Lyman B. Wharton of the 59th Virginia Infantry had an elegant gray uniform made, complete with black lapels. On each lapel he put a Latin cross, an insignia for chaplains that the US Army would eventually adopt.[5] Others simply reported in whatever they wore at home, possibly a black suit with a white shirt and a wide-brimmed hat. There were few overcoats at first because many did not think the war would last long enough to require one.

Historical Library and Archives, Nashville TN; Consolidated Service Records of Confederate General and Staff Officers, microfilm drawers 277, 278, Georgia State Department of Archives and History, Morrow GA.

[4] Herman A. Norton, *Struggling for Recognition: The United States Army Chaplaincy, 1791–1865* (Washington DC: Office of the Chief of Chaplains, Department of the Army, 1977) 132.

[5] Chaplain Wharton's uniform as displayed at the National Military Park Headquarters, Fredericksburg VA.

Memoirs, 1860-1862

"I would preserve the Union..."

James Petigru Boyce, Chaplain 16th South Carolina Infantry

James P. Boyce was born in Charleston, South Carolina, on 11 January 1827. His father, Ker Boyce of the Newberry District, was one of the wealthiest men in the state. James attended the College of Charleston for two years and then Brown University in Providence, Rhode Island. After his graduation from Brown in 1847, he went to Princeton for two additional years of study. He was ordained in December of 1851 and became the pastor of the First Baptist Church in Columbia, South Carolina. In 1855 he became the Professor of Theology at Furman University. In 1858 he was elected to the faculty of theology at the Southern Baptist Seminary in Greenville. In 1861 he volunteered to serve as chaplain of the 16th South Carolina Infantry at Charleston and on John's Island. His letters to his brother-in law, Henry Allen Tupper, chaplain of the 9th Georgia Infantry, and to his sister, Nancy J. Boyce Tupper, reveal some of his reservations about the war even as he determined to remain loyal to his state.[1]

To H. A. TupperDecember, 1860[2]

I have been all along in favor of resistance, by demanding first new guarantees, and if these were not granted, then forming a Southern Confederacy. If you Georgia people come in, we are safe enough; though we shall yet suffer, because the plan of co-operation has not preceded secession.

---

[1] Rev. Henry Allen Tupper (1828–1902) was pastor of the Baptist Church in Washington GA for nineteen years and a Confederate chaplain early in the war. In 1872 he became the corresponding secretary of the Foreign Mission Board of the Southern Baptist Convention and the principal supporter for the missionary work of Miss Lottie Moon in China.

[2] John A. Broadus, *Memoir of James Petigru Boyce* (New York: A. C. Armstrong and Sons, 1893) 184–85.

We are going to have the Confederacy of New England, the Free City of New York, the Confederacy of the Middle States, and that of the West—or the two united—and that cutting through our Southern territory to the Gulf, the Confederacy of the Border States, that of the Cotton States—Texas standing alone—and the Confederacy of the Pacific. Alas, my country!...I know I am cautious about taking any step without arranging for the consequences. I have always had such a desire for justice, even to my foes, that I wish to leave no one any ground to charge me even with failure in form. I do wish to see the North put entirely in the wrong, by making them dissolve the Union, if it must be, through refusing to grant what we ask. And again, I have always been old fogy enough to love the past, with all its glorious associations. Moreover, I believe I see in all this the end of slavery. I believe we are cutting its throat, curtailing its domain. And I have been, and am, an ultra pro-slavery man. Yet I bow to what God will do. I feel that our sins as to this institution have cursed us,—that the negroes have not been cared for in their marital and religious relations as they should be; and I fear God is going to sweep it away, after having left it thus long to show us how great we might be, were we to act as we ought in this matter.

January 10, 1861
To Nancy

I am proud to say that I love my State, and my whole country, too well to support the present movement. It is to me one of the proudest recollections of my father that he helped so manfully in 1852 to stay this folly; and were he only here in 1860 and '61, I feel well assured where he would stand.[3] The country his father bled for, and for which he himself gave his strength and means in 1852, is still dear to me. Nor do I yet despair; I believe that ere many months have gone by we shall all be safe again under the folds of the glorious Stars and Stripes of our own United States. I believe that the Southern States will yet present their ultimatum to the North, and when they do, that it will be accepted. If not, then I am ready to leave them;

---

[3] Following the Compromise of 1850, which admitted California to the Union as a free state, the South Carolina General Assembly called for a Southern Convention to meet in Montgomery AL in January 1852. The object was to discuss secession from the Union. A hot debate ensued in South Carolina between those who favored secession and those who thought the state should remain in the Union. See Walter Edgar, *South Carolina: A History* (Columbia: University of South Carolina Press, 1998) 344.

though I believe in so doing we have nothing before us but constant civil discord, until slavery will be entirely abolished. It is as a pro-slavery man that I would preserve the Union. God deliver us from the follies to which, out of it, the fire-eaters will try to carry us, and the civil discord that will thus come on us! As sure as we do not arrange some propositions for the North, we shall have to go through a long and bloody war.

During the winter of 1861–1862 Chaplain Boyce served as chaplain of the 16th South Carolina Infantry in their coastal camp and earned high praise for his pastoral work and for his "able and feeling" sermons from Colonel James McCullough, the regimental commander. In 1862 Boyce was elected to the South Carolina Legislature from the Greenville District and subsequently served as aide-de-camp to Governor A. G. Magrath. In this capacity Lieutenant Colonel James P. Boyce was acting Provost-Marshal of Columbia at the time of its capture by Major General W. T. Sherman. Boyce claimed to have been the last Confederate officer to leave the city ahead of the invaders.

After the war Boyce gave his attention to revivifying and relocating the Southern Baptist Seminary from Greenville to Louisville, Kentucky. He served on the faculty as professor of systematic theology and chairman of the faculty for eleven years. During that time, from 1877 to 1888, he also served as president of the Southern Baptist Convention. In 1887 he was awarded an honorary LL.D. degree from Brown University. Professor James P. Boyce died in Pau, France, on 28 December 1888 while on a trip with his wife and daughters.

"I am now en route for Richmond..."

Chaplain James M. Campbell, 1st Georgia Infantry Regiment, Army of Northern Virginia

James McDonald Campbell was born in McMinn County, Tennessee, on 8 October 1830. He was the fifth of eight children of Andrew and Sarah Campbell, originally from Augusta County, Virginia. In 1833 the Campbell family moved from Tennessee to Cherokee County, Alabama. James grew up farming with his father, sometimes working for a peck of corn or twenty cents a day. He possibly attended the secondary school in Gaylesville, Alabama.

When James Campbell was fifteen years old, he was converted and joined the Oak Bowery Methodist Church northeast of Gaylesville. In 1853 he was admitted into the Alabama Conference of the Methodist Episcopal Church, South, as a preacher on trial. In 1855 he was appointed as pastor to the Geneva Circuit in southeast Alabama under the supervision of the presiding elder, Reverend Stephen F. Pilley, two of whose sons would also become Confederate chaplains.

In 1861, while serving as the Methodist pastor in Warrington, Campbell enlisted in the 1st Georgia Infantry Regiment of the Provisional Army of the Confederate States then training at their camp in Pensacola, Florida. In May of 1861 he was elected and commissioned as their chaplain. Campbell accompanied the regiment to Virginia and then across the mountains into what became the state of West Virginia. In his letters to his family, he reflects on travel to Virginia and the hardships of camp life.[1]

Pensacola, Fla.
May 30th/61
My Dear Mother,
I am now in route for Richmond, Va. I am the Chaplain of the 1st Georgia Regiment[,] and that regiment received orders this morning to strike their tents and repair to Richmond, Virginia. In one hour after the order was received, almost the entire regiment (900 men) were marching.

---

[1] Original spelling and punctuation, or the lack of it, have been preserved except in cases where confusion or lack or clarity for the reader might result.

We will take the cars here tonight and go by railroad to Va. I am pleased with the change as I have always had a desire to visit this country, and it was becoming very dull here. I will mail this on the rout [sic]. I suppose we will pass through Kingston, Ga. and Knoxville, Tenn. Oh how I would like to astonish you all by calling on you as I pass on but that pleasure will be denied me. There is no probability of a fight here. Our forces are ready, but our policy is not to make the attack and I do not think the other side will. The enemy could not throw hot shot and shell into the Navy yard and burn it before we could reduce Fort Pickens. Write me with the following directions: Rev. J. M. Campbell, Chaplain, 1st Georgia Regiment, Richmond, Va. I will finish this letter on the rode [sic] if I can. I will write when I reach Richmond.

　　Your son,

　　James

　　Montgomery, Ala.

　　May 31st/61

　　I arrived at this place this morning and will leave tonight. I wish some of you to write me where father was born, the precise neighborhood as nearly as possible and all the places he lived in Virginia. I may visit some of them. I left a box of books and a trunk with Dr. L. C. Smith at Pensacola. I will write to him today to send them to Rev James A. Heard of this place, so that should I from any cause to die, you will know where to find them.[2] I left no unsettled business in Warrington. I do not expect to die in Va. but have given [them to Reverend Heard] knowing the uncertainty of life under all circumstances and should I fall among strangers you would know nothing of them books and clothing. I take nothing more with me than what is absolutely necessary.

　　This is an awfully hot day. I hope it will not be so hot in Va. I wrote Mr Moor but have received no answer.

　　Your son,

　　J. M. Campbell

　　Richmond, Va.

　　June 6th 1861

---

[2] James A. Heard, pastor of the Methodist Church in Montgomery and secretary to the Alabama Conference.

Bro[.] Joe,

I arrived at this place yesterday morning and will remain here till the five companies that are behind come up[.] [W]e will then go to some point on the line[;] I will write you when we get marching orders. I wrote you from Montgomery telling you that my Regiment (1st Geo Reg) had been ordered to this place and that I was then en rout to this place.

Our forces and the northern are having some scurmishes along the line. From what I can learn I think that in a few days you will hear of a large battle, both sides are concentrating their forces and advancing: a collision must be the result. Our troops are sanguine of success.

I was astonished to find the mashinery of the war manfacture of munitions of war. Take my morning walk with me and I will show you what I saw. We walk down from my hotel (The Spotswood House) to the R.R. depot, then up the canal, and by the way canal boats are much less than my dreams made them. We come to a gate where we find a soldier in gray uniform gun on soldier [shoulder?] who says no one can be admitted except on business. I ask him to send in my card, he looks at my brass buttons and star and ostrich feather in my hat, for the way again I have dressed enough of the military to let the world know that I am an officer, this I have done not that I wanted to make a show but to save myself a great deal of trouble which I would have in citizens dress, but to return to the walk. The sentinel said walk in. I did so and saw in one building about one hundred and fifty girls and women making cartrige and caps for guns. In another room men making boxes for said cartriges. Pass into another room mashinery is boaring out ten inch columbiads, next room molding some other rooms making gun carriages and everything else that we want.[3] Do you now remember when we were little boyes how Father loved to talk of his boy visits to this ancient city[?] I then thought that when I got to be a man I would go and see that city of wonders. Here I am now, but alas! The world is not what my boy fancy depicted. Still I have no reason to complain. God has been good to me, and his blessings have been more numerous than his judgment and I can trust him. I feel that I am in the line of duty.

As you receed from the river you ascend a hill[;] on the hill stands the capitol of the State surrounded by a substantial iron rail fence which encloses, I suppose about five acres of land covered with beautiful grass and clover except the walks which are either made of brick or gravil. In this

---

[3] Columbiads were large cannons.

enclosure are four monuments or statues. Washington is larger than life mounted on a bronze horse, the horse mounted on a granit piramid. About half way below stands Patric Henry on a table or nich of the said piramid grasping a scabbord containing a sword and holding it out as if it had been lying near him and he had grasped it in the heat of his speech. He looks the impassioned orator. On his left stands Mason with a pen in his right hand and a book with paper cover in his left.[4] He has a bold frank face with goodness and strength strongly marked. On Mason's left stands Jefferson with his right hand thrown back against his breast grasping a pen, his left hand holding his cloak under his right arm and his eyes cast down as if in deep thought. These are all in bronze. About fifty yards from these stand Clay in marble on a granite pile. Near the capitol there is a beautiful fountain throwing water from about twenty jets over in the center and the remainder about ten feet from the said center causing the water to converge to the center form a circle, then falling in a pool or reservoir.

The capitol is of gray granite and has the appearane of ages. I should have said that the grounds surrounding the capitol are covered not only with clover and grass but also with a beautiful grove of elm and sicamore principally of the former. In the central room are the statues of Washington and Lafayett, in this building a large library. I must close my imperfect description of this city.

June 8th

Since commensing this letter I have learned that our regiment will start tomorrow for Phillippi west of the blue ridge.[5] It is in Barber County, a new county made a few years since. It is about three hundred miles from this place. We will have seventy miles marching. We will go through the country where Father was raised. We will pass through Stanton. I will write you and let you know where to address me.

Pray for us.

Your brother,

James

Laurel Hill, Va.

June 30th/61

My dear Brother,

---

[4] George Mason, Revolutionary War patriot.
[5] In West Virginia.

Two of your letter have been forwarded to me. I wish I had received them in Richmond. I spent two days in Staunton[,] made the acquaintance of a Presbyterian minister by our name and heard the names of Grotter, White, York, etc., but studiously avoided a conversation about our Father's birth place and family, knowing that I would only show my unpardonable ignorance by a confession of ignorance of our family. I have often thought that I would some day visit Va. and hunt up our relatives forgetting that I ought then to have collected the facts that would have enabled me to identify them. Before I received your letter I was even undecided of the county in which he was raised. I am now one hundred and twenty miles from Staunton and may not visit it again. Take your map of Va. and draw a line from Beverly in Randolph Co. to Phillippi in Barbour County, bending the line to the east in the shape of a rainbow. Stoping half way (15 miles) you are at our camp.[6] Enclosed you will find a rough draft of our camp and be sure you allow no one to copy it or possess it in any way.

A sentinel while on post shot a soldier and killed him instantly a few days since. The sentinel was on an out post where all outside the line were expected to be enemies. The unfortunate man had been standing on post and when relieved he passed outside the line. The man who had relieved him, not knowing it, shot him for an enemy.

The army is a (almost) perfect machine, every thing is down by rule. From the beating the drum at daylight in the morning to the signals for putting out the lights at 9 oclock at night.

General Garnett is in command here, with a force of about four thousand men and eleven hundred at a camp about twenty miles from this camp.[7] The enemy is encamped at Phillippi, fifteen miles from us. I have heard so many report about their strength that I cannot venture a guess. I suppose our General is posted. We can whip four times our number if they will attack us here. Our men are in fine health. Measles are making their appearance and will give us trouble.

This is Sunday and it is raining so that we can have no service. I am quartered with Capt. F. G. Wilkins of the Southern Guards from Columbus, Geo.[8] I have a narrow shuck mattress, two pare of blankets and a trunk of clothing and my camp equipage is all told. Our Reg. is furnished with good tents and we are as dry as if in a house. Our eating is the worst

---

[6] In West Virginia, northwest of Staunton.
[7] Brig. Gen. Robert S. Garnett, killed in West Virginia.
[8] Capt. Francis G. Wilkins, Co. B, 1st Georgia (Ramsey's) Infantry.

feature, we have plenty and that would be good if prepared right. Our biscuits are very different from those we were raised on. I do not know what I would give for a dinner at home. It makes me hungry to think of *clean* milk and butter and well baked bread even if there was not even salt in it. Do not believe that I am suffering for quanity *but the quality*. Oh the cooking. Everything else is better than I hoped for.

I cannot give you any clue at our future action. Gen Garnett has made a requisition for more troops, we may await their arrival before attacking the enemy. I cannot tell[;] I will keep you advised of all important changes.

The mountain scenery throu the rout from Richmond and more particularly from Staunton to this place is worth a trip to Va.

Direct your letters to Beverly and they will be forwarded to me.

Your brother

James

P. S. What has been done with my buggy[?]

Monday morning

July 1st/61

The rain ceased yesterday afternoon and we had servis in camp. I was standing on the ground, a camp stool by my side and my books on it. And a large crowd gathered around me, after having preached about twenty minutes the rain began to fall and I stopped short and said you are dismissed, and all went to their tents. We will have prayer meeting tonight.

There is much wickedness in camp for which I reprove them boldly.

I promised to enclose in this letter a draft of our camp but I have decided that it would be imprudent. It might fall into the hands of our enemy and do much damage.

There are many *tories* in this country[—]men of northern birth and education.

No new developments since yesterday.

Your brother

J

Staunton Va

Nov 28th 1861

My Bro. Joe,

I came to this place about a week since to look after our sick, the weather being so bad I could not preach in camp. I will remain here a few days. My regiment left Camp Bartow last week, has been stoped a few days, and is expected at "Buffalo Gap" ten miles from this place in a few days. I think we will be sent to Manassas, but do not know anything definite in reference to the future. There is a rumor here this morning, that the forces are fighting at Manassas.

I am once more out of the snow but will not remain so long. If I remain here this whole country will soon be covered with [B]oreas' white vestment.

I am very anxious to return south, if my regiment is not sent south I will make an effort to be assigned to duty in the south. I am coughing, but not severely. My health is very good, but I fear the cold, and cannot stand it in tents. If my regiment goes to Manassas and there is a prospect of a battle, I will go with it. If it remains in the mountains, I will go to Richmond and ask [for] a transfer. At this point, an officer came into my room and tells me that the 1st Geo, 3rd Ark and two Va regiments will be at Buffalo Gap tomorrow evening and have orders to go directly on to Manassas and that a battle is expected to commence at that place today covering an extent of country some sixty miles in extent and perhaps will last several days. I will not leave my regiment while they have a prospect of an engagement. If the fight should come off you will hear of it by telegraph before you get this. I will keep you posted in all important movements, if I don't write it will be because there is nothing of importance to write.

Our forces have left Camp Bartow. Two thousan are stationed on the top of the Allegahny mountain nine miles this side of Camp Bartow, where they have gon into winter quarters.

I would warn you against "rumors." I have told you that a fight is expected at Manassas but, you know (or if you do not know it is so) such rumors are frequent, and may not amount to anything and if not we may go south.

There is some excitement here in consequence of a cold blooded murder, which was committed on a citizen of this place last night by a soldier from Tennessee.

Write me at Richmond and your letter will be forwarded to me.

Our Gen. Jackson has been appointed Major General of the state forces of Geo. and left here this morning for Geo.[9]

Your brother

James

---

[9] Brig. Gen. Henry R. Jackson (1820–1898) of Savannah GA.

Richmond Va
Dec 7 1861
My dear Mother,

I have been at Staunton for the last two weeks with our sick, and came to this place on yesterday to get a discharge for one of our men, and will return to Staunton on tomorrow. Our regiment left Greenbrier last week, together with three other regiments. I learn that they have stopped at Winchester, and have not gon on to Manassas as they were expected to do. I expect to join them next week. If a fight should come off at Manassas we will be near, and can go down in a few hours so we will have an opportunity of sharing the dangers and glory of a second defeat of the "grand army" of the north. A fight is very doubtful as to time, but certain in result. The Yankee will certainly be defeated if they attack us. If they attack us at Manassas with any force they can bring, their defeat is beyond a doubt. Our men are anxious for the fray.

I must mention the name of one of my best friends, I mean, but in this state, I speak of Dr. Wm. B. Young of Staunton. A nobler man I have never met at any time. When I was sick in Staunton, after the retreat, he learned that a "Royal Arch Mason" was sick at the American Hotel, he took me to his house treated me like a *brother* and has shown me every kindness from that to the present time. He is a member of the Episcopal Church. His wife is clever as he. No worthy soldier has ever been turned from his door.

I am standing the winter finely and as we are out of the mountains I hope I will get along pretty well. My health is good.

Thinking that you might need some money to pay taxes I enclose you ten dollars. My salary is fifty dollars per month and my expenses thus far have kept par with it. Our sick are at different places, and I have to look after them.

Write me at Staunton and it will be forwarded to me. There is nothing here of importance. Our cause is looking up. I read Lincoln's message today, it is very *tame*.

Your son
James

Winchester, Va.
Dec 16th 1861
My dear Sister Lizzie,

You have learned from my letter written in Richmond that my regiment left Greenbrier some days since. We are now encamped two and a half miles from Winchester. This is the most pleasant location we have had since we left Pensacola. I have a nice warm room within our lines and will do well while we stay here. Since we left Greenbrier our forces which were left on the Allegahny mountains have been attacked by three times their number, and after seven hours hard fighting drove the Yankees from the field. I have not received the particulars but from what I hear I think it, all things considered, the most desperate fight of the war.

Gen. H. R. Jackson has gone to Georgia to command the Geo. forces. Gen Thomas Jackson, who is usually called "Stonewall" Jackson, is our present commander. He left here this morning with the "Stone Wall" brigade which was formerly commanded by him as brigadier General, but now is being a Major General, Brigadier General Garnett (cousin of the Garnett of Laurel Hill notoriety) is in command of his old brigade and he is commander of all the forces of this division. The destination of himself and the brigade he took with him is kept a secret, but I am verry certain they are to cross the Potomac and destroy a Canal dam or dams. Our brigade of four regiments (1st Geo, 3rd Ark, 23rd and 37th Va) are the only troops in the immediate vicinity of Winchester. We have orders to keep one days cooked provisions constantly on hands, that we may march at a moments warning. If Gen Jackson has gon to the Potomac and the Hessians crowd him we will go to his assistance. If a fight should occur at Manassas, we can runn down on the railroad and take a hand with them. If neither of these, we will in all probability winter here. The object in destroying the Canal is to cut off the supplies Washington receives on it.

The weather is not cold for this climate, nothing to compare with Camp Bartow. This you know is in "The Valley of Virginia" and from Staunton to this place it is one of the finest countries I ever saw. We are thirty miles from the Potomac and I will keep you advised of all important movements. Write me all the news.

I left one of my trunks at Dr. W. B. Youngs at Staunton[;] I am now lodging in Dr. Luptons house but eating with myself.[10]

Your brother

James

Sell my buggy for a good note due next Christmas.

---

[10] Possibly Dr. William Lupton, later assistant surgeon in the Army of Northern Virginia.

In April of 1862 Chaplain Campbell resigned his position as a chaplain to become Captain of Company E, 47th Alabama Infantry Regiment, attached to the Stonewall Brigade in Richmond. He was wounded at Cedar Mountain on 8 August 1862. He recovered and was present during the battles of Second Manassas, Fredericksburg, and Gettysburg where he commanded the regiment during Lee's withdrawal to Virginia. On 15 May 1864, Major James M. Campbell was killed near Spotsylvania Courthouse by a sharpshooter's bullet. Colonel William C. Oates, later Governor of Alabama, wrote that Major Campbell "was a good officer and a very gallant man. He did his whole duty manfully and well."[11]

---

[11] Edmond Lee Rice, ed., "Civil War Letters of James McDonald Campbell of the 47th Alabama Infantry Regiment with a Brief Sketch of His Life," p. 5 of the undated manuscript (call no. E495.5 47th.C3) in the search room of the Georgia State Department of Archives and History, Morrow GA.

"I was elected chaplain"

Chaplain Charles T. Quintard, 1st Tennessee Infantry Regiment, Army of the Northwest[1]

Charles Todd Quintard was born in Stamford, Connecticut, on 22 December 1824. He attended Trinity School in New York City and received his Master's Degree at Columbia College. He then took up medical studies and received his Doctor of Medicine degree from the University of the City of New York in 1847. For two years, from 1849 to 1851, he practiced medicine in Athens, Georgia. In 1851 he accepted the chair of Physiology and Pathological Anatomy in the Medical College of Memphis, Tennessee.

Following a close friendship with Bishop James H. Otey, first Protestant Episcopal bishop of Tennessee, Quintard became a candidate for Holy Orders in 1854. In 1856 he was ordained a priest and became rector of Calvary (Episcopal) Church in Memphis. In the latter part of 1856, at the request of Bishop Otey, the Reverend Dr. C. T. Quintard moved to Nashville to become the rector of the Church of the Advent. It was there he entered the military chaplaincy at the urging of the home guard.

While rector of the Church of the Advent, Nashville, I was elected chaplain of a military company of somewhat more than local fame, known as the "Rock City Guard."[2] This election was only a compliment shown me by the men who composed the Guard. I was not a military man nor had I any fondness for military life. So I regarded myself as chaplain only by courtesy. But on Thanksgiving day, 1860, the Rock City Guard and other military organizations of Nashville requested me to officiate at the Thanksgiving services to be held under their auspices.

The services were held in the Hall of Representatives in the State Capitol, and there was an immense congregation present. It was a time of great anxiety[,] and the occasion was a memorable one. Rumors of approaching war were abundant, and the newspapers were filled with discussions as to the course the South would pursue in case Mr. Lincoln,

---

[1] The Army of the Northwest was the collective name applied on 8 June 1861 to Confederate units under the command of Brig. Gen. R. S. Garnett in northwestern Virginia (now West Virginia).

[2] Arthur Howard Noll, ed., *Doctor Quintard, Chaplain CSA* (Sewanee TN: The University Press, 1905) 10–19.

then recently elected, should take his seat as President of the United States. The subject of my discourse was: "Obedience to Rulers,"—my text being: "Righteousness exalteth a nation; but sin is a reproach to any people." (Proverbs, xiv, 34.) My sermon was what might be called "a strong plea for the Union."

In December, South Carolina seceded, and on the 18th of the following April—after a bombardment of thirty-four hours—Fort Sumter surrendered and the Civil War was fairly begun. President Lincoln at once called for seventy-five thousand volunteers to serve for ninety days and put down the insurrection in South Carolina. Tennessee being called upon for her quota, responded through her Governor, Isham G. Harris—"Tennessee will not furnish a single man for coercion, but fifty thousand, if necessary, for the defence of her rights or those of her Southern brethren." This undoubtedly expressed the sentiments of the vast majority of Tennesseans, who did not favor secession and deplored war, but who were nevertheless determined to stand with the people of the South.

In the Spring of 1861, the States of Virginia, North Carolina and Arkansas, which had hitherto refused to secede, joined their fortunes to those of the already seceded states; and in June, Tennessee decided to unite with the Southern Confederacy. She was slow to draw the sword. In April, the Rock City Guard, now enlarged into a battalion, was mustered into the service of the State. Subsequently a regiment was formed, consisting of the Rock City Guard and the following companies;—The Williamson Greys, of Williamson County; The Tennessee Riflemen, and the Railroad Boys of Nashville; The Brown Guards, of Maury County; The Rutherford Rifles, of Rutherford County; and The Martin Guards, of Giles County.

This was known as the First Tennessee Regiment. The field officers elected were: Colonel George Maney (afterwards made a Brigadier-General): Lieutenant-Colonel, T. F. Sevier; Major, A. M. Looney. Lieutenant R. B. Snowden, of Company C., was appointed Adjutant; Dr. William Nichol, Surgeon, and Dr. J. R. Buist, Assistant Surgeon.

On the 10th of July, 1861, orders were received by the regiment to repair to Virginia. Being very urgently pressed by members of the Rock City Guard and their friends in Nashville to accompany the regiment as chaplain, I resolved to do so. This, of course, made it necessary for me to break up my household. I removed my family to Georgia, left my parish in the hands of the Reverend George C. Harris, and prepared to join my regiment in Virginia.[3]

My route was through Knoxville and Bristol. At the latter place, which is on the boundary line between Tennessee and Virginia, I missed the train for Lynchburg by an hour, found all the hotels crowded, and the railroad pressed to its utmost in conveying troops.

While waiting I visited two sick men from Nashville of whom I had heard, and then strolled out to camp, a mile from the town. There I witnessed the execution of the sentence of a court-martial upon two private soldiers convicted of selling whiskey to other soldiers. The culprits were drummed around the camp, riding on rails, each with three empty bottles tied to his feet, and a label, "Ten Cents a Glass," pinned to his back.

At Lynchburg I missed connections for Richmond Saturday night and so spent a very pleasant Sunday in the former place. I found Lynchburg a very quaint old town, built on steep hills, from the foot of which the James River finds its way sluggishly to the sea. I preached at St. Paul's Church on "The Love of God."

Arriving at Richmond, I found the place so crowded that I began to think I would not be able to get even a lodging. The Spottswood and Exchange Hotels were crowded to overflowing, and I could not get the sign of a room, though I did succeed in getting some dinner at the latter house. But calling on the Reverend Mr. Peterkin, I was asked to stay with him, and had for a co-guest the Reverend A. Toomer Porter, chaplain of the Hampton Legion,—after the war a prominent educator and founder of a famous school in Charleston, S.C.[4]

At the Rev. Mr. Peterkin's I had the pleasure of meeting the Rev. William Nelson Pendleton, then a Colonel in the Confederate Army, afterwards a Major-General in command of Lee's Artillery. He had been in command of the artillery that did such execution at the battle of Manassas, and gave me a most interesting account of that fight. There was not a masked battery on the ground. His guns were within two hundred yards of

---

[3] Rev. George C. Harris, Episcopal minister, later chaplain of the 26th Tennessee Infantry, CSA.

[4] Rev. Joshua Peterkin whose son, Lt. George W. Peterkin, was aide-de-camp to Col. Pendleton. After the war George W. Peterkin entered the Episcopal ministry and became the first Episcopal Bishop of West Virginia. Anthony Toomer Porter (1829–1902), Episcopalian chaplain of the 25th South Carolina Infantry Regiment and the Hampton Legion.

the nearest of those of the enemy and within four hundred yards of those that were at the greatest distance. Yet he did not lose a man....

On the Sunday I spent in the city that was shortly afterwards to become the capital of the Confederate States, I preached at St. James' Church in the morning, at the Monumental Church in the evening, and again at St. James' at night.

Another interesting incident of this visit to Richmond was in regard to the Rev. John Flavel Mines, a chaplain in the Federal army, who had been captured, released on parole, and had been for two days at the Rev. Mr. Peterkin's house, where I met him.[5] By order of General Winder he was rearrested, and the poor fellow was quite crushed by the idea of having to go to prison.[6] He was especially fearful of contracting consumption, of which some of his family had died. He wrote two piteous letters to me begging me to intercede on his behalf. After two efforts I succeeded in visiting him in the afterwards famous "Libby" prison, where I found him in company with the Hon. Alfred Ely, a member of Congress from Rochester, N.Y., who had been captured at Manassas. I did all I could to cheer the prisoners up. Mr. Mines subsequently renounced the ministry and accepted a colonel's commission in the Federal army....

On my way to my regiment I found in Staunton, Virginia, that the Deaf and Dumb Asylum was used as a hospital, and I wrote to the Editor of the Nashville "Banner" asking contributions from the citizens of Tennessee for the sick and wounded and advising the establishing of a depository at Staunton under the supervision of the Rev. James A. Latané. The citizens of Staunton made up two boxes of stores and comforts for the sick of my regiment. I preached in Staunton Sunday morning and night and left for Milboro. I went thence to Huntersville, which I reached on the 21st of August after a bit of just the toughest travel I had ever made. I found Jackson's River so swollen by rains that it was impossible to ford with the stage. The passengers mounted the horses,—two on each horse,—and forded the stream.

I finally reached Colonel Fulton's camp, over the worst road I ever traveled, and thence found Huntersville—a most wretched and filthy town in those days, where there were many sick soldiers in a meeting-house, in

---

[5] John Flavel Mines (1835–1891), Episcopalian chaplain of the 2nd Maine Infantry Regiment.

[6] Brig. Gen. John H. Winder (1800–1865), provost marshal of Richmond.

public and private buildings and in tents.[7] Huntersville was twenty-seven miles from Valley Mountain where our troops were stationed. I was very anxious to get on for there was a battle daily expected.

Resuming the journey in an ambulance, I had to leave it within a mile in consequence of the wretched state of the roads, and walked all day over the most horrible roads, the rain at times coming down in torrents. I felt occasionally that I must give out, but finally reached Big Springs and received a warm welcome from General Anderson, General Donelson, Colonel Fulton, Major Duval and other officers.[8] My clothes were so wet that the water could be wrung out of them and my first care was to dry them. That done, I set out for the camp at Valley Mountain three miles distant, and reached it on the morning of Friday the 23rd of August, which happened to be the first clear day I had seen for more than a week.

The following Sunday I began my duties as chaplain, and had services in camp which were well attended. That week our scouts had a running fire with the enemy's pickets, and one of our lieutenants captured a Federal soldier. As it was the first achievement of the kind by any of our regiment, our camp was greatly enlivened by it. About this time I was appointed Assistant Surgeon, but I did not wish to accept the office as I felt that it might separate me from my regiment. I do not remember, however, any time throughout the war, when there was any opportunity offered for me to assist the work of the surgeons that I did not do it.

One afternoon a courier arrived at Colonel Maney's headquarters with orders for the regiment to report to General Loring.[9] While Colonel Maney was reading the order, a sudden volley of small arms resounded through the mountain, and some one, thinking the Federal forces had attacked General Lee's position, ordered the long roll beaten.[10] This startled the camp[;] every man seized his gun and cartridge box, and the regiment was at once in line. For at that time the boys were all spoiling for fight.

---

[7] Huntersville is in Pocahontas County, West Virginia. Col. A. S. Fulton commanded the 8th Tennessee Infantry Regiment.

[8] Maj. Gen. Samuel R. Anderson (1804–1883) and Brig. Gen. Daniel S. Donelson (1801–1863) of Tennessee. Gen. Donelson was the nephew of President Andrew Jackson.

[9] Col. George E. Maney (1826–1901) of the 1st Tennessee Infantry and Brig. Gen. William W. Loring (1818–1886).

[10] Gen. Robert E. Lee (1807–1870). This was Gen. Lee's first field command in the Civil War.

I well remember how good Mrs. Sullivan, the wife of an Irish private and a kind of "daughter of the regiment," drew off her shoes and gave them to a soldier who was barefoot.[11] The boys started off for General Lee's headquarters without rations, without blankets, and many of them without coats or shoes. In this plight they reported for duty. It was altogether a false alarm. A regiment had been on picket duty and was firing off guns in order to clean them. Nevertheless it happened that the action of our boys was in conformity to an order received regularly enough about five minutes later, requiring our regiment to take position within a very short distance of the enemy's entrenchments, and the regiment remained out in consequence from Friday morning until Sunday, in full view of the enemy.

A few days after this General Lee determined on a movement on the enemy holding a fortified position on Cheat Pass.[12] The camp became a scene of great animation in anticipation of an important impending battle. To me it was a memorable week beginning on Monday[,] September 8th—a week of such experiences as I had never dreamed would fall to my lot, and of such fatigues as I never imagined myself capable of enduring.

In 1865, after the war ended, the Reverend Charles T. Quintard was elected and consecrated the second Episcopal Bishop of Tennessee. In 1866 he began raising money to establish the University of the South at Sewanee, long the dream of his predecessor, Bishop Otey. As vice-chancellor of the University he was instrumental in designing the campus and raising funds for institutional growth. In 1868 the University of Cambridge honored him with the LL.D. degree. Bishop Quintard's ministry lasted another thirty years. When he died on 15 February 1898, he had served for fifty-one years as a physician, forty-two years as a priest, and thirty-three years as a bishop of the Episcopal Church.

---

[11] Wife of Pvt. Patrick Sullivan killed at Kernstown VA in 1862 while serving in the Stonewall Brigade.

[12] The battle for Cheat Pass at Cheat Mountain, West Virginia, 10–15 September 1861, resulted in a Confederate defeat, Gen. Lee's first in the war.

"I left my little church…"

Chaplain George G. Smith, Phillips Legion,
Army of Northern Virginia

The Reverend George Gillman Smith was born on 24 December 1836 in Sheffield, Newton (now Rockdale) County, Georgia. He was baptized when quite young by Bishop James Andrew and united with the Methodist Episcopal Church in Atlanta in 1846. During his youth, he was the first newsboy to sell newspapers in Atlanta. His initial schooling was in Oxford, Georgia, when Emory College was just getting started. He was licensed to preach by the Quarterly Conference of St. John's Church in Augusta and admitted on trial in the Georgia Annual Conference in Washington, Georgia, on 9 December 1857. Smith served brief appointments on the Waynesboro and Forsyth Circuits and was the "junior" preacher in Macon in 1859 under the supervision of the Reverend Harwell H. Parks. In September of 1859 he married Sarah Joanna Ousley.

In 1861, at the age of twenty-five, Smith was appointed to the Methodist Church at Cedartown, Georgia, but remained there only part of the year. Colonel William Phillips, commander of the Phillips Legion, asked him to take the chaplaincy of his command for service in the Army of Northern Virginia.[13] Smith's memoir of his ministry as a chaplain, written at Macon, Georgia, in 1864 reveals how close he came to death as a result of a wound he suffered in Maryland, and how glad he was to come home.

---

[13] Rev. G. G. Smith's unpublished memoir of his ministry as a chaplain is filed under his last name in the Special Collections catalog in the Special Collections department of the Robert W. Woodruff Library at Emory University, Atlanta GA.

Near Macon July 13, 1864

The state had seceded from the General Government...and it became evident that we would become seriously involved perhaps in war. I had always been most ardently attached to the Union[,] and the previous election had voted for Bell & Everett with the hope of saving it[,] but there seemed to be now no choice between the Abolition of slavery and Secession.[14] To secede might, but would not we thought, involve war. When[,] however[,] the step was taken and when it was too late to retrace it, it became apparent that we were to be driven into the most desperate strife. I of course felt as a southern man[,] and when the war was declared[,] I determined to take my part in it. The result was that I left my little church and entered the Army as Chaplain in August, immediately after we had won the battle of Manassas. I cannot think now I acted prudently, I cannot think that I would have so hastily if I had the same circumstances around me now[,] but I was young and ardent and as such I acted on the impulse of the hour—

My campaign in the army was full of incidents and too full for account in mere autobiographical sketch. Our first camp was at Lynchburg. I returned home and made a hasty trip through Georgia securing hospital supplies for the Regiment. I joined the Regiment in September[,] and we were soon after ordered to West Virginia. I came with the Cavalry[,] and on the 29th September 1861 we were at Jackson's River. From thence over the mountains to Lewisburg at which village I was most kindly entertained by my kind friend Mr. James Montgomery. The country through which we had passed up to this time was wild and mountainous. We found ourselves now in a most charming country albeit the heavy increasing rain had chilled all its loneliness. I did not tarry long but to rejoin the regiment I hurried forward to Sewell Mountain which they were encamped with the united armies of Wise, Loring, and Floyd under command of Genl. Lee.[15] We remained here some days[,] and when Genl Lee was for once outwitted by Rosecrantz who had retreated[,] and we were ordered further to the West by

---

[14] Punctuation in brackets has been added for clarity. Original style and capitalization have been preserved.

[15] Part of Gen. Robert E. Lee's operations in West Virginia from 28 July to 30 October 1861. Lee's subordinate commanders were Brig. Generals Henry A. Wise, W. W. Loring, and John B. Floyd. A combination of bad weather, disease, and poor tactical coordination resulted in the failure of the Confederate forces to achieve their objective of defeating Brig. Gen. William S. Rosecrans's Union troops at Cheat Mountain, West Virginia. This was Lee's first field command and first defeat during the Civil War.

him and marched with Genl Floyd toward the Kanawa Valley. We encamped for several weeks near Cotton Hill which is upon the banks of the Kanawa river. My stay here was one of constant anxiety. The sick, the suffering, the dying were everywhere. At last barely escaping Rosecrantz we retreated[,] and the army encamped at Dublin. I left them at Piney and hurried forward to my family at Macon. I found them well and my little boy grown to be a big baby.

Conference convened at Atlanta and here I was ordained an Elder and returned to the Army as Chaplain.[16] In the meantime our regiment was ordered to South Carolina[,] and we were encamped on the coast near Beaufort. The change was delightful[,] and my health which was not strong was soon restored. We remained here inactive. I can never sufficiently regret that I was not more active religiously. I had prayer meeting however at my tent, visited the hospitals, and preached repeatedly—and did all I could to make the Christian example felt[,] but I might have done more. In August we were ordered to march[,] and we were soon before Richmond. From Richmond we were ordered to the Army of Northern Virginia and we began at Gordonsville our campaign to Hagerstown. I have elsewhere a record of this march. I do not like to refer to it and never do so without pain. The 11th September 1862 at the battle of South Mountain[,] while endeavoring to save my regiment from slaughter[,] I was shot through the neck.[17] The effect of the wound was almost fatal[,] and but for a series of wonderful Providences I know I must have died[,] but God watched over me & cherished me with more than a Father's care.

I was taken into the family of a good woman Ann Bombarger in Boonsboro, Maryland.[18] I lay vibrating between life and death for over 3 weeks. I wrote to Mr. Charles Baker of Baltimore of whom I had heard much and everything good and he sent for me to come to his house. At last I was able to make the trip and permission given by the Provost Marshall, I was carried in an ambulance to Frederick and thence to Athol, Mr. Baker's residence near Baltimore.[19] I was there in October 1862 when I first was

---

[16] Smith was appointed a chaplain from the Rome GA district in December 1861.

[17] During the Antietam Campaign.

[18] The US Census of 1860 shows Ann Bombarger, age twenty-nine, living in Boonsboro with her mother Rebecca Heck, age sixty-five, and Eugene Bombarger, age eight. Boonsboro is between Frederick and Hagerstown MD.

[19] Charles Joseph Baker (1821–1894) a wealthy Methodist businessman who sympathized with the South. Baker was a newspaper publisher, railroad executive,

received into the bosom of that family who have been endeared to me by so many remembrances of kindness undeserved and unexpected. I was very feeble[;] at last I was able to take the boat from Baltimore to Fortress Monroe and early in November I reached Richmond. Was my darling wife living[?] Had she heard the sad story of my being wounded and then had she heard of my promised recovery[?] Had the shock proven too much for her or was she hopefully awaiting my return[?] I telegraphed Macon and received no answer till I left Richmond. I was in Petersburg at the house of my good friend & Bro Charles H. Hall[20] when I received the Telegram that she was well and waiting for me. It was not long before I was with her again. Oh the rapture of the hour when I clasped her once again to my heart.

The Conference of 1863 placed me on the superannuated list and for the next year I was to receive a small dividend from the Preachers Aid funds. In the meantime extensive preparations were being made by the Enemy for an advance upon us. The lines of entrenchments were to be around my house near Macon and very reluctantly we decided when Johnston was removed to change our place of residence to Lowndes County. We moved to Ousley's Station in Lowndes County in October 1864 and by Christmas were in our own log cabin.[21] But for the war my life would have moved calmly enough along.

After Rev. George Smith's health recovered, he held revivals in Valdosta and Quitman, preaching in schoolhouses and in an old store. He traded snuff tobacco, yarn, cotton and wool cards to supplement his income. In 1866 Smith took an appointment as a pastor in the Baltimore Conference. From 1868 to 1870 he preached at Lewisburg, West Virginia, where his wife, Sarah, died. From 1870 to 1888 he served Methodist churches in Dalton, Marietta, Barnesville, LaGrange, Milledgeville, Gainesville, and Madison, Georgia. He wrote five books including The History of Georgia Methodism *and* The Life of Bishop Francis Asbury. *He received the honorary Doctor of Divinity degree from Emory College and was elected vice president of the Methodist Historical Society of New England. He superannuated, or retired, in 1888 from the itinerant ministry; but when he could*

---

and later president of the 2nd branch of the Baltimore City Council. His estate, Athol, originally comprised 617 acres in what is now metropolitan Baltimore.

    [20] The Rev. Charles H. Hall (1831–1872), pastor of Washington Street Methodist Church in Petersburg.

    [21] Ousley's Station was between Little River and Kinderloo Station southwest of Valdosta GA.

no longer stand or sit in the pulpit, he preached from his fireside in his "rolling chair." His contemporaries remembered him as sound in doctrine, always intensely spiritual, having interpreted his call to preach the gospel as a call for life.[22] *He died in 1913.*

---

[22] Memoir of George Gillman Smith, D. D., North Georgia Conference Minutes, The Methodist Episcopal Church, South, 1913, Pitts Library, Candler School of Theology, Emory University, Atlanta GA.

Chapter 2

Ministry in the Camps

Take your share of suffering as a good soldier... II Timothy 2

Although there were no duties prescribed for them in the *Regulations for the Army of the Confederate States,* chaplains were always under the watchful eye of their commanders, their fellow officers, and their soldiers as they designed and performed their ministerial tasks.[1] Chaplains had to earn the respect of the men in their camps and on campaigns where incompetence or cowardice would not be ignored.

A Baptist chaplain of the 13th Virginia Infantry, J. William Jones wrote to the *Religious Herald* in Richmond, "Send us the names of *good men*; and here I repeat, we want *none others*—our object being not merely to fill up the regiments with nominal chaplains, but to fill up the vacancies with *efficient, working* men. We want *effective Gospel preachers*, whose burden shall be Christ and Him crucified."[2]

In a letter dated 14 November 1864 to the Reverend C. K. Marshall, Colonel A. E. Reynolds of the 26th Mississippi Infantry discussed his requirements for a chaplain who would fight himself when necessary:

> I have been exceedingly unfortunate with my chaplains, none have done me any good; all have become indolent and neglectful of those duties they could make themselves most careful in; hence I persuaded them to resign and go home. For two years I have had

---

[1] War Department, *Regulations for the Army of the Confederate States, 1863* (Richmond: J. W. Rudolph, 1863) 22.

[2] Charles Pitts, *Chaplains in Gray* (Nashville: Broadman Press, 1957) 46.

none preferring to be without rather than have one who does not command the respect of my men. At this period of the war no official will be respected in camp unless he is a working man. A man should not be afraid to fight if necessary; always be ready to wait on the sick and administer to the distressed and should ever be at the right place at the right time.[3]

With latitude from their commanders, chaplains performed a wide range of duties as staff officers and as pastors to the command. Kensey Stewart, the Episcopal chaplain of the 6th North Carolina Infantry, traveled to London on a mission to get prayer books published. Chaplain Ballard S. Dunn of the 1st Louisiana Infantry also went abroad, not for prayer books but to buy arms for his regiment. Father Darius Hubert, the Roman Catholic chaplain of the 1st Louisiana, and Baptist Chaplain William Gwaltney of the 1st North Carolina Infantry served as lawyers and administrators for soldiers killed in action. Chaplain William A. Crocker, a Methodist of the 14th Virginia Infantry, formed the Army Intelligence Office in Richmond with the mission of locating missing, wounded soldiers and reestablishing communication with their families.[4]

The most important objective of the chaplains' ministries was to prepare soldiers for battle—to fight the enemy with courage and conviction, and to endure defeat, disfigurement, disease, or death if necessary. It was believed by many, Lieutenant General "Stonewall" Jackson among them, that a Christian soldier was the bravest and best soldier because his faith would overcome his fear. Divine Providence would give the victory to the righteous, so soldiers must be converted to the Lord's Army. Many soldiers simply wanted the assurance that they were "saved from the wrath to come," regardless of how well or how poorly they fought. To meet these needs, chaplains pressed forward to "do the work of an evangelist," as St. Paul had

---

[3] National Archives microfilm drawer 277, roll 59, Consolidated Service Records of Confederate General and Staff Officers, record of Chaplain M. B. Chapman, 26th Mississippi Infantry, Georgia State Department of Archives and History, Morrow GA.

[4] Herman A. Norton, *Struggling for Recognition: The United States Army Chaplaincy, 1791–1865* (Washington DC: Office of the Chief of Chaplains, Department of the Army, 1977) 156.

written in his second letter to Timothy, one of the books in the New Testament treasured for advice to ministers and chaplains alike.[5]

Preaching evangelistic sermons was important because only about a fourth of the Confederate soldiers were members of a church at the beginning of the war. Many were barely literate and had trouble reading the Bible for themselves. Two thirds owned no slaves and were prone to grumble that this was "a rich man's war, but a poor man's fight," especially after April of 1862 when the Confederate government allowed paid substitutes to be provided for the draft.[6]

For soldiers, chaplains brought a gospel message of individual worth, hope, encouragement, and faith in God. Chaplains also provided Bibles, tracts, newspapers, visits to the sick, and a willing hand to help the men write to their families back home so their families would know what had happened to them. There were also baptisms, communion services when supplies could be obtained, a rare wedding when romance would not be denied, and ministries to hospital patients and to prisoners of war when they had no chaplains of their own. On occasion, when there was time and bodies could be recovered, they conducted funerals.[7]

The chaplains' work of preaching and teaching was usually tied to weekly Bible studies or prayer meetings.[8] If there was no fighting, the basic schedule of preaching services and prayer meetings followed a pattern—meetings at night during the week and in the afternoon on Sundays. The observation of communion, or the Lord's Supper, was sporadic because literature and elements were scarce. Baptisms, often in rivers or creeks, were numerous and mostly followed extended preaching services by a battery of preachers of different denominations.[9]

---

[5] William C. Davis, et al., *Faith in the Fight: Civil War Chaplains* (Mechanicsburg PA: Stackpole Books, 2003) 78. Hereafter cited as Davis, *Civil War Chaplains*.

[6] "Persons not liable to duty may be received as substitutes, under such regulations as the Secretary of War may prescribe." Edward McPherson, *The Political History of the United States of America during the Great Rebellion* (Washington DC: Philp and Solomons, 1865) 118.

[7] As in the case of Lt. Gen. Leonidas Polk's funeral conducted by Chaplain Charles T. Quintard at St. Luke's Episcopal Church in Atlanta in June 1864. See Arthur Howard Noll, ed., *Doctor Quintard, Chaplain CSA* (Sewanee TN: The University Press, 1905) 98.

[8] J. William Jones, *Christ in the Camp, or Religion in the Confederate Army* (Harrisonburg VA: Sprinkle Publications, 1986) 468.

[9] Ibid., 469.

Singing hymns, either from memory or following a hymn leader who might have a small hymnal with words if not music, was an important part of camp and hospital worship. Hymns sung by soldiers frequently reflected both their fears and their faith. Just before the battle of Chickamauga in 1863, chaplains in the Army of Tennessee urged the soldiers to remember the promises of God.[10] But many of these soldiers, especially from Longstreet's corps, had also been at Fredericksburg and Gettysburg. They remembered the horrific casualties that one day could bring. The hymns they sang included the poignant lines, "Rock of Ages, Cleft for Me, Let Me Hide Myself in Thee;" "Jesus, Lover of My Soul, Let Me To Thy Bosom Fly;" and "There is a Fountain Filled With Blood, Drawn From Emmanuel's Veins, and Sinners Plunged Beneath That Flood Lose All Their Guilty Stains." These were hymns not only of faith, but also of hope.[11]

---

[10] Sam R. Watkins, *Co. Aytch: A Side Show of the Big Show* (New York: Collier Books, 1962) 103. Private Watkins of the 1st Tennessee Infantry had both critical and laudatory comments about Confederate chaplains on pages 103 and 132.

[11] Davis, *Civil War Chaplains*, 79.

Sermons

The Spirit of the Lord is upon me, because he has anointed me to
preach good news...
Luke 4:16a

Sunday worshippers were sometimes distracted by general camp noises: frying bacon, yells from adjoining regiments, oldtime fiddlers, running horses, and units drilling to the shouts of their sergeants. The weather was another frequent handicap to worship. Rain, wind, and snow would frequently trump preaching, but not always. One regiment reportedly stood for thirty minutes in a rainstorm to hear a sermon; another, fourteen of them barefoot, stood for a preaching service in the snow.[1]

Some obstacles to worship were completely unforeseen as was the situation faced by a Methodist chaplain in 1861. He addressed a regiment of Louisiana soldiers who knew very little English. At the close of the sermon, to which the troops listened attentively, the commander told them to remember what the minister said, "for there is no knowing but in less than six months every damned one of you will be in hell!" At this point a voice from the ranks called out, "Three cheers for hell!" and they were enthusiastically given. The preacher asked why the men were cheering for hell. The colonel responded, "The boys don't know much about the scriptures. They think hell is somewhere between Montgomery and New Orleans and they are anxious to get down in that neighborhood."[2]

In spite of these distractions, worship in the army was generally well attended. The majority of Confederate chaplains focused on basic evangelical sermons that stressed the righteousness and mercy of God, the importance of individual salvation and the path of Christian morality as revealed in the Scriptures. Most did not preach sermons on the right of secession or offer justifying arguments for the war. They realized that

---

[1] Herman A. Norton, *Struggling for Recognition: The United States Army Chaplaincy, 1791–1865* (Washington DC: Office of the Chief of Chaplains, Department of the Army, 1977) 146.
[2] Ibid., 147.

discussing politics in the field produced few converts. Chaplain John C. Granbery of the 11th Virginia Infantry wrote:

> Chaplains and visiting ministers determined not to know anything among them save Jesus Christ and Him crucified. It was always assumed that the cause for which they contended was righteous; on it was invoked the divine blessing, and the troops were exhorted to faithful service. But the grounds of the war were not discussed; constitutional and historical questions were passed by, except a certain local coloring, such as illustrations drawn from active military life and appeals based on the perils of war.... Eternal things, the claims of God, the worth of the soul, the wages of sin which is death, and the gift of God which is eternal life through Jesus Christ our Lord—these were the matter of preaching.[3]

Sermons by the chaplains varied widely, but the majority stressed what became known as "God's Plan of Salvation," taken directly from the Scripture: A) " For all have sinned, and come short of the glory of God," (Romans 3:23); B) "Christ died for our sins according to the scriptures; And that he was buried, and that he rose again the third day," (I Corinthians 15:3–4); C) "I acknowledge my sin unto thee and mine iniquity have I not hid," (Psalm 32:5); and D) "But as many as received Him, to them gave He power to become the sons of God, even to them that believe on his name," (John 1:12). For soldiers who could not read, the verse from John 3:16 might be sufficient: "For God so loved the world that he gave his only Son, that whosoever believes in him should not perish but have eternal life" (John 3:16). For those who did not know if they would survive the next battle, baptism and even church membership were offered.[4]

In addition to the four Gospels and the letters of Paul the Apostle, the book of Revelation was popular for sermons because it held both the exhortation, "Awake, and strengthen what remains and is on the point of death, for I have not found your works perfect in the sight of my God" (Revelation 3:2), and the promise, "...he who sits upon the throne will shelter them with his presence" (Revelation 7:15). The first text from Revelation was a popular one for Chaplain J. William Jones of the 13th

---

[3] As cited in Jones, *Christ in the Camp*, 14–15.
[4] Ibid., 525.

Virginia Infantry, the second for Chaplain Charles James Oliver of Cabell's artillery battalion.[5]

If political ethics were not favored, basic Christian morality was. Gambling, drinking, swearing, profaning the Sabbath, and other sundry sins became favorite topics for discourses and sermons. Soldiers were reminded, "we have little to hope for, if we do not realize our dependence upon heaven's blessing and seek the guidance of truth."[6]

Baptist Chaplain R. W. Cridlin of the 38th Virginia Infantry convicted gamblers very effectively by using religious tracts to shame them:

> I entered a tent and found two young men engaged in a game of cards. At first they seemed ashamed, then they braced up their failing courage (if courage it was) and continued the game. I kindly asked if I could take a hand. Waiting for my turn, I first threw down *Evils of Gambling*; then *Mother's Parting Words to her Soldier Boy*. I found that the game was mine. At the sight of the word "mother," the tears rolled down their cheeks as they both exclaimed: "Parson, I will never play cards again!"[7]

Excessive consumption of alcohol was more difficult to curtail since whiskey was abundant in the Confederate armies and was used frequently by surgeons as an anesthetic if none other were available. Chaplain W. W. Bennett of Richmond cited figures of massive proportions for the production of whiskey: 50,000 bushels of grain used monthly in one county in Virginia by the distilleries there; 150 distilleries in operation in one South Carolina district; and 64,000 gallons of whiskey manufactured *daily* throughout the Confederacy in 1862.[8] Drunken soldiers were dangerous, profane, and often useless, not to mention frequently out of rational control of themselves.

General Braxton Bragg issued a general order attempting to control the vice: "Commanders of all grades are earnestly called upon to suppress drunkenness…the largest portion of our sickness and mortality results from it; our guardhouses are filled by it; officers are constantly called from their duties to form court-martials in consequence of it; inefficiency in our troops,

---

[5] Ibid., 469.

[6] Ibid., 42.

[7] Ibid., 479.

[8] W. W. Bennett, *A Narrative of The Great Revival Which Prevailed in the Southern Armies* (Philadelphia: Claxton, Remsen and Haffelfinger, 1877) 37.

and consequent danger to our cause is the inevitable result."[9] President Jefferson Davis was more direct. On 1 March 1862, he prohibited all distillation of spirituous liquors within ten miles of Richmond. He directed that the distilleries be forthwith closed, and the establishments for the sale thereof closed.[10] Nevertheless, there were testimonies of chaplains in the summer of 1864 who found Confederate soldiers wounded on battlefields with canteens filled not with water, but with whiskey.[11]

In sum, the ministries of chaplains in camp depended on the weather, on the expectations and support of their commanders, on the proximity of the enemy, and on whatever resources they could scrape together. They were dependent on churches and denominational officials for religious literature because there were no military supply channels for ecclesiastical items. Above all, as battles progressed and casualties mounted, the ministries of pastoral care and hospital visitation became more pressing and consuming.

---

[9] Ibid., 38.

[10] Edward McPherson, *The Political History of the United States of America during the Great Rebellion* (Washington DC: Philp and Solomons, 1865) 121. This was a slightly ironic order from Jefferson Davis since he was court-martialed as a cadet at West Point and almost expelled for consuming spirituous liquors.

[11] Chaplain Milton L. Haney, *The Story of My Life* (Normal IL: privately published, 1904) 201. Chaplain Haney, of the 55th Illinois Infantry, USA, was awarded the Medal of Honor for heroism during the battle of Atlanta. He wrote that Gen. Hood "ordered whiskey barrels to be opened that the boys might fill their canteens, for this was their last battle and they would drive the Yanks out of the country."

Memoirs, 1863-1864

"Why am I here?"

William F. F. Broaddus, Post Chaplain, Charlottesville

The Reverend William Francis Ferguson Broaddus was born in Culpeper County, Virginia, on 30 April 1801. He was ordained at age twenty-three and held five Baptist pastorates in Loudoun County over the course of the next sixteen years. In 1840 he moved to Lexington, Kentucky, where he served two churches. In 1851 he worked as an endowment agent for Columbian College in Washington, DC, and was so successful in raising money that the faculty granted him an honorary Doctor of Divinity degree in 1854.[1] In 1855 he became the pastor of the Baptist Church at Fredericksburg, Virginia.

An outspoken advocate of secession, Broaddus was arrested by US. authorities and imprisoned in "the Old Capitol Jail" in Washington, DC. Following his release, he moved to Charlottesville, Virginia, where he accepted a commission as a confederate post chaplain with responsibilities for ministry to the wounded in the Charlottesville hospitals. In 1863 he left Charlottesville to help preach a revival at Winchester for the soldiers returning from the Gettysburg campaign.

As a part of his pastoral duties, Chaplain Broaddus wrote a pamphlet for soldiers in camps throughout Virginia titled, "In Camp." His intent was to offer a justification for serving in a defensive war.[2]

---

[1] Columbian College is presently part of George Washington University in Washington DC.

[2] William Francis Ferguson Broaddus, Confederate Imprint, B 1574, number 47, Western Reserve Historical Society, Cleveland OH.

In Camp
By Rev. Wm. F. Broaddus, D.D.

Here I am, far from home, and loving friends, and long-cherished associations: from all that makes life dear to me. And why *am I here?* Was it merely that I might be an actor in scenes novel and exciting, that I turned my back on the delights of home, and subjected myself to the untold trials and privations of camp-life, and to the fearful dangers of the battle-field? Let me consider. If I can satisfy myself that I am *right* in being here, conscious rectitude will reconcile me to my present privations, and nerve my arm for the deadly conflict, whenever I may be called to meet it.

1. *I am here*, because a numerous and powerful enemy has invaded my country, and threatened our subjugation. Long had the two sections of this great country, lived together in harmony, under a "Constitution" framed by men whose wisdom and integrity have seldom been equalled. The manufacturing and commercial pursuits of the "North," and the agricultural habits of the "South," seemed to create a mutual dependence, which by many was supposed to constitute a bond or union, too strong to be broken. For many years this bond was held as sacred, and all over the land a spirit reigned, ready to respond to the sentiment, "palsied be the tongue that would utter the word *disunion*." While this harmony, so delightful to remember, continued, the country prospered to a degree which astonished all Europe. But evil counsels at length obtained in the heart of the great *North*, and by steady encroachments, pressed for years, the sacred safeguards provided by the *Constitution*, were, one after another overthrown, and one section of the country was found using the power which numerical strength supplied, to oppress the other. *This brought me here.*

2. *I am here*, because those who once called us *friends*, now call us *rebels*, and openly proclaim their purpose to subjugate us, simply because we claim the right to interpret the Constitution for *ourselves*, though they loudly claim the same privileges for *themselves*. When we found that the difference between us and our Northern brethren rendered it impossible that we could any longer live peaceably under the same government, we sought by all honorable means to secure such a compromise as would make us separate nations, each interested to maintain, with regard to the other, the kind of feelings of good neighborship. But our propositions for a compromise were treated with scorn and contempt; and we were made to understand, by many *indirect*, but at the same time, *practical* demonstrations, that we must submit to the will of a *majority*, whether that majority should conform to the

Constitution, or govern its course by its own sectional interests, and selfish ambition.

3. *I am here*, because I believe that *defensive* war is justifiable. True, nothing can be plainer than that war in itself is unnatural, and would never come to pass, if all men should observe the law that bids them love others, as they love themselves. But when my fellow man so far forgets this law, as to assail my personal rights, my property or my friends, this same law which binds me to love him, requires me to *compel* him if in my power to respect all my rights. The present war, is on our part, emphatically a war of defense; and would not lose its *defensive* character, even if in prosecuting it, we should find it necessary to advance into the very midst of the enemy's territory. Camp-life has no charms for me; nor would I seek the battle-field, for its own sake. To dwell in the midst of my loved ones at home, would be far more agreeable to every feeling of my heart, than to encounter either my present, or prospective experiences. But, more than all other earthly good, I covet for my friends, as well as for myself, the privilege of choosing the civil institutions under which we live. To secure this privilege *I am here*; and would regard myself as unfaithful to my country, and my country's God, if I should for a moment shrink from the just responsibilities of a soldier's position.

4. *I am here*, under a stern sense of duty. I am impressed in some degree (may I be more and more so) with the obligations that rest upon me as a soldier. My health must be cared for, my morals must be guarded against the seductive power of evil examples, and all the duties of a soldier I must faithfully discharge. I owe all this to myself, to my friends, my country, and my God. Determined then, to occupy my place here, with honor to myself, with comfort to my friends at home, and with some advantage to my country's cause, I cheerfully consent to be a soldier—to lead a soldier's life—to bear a soldier's burdens—to die, if need be, a soldier's death. God grant that I may never fail of the *true* soldier's spirit!

5. *I am here*, not knowing what destiny awaits me. Many, (O how many!) through the exposure of camp-life, contract diseases, which they would probably have escaped had they remained at home; and dying far away from home and friends, now lie buried in a "stranger's grave;" while many others (O how many!) fall in the midst of the dreadful clash of arms, and scarcely find a decent burial. And who am I, that I should escape from both these contingencies! This thought may well awaken emotions in my bosom, which some would consider unmanly. To me they seem rational, and

worthy of one who believes himself, as I do immortal; and I will, therefore, strive to cherish them—and yet I desire ever to bear in mind, that everywhere God is with me. Putting my trust in Him, if I must fall in this campaign, whether by disease or by violence, may those who witness my end, have it in their power to testify to the dear friends that survive me, that I "died at my post." With such feelings and sentiments *I am here;* and committing myself, for time and for eternity, to Him who stands pledged to men and angels, that those who trust in Him shall be sustained in their cause, I desire quietly to await whatever His wisdom and goodness may appoint.

Addendum

Soldier! The writer of the above lines, who has one son, and several near relatives, and many, many dear friends in our armies, would fain put one more thought into your heart: and O how it would swell his heart with love *to* you, and joy *in* you, if he could learn that upon reading the above lines, you should cry out with heartfelt enthusiasm to your comrades around you:

"*I am here*; and if God spare my life and health, *here I intend to be*, until my country no longer needs the work I am now doing. I did not volunteer for a holyday [sic] amusement. I did not come to camp seeking ease. I came to aid a good cause in danger, and while the danger continues, *I will be here.* What if others prefer to stay at home, and make money, while I am passing through these toils! Will *their* failure to discharge *their* duty excuse *me* from *mine*? What if, either by the culpable neglect of unworthy officials, or the slender means possessed by the Confederate Government, my physical wants have been scantily supplied, and my hardships have thereby increased! Do my sufferings make my country's cause less dear to me? Shall I desert a cause, for which I have already suffered so many privations? No! no! no! Perish the unworthy thought! Come, comrades, here's *in for the war*! I have drawn my sword, and thrown away the scabbard; and my sword is not to be laid down, unless wrested from me by the hand that is stronger than all, until the nations of the earth (including the proud, boasting *North*) shall confess that we are not "Rebels," but a nation of freemen, that "know our rights, and knowing, dare maintain them."

After the war Dr. Broaddus moved back to Fredericksburg where he devoted his energies from 1868 to 1872 to pastoral work in the Baptist Association and to raising money for children of disabled and deceased Confederate soldiers. He died in Fredericksburg on 8 September 1876 at age 75.

"Trying It On"

Charles Holt Dobbs
Chaplain 12th Mississippi Infantry CSA

Charles Holt Dobbs was born in St. Francisville, Louisiana, on 9 July 1835. His father, Henry M. Dobbs, Jr., and his mother, Thekla Nubling, were originally from Dutchess County, New York. Charles Dobbs graduated from Centre College in 1859 and Danville Theological Seminary in Danville, Kentucky, in 1861. He was ordained by the Central Mississippi Presbytery and served as the pastor of the Oak Grove, Mississippi, Presbyterian Church from 1861 to 1863. He was the chaplain of the 12th Mississippi Infantry Regiment, Army of Northern Virginia, from February 1863 to September 1864, and was at the battles of Chancellorsville, Gettysburg, Spotsylvania, and Cold Harbor.

Chaplain Dobbs wrote "Reminiscences of an Army Chaplain" as a series of weekly articles for the Presbyterian Christian Observer *in 1874.*

Reminiscences of an Army Chaplain

Trying It On

Having gone out to the army in order to do good, I was anxious to serve the Lord in any way I could. It was, however a new work to me.[1] So I inquired if there was any other chaplain in the brigade. I found one Sunday morning, he[,] as partner to the sutler, and was selling goods on Sunday; I thought it was best not to cooperate, went back to my regiment, got the drums to beat a tune, and about fifty men gathered around me in the snow. I stood on a low stump and preached my first *extempore* sermon. The Lord was with me. Some base fellows came out of their tents about the midst of the service, and getting as near to the congregation as possible, spread an oil cloth and commenced a game of cards for money, cursing and swearing with all their might. This was discouraging.

---

[1] Chaplain Dobbs reported to the 12th Mississippi Infantry Regiment on 5 February 1863, near Fredericksburg VA. The 12th Mississippi Regiment was in Posey's brigade of Anderson's division, A. P. Hill's corps.

On Monday a young man came to me and suggested that, as there [w]as a young man in the regiment who was a preacher, and was willing to take the position of chaplain, I ought to resign in his favor. I told him I would take it into consideration. I went to this man, whom I found to be a Christian gentleman and an excellent soldier.[2] It seemed he had made application for the position, but not through the proper officers. I learned, too, that he could not get the position even if I were away. I explained that I had been solicited to take this position, without any knowledge of his existence. I found, however, there was friction here, which I regretted but could not help.

I became very low spirited and entreated the Lord for help. I was without any spiritual association, was young and inexperienced. During the week I determined to go to Richmond to get a supply of religious tracts, papers, etc. I must mention here dear Mrs. Brown, of the *Central Presbyterian*. Her encouragement, her advice, her earnestness, gave me new hope and new life. While there I called around at the office of the *Christian Advocate*, where I made myself known as a chaplain. While there a young servant of the Lord, I have no doubt—he was a boy of some 18 years—gave me a catalogue of a Christian association organized in Hood's division. "This," he said, "has enabled us to accomplish wonders."

The plan was to get all members of the church, of any name or denomination, to come out, enroll their names, assist in the conduct of prayer meetings, Bible classes, etc. The idea struck me as an excellent one, and I determined to put it into execution immediately.

On my return, I announced my plan to a few Christians known to me in the regiment. At night a great fire was built[;] we sang a hymn, which was the summons for some sixty or seventy-five men to gather together. I stated my plans, and there were ten names enrolled that night, the next night some twenty more, and on the third night a large number from the other regiments in the brigade, and among them a preacher, who, when the opportunity was given, made a few remarks. When he finished, one man in the audience rose and with a choking voice said, "[M]en, pray for me, I am a back-slider." And another rose and said, "I am a great sinner, pray for me." And we did; it was good to be there.

The next night and the next, and on, there were meetings, until we moved camp upon the Rapidan river, and there we commenced again, and

---

[2] Pvt. Alexander A. Lomax, Primitive Baptist preacher in Company I, was later commissioned as the chaplain for the 16th Mississippi Infantry on 8 January 1864.

night and day we went on, and souls were converted. One day while some brother was praying, the long roll beat, and the meeting broke, the man hurried away, and in half an hour every living soul had moved from that encampment and we were all upon the war path.[3]

I followed the men not knowing what I would do.

My First Experience of a Battle

As I said in the last, I followed the men, not knowing what I would do.

Soon we came to the plank road, leading from Fredericksburg to Orange C. H., and here the men were formed into a line of skirmishers, to feel for the enemy's position.[4] Some soldier said to me: "Mister, if you want to fight, you can have my gun." I thanked him, and told him I did not come out for that purpose; I was only waiting till the battle commenced, to assist the wounded.

Gen. P., our brigade commander, met me pretty soon after this, and advised me to go back to the hospital and I would soon have my hands full. He was pale and thoughtful; he was a good and true man, as well as brave; but he knew many a heart would mourn for that day's work.[5]

After some time, I found the field hospital and offered my services to Surgeon _____.[6] He very impertinently remarked: "You had better take a gun and go to the front; I have no use for you." Upon the impulse of the moment, I said: "I know my place, sir; I mistook you for a gentleman," and turned away, feeling as if I had done wrong.

Soon after this, skirmishing commenced upon our front and the wounded were brought in.[7] There were no arrangements made for their accommodations, and one of those cold spring rains set in. The hospital was in an old corn field grown over with grass, and there were the furrows, like the waves on the river, which follow a steamer. My thought was for the comfort of the men. I had a couple of fly tents, about one and a half yards square, and some of the wounded men had others. I sent word by the ambulance drivers, to the men to bring in their oil-cloths, flies and blankets.

---

[3] Anderson's division marched west toward Chancellorsville to counter Federal Maj. Gen. Joseph Hooker's move toward Lee's left flank, 29 April–1 May 1863.

[4] The road leading to Orange Court House VA.

[5] Brig. Gen. Carnot Posey (1813–1863), a Mexican War veteran and former colonel of the 16th Mississippi Infantry Regiment. Appointed brigadier general on 1 November 1862.

[6] Dr. M. S. Craft of Hinds MS was the regimental surgeon.

[7] Battle of Chancellorsville, 2 May 1863.

These small tents I put up on the shape of a letter A. They reached across two furrows, and by digging a trench on the upper side and making a dam there to turn the water, I could get two men under one tent, one in each furrow. I gathered pine leaves and small branches and put these upon the ground, filling the furrows; over this spread an oil-cloth, then a doubled blanket. This made a good bed, so we thought in those days. After working this some time, I heard someone ask the surgeon: "What shall we do with these men?" His answer was gratifying: "Go, ask the chaplain." After this the surgeon treated me like I had been his brother.

About dark there came in a man very near death's door. He was badly wounded, and had bled until there was no color in his face; he was ghastly. I found it was one who had recently joined the Church. He talked calmly of death. I read several portions of Scripture, talked and prayed with him. He gave me some directions about his little effects, sent a message to his mother and sister, and very soon fell asleep.

The night wore on, the wind blew, the rain poured, and it was terribly dark. During the night our command was ordered back from Chancellor's toward Fredericksburg. They marched all night long, now advancing, now falling back; now to the right, and now to the left, until finally a line of battle was formed near the brick church, where upon the next day, they fought the Federals, who were trying to take us in the rear. During this day the battle raged fearfully upon this line, and success crowned our arms.[8]

It was here I had my first sight of a battle-field, just after a battle. I think it was four or five days afterwards I went over this field while our men were burying the Federal dead. The ground was strewed with their dead bodies, now swollen to three times their natural size, and their faces were as black as their clothes. It was a sad, sickening sight, and haunted me for days.

The next was the great fight of the "Wilderness." Soon in the morning a prisoner, wounded in the arms, was brought into the camp. He was in fine spirits. He believed he was within a few miles of Richmond and said: "We have got you now. We have found out your Stonewall this time. Fightin' Joe knows a thing or so. I tell you, Jackson thought he was taking us in the rear, but we trapped him and his whole command."[9] I suppose he thought so. We did not. But his confident tone and exuberant spirits troubled us somewhat.

---

[8] Battle of Salem Church, 4 May 1863.

[9] Maj. Gen. Joseph Hooker, USA, commanding the Army of the Potomac, and Lt. Gen. "Stonewall" Jackson, CSA, commanding Lee's Second Corps, Army of Northern Virginia.

Hospital at Chancellor

All during the first day at the hospital there were no rations, the men when wounded would usually leave their haversacks. The surgeon's commissaries were not to be found. A report came in that the Yankee cavalry had intercepted our supplies, and the wagons had turned back. They did not come that day. Two days hard work and a whole night lifting wounded men, talking, praying, dressing wounds, writing letters, one after another, sometimes three or four things all needing to be done at once. Hungry, tired and sick for rest, the second night wore on. One poor fellow lay senseless, shot though the head. The doctors said nothing could be done for him. He lived about two weeks, never able to speak or eat, seemingly entirely unconscious, and finally died, I think from starvation.

About this time a man from a Georgia regiment came to me, a most hideous sight, his under jaw was broken and hung down, his beard and clothes were all covered with blood. I showed him his hospital. He recovered. A poor fellow was brought in one day with his leg shot off about half way the thigh; the bones were not splintered.. Some of his comrades had gathered up the flesh and corded it with a shoe string, thinking they had caught the artery. It was kindly meant, but the artery was not caught. It was a ragged wound, and the blood coagulated, and the artery was severed. The jagged ends and coagulated blood had stopped the bleeding. The surgeons amputated the limb and the man recovered very rapidly. But why go on narrating such scenes. Alas! How many brave and noble men were slain or maimed, or laid long upon beds of suffering. Late in the evening of the third day the wagons had not come, and my hunger was of a most distressing character. It looked like starvation. While thinking of my hunger, I saw a man riding by with a huge chunk of corn bread. I stepped out and *begged*. He gave me a small piece; it was delicious.

About dark, however, two wagons came in. There was great rejoicing, the poor fellows looked longingly out of their hollow sunken eyes as the barrels, bacon and sacks were taken out of the wagons; but the peculiar luster and wistful desire faded when it was announced, bacon and *hard tack*. If the reader was ever a soldier, he remembers *hard tack*, and if he was in Anderson's division at that time, he will remember that hard tack, for it was very hard.[10] I chewed on it until my jaws pained me, but was not a whit less hungry at the end of the chewing.

We made *cush*, a word I presume coined expressly for the stuff. The tack was dropped into boiling water, and when soft, it was fried with bacon grease, and a little *mild onion*, a very strong kind of garlic that [g]rows extensively upon all the commons in that portion of Virginia. It is hardly worthwhile saying, this was not a savory dish, but it filled up, and that was what we needed, only the poor fellows who were wounded required nourishing food. They were kept up on whiskey. The next day, however, we got extra rations—beef, flour, sugar, molasses, and a very little coffee.

I saw at this hospital, a pile of human limbs as high as an ordinary table. The surgeons were skillful, prompt and kind. Only one died under the knife; his case was almost hopeless at any rate. On the morning of the third day another wounded prisoner was brought in. He was very much dejected. After a little talk he says, "Well, it is no use, every time we get things fixed to our own notion, and think we have got the Rebs right where we want 'em, old Jackson turns up in our rear and upsets all our plans; it is too bad." This poor fellow was painfully wounded in the arm, but our but our surgeons saved his arm for him, by skillful dressing, etc.

Stonewall Jackson

I do not attempt to write history in these papers; I design merely to give an account of events and incidents, and their religious bearings, which came under my observation, or which I gathered from trusty witnesses. It is certainly true that the good which men do lives after them. Gen. Jackson exerted a great moral influence upon the chaplains, the officers and men of the army of Virginia. His godliness, his simplicity, his sincerity, his spirituality, were themes which never grew stale. The ungodly as well as the pious revered and honored him, as well for his earnest, religious zeal, as his soldierly qualities.

Whenever he rode through the camp, the air resounded with cheers. On the morning that our meeting was interrupted by the long roll, Gen. Jackson, with his staff, rode past our command. The men cheered loudly, and after he had passed you could hear on all sides, "Look out, boys, old Jack is on the war path;" "he's got on his new suit;" "bloody work ahead;" "old Jack has on his war look;" "he is wide awake;" "he is riding at his

---

[10] Division of Maj. Gen. Richard H. Anderson of Hill's corps.

fighting gait;" etc., etc. Sometimes after this I learned the following particulars from and [*sic*] eye witness:

Gen. Jackson first asked Rev. Dr. Lacy, his chaplain, if he could not pilot him through the wilderness, by some road to the left of the plank road, by which he could get into that road two or three miles beyond Chancellors.[11] Dr. Lacy, not having lived there for a number of years, sought out a trust farmer as guide. This man informed him that there was a road which led into the plank road a half mile beyond Chancellors, and another five miles beyond. Gen. Jackson chose the latter, and sent one brigade upon the former, some of whom were captured, and left the impression that their whole command was captured. And here is where prisoner number one got his impression. History, however, tells us how Gen, Jackson succeeded in planting his batteries, and forming his lines within a few hundred feet of Hooker's reserves. Prisoner number two gave us the first intimation of this grand flank movement. Soon after this, however, came the intelligence that Gen. Jackson was seriously wounded, and was suffering from pneumonia, and the joy of victory was turned into sorrow. I believe I could have laid my hands upon a thousand men who would willingly have died in his place. Many of our men now lost heart in the success of the Southern Cause. It was not from lack of confidence in Gen. Lee, but there was none who could execute like Stonewall Jackson.

When the news came, as come we all felt it must, that the great General was dead, the whole army wept, and every man pronounced his eulogy.[12] They talked of his piety, his earnestness, his interest in them, his love for souls. They talked of his natural traits of character and of his generalship; they lived over their army life, in which he was the hero.

A chaplain said: "I met him one day, and thought he was a captain of artillery, but he talked so well and was so thoroughly posted as to a chaplain's duties, and gave me so much valuable information and advice, that I was not surprised when they told me he was Stonewall Jackson."

A private said: "He spoke in the prayer meeting, a few words, but they were so earnest that I shall never forget."

Another said: "At meeting he came and sat down on a log by me, and would not let me get up to make room for him. He knelt down by me and prayed; it was so natural, so earnest."

---

[11] Chaplain Beverly Tucker Lacy, former pastor of the Presbyterian Church in Fredericksburg VA was Jackson's "Corps Chaplain."

[12] Lt. Gen. "Stonewall" Jackson died on 10 May 1863.

Another said: "He shook hands with me, and urged me to give my heart to God." Thus, all over the army, men of every rank and condition pronounced his eulogium. And all had some action, some word, some pleasant recollection, which doubtless now they tell to their children, with tears in their eyes, as they think of the great and good man, who has "crossed over the river, and is at rest under the trees."[13]

Blessings—Incidents

The work of grace, so propitiously commenced previous to the battle of the Wilderness,[14] was only interrupted and not discontinued. Several who had made profession of faith had been called to rest. Some were discharged on account of wounds, and some were on furlough. There was, however, at this time a large addition to the association. Persons who, hitherto from shame, not having taken their stand as Christians at first, others from want of sympathy, others from indifference, now came out and joined in hearty cooperation and swelled our ranks wonderfully. We organized a daylight prayer meeting, at which there were generally over a hundred. At ten o'clock daily, we had inquiry meeting, at which there was always a goodly number, at which I attempted to instruct the hearers in the fundamental truth of the gospel.

There were many blessed conversions. A young man would make a profession of his faith, and at once would commence to pray in public. God dealt very graciously with us in those days, and many souls were brought to Christ.

Every experienced Christian knows, that in order to a healthy growth in grace, there must be exercise of the gifts. We know, too, that where there is a vigorous Christian there will be vigorous works.

About the borders of the Wilderness, and near the encampment of our brigade at this time, were a good many poor families. Their natural protectors being absent, many of them were reduced to the verge of starvation. Some of them were without any of the comforts of life. A plan was now set on foot, and from our scanty rations we furnished a number of families with provisions.

---

[13] Paraphrase of Jackson's last words, "Let us cross over the river and rest under the shade of the trees."

[14] Chaplain Dobbs remembered the Battle of Chancellorsville as the first of the battles fought in the Wilderness area of Virginia.

Early in June, there were evident signs of an active campaign. All unnecessary baggage has been packed up and sent to Richmond; new shoes, new and better guns were furnished, a few suits of new clothes, (by which I mean pants, for that was about the only article of clothing the Government ever furnished), with various other signs, admonished us that we would soon experience a severe campaign. Our rations were now very meager; nineteen ounces of flour, one-third of a pound of bacon, daily, and three ounces of rice once per week, constituted our living. The idea was to give us just enough to sustain life. About this time a soldier came in and announced a poor family near, where the children in rags had followed him a long way, asking for something to eat. Rev. B. T. L. was preaching for me that day.[15] After the service I announced the condition of the family, stating that I had taken measured to find out the truth about their need. Thereupon, I proposed that we all should fast one day, and furnish the family with the results, and that we would give them the extra blankets, tents, etc., which we could not carry.

The result was, we sent to that family about four barrels of flour and nearly three hundred pounds of meat, for there were a thousand brave and noble-hearted men who fasted all that day. As they came up, mess after mess, with their pans and trays and buckets containing their day's rations, I thought of the poor woman who cast in her *mite* into the treasure and received the Savior's commendation. There was a wagon load of overcoats, blankets, tents, skillets, pots, etc[.], that was sent in addition—articles which in those days, she could readily exchange for clothing, etc.

The nobility of the action consisted chiefly in the unostentatious, cheerful manner in which it was done, together with the purity of the motive. I record it here to show the spirit of these men.

Gambling—An Incident

At this time I had been chaplain about four months. How much the Lord had accomplished for us during this short period! But still the amount of gambling and swearing was fearful. One of the greatest difficulties I found in the way of reform, was in the want of confidence in chaplains as a class. Whatever may have been the character of the men who sought this position at the breaking out of the war, in other portions of the army, in our brigade at least, it had been obtained by men without principle. One was well nigh

---

[15] Chaplain B. T. Lacy.

drummed out of camp for his inefficiency; another as I have stated, was in partnership with the sutler, and sold goods on Sunday, and cheated the young boys, of whom there were many in our brigade, out of all their wages.

After I had in a measure overcome these prejudices, by manifesting an interest in their spiritual condition, my position became exceedingly pleasant, and many men who rudely insulted me in the beginning of my work, now became my warmest friends, even where they did not until long after this, attend upon my preaching.

A great many of the men seemed to be hopelessly given up to gambling. Not far from the camp was a spot called "Hell's Half-acre." There thousands of men, from all the neighboring brigades assembled and played at "chuck-a-luck" from morning till night.[16]

On pay day as soon as certain characters drew their pay, they never thought of buying anything to eat or wear, but would sit down and play until every cent was gone. There was a certain officer, who in a few weeks would have it all. There were sets of men in the ranks who could "clean out" everybody else, and at headquarters would take it all in from them. He never drew any pay himself, and generally had thousands of dollars by him. I am glad to say the time came when Othello's occupation was gone, and this man could get up a game only between a commissary and a quartermaster or so.[17] It was terrific to see these men swarming about "Hell's Half-acre" swearing, betting and quarreling from early dawn till dark. Finally, however, Gen. Wilcox, commanding a neighboring brigade, with about a thousand men dashed upon them one day, capturing numerous banks and bankers.[18] The money was confiscated and the prisoners put on double duty. Some of the bankers were made to parade for several hours a day for weeks, with big logs on their shoulders, before the tent of adjutant.

This in a measure broke up the game of "chuck-a-luck," but for a long time gambling was carried on all over the brigade. The great want, however, was good reading. True, we had a great many religious papers and tracts; but there were few Bibles to be had, though they were eagerly sought after. This want, however, was somewhat remedied by men forming classes, and

---

[16] A card game in which the players try to trump one another's hands (similar to poker).

[17] Chaplain Dobbs carried a copy of Shakespeare's plays with him during the war.

[18] Brig. Gen. Cadmus M. Wilcox, CSA, West Point class of 1846 and former colonel of the 9th Alabama Infantry Regiment. Promoted to major general on 13 August 1863.

reading aloud by turns. In this way I have known a group of men to read the Bible through in two months, and many of them acquired a great familiarity with the Scriptures.

About this time there occurred a very melancholy event, which had its effect in deterring many from cards. A young man of good parentage, a druggist by profession, a good soldier, a warm-hearted, genial fellow, beloved by his comrades, sat up one night playing cards and eating a supper at the cost of the loser, was taken with violent cramps during the night and walked over to the surgeon's tent, awakened the hospital steward and asked for the morphine. The steward, half awake gave him the bottle, saying, "Take some, and examine which you get to your tent, how much it is; you are a better druggist than I am." P. poured some in his hand; but violent pains seized him before he got back, and he licked it out of his hand. Some time after this, his companions becoming alarmed at his deep sleep, woke the surgeon and myself. We worked with him all night. We aroused him sufficient to get from him what he had done, but before morning he was dead.

It was a sad blow to his many friends. Those who were killed in battle, or died of disease in the army, were remembered and mourned, with the consolation left to them that they died while on duty. But how sad the reflection to his comrades was that last evening, and what could they write to his friends at home!

Ho, for Pennsylvania!

As the month of May, 1863, advanced there were preparations on all hands for an active campaign. The wagons were all put in repair, the ordinance department supplied with fresh ammunition; there were drills, marches; issues of three days' rations, frequent alarms; fancily dressed couriers galloped to and fro in every direction; all extra baggage was ordered back. The old veterans said: "We will not be idle much longer."[19] The commissaries and quartermasters assured an extra air of importance and an extra knowing look.

Squads of men discussed the campaign, fought many battles, captured Washington City, caged Messrs. Lincoln and Stanton, and dictated terms in "Africa."[20] Some knew from headquarters that Gen. Lee had maps of every by-path and dirt road and turnpike, of every town and farm and house to

---

[19] Preparations for the Gettysburg campaign.
[20] President Abraham Lincoln; Secretary of War Edwin M. Stanton.

Philadelphia, Baltimore, etc. Everybody knew by intuition that we were bound for Pennsylvania, and the whole army was eager to be on the move. What glorious living they would have! How they would pay back the Yankees for what they had done in our country! This, however, they knew to be "Buncombe."[21] The most of them were as much above plundering as the best citizens in the land today.

It [w]as a beautiful and bright morning that we broke up camp and left the spot hallowed to many of us by the blessed work of grace we had there witnessed. Our route was through Culpeper county, in sight of the famous Cedar Mountain, by way of Front Royal, over Snicker's Gap, through Winchester, Williamsport and Chambersburg to Gettysburg. This march was certainly one of the best conducted on record. Everything was arranged and executed with consummate skill.

The army was divided into three corps. Gen. Jackson's old corps, now under command of Gen. Ewell, had gone in advance and had won a great victory at Winchester; the other two corps, under command of Gens. A. P. Hill and Longstreet, respectively.[22] Of these, one went in advance one day, the other the next. The same order was observed with the divisions, the brigades and regiments. The brigade first today was last the next day.

If one division took up the line of march at 3 o'clock, A.M., today, it went into camp at 2 o'clock, P.M., and cooked three days' rations. The last brigade would not take up the line of march until 10 o'clock, A.M., and of course did not go into camp until about 9 o'clock, P.M. The wagons were not seen by us, only every third day, we found them upon the ground when we went into camp. Usually the greatest trial to a soldier upon the march was the wagons. Something would detain one wagon, and this would bring the whole train to a halt, then the men who were behind would close up, and be jammed together in the road. In a few minutes the line would stretch out again; and by the time the men would get well started, there would be another halt. Every infantryman, who has ever marched under such circumstances, will bear me out in the statement that nothing is more annoying or tiresome than these sudden halts and starts. In the march to Gettysburg there was no interruption of this kind. The wagons, I presume, went by a parallel road usually, and we saw nothing of them only at regular intervals, when rations were issued. It was all like clock-work.

---

[21] The modern word *bunk* (meaning *nonsense*) originated from a speech by a congressman from Buncombe County, North Carolina.

[22] Lt. Generals Richard Ewell, A. P. Hill and James Longstreet.

There was only one exception to this regularity of encampment, and that as at Shenandoah. We crossed just above the junction of the North and South Fork. On this day I borrowed a horse and went in advance of the army, to try and swap a gold watch and chain for a horse. I knew that these articles would be worth more to the citizens of that country than Confederate money, and so invested all my money for that purpose. I had not succeeded in making the purchase, and so waited on the far side of the river for my regiment. In the meantime, there came up a tremendous rain. The heavens were black with the thick, threatening clouds, peals of thunder followed quick upon vivid flashes of lightning, and there I must wait. Night set in, and still my regiment came not. Soon it was pitchy dark; not an object was visible two feet off.

As I stood there upon the banks of the Shenandoah, in the rain and darkness, I called out occasionally, "What division is this?" Finally a familiar voice answered: "Bejabbers, parson, its yer own regiment, an' jist let me have the Colonel's horse if yez have him there, an' fall back into the ranks." It was Jimmy, one of an Irish company in our regiment. I remonstrated, but Jimmy took him and I fell in. After marching some half a mile more, we were filed off to the right. The darkness was oppressive, and the confusion unbounded. Men were calling out for their companies, regiments and divisions. Everywhere you could hear "Company A," "Company C," "Twelfth Alabama," "Sixteenth Mississippi," etc., all jumbled and mixed. At last some stentorian voice, sounding high above all the rest asked: "Where is Company Y, 799th North Carolina Tar Heels?" Then was confusion doubly confounded.[23] In the course of time, however, we reached a fence where we were halted for camp, and the men were not long in making fires. In the meantime the rain ceased, the thousands of fires lighted up the old field, and the men lay down to sleep. I found myself among my Irish friends, drenched to the skin and hungry as a wolf. On such a night as this one place was as good as another, and amid the sons of the Emerald Isle I concluded to stay. I got a great rock, rolled it up to the fire, sat down to toast my toes, and with my head on my knees, was soon in a profound slumber.

In the course of an hour or so, I was suddenly awakened with the sensation of having had an icicle thrust down my back. It was soon explained. A gentle shower had fallen, filling my hat brim, which finally gave way and poured the stream down my back. How many times this was

---

[23] Illustrative of soldiers' humor.

repeated during the night I do not know. The morning, however, came at last. The clouds lifted, the sun came out cheerily and myriads of dew drops danced upon the foliage like diamonds; the birds sang their merry carols in the trees, and the soldiers joined in the chorus as they cooked their three days' rations. I got "Old Winny," the Colonel's extra mare, led her off down a ravine, gave her some corn, and lay down upon a huge sandstone rock to nap, with "Winny" tied to my foot. When I awoke it was near the middle of the day. Everything was as still as the shades of death not a human being was in sight. The beaten road told me the direction the army had gone, and about night-fall I came up with my command in camp. Supper was spread and my mates were wondering where I could be. As I had eaten nothing since dinner the day previous, I did ample justice to the biscuit and bacon.

The men upon that march I presume will never forget the abounding hospitality of the good people at Charlestown.[24] There were hundreds of lovely women who greeted us with waving handkerchiefs, their smiling faces, and, excuse me if I say it, more than all with an abundance of meat and bread and butter-milk, cakes, custards, etc., such as the good and virtuous women of Virginia knew our craving appetites longed for. But hungry as we were and delicious as were the viands, the smiles and bright faces of the old and young who gathered there upon that day, did most to cheer our hearts and nerve us for the hardships which soon after gathered about us.

I am not a Virginian by birth nor adoption. Far as our homes were from Old Virginia, we learned to love her as a foster mother. She bore her breast bravely to the storm. There many of my friends found a Savior precious to their souls; there many a one poured out his heart's blood, and lies buried beneath her soil. I utter but the oft-expressed sentiment of the Southern soldier when I say, God bless the noble men and women of Virginia.

In the Enemies' Country

How different things appeared in Pennsylvania from what they did in suffering, over-burdened Virginia.

Magnificent turnpike roads in perfect order, fences in excellent repair, beautiful barns everywhere were signs of thrift and prosperity; while in Virginia the great burden of war, of armies camping, marching and fighting, had devastated and defaced the country until there were nowhere signs of

---

[24] In West Virginia.

thrift or prosperity, and in some places even of habitation; fields were fenceless, houses without tenants, barns, stables, etc., falling down or torn away to kindle fires, or build winder quarters. But here in Pennsylvania everything indicated the highest degree of prosperity. At a little town called Greencastle, just on the Pennsylvania and Maryland line, I witnessed a war of words, and the thorough defeat of some women, which was decidedly amusing. I would preface this incident with the remark that, as far as I could learn, our soldiers were exceedingly polite to all the inhabitants of that country, and especially to the females, except where they were attacked, in which case they usually gained the victory.

Three very genteel-looking women were standing upon the perch of a small frame house which came out to the sidewalk. A lot of soldiers were driving several hundred head of cattle by the house. One of the females called out to the others: "Jane, come here and look at the cattle these nasty, dirty rebels have stolen from us and are driving off." A lank Confederate stopped, and with very solemn mien, polite bow and soft tone of voice, said: "Madam, indeed your [sic] mistaken. Do you see that old brindle cow over there?" "Yes," she responded, a little curt. "Well, we bought her way down in old Virginia, and she has had all these calves since we left there." The ladies gave in and our Confederate marched off, whistling the medley of Dixie Doodle. About this time a general order was issued, forbidding the men appropriating to private use or food anything found in the enemies' country. This order was generally obeyed, except in regard to fowls and small pigs, and now and then a lamb. I think, however, on the 2nd day of July, 1863, from the Potomac to Chambersburg, not a single chanticleer was left to announce the approaching day. Some amusing incidents occurred about this time.

Hearing a great shout just ahead, I pushed forward to learn what was the cause. As I approached I heard: "Run, Bill! Run, old 'oman! Give it to him!" etc. It seems a drummer boy had got over into an old Dutch woman's yard to catch her last Bramah cock, and the old woman saw him. So gathering a barrel stave, she took after Bill. Bill gained on the cock and the old woman gained on Bill; thus they ran several times around the yard, till finally the cock assayed to go through the fence. Bill stooped to pick him up and the old woman came down with such force upon the young drummer that it drove him head-foremost against the fence with a terrific thump. But Bill held onto the chicken, slipped out by the old woman and escaped. This chicken, however, was dearly bought, for he had to beg a ride in the ambulance where he lay down, as he did for several days on account of the severe blow given by this old lady.

Within the Lines—Incidents and Events

There was a company connected with a regiment in our brigade, most of whom were Irish. They were good soldiers and true, full of fun and frolic. They were exceedingly loyal to their colonel, who was very kind and lenient to his men, and withal lacking in discipline according to the standard in that army.

The men were hungry for hog meat. Two of them killed a fine, fat porker and sent up a piece to Col. V., who ate it and said nothing.[25] A few days after this they determined to try a little practical joke upon the Colonel. They went out, killed a hog, and awaited in ambush, near where they knew the Colonel would pass. Soon they saw him coming, and as if by accident, stepped out facing the Colonel. There was no way to get around; he saw them with the hog. So, very sternly: "What are [you] doing with that hog?" "We are taking him to camp to eat him, sir!" "Didn't you know it was a violation of orders, and you are subject to a court martial?" "Yis, Colonel, but this Pinnsylvany hog tried to bite us, bejabers! Would ye's expect a man to stan' still an' lit an innimy's hog bite ye's?" "No, men, you are right. Don't let these Pennsylvania hogs bite you."

After this all the sheep and poultry became alarmingly dangerous whenever any of Col. V's men were about. Doubtless this colonel was an exception, for I heard of such doing nowhere else.

The citizens of that country were peculiar in their mode of living. The houses, at least on the outside—for I was not inside a residence during our entire stay there—were very common looking; generally one-story log houses. The barns, however, were magnificent; their pig-sties were two and three stories, handsomely ornamented with cornice, etc. In every yard was a bake-oven, and they made bread but once a week—very large loaves and very sweet bread. Their butter was rich and elegant and the milk delicious. They gloried in "spread"—and no wonder. This spread was prepared by slicing the bread in slices half an inch thick; over this was spread a good coating of butter, that is, just enough apple butter so that when you took one

---

[25] Lt. Col. Ward G. Vaughn, 19th Mississippi Infantry.

bite, your nose would measure another. N.B. Long-nosed people generally have a proportionately large mouth.

It was common to see several soldiers around a door, and good housewives busy making spread and passing it out, and these hungry Confederates starting off as they were served, at a double quick, to catch up with their regiment, eating as they went, and their places taken by others eager for "spread". The bread and apple butter, or "sarce", as some of them called it, rapidly disappeared. For the women had heard wondrous stories of rebel cruelty, and many of them expected to see barbarians, stealing and carrying away everything movable. But I neither saw nor heard of any plundering. I think I knew the spirit of these men. I was familiar with most of the privates in my regiment, and thought it was above the average in intellect and standing at home. I think their feelings upon this subject were common to most of the volunteers in our army. If any man had gone to plundering houses, or stealing from individuals he would have been drummed out of the regiment. I am sure this was the spirit of those men. They would have spurned from them one who was base enough to insult the women and children, or who would have appropriated to his own use the private property of citizens there. There were exceptions. There were some regiments in the Southern army which would have robbed, and perhaps did to a limited extent, but they kept it hid from their fellow-soldiers, or they would have received the punishment they deserved.

Chambersburg—Incidents

Perhaps it has never occurred in the history of wars, that a half-clad, half-starved army should enter a beautiful, wealthy and thriving town, amongst its most bitter foes, and commit as few depredations and make as few demands, beyond what was essential, as did Gen. Lee's army in Chambersburg.

There was no general plundering. No sane man would expect to see eighty thousand men together and no rogues. There were, no doubt, individual cases, but they were exceptional.

Some wags in our army got off some practical jokes, in themselves amusing, though not altogether innocent. A short, thick-set, jolly-looking rebel, with a round, red face, a little gray eye ever sparkling with fun, a big mouth always fixed for a laugh, ragged and dirty and unshaven, espied a well-dressed citizen, sitting on the pavement smoking a cigar, with his heels resting high upon a tree. Our rebel stopped and eyed the luxurious-looking enemy; he saw his fine felt hat. Our rebel took off his own old wool hat, the crown of which he had pushed with a stick until it was stretched to a point like an old-fashioned sugar-loaf; the rim was notched into scallops, and the crown was full of fancily-cut air-holes. With this he walked up to the citizen, and with one hand seized his hat, while with the other he put his old wool hat upon the citizen's head, and walked on unconcerned, not even smiling.

The indigent citizen knocked the old hat off and jumped up to kick it off the pavement, when a lady rushed out of the house with a pair of tongs, saying, "O, Tony, don't pollute your foot with the dirty thing!" and daintily lifted the hat and threw it off the pavement. Our rebel turned and watched the proceeding, and with a merry twinkle in his eye said, "A good swap anyhow," and walked off, whistling the medley of Dixie Doodle.

A poor fellow whose feet were in a deplorable condition, protected only by some old shoe-soles strapped around his ankles, saw a gentleman walking upon the pavement in Chambersburg, with an elegant pair of boots. Johnny saw the Yankee give a wink, saw him look down at his boots, saw him stick out his foot in a peculiar way. Our rebel took the hint, walked up to him, halted him, saying: "Mister, a pair of boots is a military necessity with me. Unless I get them, there will be one soldier less to do battle in the Confederate army. This, sir, you can see: look at my feet. So, sir, *come out of your boots.*"

The citizen, looking down at the man's feet, said: "You are right. your request is moderate, and since your reasoning is sound and your demand imperative, take them."

The complexion of that man's politics was afterwards found to be of the right hue, so I was told.

Occasionally we saw persons standing back in their rooms, waving handkerchiefs, and the soldiers would cheer loudly at such demonstrations, though they had but little confidence in the rebel proclivities of any Pennsylvanian.

Soon after we left Chambersburg, we came upon the headquarters of Gen. Lee. He was sitting in his tent door, not far from the road-side, with his hat off, conversing with some officers. As regiment after regiment passed by they cheered vociferously, which as acknowledged by a bow from the great and noble man.

The road from Chambersburg to Gettysburg, a beautiful, smooth turnpike, was lined on either side by magnificent cherry trees laden with the delicious fruit, fully ripe at this time. I suppose fruit was never enjoyed more. Notwithstanding there were hundreds of these trees, all very large and laden with fruit, in a few hours it was all gone. All the smaller limbs were stripped off. the road was filled as far as the eye could reach, with moving branches.

It was near here that a Louisiana regiment came upon a patch of sorghum cane, and cleaned it out entirely. Here also a North Carolina regiment came upon a clover field and thought it was a "goober" (pindar) patch, and the whole regiment broke ranks and commenced grabbing.[26]

Gettysburg

The battle progressed fearfully. We could hear the booming of the guns, the bursting of shells and the roar of artillery for miles to the right and left. I advanced toward the front, and by chance saw Gen. Lee, his staff and several generals in a prominent position, evidently viewing the field of battle. Going forward I took my position near them, and there the grandest scene I ever witnessed burst upon my view.[27] The central lines of both armies were in full view, the enemy upon an elevation beyond, and our lines upon the great flat, with rising ground here and there. The roar of artillery and musketry was almost incessant. Soon, however, I could only distinguish the lines by the denser clouds of smoke and the bright flashes of fire.

Pretty soon I saw upon the turnpike to my left, there emerged the long lines of ambulances, and I could plainly hear the groans and cries of the poor fellows whose mangled limbs and painful wounds were as yet undressed. I hastened back to the hospital where I found a few of our own men slightly wounded. My brigade was held in reserve.

Upon the day previous, as the men advanced to the front, I rode along with them.[28] A greater number came to me and gave me a finger-ring, a locket, a purse, or some other memento or keepsake, with the invariable request, "Parson, if I am killed, send this to my mother, wife, sister, or to the person whose name you will find in the package." In the latter case usually accompanied with a knowing look, "You understand, Parson." Soon I had in trust about thirteen thousand dollars in Southern money. This, with the

---

[26] "Pindar" is the African Congo word for peanut.

[27] Pickett's Charge on 3 July.

[28] On 2 July, the 12th Mississippi Infantry formed the reserve for the rest of Posey's brigade which was attacking through the Peach Orchard. Because they were in reserve, the casualties for the 12th Mississippi were comparatively light: seven men were wounded.

rings, the pocket-books, etc., filled a large haversack. They caused me a great deal of uneasiness and several sleepless nights. Finally I rolled them up in an oil cloth and put them in the medicine chest. The surgeon was now one of my warmest friends, and did all in his power to make me comfortable.

It was not long until my brigade was in the thickest of the fight, and the wounded came pouring in. As fast, however, as their wounds were dressed, they were sent to a large seminary building in the rear of Gettysburg.[29] Upon the third day I mounted my horse and started for this hospital. After riding some distance I sent my horse back, on the advice of a surgeon whom I met coming from there. Soon after I commenced the foot journey, I met numbers of men who had been slightly wounded and were sent to this hospital and were not returning, determined to walk to Staunton, rather than be captured.

Many of them I knew, and they tried to persuade me to return, as I would be captured. I was bent, however, upon the work of ministering to those poor fellows, so on I went. But presently I came to a picket, who refused to allow me to pass. Suddenly I thought of the haversack containing the money, etc., entrusted to my keeping, and I hastened back to the hospital, where I found everything packed, preparatory to a backward movement. There was no haste, however, no undue confusion, and nothing like a panic.

As we fell slowly back, requisitions of horses, medicines and clothing, were made upon the various towns. The army moved with great, good order, considering the disastrous results. The army fell slowly back to some point near the Maryland line, where we waited two days, anxious for the enemy to attack us. We were defeated, but not demoralized, and our boys were anxious to retrieve the loss.

Doubtless we would have remained in this position longer, but the Potomac was now rising very rapidly from recent heavy rains, and prudence I presume, dictated the policy of placing the river between us and the enemy.

In a little town—I have forgotten the name, it was in Pennsylvania— the surgeons were making some extensive purchases of drugs. The druggist complained very much of the kind of money he was to be paid in; but when it came to a settlement, disputed some time about a difference of twenty-five cents, and would not be satisfied until it was paid.

---

[29] The Lutheran Seminary on Seminary Ridge.

The wounded men who could not obtain places in the ambulances, commenced *capturing* buggies, carriages and spring wagons wherever they could be found; and so they passed on and made their way to Staunton. This, however, was a military necessity. The men must either fall into the hands of the enemy or take some conveyance to ride in. I know in the Northern army, this would have been considered a slight offense. If the people of Pennsylvania only knew how our people suffered at the hands of Sherman, Sheridan and Wilson, and even by the army of the Potomac under its best discipline, they would today thank God for the discipline and humanity of the Southern soldier.[30]

After waiting two days for Meade to attack, Gen. Lee crossed over the Potomac.[31] In the move I found myself separated from the division. Soon I reached Williamsport, where the cavalry, the commissary, quartermaster, ammunition and artillery departments were crossing. The river was rising rapidly, and I determined to cross. The water came up on my saddle-skirts, but we all got over without accident. On the Virginia side the turnpike followed down the bed of the river for several miles. On the Maryland shore the bank was a high bluff, and as we passed down this road I thought what a trap if the enemy should come upon that side. But when we came to the point where the road diverges from the river, I found a pontoon bridge being laid. Gen. Longstreet was up to his waist in the water[,] working as hard as any of the detail.[32] The rain was still coming down, and a cold wind had set in from the west.

About dark the last of the trains passed beyond the bridge and the infantry commenced to cross over. I afterwards learned that the infantry marched down a dirt road parallel with the river on the Virginia side. All night long in mud almost knee-deep, in pitchy darkness, the poor fellows marched. Many of them left their shoes sticking deep down in the mud, and surely when they went into camp the next day they were the most woe-begone, bespattered set of fellows in the world. Though they had marched only three or four miles, the tramp was the most tiresome of any day's march of twenty miles since we had left Virginia.

---

[30] Maj. Generals William T. Sherman, Philip H. Sheridan, and James H. Wilson who periodically devastated large portions of the South.

[31] Maj. Gen. George G. Meade and Gen. Robert E. Lee.

[32] Lt. Gen. James Longstreet was the I Corps commander in the Army of Northern Virginia.

Learning at the bridge from a friend, that my command was bringing up the rear and would not be along till morning, I rode to the top of the hill where I fell in with some cavalrymen, and with three or four of these took possession of an old shanty. Finding I was a chaplain, they treated me with great kindness. Each of these men stood guard over the horses, alternating every two and a half hours.

They refused to allow me to go on guard; and though I had a good many of the treasures committed to me by men who were wounded, and which I had no opportunity as yet to deliver up, I slept soundly with my saddle for a pillow.

The army was marched with some degree of regularity back to Culpeper[;] thence we crossed the river and went into camp near the Rapidan bridge, some three miles from Orange C. H.[33] During the march to and from Pennsylvania, we usually rested on the Sabbath and had preaching. These services were well attended, and besides the Sunday service we had a prayer meeting daily, sometimes in the morning and sometimes in the evening, according to the time of day we camped or broke up. These services were instrumental in doing great good. Numbers of the men kept up their Bible reading. Still, the profanity in my regiment was alarming. Most of the men had too much respect for me to swear in my presence, but I heard enough of it. It is singular that men will swear, who have enough good breeding to refrain from it while in the presence of a poor servant of Him whose name they blaspheme!

Aunt Polly

In the first revolution we read of Polly Pitcher, notorious for carrying water to our wounded men in some battle during that great struggle for independence.[34] But Aunt Polly, as she was known to me, is more worthy of note. She lived in Culpeper C. H.,[35] and if she lives yet, I would say in behalf of thousands who knew, *Hale, Aunt Polly!* Glorious and gentle woman, kind of heart and earnest in spirit. Aunt Polly had coffee hid in her cellar, sugar concealed in her trunks—pure, good Rio and Java—whole sacks of it, at that.

When we reached this point in the retreat from Gettysburg, Aunt Polly commenced serving the soldiers; day and night she made coffee and biscuit—ah, such biscuit, so white and flaky and sweet, so abundant and so

---

[33] Orange Court House.
[34] Molly Pitcher was the heroine at the Battle of Monmouth in 1778.
[35] Culpeper Court House.

free and good. Sweet, kind-hearted, old Aunt Polly looked so happy when she saw the sick and hungry men devouring her provisions. True, she was not alone; there were many other women there who helped her; but hers was the master-spirit; she was in the hospital, in the camp everywhere, like a good angel that she was.

One day she came into the hospital, and there was a poor fellow wounded in the head. The doctors said he was past recovery, and so left him alone to die. Aunt Polly came in and saw him lying, his hair all clotted with blood, his great, strong body as still as if death had already taken hold upon him. "What," she says, "can nothing be done for this poor man?" "Nothing," said the surgeon; "he is past recovery, and there are so many here that we can help, that we must give them all our attention." "Give him to me, then; perhaps I can do something for him." "Certainly, Aunt Polly, he is of good parentage, a faithful soldier and an honest man." "And one that needs attention," added the good angel of mercy. Pretty soon she had washed away the clotted blood from his hair, bathed his hands and face, and commenced to moisten his lips with a little spirits. In a few hours after this the man opened his eyes, gave an intelligent look, and evidently fell into a doze. She had succeeded in getting him to swallow several spoonfuls of toddy. Soon after this she had him moved to her own house, where she nursed him with the tenderness of a sister. The man recovered rapidly, and in about six weeks went home on a furlough.

Aunt Polly was one of a glorious and blessed band of women, who, in every part of the South, hovered about our hospitals, who, by their labors, their attentions and words, saved many and many a soldier from an untimely grave.

The Revival

Some time during the early fall of 1863 we took up our quarters permanently near Rapidan railroad bridge in Orange county. Soon after, the Federal army encamped in Culpeper, opposite, and there the two armies remained in sight of each other for many months. Regular services were now commenced. There were two other chaplains in the brigade and we united our services and carried on the work in harmony. No one asked what denomination the preacher was connected with. The men came together to hear the word preached. Whenever I could obtain assistance, I generally went to some other regiment and preached. There were several brigades in our corps that were without chaplains, and among them were thousands anxious to hear the gospel. It was customary amongst us to use the mourner's bench, generally merely to know who were specially interested in their soul's salvation.[36] It was our custom to offer a prayer in their behalf—invite them to the morning prayer meeting and inquirers' meeting.

At sunrise in the morning we gathered together for prayers; at ten o'clock, conversation with inquirers; at eleven o'clock, preaching. The afternoon was usually spent in reading scripture, or such religious reading as we could procure.

My library consisted of a Bible, a short commentary on the Scriptures, furnished us through Dr. Moses Hoge of Richmond; "Hedges' Outlines of Theology;" a book of sketches for sermons which was given me by a friend, and proved a friend in need on several occasions.[37] These, with Shakespeare, made up my library. We were furnished, however, with many copies of Presbyterian, Methodist, and Episcopal papers, besides numbers of tracts. These I distributed to the men, carrying them about from tent to tent like a newsboy. Generally they were glad to get them. Now and then, however, I was rebuffed; but generally, by perseverance and prudence, in the course of time succeeded in overcoming these prejudices, and in some instances these very men became the most earnest Christians.

At the close of our night services, after a prayer for those who were forward as seekers of the Lord, an invitation was given for the men to join the church, their names were taken down, and then they were asked—What Church do you wish to join? If the Presbyterian, I received them on profession of their faith, and gave them a certificate, which was usually acceptable to their sessions at home; if the Methodist Church, I received them on profession into our church and gave them a letter to their own church, which, as far as I know was always accepted by them.[38] Those were days of probation in the Methodist Episcopal Church, South, and the men did not want to be probationers. They could not find it in the Word of God. If the men wanted to go into the Baptist Church, their minister was usually there, and we would go together to the river, and I would take part by

---

[36] Mourners' benches were put in front of the congregation during these services for those who were convicted of sin by the sermon or who were in special need of prayer.

[37] The Rev. Dr. Moses D. Hoge (1819–1899), Presbyterian chaplain at Camp Lee VA.

[38] Chaplain Dobbs received the soldiers into the Presbyterian Church and then gave them a letter of transfer to the Methodist Episcopal Church, South, thereby avoiding probationary membership for them.

praying with and for them, or making some remarks appropriate to the occasion. There was no sectarian feeling, no bitterness, no strife. The Spirit of the Lord was present there, and where that Spirit is there is Liberty. Ours was a glorious, blessed liberty. We had one heart and one desire.

Some time after the battle of Gettysburg, I think it was in September, 1863, while we were in camp at Rapidan Bridge, without previous warning and to the surprise of the whole army, the long roll beat, and with breakfast cooking, we were marched up the river at a rapid rate. At some road several miles above the bridge, we crossed to Culpeper county, and winding around through fields and forests, we came into a road beyond Culpeper C. H., in the rear of Gen. Meade's army. Here we stopped to cook rations, at which the men were so much incensed they would not eat them in some instances. Why? We were about to bag the Yankee army—this is what our men believed; and what was the universal opinion of these soldiers was generally true. However secretly a campaign was planned, these fellows were sure to guess pretty close at what was designed. And, sure enough, the Yankee army strung out upon a rapid retreat, and we after them; a portion of our forces engaged the enemy. During the next day we could hear the guns as we marched, and before we had advanced far we saw the evident signs of a retreating army—guns, canteens, blankets, overcoats—in fact all the paraphernalia of an infantryman's outfit were strewn upon the road, and the farther we advanced the more numerous were the signs. The bands played lively airs, and from a steady march we advanced to a double quick.

The citizens hailed us with joy. They told us the Yankees were running, with their tongues hanging out of their mouths, and the provost guards were pushing them forward at the point of the bayonet. We were not tired; it was more exciting than a fox chase. As a minister of the gospel, in these calmer hours I am ashamed of it, but it was even so; like a spirited horse in a deer chase, we did not get tired. But the cooking of the rations I suppose, did the work. When we came upon the enemy it was not far from the old Manassas battlefield. We came upon the brow of the hill, and in the midst of an immense plateau, in the center of which was a railroad out, lay the object of our search. Guns were stacked, they were lolling upon the ground, bathing in the creek, sunning themselves like terrapins on logs. They evidently had no knowledge of our presence, for we were massed in the thick woods. Just as we were wondering what was to be done, Gen. Lee, with several officers, rode up to where I was standing and took the view in with their field glasses. Just then one of our batteries let a bombshell drop right in the enemies' camp. The effect was like magic. In a moment every Yankee had his gun and fell into line.

Those who have never witnessed the evolutions of well trained soldiers, can form no idea of the rapidity of their movements. In an instant their line was formed, their guns wheeled into position, and the shells came flying about us like leaves in autumn. Gen. Lee turned to a general beside him and said, with a flashing eye, "Sir, you have ruined it all." The other general said it was not his fault; the gun was fired contrary to orders. I never knew what was the plan; there was no battle fought. Our men got into a skirmish, in which our brigadier general was badly wounded in the thigh.[39] Finding there would be no general engagement, I went back with General P_____. There were three or four guards, General P's son, a cook and myself. I went along by request of the surgeon to dress the wound. Gen. P_____, as I have said, was a good, brave and sincere man, very much beloved by all his command. He was greatly reduced from loss of blood. the wound was a painful one in the thigh, and he became feverish and exceedingly nervous during the first day's ride. At night we camped at a deserted mansion, near the O. and A. railroad. But the events of this night and next day I must occupy another paper to tell about.

A Big Scare—Devastation

Notwithstanding the handsome old mansion was without an inhabitant, when we reached there Gen. P. would not consent to go into the house. It was about an hour before sunset when we stopped. The camp was pitched in what once had been the front yard. The General was taken out. I dressed his wound and went out to feed my horse. While busily employed in this, I heard approaching horses at a gallop. Looking in the direction of the sound, I saw two negro men advancing rapidly at full speed. They were dressed in full Yankee uniforms with all the accouterments of cavalrymen, even to the sword, the carbine, the boots and spurs. Right on they came at full speed. I sprung behind a bush and quick as thought made up my mind. In my saddle-pockets which I had laid fortunately by the bush, were a pair of Gen. P's pistols. Snatching one of these, I stepped out, bold in appearance, but with my heart in my throat, said sternly, "Halt!"

Quick as thought they stopped, dropped their guns and said, "Laws 'a mercy! Massa, don't shoot. We ain't no soldiers."

---

[39] Maj. Gen. Posey was wounded on 14 October at Bristoe Station and died on 13 November 1863.

On inquiry, I found that they were loyal servants belonging to the owner of the mansion, and had been sent over by their mistress to offer us the use of the house. They brought us the keys, and we put Gen. P. in a comfortable bed.

No description in words can given the reader any idea of the desolation of this portion of Virginia. The fences were all burnt, the forest and ornamental trees all cut down, and in some cases the houses were torn down, the lumber burned up and the brick carried off to build chimneys for winter-quarters.

On the next morning we found in a field hard by, a Yankee camp which had been suddenly deserted. It reminded me of Byron's Senacherib [sic], except the dead soldiers.[40] There were their tents, their arms stacked, their provisions, and all other paraphernalia of well equipped soldiers in camp.

About 10 o'clock we left this camp and took up our journey. In about an hour we fell in with the army on the railroad track, which they were tearing up and burning. The ties were piled up and the iron put on them. The heat was so intense that the rails bent almost double. It was astonishing with what rapidity the road was torn up and set on fire. As we advanced to the Rappahannock River, the work of desolation was greater; for it was here the Northern army had spent the previous winter.

In one place there was pointed out to me the site of a flourishing village of the year previous. Not a trace of it could now be seen; not even the foundation of a house. For miles and miles were rich fields bare now as a Western prairie; no fence, nor house, nor tree, nor shrub. There was not a living thing there but our army, and no signs of life. At the Rappahannock Bridge trains on the railroad came up to meet us, bringing supplies and the mail.

We remained in camp here and about Culpeper for some time, and finally returned to our old camp at the bridge where we found our bunks and tents, into which we went and remained without interruption until the following spring.

Revivals—Incidents

As the winter of 1863–64 drew on, it was determined to build a chapel. Some thirty men got together, and in the course of a few weeks—we were interrupted by rain—we had a comfortable log house forty feet by twenty,

---

[40] From "The Destruction of Sennacherib" by George Gordon, Lord Byron, English poet.

with one window, a door in the side, and a large fireplace in each end. We rived boards and fastened them on the roof with poles pinned over them. It was a comfortable house and a glorious place—a blessed Bethel, where we soon learned to sing Ebenezers.[41] Within this chapel we had benches made of pine logs split in half, the split side up, and the round side checked with rocks to keep it from rolling.

When the men came there to worship, they reverently sat with earnest gaze and wistful attention riveted to the preacher as long as he spoke, no matter how dry or uninteresting the manner of the messenger. What they seemed to desire was the message. You seldom heard one say, "Ah, that was a fine discourse," but they came daily, seeking information upon some point made. You would see groups of men looking into their Bibles to find Scripture for it.

You never saw them turning their heads to see who was coming in. No unusual noise, nor gathering of men, ever seemed to disturb their devotions. In our brigade were a great many young men just grown, some still in their teens, and many of them beardless. A great many of these were converted.

One night, after preaching had been over some time, a young man, a warm friend of mine, came to my tent and asked me to follow him. I walked some distance, I suppose a mile or two, where we entered a thick woods beyond the camps, away from the noise and clamor, until we came to the brow of a hill, and pointing down in the valley below, not more than thirty steps were some forty or fifty of these young men around a great log fire holding a prayer meeting. It was one of the sublimest pictures I ever saw. Those pure, bright faces, as peaceful and happy as the angels in the presence of their Father. [I]t was good to be there. All unknown to them I and my companion sat down and drank in the sweet notes of their hymns, and joined our hearts in their youthful petitions. Ah, boys, me-thought, if your mothers and sisters could see what I behold, how it would gladden and cheer your desolate hearts.

---

[41] Bethel means "house of God." Ebenezer in Hebrew means "stone of the help" and refers to a stone set up by the prophet Samuel after a defeat of the Philistines as a memorial to the help God provided to Israel (I Samuel 7:12). In the hymn, "Come Thou Fount of Every Blessing," the second verse reads, "Here I'll raise my Ebenezer, Hither by Thy help I'm come; and I hope by Thy good pleasure, safely to arrive at home."

One day a Baptist minister, who had recently received the appointment of chaplain to a neighboring brigade,[42] sent for me, as there were several he said, who wanted to join the church some the Presbyterian, some the Methodist, and some his own. Brother B. was an earnest man, and withal a faithful and most excellent preacher. He had not, however, witnessed many scenes in army revivals. His own soul was full, but he did not know that many others were like him. He asked me to preach, after which he requested to me to take the usual steps to find out who wanted to confess their faith in Christ.

After a short sermon, I requested all who wanted to join any church to occupy certain seats. There was sitting room for about eighty persons, while we sang a hymn the men came up in numbers until every seat was filled, and others were standing near or sitting on the ground. Brother B. came up, "Certainly they did not understand you." But they did, and there were over eighty that day, and afterwards many more.

I neglected to say in the proper place, that our meetings at this encampment received a great impetus by the earnest preaching of Rev. B. T. Lacy, then corps chaplain.

Horses and Horse Doctors

In that portion of Pennsylvania through which our army passed, there were notable horses for size and clumsiness, unsurpassed I presume in the world. The quartermasters had orders to buy horses, *ad infinitum* at $125, good, bad, indifferent, large and small, old and young, so much, no more, no less[;] these were not the orders, but $125 for a good horse; and good is an adjective admitting of comparison, and is an extremely relative term as regards horse-flesh, influenced by whose spectacles you look through. So they bought horses. But a wag remarked they ought to have bought a Pennsylvania iron mine foundry, and rolling mills to keep in iron and nails. Those horses, called Conestogas, why I don't know, had very large feet.

The quiet and frugal inhabitants of that country treated their horses with as much tenderness and care as their children, and some of them loved them as much, some more. The great elephantine monsters were hitched to the ambulances, the wagons, caissons and cannon, and the poor horses of the army driven behind, and they looked grand, so fat, so sleek, so large and strong. Alas! [I]t is not all gold that glitters. Their great feet beating with

---

[42] Chaplain Edward B. Barrett was the Baptist chaplain of the 45th Georgia Infantry.

such tremendous force against the hard pikes soon tore them up, and before we had advanced many miles, these big horses were led, and the poor old horses which had served so long and so well, were again put to hard work.

I had afforded one Pennsylvanian great relief[;] the quartermaster was about to "press" him for $125 confederate money, when I stepped up and offered my watch and chain. The bargain was concluded in a trice. Mr. Quartermaster seemed satisfied, I was, and I know the seller was. The horse was a good one, but I paid for him all that he was worth.

One day "Hessian" my horse got sick. One man said he had kept a livery stable, was raised amongst horses and he knew what ailed him, it was "botts" and he knew a dead sure cure, so John mixed a bottle of stuff, and swinging Hessian's nose high in the air, he poured it down his unwilling throat. But poor Hessian stood trembling with pain, and then staggered off and lay down. "Blind staggers" said Jim, and Jim was an oracle among horsemen. And so Jim mixed a dose, drenched my poor Hessian again but all to no purpose.

"Colic," said dry old Pete, "colic, colic," chimed in a quartermaster sergeant, a hospital steward, and three wagon drivers, and Whitman "knewed it was colic from de fust." Hereupon every man had his remedy, but I concluded Hessian had better die in peace, so with a rope long enough for him to lie down and get up I tied him to a limb and went to my tent. Soon after this the assistant surgeon and regimental commissary rode up on their Pennsylvania mares, and hitched on either side of Hessian. Not long after this I was aroused from reveries by some terrific thumps and the sudden appearance of Whitman. "Sir, dem mars is killing Hesay." I hastened out and sure enough he was between two mares, these friendly horses were drumming upon his sides.

I thought, well surely my horse will die before morning, and I led him out into an old field and turned him out. But he did not die. Next morning he had his head in the tent door, looking as hungry as his master felt. He was well again, thanks to the Pennsylvania mare doctors.

Winter of 1863–64

During the long winter nights there was ample time for improvement. Many of the young men had come from school into the army, and many who would have received a collegiate education, were now deprived of every opportunity of study. So, classes were formed, school books purchased—grammar and arithmetic, Latin and Greek, law and medicine were taken up, and in the afternoons and of nights after services, the little chapel was turned into a university, and the lawyers and doctors and teachers, who were now in rags and tatters, unshaven and shabby-looking enough, sought mental recreation in renewing their professional studies in instructing others. There was a masonic lodge organized, and degrees were conferred and lectures given. And with devotions and studies, cards were laid aside, and except among the surgeons and quartermasters, scarcely a game of cards could be gotten up. As the spring advanced, our meetings seemed to deepen in interest. The little chapel would not hold the half of the congregations, and when the weather would admit, services were outdoors.

About this time there came a young man to the meetings for the first time, and at once he became deeply interested. I found he was a Presbyterian, but had not been attending because he thought it was all excitement, and that all kinds of trickeries were being used to get men into the Church. When he saw how the meetings were conducted, he at once joined in heart and soul. He had been absent several months from a wound, during the first part of my ministry, and hence was not there to grow up with the work.

Only once do I remember ever to have witnessed any unusual excitement, and that continued during two nights. Some young men who had been brought under conviction, and were very deeply impressed with a sense of their sins, remained kneeling after the congregation was dismissed, giving way now and then to convulsive sobs. I talked with them awhile, but could get no response from them. Finally, I left them in the care of several earnest young men who agreed to remain with them. Along towards morning they seemed at once to take in the plan of salvation and believe in Christ as their Savior. As far as I can now remember, their deportment was consistent after this. There was also another case, very similar to this one. Generally, however, there was no excitement and no attempt at anything of the kind. Presbyterians, Methodists, Baptists and Episcopalians were all one in their worship.

As I have said as the spring of 1864 approached, a greater solemnity seemed to pervade the meetings; the religious feeling was silently and surely gaining ground. As we met there was an undefined feeling that with many, our earthly intercourse would soon end, and our meetings below exchanged for those in heaven. Still, I do not think many joined the Church from fear of death. We watched their religious convictions; we conversed with them in private, and found them generally giving every evidence of genuine faith and repentance. Their consistent lives, their earnest prayers, their solemn warnings and entreaties to companions, their zeal and love for the truth, were fruits which evinced a good tree.

The Lord be praised for those glorious manifestations of His grace and power!

The First and Last Communion of the Lord's Supper

As the spring advanced, the orders for drill, for sending back extra baggage, the issue of rations for several days, and orders to cook three days' rations, all these and numberless other indications were sufficient to warn us that our peaceful encampment in Orange county was about to come to a close. The religious impression seemed to deepen. Our congregations were now much too large to be accommodated in the chapel, and so when the weather would permit, the services were held outside. I had a great deal of assistance at this time, and crowds came out to hear the Word of Life, and many were daily added to the church.

On a Monday morning we determined to celebrate the Lord's Supper on next Sabbath. The trouble before was to procure the bread and wine. So two men started out on four days' leave of absence to procure the bread and wine. The week wore on and there was no news of our scouts. On Friday one of them came in unsuccessful. He said he had walked a hundred miles or more and could get no wine. It was late on Saturday evening. There were about five hundred men assembled for prayer. We were all despondent. There were some forty persons to be received the next day. Dr. Witherspoon was to preach for us,[43] and we had our hearts set upon meeting around the table of our dear Lord before we commenced another campaign. I was about to dismiss my congregation when, looking up the long hill, we could see a full mile, I saw Leonard, one of the scouts. He held in each hand a bottle of wine, and held them high above his head and came in a run. Pointing toward him I announced the communion for the morrow, and commenced singing the long metre doxology to Old Hundred.[44] The whole congregation arose *on masse*, and such a spiritual, soul-stirring doxology I never before heard. But our fears were not yet past. Leonard told us nearly

---

[43] Chaplain Thomas D. Witherspoon (1836–1898) of the 48th Mississippi Infantry.

[44] The "Old Hundred" tune was used often for the doxology, "Praise God from whom all blessings flow."

the entire army was on the move. Gen. Grant was crossing the Rapidan, the skirmishing had already commenced.[45] It was an uneasy, restless night we spent, and about nine in the morning we assembled for worship. A kind Providence favored us, for while the entire army was on the move and engaged in heavy fighting, our command alone remained quietly in camp all that blessed Sabbath morning.

Bro. Witherspoon preached one of his characteristic, earnest gospel sermons, at the conclusion of which some forty men stood up, professed their faith in Jesus Christ and were baptized. After this between four and five hundred men gathered around the table of our Lord, the majority for the first time and a large number for the last time on earth. It was a blessed and hallowed occasion. Late in the evening the long roll beat, and all night long we were on the tramp. Early in the morning some of our men were engaged in a skirmish and before the hour on which we had assembled the day before, two of our communicants went into the presence of Him, whose love in death they had celebrated on earth the previous day. Our forces were not, however, heavily engaged at this point[,] and we soon found ourselves marching at a double quick towards Spottsylvania C. H.[46]

I do not know remember how long we remained in the position in the Wilderness, nor how long we were in going to Spottsylvania. They may have been fighting between these two points; if so, it is a blank in my memory. The terrible scenes near Spottsylvania, however, are deeply impressed upon my mind. I shall never forget them.

Soon after the hospital was located at Spottsylvania, near the old courthouse, our men were engaged pretty heavily. Quite a number were wounded, but very few killed. I think there was something over a hundred wounded, and about the same number of prisoners; all were thrown upon our hands. For some reason our brigade commissaries were not brought up, and we were short of rations. In fact, there was nothing for these wounded men. The negroes, cooks, etc., who usually swarmed around our hospital, had stampeded during the march, and had not found our place of encampment. Here were from one hundred and seventy-five to two hundred wounded men, and nothing for them to eat. We had an abundance of tents, bed clothes, etc., but the wounded men had already been suffering with hunger, and most of them were appalled when they found nothing to eat. I

---

[45] Ulysses S. Grant (1822–1885) was promoted to Lt. Gen. on 9 March 1864, and given the title "General-in-Chief" three days later on 12 March 1864.

[46] Modern spelling is "Spotsylvania."

saw that our soldiers bore it with a great deal more patience than the prisoners. They could not or would not see that it was one of those unavoidable accidents of war.

My heart was grieved for the intense suffering of these men, who, to add to their wounds and their consequent weakness, must now endure the additional pangs of hunger. Pretty soon, however, I bethought me of Dr. Gaston, division surgeon, a Presbyterian elder, a humane Christian gentleman.[47] I rode over to his quarters, stated the sad condition of affairs, and implored his assistance. It seems that I reached him in the nick of time. He furnished me flour, bacon, rice, sugar, coffee, and beef. I went back in triumph, and the men hailed my arrival with cheers.

But how was I to get provisions cooked for such a number of men? It did not take long to decide. Gathering together the men who were slightly wounded, I assumed command of the squad. Happily a negro boy, connected with the regiment as a servant, came up. Fortunately, he was hungry and at once volunteered his services. Being commander-in-chief, or what was better, commissary general, I ordered Jim, the colored man, to bring wood.[48] The others could help cook, *i.e.*, fry the meat, bake the biscuit, make the coffee, etc. But I alone was physically able to make up the bread. There was a huge, fresh-cut oak stump close to the fires. Trimming the splinters from this, I used it as a *biscuit-board*.

There were at hand immense camp kettles, holding from twelve to fifteen gallons each; in these we put the beef to boil for soup. I found in one of the wagons an immense club, something like a rammer for packing the dirt around fence-posts. I put about a half bushel of the flour on the stump, poured water in the hot bacon grease, and with this mixed my dough and beat it with the handspike. Then one batch of dough was ready, I divided it among several wounded men, who made out the biscuit upon newspapers and tent-cloths, and another squad of men baked them in skillets. There were several very nice old hams with the bacon, and as fast as the bread was done, it was given with the bacon and coffee to the most needy first. This process continued for several hours, until the soup was done, which we thickened by dredging a little flour into it, and was served in tin cups, with boiled rice. The beef was then baked. Steaks were fried and given to those

---

[47] Dr. J. B. Gaston, formerly of the 14th Alabama Infantry, the division surgeon for Anderson's division.

[48] A tongue-in-cheek promotion for Chaplain Dobbs. References to the black servants who accompanied the 12th Mississippi Infantry.

who desired them. But all day long I mixed and beat the dough[,] and still the poor fellows wanted more. Jim relieved me now and then when he had a surplus of wood. It required a good deal of tasting to get the food properly seasoned, and that is the way *the cooks* dined.

Among the prisoners was a big, strapping fellow, wounded in the foot. I took him some biscuits, ham, soup and coffee. He looked at it, and curling his monstrous, ugly lip, said: 'Is this all you can give a poor wounded prisoner?"

He saw the flash of my eye and looked down. In a second my anger was gone. I explained my position as chaplain; my efforts in their behalf were purely voluntary. He at once apologized, and said he could see that I gave him what our men had. There was no difference made between the prisoners and the Confederates.[49]

Our men in the army never knew what it was to have luxuries; no more did the citizens of the South, with rare exceptions. This is the mistake Northern men have made. Our people did not have them and could not get them. And the above bill of fare was something extra; it was the only time during all my connection with the army, that there was such an abundant issue. And at night there was not a thing left, and some of our own men who were brought in late had nothing.

Hospital at Spottsylvania

Long before Gen. Grant commenced his campaign, during the winter previous—before Grant assumed command of the army of the Potomac, Gen. Lee, with great foresight, had built ice houses along the line upon which we fought, and had them filled with ice. I do not know why it was, but the men found breast-works and rifle-pits, and the hospital corps found ice for the sick—and oh, what a luxury it was to the poor wounded, feverish sufferers!

Long after dark upon the night of the day that I assumed the position of chief cook, wounded men were brought in. The enemy had made some desperate charges upon our lines, but up to this time had been successfully foiled, so that, while our wounded were not numerous, there were enough to keep me busy. Every now and then a shell would go whirring over our heads, bursting near the camp, scattering fragments all around.

---

[49] Chaplain Dobbs's reference to ministering to prisoners of war may have also been a counter-point to the charge that Confederates deliberately starved Union prisoners as at Andersonville GA.

For two days and nights the war of artillery had been almost incessant. Worn out as I was with the fatigues of marching on Sunday evening and night, the labors of Monday and Monday night, and the cooking of Tuesday, it seemed impossible to endure longer. Truly the spirit was willing, but the flesh was weak; and notwithstanding there were duties still pressing, I laid myself down for a nap. I was soon oblivious to shells, groans, and the constant tramp and talk. In an hour or so, however, I was awakened to attend upon a dying man. He was a stranger to me and from another brigade. He gave his father's address at Canton, Miss. "Tell them I died happy. Jesus Christ is my Savior—and oh, what a Savior He is!" He gave me a small keepsake for some of his family, and fell asleep. I helped with my own hands to dig his grave and bury him in a blanket; and there beneath that pine grove not far from the spot where he was wounded, his body awaits the resurrection morn. I wrote to his friends and sent him mementoes, but I never heard if they received them. His name I have forgotten. I put it down in my *notes*, but these were lost with all my papers, by the express company, which fact throws me entirely upon my memory for the facts contained in these reminiscences. The long, weary night wore on—weary because of the sad scenes I was called upon to witness. At length the morning dawned; it was cloudy and there was evidence of rain. Very early in the morning our brigade came marching by the camp. I went out to speak with the men, and for this purpose walked with them a mile or so.

I learned from them the sad news of the surprise and capture of a large portion of Johnson's division.[50] The men were wearied and fagged with incessant fighting. They knew they were going to try to recapture the lost position. I marched with them to the point of departure from the road, where occurred one of the most thrilling incidents of the war. Gen. Lee was here, awaiting their arrival. With tears in his eyes, he told them they were about to undertake one of the most hazardous and dangerous duties possible. Many of them, perhaps all, would be sacrificed, but unless it was accomplished, ruin to or army must follow. He said he would lead them—not because he lacked confidence in the skill of their officers, or the bravery of the men; but he would and should share the danger with them.

To this the men would not consent. They said: "If your life is endangered, we cannot fight; if you are killed, our hope is gone. Trust us, trust us, General Lee; and if it is in the power of men, we will take the

---

[50] Maj. Gen. Edward "Allegheny" Johnson's division was captured at Spotsylvania's "Bloody Angle."

position." Thus they plead—and the great man, wiping his eyes said, "God be with you;" and giving another the command, with instructions, rode off.[51]

I learned from the men afterwards that this position was in an angle of the line, and was held by three corps of the enemy with an immense amount of artillery. Approaching as near as possible the enemy's position, they formed a line of battle under a murderous fire, and with the well known "yell", bounded forward; and though a third of them fell the rest retook the first line.[52] A vigorous attack was made upon another part of the enemy's line, which drew off a large part of the opposing forces, and other troops were sent in to our relief. It was at this point that a white oak tree, a foot through at base, was cut down by the minnie balls, and falling upon our line, killed two men from Branch's N. C. brigade.[53]

It is not in my line to give an account of the battles; only those who have access to public documents can do this. I only give the above statements as I got them from eye witnesses.

Spotsylvania—Incidents

Those of our men who were wounded in that terrific charge mentioned in our last, were in a most deplorable condition. All who were able to do so, crawled back, keeping as close to the ground as possible. The ambulance corps could do nothing. The bullets and shells continued to fall there like hail. To add to the calamity and suffering, it commenced to pour down rain in torrents. At night the fire was kept up; but as it was dark there was but little execution. And though several of the ambulance corps were wounded, they succeeded during the night in bringing off those of the wounded who were living. Some few were wounded in several places[,] shot while dying upon the ground. All night long as the ambulances came in, our hearts were wrung with the ghastly wounds and terrific torture endured by the poor fellows, some of whom might have been saved, had they received medical aid sooner; but were now past hope.

---

[51] This story of Gen. Lee's appearance was repeated in several histories of the 12th Mississippi Infantry and their attack at the "Bloody Angle" on 12 May 1864.

[52] A casualty report in June 1864 showed that the 12th Mississippi lost thirty-eight soldiers, killed, wounded and missing out of 114 fit for duty. In 1862 the regiment numbered 1,013 men. About forty were surrendered at Appomatox Court House in April 1865.

[53] The brigade was named for Brig. Gen. Lawrence O. Branch (1820–1862) who died at Antietam.

As they told of their wretched condition, lying there in the cold and rain, under the thick hail of bullets flying all around them, of shells bursting and whirling over their heads; now seeing some poor fellow mangled just beside them with fragments of shell, their efforts to sink down into the most earth even a little, or get close beside a dead companion to shield them; indeed there were tales of horror and anguish sufficient to touch the hardest heart. Some of them were delirious with fever, and talked to the friends at home. A mere lad called out, "Mother, mother! How sweet to have you here to minister to my wants!"

But this mother in her far off Southern home, knew not that her son lay there lisping her fond name in a wild delirium of joy because he thought she was near. A middle-aged man addressed his wife and besought her now to lift the great weight from his body, now to bring the children near and let him kiss them ere he went to battle. Such are but a specimen of the heartrending scenes of those fearful times.

Among the killed was H_____, a young man who had joined the Church and communed with us on that last blessed Sabbath before this. Though but three days had passed since then, it seemed like as many weeks. I had given H_____ a Bible, one of some thirty or forty given me by a Sunday school in Orange county. This Bible he carried in his breast-pocket. The first ball struck the Bible on the edge and penetrated about halfway through and stopped. The force of the blow knocked him down, and as he recovered himself another ball struck him in the forehead and killed him instantly. His comrades brought me the Bible and showed me that the ball tore through and the point rested upon, I think, "The blood of Jesus Christ, His Son, cleanseth from all sin."

About this time I learned that a Federal General had been brought into the hospital, mortally wounded. On inquiry I found it was Gen. Wadsworth.[54] A man who stood high among our men as a gentleman and a soldier. He was mortally wounded in the head, if I remember correctly. I went in and did all in my power to arouse him, telling him his critical condition, asked him if there was no message to his friends, but he was in a deep coma, and no human voice could wake him. His noble countenance was unmoved, and his large frame lay as still and quiet as death itself. He did not live long, and his body was sent through the lines by a flag of truce.

---

[54] Maj. Gen. James S. Wadsworth (1807–1864), US Army, died 8 May 1864, at the Wilderness.

A Pastoral Sketch

Upon the day following the events recorded in my last, the rain continued off and on all day and night. During the day most of our wounded were sent over to the division hospital, about two miles off; and as night came on in wrapped myself in my oil-cloth and blanket and lay down under a large tree. And though the water ran in a stream under my body, I slept until awakened by the hospital steward, saying his brother had been killed, and I must go with him to get his body. I felt it was a useless expedition, but could not say no to one in such deep distress. Getting into an ambulance, we drove as near the line of battle as possible, where we waited to find the way to the regiment. Soon after this one of the men came back for ammunition, and told us we could do nothing; that when there was a lull in the fighting the ambulance corps would bring his body in. This they did in the morning, and the brother and I with another buried him.

After this I rode over to the division hospital, where I found several hundred men, without a chaplain; and what is pertinent to this sketch, the men from my brigade were without medical attention. Several surgeons had been detailed for this work, but they were devoting all their time to those men who were from their own commands.

Among the sick here was M___, from Co. H, of our regiment. He was very ill and suffering greatly with pneumonia. M____ was of a singular disposition. He had never attended church, he would never receive a paper, a tract, or even a word from me. He was absolutely unapproachable by me or any other preacher. He regarded all of the profession with suspicion and contempt.

But here he was in agony and pain, and to this time had no attention whatever. When I addressed him he turned and looked me right in the eye for a moment, and I saw that all his prejudices were gone. I again applied to Dr. Gaston, who went with me and ordered such things as he thought necessary, and gave me a blank requisition on the commissary, requesting me to see to their physical wants.

This hospital was in a very large tobacco barn at Mr. Stuart's. Mrs. Stuart very kindly offered to make delicacies for the sick, and have such things cooked as were needful.

I put a large blister on M_____, and afterward dressed it. I procured for him milk and gave him such other food as Mrs. S. could make. I found that the Lord was gradually opening M____'s heart to receive the truth. For some time his life seemed to hang on a thread. Our surgeon, during the lull in the fighting of the next two weeks, had ample time to come over and visit our men and prescribe for them. There I remained, however, as nurse, chaplain, etc. M____, as he began to recover, could not restrain his expressions of gratitude, his sorrow for the rude manner in which he had treated me; but above all I was most rejoiced to see him in possession of an intelligent faith.

"Sir," he said, "I had no claims upon you. I looked upon you with mistrust. I thought preachers only sought their own case, but I saw there was a power in your religion, an now I thank God that I begin to see how it is, and Jesus Christ is a very precious Savior."

Soon after this, when he was removed to Richmond, I put pine branches under him together with all the blankets I could get, procured him a canteen of milk and some ice, and rode beside the ambulance until we arrived at Hanover Junction, where he was taken out of the ambulance and laid upon the ground beside the railroad track awaiting the trains for Richmond. On every side were the sick and wounded. Near us the whole army was passing. M____ called me and said: "Parson, read a few verses of Scripture and pray with me once more." And there upon that beautiful May morning, in the presence of hundreds, M____ acknowledged his faith in Jesus Christ. I gave him a letter to the chaplain at Howard's hospital, and never saw him again.

Wounded Men—Falling Back

Notwithstanding there was a lull in the fighting at Spottsylvania from about the 10th of May to the 21st, yet the rattle of musketry and the bursting of shells as almost incessant and extremely wearing upon the nerves. And during all this time my labors were not in the least diminished. I know much of it was self-imposed, but I did it in order to win souls.

G____ was wounded in both arms—one was taken off about three inches below the socket; the other had three inches of the bone removed between the shoulder and the elbow. He was the most helpless creature I ever saw. Both arms commenced sloughing and were very offensive. I helped to dress his wounds every day. Of course such an immense drain on the system required nourishing food and a good deal of stimulus. He became very nervous and was completely unmanned, and became as fretful as a little child. Of course we had to feed him; the bits of meat or bread were too small or too large, the soup was too hot or too cold; the spoon was put too far in his mouth or not far enough; now he wanted his nose scratched, or his head, or his eye itched, or his toe. It required a good deal of patience, but he finally got well and had pretty good use of his resected arm. He married and a few years after the war he was keeping an eating-house at a railroad station, where he succeeded well.

H____ was a mere boy; his right leg was amputated above the knee. He lay there as patient as a lamb[,] no murmur, no complaint fell from his lips. One morning he woke up crying bitterly. I went to him and asked what troubled him. "Oh, sir," he said, "I thought I was sleeping with my little brother at home, and my foot, the one that was cut off, itched and I tried to rub it against the other, and I moved this stump; the pain woke me—and oh, it was such a shock to think I would always be a cripple." I told him that this was a sensation he would often experience—perhaps for years to come. I told him that, with a good cork leg he could walk very well and that God would give him work to do. He was a Christian and said, "he was resigned to the will of his Heavenly Father; he did not want to complain, but the shock was so sudden."

K____ was another young man. A minnie ball had opened the knee joint. The surgeon insisted that his leg should be amputated at the knee, otherwise his recovery would be very doubtful. He was so violently opposed to the operation, the surgeon said he knew he would never recover unless he could be persuaded to consent! To this end I plead with him, but it made no impression. He had known of a similar case where the surgeons desired to operate, and the man had opposed it and recovered. He thought he would recover also. I saw him about a month afterwards in the hospital at Richmond. He was a living skeleton[,] the flesh seemed all gone; he was full of bed sores. His wounded limb was swung up in a cloth; it was four times its natural size and full of worms. Poor fellow! He died in great anguish. He deeply regretted his folly when it was too late.

Sickness—Hospital Experience

Under the wear and tear of these four weeks I found my physical strength was going away. When we arrived at Cold Harbor a misty, cool spell of weather set in. My duties increased; there were many inquirers for truth; men would come in as opportunities arose and seek me out for religious conversation. The wounded, the sick, the dying, required constant care. About this time our rations, which consisted of meager supplies of cornmeal and bacon, were increased. We were all very hungry—hungry all the time. When I was at the hospital in Spottsylvania, I could have drawn for myself, but I had no right to do so; for the numbers who preyed upon our rations before they reached us, diminished them by one third, and I had learned to look with great horror upon such swindling.

The increase of rations had a disastrous effect, and sickness increased fearfully. About the 1st of June while at Cold Harbor, I was taken suddenly down in the midst of my duties—a raging fever with violent vomiting and purging. I was put into an ambulance and sent to the hospital at Richmond, where a most remarkable Providence interposed for my deliverance.

I have spoken in a former letter of my young friend G_____, a private in company A, who followed my example in kneeling down to pray in the presence of his mates on the second night of my arrival in camp. On the last day of May, while out upon the battlefield, G_____ heard of my illness, and that I was next to be sent to Howard's hospital next morning.[55] He wrote a note in the midst of a fierce conflict, to a brother-in-law, Dr. Bagby, who was an assistant surgeon in that hospital, asking him to give me every attention in his power.[56] The letter reached Dr. B_____ the morning after my arrival.

I knew nothing of my journey to Richmond. When I came to myself in the night, full of cramp, vomiting every little while, I found myself on a clean bunk, with rows and rows of men as far as I could see.[57] The doctors gave me opiates, and that seemed to unsettle me more.

About sun up Dr. B_____ came to me; "You are chaplain _____? "Yes, sir." After a close examination, he went off to consult with the surgeon who had been waiting on me. When he returned he said: "Your case is a very critical one; unless you get relief soon, you must die." I told him I was aware of it. I remember I felt no uneasiness about dying. After sitting a while, he said: "Is there anything you want? Does your stomach crave something?" Though at that time I prided myself in not knowing the difference of taste in liquors, I craved an ice-cold toddy. I had taken one when a lad, from a physician, and there was a longing for what I had not tasted for fifteen years, and then but once. He said: "If you can take this, you

---

[55] The General Hospital at Howard's Grove was one of several Confederate hospitals in Richmond. It was designated to receive casualties from Mississippi regiments as other hospitals received the wounded from other states.

[56] Dr. George W. Bagby (1828–1883), a graduate of the University of Pennsylvania Medical School and editor of the *Southern Literary Messenger* in Richmond, was a volunteer doctor who assisted the commissioned army surgeons.

[57] Chaplain Dobbs was admitted to the General Hospital at Howard's Grove in Richmond on 19 September 1864.

will get well." He made me a weak toddy, of which he gave me a teaspoonful every ten minutes. Soon I went to sleep and awoke in several hours refreshed, my stomach quiet, and ready for vigorous treatment.

I remained here for several weeks and saw many strange sights.

What I Saw in the Hospital

After the second or third day, I was somewhat improved, and was sufficiently from under the influence of opium to see and hear what was going on. Opposite and about three bunks from me was a quartermaster. I knew him at once, and wondered what he was doing there. He was not wounded, and not much sick; *he was recruiting*. It was not long after my first observation of him, that I saw a beautiful young lady come tripping lightly on, scattering her smile like dew drops on us all; but an she went, past the ragged privates, past the tattered lieutenants and captains, past one Colonel suffering with wounds, on to the well dressed, clean shaved, good looking quartermaster. Thinks I: Has this angel of mercy no higher mission than this? None. For him alone she brought her dainties, her flowers and her words of cheer.

Pretty soon after this, came in another; tall, but homely and rather awkward; an intelligent, sympathetic face was partly concealed by her gingham sun-bonnet. As she passed, she turned her head slightly as if to see if I were the one she wanted. The tears were coursing down her pale cheeks. Surely, thought I, she is one of those sweet angels of mercy, of whom I have heard so much. She stopped beside a poor, ragged private, badly wounded and suffering. She spoke low, but I heard; "We could spare you but little today. I made a little by washing some clothes for a neighbor, but everything is so high. Here is an apple; I gave nearly the price of a half day's work for it, but if you only enjoy it."

The next day she came at the same hour, and every day as long as I was there. When I was able to walk, I threw myself in her way and asked her if that man was a relation of hers. "No, sir."

"Did you know him before he came here?" "No, sir; he was a stranger."

"Will you tell me why you selected him out of all these men as the recipient of your kindness?"

"O sir," she answered, with much simplicity, "he was the poorest, the most needy and friendless."

God bless the noble women of Richmond! There were many of them who became ministering spirits. The rich divided their wealth, the poor their little. Many of them gave all their time and substance, and absolutely beggared themselves to alleviate the wants of the sufferers; and while a few ministered only to the well dressed officer, the great majority made no distinction between private and officer, except according to their necessities.

While in this hospital, I met with quite a number of my army friends. Among these was a young man who had been raised by a pious aunt in South Carolina. For a long time he had been under a deep conviction of sin, and was now in a sad state of religious melancholy. I soon found the true cause was his wretched physical condition. A few days after this he went home on a furlough, and I doubt not, with health, he became happy in trusting in Him who died for him.

One day Dr. B. came in to see me, and said, "Your young friend, Billy G_____, had his leg shot off, and was taken prisoner on the day he wrote that note to me. He is young, strong and healthy, with a cheerful spirit and a brave heart. I do not fear for his recovery."

After the close of the war, I met my friend, hale and hearty; but sure enough, he had lost a leg. In the few moment conversation between us, he thanked me for the friends from Kentucky I had induced to interest themselves in his behalf. "Say to them I shall never forget them; they ministered abundantly to me."

After I had been in the hospital some days, Dr. Bagby gave me and a friend the benefit of an invitation from Capt. Wm. Old of Amelia county, to come out and recruit.[58] I was weaker than I ever was before, but my friend, Dr. D., who was wounded in the shoulder, helped me to walk to the depot. Ah, but it was grand. The pure, fresh air; the lovely old mansion; the generous hospitality of the captain and wife; what a green spot in the memory of all those months of horror!

Virginia Hospitality

With the pure air, the genial society, the excellent diet and kind nursing we received from Capt. O. and his most excellent wife, Dr. D. and I recovered rapidly. Some time in July, I determined to run up to Petersburg to see how the men were getting on. I found the poor fellows suffering for want of vegetable diet, and on my return I told Mrs. O. and some other ladies of the condition of affairs. At once a committee was appointed, and in a few days the entire community for miles around was informed that upon a

---

[58] Cpt. William Old, Asst. Quartermaster

certain day all kinds of vegetables would be shipped to the army. Dr. Gaston furnished me two box cars, which were filled to overflowing with boxes, barrels and crates of all the vegetables of the season.

When I arrived at camp, I found we were just in the niche of time. There were about one hundred and twenty men who had been wounded the day pervious. Rations of beef were issued, and the poor fellows luxuriated in soup, rich and elegant. Our Amelia friends repeated their kindness in a few weeks afterward. Soon after my return to duty, I relapsed and could not gather strength for the laborious duties. I remained in camp at Petersburg, and in the midst of great suffering and weakness, performed my duties for about two months longer.

At night the illumination from our encampment was magnificent. The enemy were throwing 100 lb. mortar shells into the city. We could follow their course through the air by the burning fuse, which looked like a shooting star. Usually these shells would burst in mid air, and the explosion was like to sky-rockets in appearance, and a sudden clap of thunder in sound. One night while here, I went with a friend to visit a family of women who could not leave the city. I was surprised when I found them living in a portion of the city very much exposed to the shells. Several houses near them had been struck, but theirs had not. I talked with them a while, and after worship, went away as soon as possible. When you could see the course of these shells in the open air, you soon became accustomed to them; but to be confined between brick walls to hear them rumbling like a half dozen carts drawn by frantic horses over a boulder pavement, was at least sufficient to make me wish myself back in camp. The ladies seemed unmoved; they were accustomed to it.

As the summer wore on, I grew worse. The men when wounded were sent off at once. I found there was little more work that I could do, and hence, in September, after an arduous work of one and a half years, I was forced to resign my position for the want of physical strength to continue longer. Of the young men, with whom my intercourse was so delightful, many of them have gone to their eternal home, and are with the white robed throng in heaven; of those who survived the war, I have met with very few. Wherever they are, God grant they may stand in their places as true and valiant soldiers of the Lord Jesus.

Chaplain Dobbs resigned from the army on 5 November 1864. He returned to Kosciusko, Mississippi, where he did supply preaching until 1867. He then accepted a call as the pastor of the Presbyterian Church in Washington, Kentucky, where he remained for seven years. Thereafter Dobbs held numerous pastorates in Texas and West Virginia until he lost his sight in 1901. He continued to serve as an occasional stated supply preacher in the Brownwood Presbytery in Brownwood, Texas, for nineteen additional years. He died in Brownwood in 1920 at the age of eighty-five.

Chapter 3

Ministry on Campaigns

Blessed be the Lord, my rock, who trains my hands for war,
and my fingers for battle...
Psalm 144

When orders came for the army to move out of camp for a campaign, chaplains placed their few possessions, clothes, books, writing paper, and blankets, either on their horses or in the baggage wagons and joined the long line of soldiers trudging toward the unseen enemy. From their surviving journals, letters and diaries, chaplains performed a number of duties on the campaigns to help provide encouragement and hope for the soldiers. Besides helping soldiers send last-minute letters back home, there were ministries of presence on the battle line, ministries of healing and prayer at field hospitals, and burial of the dead when possible.

Some chaplains were not content to minister to the spiritual and physical needs of the troops, but felt obligated also to take a hand in the fighting. Although the official position of both the United States and Confederate governments was that chaplains were noncombatants, there were chaplains on both sides who bore arms.

From the beginning of the recruitment effort in 1861, there was a call for every patriot to volunteer, clergy and laity alike. President Jefferson Davis had declared on 29 April 1861, just two weeks into the war, "We feel that our cause is just and holy; we protest solemnly in the face of mankind that we desire peace at any sacrifice save that of honor and independence; we ask no conquest, no aggrandizement, no concession of any kind from the States with which we were lately confederated: all we ask is to be left alone."[1] This "just and holy war" resonated with many young ministers who volunteered for the army in 1861 and 1862, not just as chaplains but also as soldiers and officers in the regiments. There were no regulations or written instructions with regard to the chaplain's place of duty during a battle and no Geneva Conventions as yet in effect, so the door was open for "fighting parsons" in the army.

Many churches and church leaders presumably approved of their young pastors and theology students serving as soldiers. In the Shenandoah Valley Baptist Chaplain J. William Jones recalled visiting the Rockbridge Artillery which contained nineteen theological students in the unit.[2] The Columbia Presbyterian Seminary in South Carolina formed its own infantry company from the student body. The six bishops of the Methodist Episcopal Church, South, the largest Protestant denomination in the South at the time, appointed 318 fully ordained ministers from all conferences to serve as Confederate chaplains but allowed 109 other ordained ministers to serve as line officers or enlisted soldiers.[3] Of course there was an Episcopal bishop already serving as a Confederate general, and other preachers and seminarians in the ranks not as chaplains but as soldiers with muskets in hand.[4]

The demographics of the clergy in the Southern states and the organization of the Confederate armies help explain this phenomenon. In 1860 half the population of the Southern states was under the age of twenty-one, and in the Southern states approximately 9,000 young men under age thirty-five were licensed or ordained preachers.[5] Many of these young preachers volunteered to serve in the Confederate armies in 1861 and 1862, but there was only one chaplain allowed for each regiment. Hence the majority of preachers who desired to serve had to decide whether to enlist as

---

[1] E. Merton Coulter, *The Confederate States of America, 1861–1865* (Baton Rouge: Louisiana State University Press, 1950) 43.

[2] Jones, *Christ in the Camp*, 21.

[3] *Minutes of the Annual Conferences of the Methodist Episcopal Church, South, 1855–1865* (Nashville: Methodist Publishing House, 1878). A copy can be found in the Georgia State Department of History and Archives, Morrow GA, and also in the Pitts Theological Library, Emory University, Atlanta GA.

[4] Reference to Episcopal Bishop Leonidas Polk of Louisiana who served as a Maj. Gen. and corps commander at Shiloh in 1862.

[5] Frank L. Hieronymus, "For Now and Forever: The Chaplains of the Confederate States Army" (PhD diss., University of California at Los Angeles, 1964) 3, 341.

privates and wait for chaplain positions to become available through attrition, or stay at home and risk the draft if they were not serving churches.[6]

Those preachers who entered the army as privates had to pitch into the fighting as their primary military duty. Chaplains who were supporting them, and who had bonded with the men, soon felt that they were expected to fight as well.

Of course not all commanders wanted their chaplains to fight. Brigadier General John K. Jackson, a brigade commander at Shiloh, reprimanded chaplains who took up arms.[7] Major General P. G. T. Beauregard thought that chaplains who were in the rear with hospitals, attending to their appropriate duties, were in their rightful place. Lieutenant General Stonewall Jackson reportedly rebuked a chaplain who advanced with the battle line. He believed his chaplains should be in the rear of the troops, praying for victory.[8]

In a meeting on 25 April 1863, the Chaplains' Association of the Second and Third Corps, Army of Northern Virginia, took up the question of where chaplains should be positioned during battle. Although they recognized that there was no absolute rule on the subject, they decided that a chaplain should be wherever duty calls, but "ordinarily it is thought wrong for him to take a musket."[9] Some should be with the ambulances, some at field infirmaries, and most wherever soldiers were at the point of death. However, each chaplain "should ascertain the *opinion of his regiment* on this subject."[10]

---

[6] The Conscription Act of 1862 exempted only clergy who were serving churches. In the Methodist Episcopal Church, South, that meant some 5,353 lay preachers on the rolls of the annual conferences were subject to the draft. See the *Minutes of the Annual Conferences of the Methodist Episcopal Church, South, 1855–1865* (Nashville: Methodist Publishing House, 1878). A copy can be found in the Georgia State Department of History and Archives, Morrow GA, and also in the Pitts Theological Library, Emory University, Atlanta GA.

[7] Kenneth W. Noe, "The Fighting Chaplain at Shiloh" (unpublished paper, Society for Military History, Madison, WI, 5 April 2002) 8. There is a copy in the US Army Chaplain Museum Library, Ft. Jackson SC.

[8] Gardiner H. Shattuck, Jr. *A Shield and Hiding Place* (Macon GA: Mercer University Press, 1987) 70.

[9] Jones, *Christ in the Camp*, 522.

[10] Ibid.

Nevertheless, it would seem from references in letters and diaries that there were a sizable number of commissioned chaplains who did not hesitate to take up arms in the ranks or even to lead other soldiers in assaults in addition to their other duties. Some of these "fighting parsons" had served first as enlisted soldiers and were accustomed to loading and firing weapons. Some wanted to demonstrate their patriotism, their dedication to their soldiers, or, at times, to build or maintain their reputations as Christian warriors not unlike their leaders, Lieutenant General Stonewall Jackson, Lieutenant General (Bishop) Leonidas Polk, Brigadier General (Reverend) William Pendleton, or General Robert E. Lee.

One additional motive for "fighting parsons" to take up arms was that in the smoke, explosions, groaning, yelling, and screaming, it was not hard to get caught up in a kind of heroic mass hysteria. At the Battle of Shiloh, Isaac Tichenor, chaplain of the 17th Alabama Infantry, "killed one colonel, a captain, and four privates" with his Colt's repeater rifle.[11] "Every man stood to his post…every eye flashed and hearts beat high with desperate resolve to conquer or die," he wrote.[12] William D. Chadwick, a Cumberland Presbyterian and chaplain of the 4th Alabama Infantry, bought a rifle at Harper's Ferry. He enjoyed choosing his own battle station and "fighting the rascals" with one of their own weapons.[13] A. A. Lomax, Baptist chaplain of the 15th Mississippi Infantry, said his rightful place was on the firing line.

Andrew Jackson Potter, a Mexican War veteran and chaplain of the 26th Texas Cavalry, seized a rifle at a battle near Bayou Bluff, Louisiana, and rode to the front to take part in the fighting. Thomas L. Duke, chaplain of the 19th Mississippi Infantry, was cited for "gallant conduct" at Chancellorsville because he "remained in front of his regiment with his musket during the series of engagements and mainly directed the movements of the skirmishers of that regiment."[14] After one engagement, William McBryde, Cumberland Presbyterian chaplain of the 5th Mississippi

---

[11] Hieronymus, "For Now and Forever," 158.

[12] Isaac Taylor Tichenor, papers, Alabama Department of Archives and History, Montgomery AL, as cited in Hieronymus, "For Now and Forever," 157–58.

[13] *South Western Baptist*, 29 August 1861, as cited in Herman A. Norton, *Struggling for Recognition: The United States Army Chaplaincy 1791–1865* (Washington DC: Office of the Chief of Chaplains, Department of the Army, 1977) 157.

[14] US War Department, *The War of the Rebellion. A Compilation of the Official Records of the Union and Confederate Armies*, 70 vols. (Washington DC: Government Printing Office 1880–1901) ser. 1, vol. 25, pt. 1, p. 873.

Infantry, found bullet holes in his shoe, haversack, back of his coat, front part of his vest pocket, his sleeve and his Bible—yet he was not wounded.[15]

Others were not so fortunate. Lucius H. Jones, Episcopal chaplain of the 4th Texas Cavalry, was wounded while ministering to a dying soldier at Glorietta Pass, New Mexico. Chaplain Edward Hudson of the 6th Texas Cavalry was hit while carrying a wounded man off the field at Newnan, Georgia, and Father Emmeran Bliemel was killed at Jonesboro, Georgia, in 1864, while ministering to the mortally wounded Colonel William Grace of the 10th Tennessee Infantry. Benjamin T. Crouch, chaplain of the 1st Tennessee Cavalry, was killed "while gallantly leading a regiment in the memorable battle of Thompson's Station."[16] Chaplain M. L. Weller, Episcopal chaplain of the 9th Mississippi Infantry, was killed at Shiloh, and Chaplain B. F. Ellison of Madison's Texas Cavalry, Arizona Brigade, was mortally wounded fighting in the front rank at Monett's Ferry, Louisiana.[17]

Possibly one of the most ironic engagements from a casualty standpoint was during the battle of Resaca, Georgia, in 1864. There Presbyterian missionary J. P. McMullen, with the 18th Alabama Infantry, saw his son killed in the first fire, so he buckled on his son's sword and led the men on "a piece further" until he too was killed.[18] Opposite the 18th Alabama was the 3rd Wisconsin Infantry, whose chaplain, John Springer, was also killed in the same action on the same day.

In all, some forty-one Confederate chaplains are known to have died during the war, thirty-two of them from exhaustion or disease.[19] Of these forty-one who died, seventeen, or almost half, expired in the years 1861 and 1862. An additional twenty were wounded during the war but survived their wounds. Only one, Dr. John P. Richardson, physician and chaplain of the 4th Mississippi Infantry, died as a prisoner of war—he at Camp Chase, Ohio, 4 March 1862. Of the forty-one chaplains who died while on duty, twelve were Methodists. Ten, of various faiths, were from Mississippi regiments. The Army of Northern Virginia lost a total of fifteen, the Army of Tennessee, eleven, and the Army of Mississippi, six. The rest of the

---

[15] Hieronymus, "For Now and Forever," 155.

[16] Ibid.

[17] Ibid., 163–64.

[18] Charles Pitts, *Chaplains in Gray* (Nashville: Broadman Press, 1957) 98. By comparison, there were thirteen US Army chaplains lost in the Korean War, and thirteen died during the Vietnam conflict.

[19] Hieronymus, "For Now and Forever," 161. The total of forty-one came from examination of 1,307 individual service records.

chaplain casualties were hospital chaplains and chaplains from units in other regions of the South.[20]

As a matter of policy, both the Union and Confederate armies regarded chaplains as noncombatants when they were captured because most chaplains reported to field hospitals to pray for the wounded and comfort the dying during battle.[21] About six, in fact, were dual professionals, trained as surgeons or assistant surgeons and also commissioned as chaplains.[22]

John J. D. Renfroe, Baptist chaplain of the 10th Alabama Infantry, stated that he usually went with the regiment to their battle line, said what he could to encourage them, and then went "to his station" at the field hospital. At Salem Church and at Gettysburg, Renfroe waited too long and was pinned down in the shooting.[23] In 1863, Dr. Joseph Cross, Methodist chaplain of the 2nd Tennessee Infantry, got caught in a retreat and was pushed into Chickamauga Creek before his regiment could fight its way out. His colonel later reminded him that his place was at the field hospital.

The major battlefields of the Civil War were often described by the chaplains as "fearful sights for Christian eyes."[24] Dr. Joseph Cross of the 2nd Tennessee Infantry described what he found among the cedar trees at Stone's River:

> Here is a foot, shot off at the ankle—a fine model for a sculptor. Here is an officer's hand, severed from the wrist, the glove still upon it, and the sword in its grasp. Here is an entire brain, perfectly isolated, showing no sign of violence, as if carefully taken from the skull that enclosed it by the hands of a skillful surgeon. Here is a corpse, sitting upon the ground, with its back against a tree, in the most natural position of life, holding before its face the photograph likeness of a good-looking old lady, probably the dead man's mother. Here is a handsome young man, with placid countenance, lying upon

---

[20] William C. Davis et al., *Faith in the Fight: Civil War Chaplains* (Mechanicsburg PA: Stackpole Books, 2003) 85.

[21] For a fuller discussion of the fluctuations in regulations regarding chaplain prisoners of war, see Herman Norton, "The Organization and Function of the Confederate Military Chaplaincy, 1861–1865" (PhD diss., Vanderbilt University, 1956) 44–47.

[22] Dr. Charles Quintard of Tennessee, Dr. John Richardson of Mississippi, and Dr. F. S. Petway of Alabama were three of these.

[23] Hieronymus, "For Now and Forever," 155–56.

[24] As cited in Jones, *Christ in the Camp*, 1986, 542.

his back, his Bible upon his bosom, and his hands folded over it, as if gone to sleep saying his evening prayer....Dissevered heads, arms, legs are scattered everywhere; and the coagulated pools of blood gleam ghastly in the morning sun.[25]

At Chancellorsville Father Sheeran of the 14th Louisiana said that the line of battle extended for eight miles and "for that distance you could see the dead bodies of the enemy lying in every direction," including those who had been burned to death by a wild fire that broke out in the underbrush.[26] These were just the human casualties, for the thousands of dead horses were just rolled into ditches or pulled to ravines.

Clearly these battlefields demanded close teamwork from the chaplains, litter bearers, and surgeons just to save a few lives. Chaplain Sterling Cherry of the 37th Georgia Infantry reported on the work of chaplains in the hospitals after the battle of Chickamauga in the fall of 1863:

> Dr. McFerrin was at Cleburn's Division hospital, where his son was, slightly wounded, and his nephew, Rev. John P. McFerrin, severely wounded, working with the sufferers. Dr. Cross, chaplain on Gen. Buckner's staff, was on the field and at the hospital. Bros. Mooney and Miller were at Stewart's Division hospital, active and industrious in attending to the wounded and dying. Dr. Petway came in good time to render efficient aid in the double capacity of surgeon and minister. Chaplain Willoughby was with the dying and superintended the burial of the dead of our division.[27]

In all, Cherry counted thirteen chaplains and two missionaries in two division hospitals, transporting wounded on stretchers, performing surgery, praying for the wounded and dying soldiers, taking last requests, and burying the dead.

By 1864 recruitment of chaplains for the armies had declined. Several states simply had no churches or church conferences free of occupying Federal forces, and therefore no way to recruit chaplain replacements. The Baltimore Conference of the Methodist Episcopal Church, South, meeting

---

[25] Ibid.

[26] Joseph T. Durkin, S. J., ed., *Confederate Chaplain: A War Journal of Rev. James B. Sheeran, c.ss.r. 14th Louisiana, CSA.* (Milwaukee: The Bruce Publishing Co., 1960) 44.

[27] W. W. Bennett, *A Narrative of The Great Revival Which Prevailed in the Southern Armies* (Philadelphia: Claxton, Remsen and Haffelfinger, 1877) 327–28.

in exile in Virginia, reportedly appointed fourteen ordained members of their body to serve as chaplains in 1864, but there are few if any military records for this group. The Methodists, Baptists, and Presbyterians did, however, increase the number of missionaries appointed to the armies. These included chaplains who had been wounded but who volunteered to return as missionaries, such as John Granbery of the 11th Virginia Infantry, those who had become increasingly involved in colporteur work such as Sterling M. Cherry of the 37th Georgia Infantry, and those who had not served as chaplains but who volunteered to serve as missionaries late in the war. The Southern Baptists furnished about seventy-six and the Methodists about thirty-two missionaries during the war.

The Presbyterians resolved in 1863–1864 to put at least one chaplain or missionary in each brigade in the Confederate armies. In 1864 the Presbyterian Committee on Domestic Missions had 130 chaplains or permanent missionaries in the field, more than a quarter of the total number of ministers in the church—the highest proportion of clergy that year of any denomination in the South. The ministers were distributed throughout the armies, with thirty-six in the Army of Northern Virginia, twelve in the Army of Tennessee, nine on the coast of South Carolina, twenty-two in hospitals in Virginia, Georgia, and Mississippi, and the rest scattered in units and hospitals from North Carolina to Florida. Moreover, the blockade-running Dr. Moses D. Hoge of Richmond, was able to bring 15,000 Bibles, 50,000 Testaments, and 250,000 copies of the Gospels and Psalms from the British and Foreign Bible Society through Wilmington, North Carolina, to the soldiers of the Confederacy.[28]

---

[28] Ernest Trice Thompson, *Presbyterians in the South*, vol. 2 (Richmond: John Knox Press, 1973) 47.

Memoirs, 1862-1864

Chaplain Isaac T. Tichenor
17th Alabama Infantry Regiment, CSA

Isaac Taylor Tichenor was born in Spencer County, Kentucky, on 11 November 1825. He attended Taylorsville Academy and remained there as a teacher and, after three years, as the principal. He was called to preach and ordained at the Baptist church in Columbus, Kentucky, in 1848 at the age of twenty-three. He accepted preaching assignments in Texas and Kentucky until 1852 when he began a sixteen-year pastorate at the First Baptist Church, Montgomery, Alabama. For two years he served as chaplain of the 17th Alabama Infantry and acquired a reputation not only as a spiritual leader but also as a sharpshooter. His letter to Alabama Attorney General Thomas H. Watts, written after the battle at Shiloh Church in Tennessee, was published in the Richmond Whig in April of 1862.[1]

Letter from Chaplain I. T. Tichenor to Alabama Attorney General T. H. Watts, Former Colonel of the 17th Alabama Infantry Regiment

Camp Watts, Near Corinth
April 15, 1862
My Dear Friend: Enclosed I send you a copy of the petition to the Secretary of War, asking that the two flags, taken in the great battle of Shiloh by our regiment, may be transferred to Gov. Shorter, to be placed in the Capitol at Montgomery. I feel that I need not ask you to do all you can to have this petition granted. They are both marked on the stripe just below

---

[1] Isaac Taylor Tichenor, diary and unpublished papers, microfilm (#0336), Southern Baptist Historical Library and Archives, Nashville TN. The same microfilm is also available at the Auburn University library. See also the Montgomery *Weekly Mail*, 17 May 1862.

the blue field "Captured by the 17th Alabama, at Shiloh, April 6, 1862." One is a beautiful silk flag, the other a large cotton one.

The loss of our regiment in killed on the field was thirteen; wounded and missing one hundred and seventeen—more than one[-]third of the number we carried into the field. Accurate information obtained on the ground, and from prisoners, satisfies me that we fought all day five times our number—and with 350 men, killed and wounded not less than 1,000 Yankees.

The dead Yankees in front of our regiment, where we first met the enemy, counted after the fight, 352. Captain Cumming's of Jackson's staff says they were piled three deep—others say it looked as if a regiment had dressed up and lain down. Most of them were shot in the head; this was caused by the fact that the enemy were formed in three lines of battle, one behind the other; and the front were lying down. During this engagement we were under a cross fire on the left wing from three directions. Under it the boys wavered. I had been wounded, and was sitting down, but seeing them waver, I sprang to my feet—took off my hat—waved it over my head—walked up and down the line, and they say, "preached them a sermon." I reminded them that it was Sunday; that at that hour (11 o'clock), all their home folks were praying for them;—that "Tom Watts"—(excuse the familiar way in which I employed so distinguished a name,) had told us he would listen with an eager ear to hear from the 17th; and shouting your name far over the roar of battle, I called upon them to stand there, and die, if need be, for their country. The effect was evident. Every man stood to his post—every eye flashed and every heart beat high with desperate resolve to conquer or die.

"They piled the ground with" Yankees "slain."[2]

Colonel, I am satisfied—more than satisfied, with the results of my labors as chaplain of the 17th. I feel in my heart a consciousness, that in no other position could I have served the cause of my God or my country so well; and I am more than recompensed for all my toils and privations. Yours,

I. T. Tichenor

---

[2] Punctuation is original. Tichenor may have been referring to "filled its street with the slain" (Ezekiel 11:6).

In 1901 Dr. Tichenor dictated this account of his part in the Battle of Shiloh for his family's records. It was preserved by his granddaughter, Annie Barnes. In this account Tichenor added more details about the battlefield and his role as a "fighting parson."[3]

Reminiscences of the Battle of Shiloh[4]

In 1859 the political unrest had reached a crisis in the incident known as the "John Brown Raid," but despite the gathering storm clouds there was still hope among the conservatives of both North and South that some settlement of the country's differences could be made. But after the assembling of Congress in December, 1860, all hope died, for congress [*sic*] showed no spirit of conciliation, and the South was advised by its representatives to prepare for the worst withdrawal from the Union. South Carolina was the first to secede, December, 1860, and six other Cotton States followed her. In February, 1861, they declared themselves the Confederate States of America, with their capitol at Montgomery, Alabama.

From February on events moved at an accelerated pace. Although Mr. Lincoln's attitude toward the Confederacy seemingly leaned toward reconciliation, the declaration of his purpose to 'hold, occupy and possess' the property of the South for the Federal Government amounted to a declaration of war, and was received as such by the South. It was at this time that the young Confederacy sent Commissioners to Washington, to effect an amicable adjustment of the swelling difficulties. Even while this peaceably intentioned group was on its way to Washington, Mr. Lincoln sent reinforcements to Charleston for the defense of Fort Sumpter [*sic*]. As soon as the authorities at Montgomery learned of Mr. Lincoln's action, they ordered the reduction of the fort. After a bombardment of thirty-two hours, General Anderson, commanding Ft. Sumpter [*sic*], capitulated, April 13, 1861.[5] Mr. Lincoln called for volunteers on April 15, and proclaimed a blockade.

---

[3] Kenneth W. Noe, "The Fighting Chaplain at Shiloh" (unpublished paper, Society for Military History, Madison, WI, 5 April 2002) footnote 36. There is a copy in the US Army Chaplain Museum Library, Ft. Jackson SC. The Tichenor papers are on microfilm at Auburn University and at the Southern Baptist Historical Library in Nashville TN.

[4] Capitalization in this section has not been modified from the original.

[5] Maj. Robert Anderson commanded the small garrison at Fort Sumter.

Immediately following these and other acts of Mr. Lincoln, Virginia, North Carolina, Tennessee, and Missouri withdrew from the Union. Both the North and South were preparing for war.

I was married on April 16, 1861, to Miss Emily C. (Cooper) Boykin, daughter of Dr. Samuel Boykin, of Columbus, Georgia. He was a prominent physician of Columbus and a scientist of no mean ability. He had a large family. Two of his sons, Samuel and Thomas, were preachers and earnest workers in the Baptist Church and prominent in the Southern Baptist Convention.[6] My wife, Emily[,] was charming and lovable. She was a fine musician and had traveled abroad. We were living in Columbus at that time, the spring of 1861. It was our honeymoon....

When the South called for volunteers, many of the members of my church joined the Confederate Army. I went in as Chaplain, with the rank of Captain. We were a part of the 17th Alabama Regiment, and Honorable Thomas H. Watts, subsequently Governor of the State of Alabama, was our Colonel. The Regiment was organized near Montgomery in the fall of 1861.

About November 1st, 1861, our Regiment was removed to Pensacola, Florida, and became a part of General Gladden's Brigade, under the command of General Braxton Bragg. The camp at Pensacola was not well equipped. There were hardships, to say nothing of discomforts, to be endured.

I was present at the bombardment between Bragg's Battalion on the mainland, and Fort Pickens at the batteries in its vicinity, on the island of Santa Rosa. The time was about the winter of 1861–62. The Command wintered near Pensacola, and in March was removed northward to reinforce the Army of General Sidney Johnston. In the reorganization which took place at Corinth, Mississippi, the Regiment (17th Alabama) was put with a Brigade,—with the 18th Alabama, Colonel Shorter commanding, the 19th Alabama under Colonel (afterwards General) Wheeler, and the 2nd Texas under Colonel Moore,—all under the command of General John K. Jackson, of Augusta, Georgia.[7]

---

[6] Rev. Samuel Boykin, born 1829, was pastor of the 2nd Baptist Church in Macon GA, and editor of the *Christian Index*. His brother, Rev. Thomas Cooper Boykin, born in 1836, was educated at in Macon at Mercer University and at South Carolina College in Columbia. In 1874 he moved to Atlanta to head the Georgia State Baptist Convention's Sunday school work.

[7] Col. Eli S. Shorter of the 18th Alabama Infantry, Col. Joseph Wheeler of the 19th Alabama Infantry, and Col. John C. Moore of the 2nd Texas Infantry.

Our Division, under the command of General Withers, was composed of the three Brigades, commanded by General Gladden, General Chalmers, and General Jackson, constituting the right wing of General Bragg's corps.[8] After various unimportant movements and operations in the vicinity of Corinth, on the 4th day of April (1862) our command moved with the Army of General Johnston out to the battlefield on the Tennessee River, and took part in the Battle of Shiloh.

Leaving Corinth about 12:00 noon on the 4th of April, we marched out ten miles in the direction of the River and encamped for the night at Monterey. The next morning, the 5th, the corps with our Regiment was advanced. We moved about two and a half miles nearer to the River and bivouacked at Meekey's Cross Roads, awaiting the arrival of General Hardee's corps, which had moved from Corinth by the Purdy Road. We awaited the passing of General Hardee and General Polk until noon.[9] We were then ordered to stay in the rear. We broke line late in the afternoon. Then moved forward to rear of camp the next day, April 6th.

We were in a depression and outlined against the enemy's tents. A canon [sic] ball crashed through. Our men were ordered to lie down. A battery had turned loose. In shooting the shells they cut the fuse so as to explode the shells in front of the line.

Instead of lying down, I sat down with my back to a big oak tree. Captain Girarday's battalion came over to the left and opened fire,—another took position on the right and opened fire.[10] The two battalions soon silenced the enemy.

We then marched off to the right about a mile, when we reached the top of a wooded ridge and faced left, in the enemy's direction, at the foot of a miry creek, with a bluff opposite, and a cleared field rising gradually to the crest beyond, covered by the enemy's camp.[11] We were ordered forward on

---

[8] Brig. Gen. Jones M. Withers, commanding the second division in Bragg's Second Corps of the Army of Mississippi; Brig. Gen. Adley H. Gladden of Louisiana, killed at Shiloh; Brig. Gen. James R. Chalmers of Mississippi; and Brig. Gen. John K. Jackson of Georgia.

[9] Maj. Gen. William J. Hardee and Maj. Gen. Leonidas Polk.

[10] Girardey's Georgia Battery from Augusta was part of Jackson's brigade. Brig. Gen. Victor J. B. Girardey of Georgia was killed at Petersburg in 1864.

[11] On the battlefield of Shiloh, Jackson's brigade was positioned on the morning of 6 April behind the Locust Grove Run, a creek that ran west to east near McCuller Field, on the left flank of the Union forces. The brigade moved forward toward

the double quick. We rapidly descended, crossed the stream, and ascended the bluff, and were ordered on the double quick up the slope, into and through the camp. We halted in the rear of the camp.[12]

In the camp's rear, which was our front, was a settlement consisting of houses, stables, shops, haystacks, etc. Beyond this was thick underbrush.

I suspected the enemy was in the underbrush, and walked up and down the line with the view of ascertaining whether I was correct. While I was investigating, a splendid gray (horse) richly caparisoned, dashed up the road between our line and the fence. The horse entered an open gate and went in a stable. The desire of capturing him was strong, but so strong was my apprehension that the enemy was concealed in the underbrush I was unwilling to risk my life to capture him.

While walking up·and down the road, trying to discover whether the enemy was in front, a bullet from the left passed close to me. I was so intent on my purpose, that is, to discover the enemy's position, that I paid no attention to it. A few moments after another bullet came even nearer, and then a third one passed close to my head. This awoke me to the fact that somebody at the left was shooting at me. I stepped behind a tree which was broken off about eight or ten feet above the ground, thus shielding myself from the fire and, fixing my gun at ready, leveled it in that direction. A fence ran parallel with the road more than a hundred yards, then turned at right angles. Just across at the fork of the roads, was a large tree behind which I concluded the foeman was concealed. Between me and that tree the ground rose for several feet, then fell again; so, from my position, it was impossible to see any object lying at the tree. While I was watching, a man darted from behind the tree, running towards the angle of the fence—a distance of about fifty feet. I was sure he was the fellow who was endangering my life, and I was ready for him. I thought,—my shot must be quick and accurate, for if he reaches the fence he will be safe. I fired as he ran. Smoke from my rifle concealed the effect of the shot, but the men on the left of the Regiment, who say it all, cheered, and someone called, 'Captain, you got him!'

So the contest ended. If I had shot him, that freed me from danger from him. If he escaped, he was beyond my reach. I was still too busily

---

Larkin Bell field on the Savannah-Hamburg Road where they encountered the 55th Illinois and 54th and 71st Ohio infantry regiments.

[12] The camp of the 55th Illinois Infantry commanded by Lt. Col. Oscar Malmborg, part of Col. David Stuart's Second Brigade of Brig. Gen. W. T. Sherman's division.

absorbed with the idea that the enemy was in front to give the incident further attention. However, it chanced that I passed that way on my return from the battlefield, at dusk. And just in the fence corner was a haversack. It contained, among other things, white metal cups and handsome stationery. There was blood on the grass, showing someone had been wounded. I always supposed the haversack was his—the man who had shot at me...

Our line was ordered forward. We passed fences and circles down in the woods where I feared the enemy was concealed. I was mistaken in my apprehension. The line of battle was not there. We found it a quarter of a mile beyond. Here was our Regiment's first fight of the day. Our line of march was nearly parallel with the stream on our left, running into the Tennessee River. We descended a steep hill, crossed a narrow, rugged, ravine, ascended the opposite slope, and halted. The left flank of the Brigade rested on the point of the ridge, where it terminated at the valley of the stream. A glance at our position showed us we were in the immediate presence of the foe. They were on the crest of the ridge beyond, and stood circling around from a point obliquely in front of our left flank to another point obliquely in our rear. Who were they? Friend or foe, the underbrush concealed them. So it was impossible to say, with certainty. Flags in that motionless air dropped on their staffs, and we could not tell one army from the other.

A few minutes decided it, so far as we were concerned. A squad of men came down the slope from the line obliquely on our front, down into the valley. They no sooner emerged from the underbrush than it was manifest that they were Federals. They incautiously approached inside our line of fire and there stopped to parley. When they discovered we were Confederates, upon our demand that they surrender, they laid down their arms and walked into our lines.

Though I had no command, as no other officer was present, the men obeyed my instructions implicitly. I instructed the detail to carry them through to Colonel Farriss [sic].[13] Meantime, our position was anything but a comfortable one. Being on the extreme left, I did not know what was immediately in front, but we had a heavy line of fire on our left which rendered our position altogether untenable. They seemed as much puzzled to know whether we were Confederates or Federals as we had been about

---

[13] Col. Robert C. Fariss of the 17th Alabama Infantry.

them. The officers in front of their line passed to and fro, to secure such view as would enable them to decide.

Before long two men, one on foot and one on horseback started directly towards us. They evidently proposed to obtain definite information as to whether we were friends or foes. As soon as I saw their purpose, I said to the men near me, 'Boys, never let those men get back alive. That is the Yankee line of battle on our flank. If they ascertain that we are Confederates they will open fire upon us, enfilading us from obliquely in front around to our rear.'

In the meantime the two men came down in the valley. A colloquy began between them and us. On our side I was the spokesman. I told them we were Confederates and demanded their surrender. I told them escape was impossible; the attempt would mean death. I urged them to accept my proposal and surrender. They did not seem to fancy their position. They stood a little distance apart, talking in tones I could not hear. I felt assured the man on horseback would attempt to escape and I advised the squad about me that his plan must not be allowed. Our own lives and the safety of the Regiment depended upon preventing his getting back.

He made the attempt. The results was [sic] as I predicted. Our men fired. When the smoke of their guns lifted and allowed me to see, he was lying on the ground and the horse was going up the hill.[14] The other man slipped up to a tree, drew his pistol, and began calling back to his Regiment that we were foes and to fire. We tried to persuade him to surrender, but he paid no attention. Some of our men wanted to go down and capture him. I prevented that, seeing that the Yankees would then have our men in a similar position. However, in spite of my order and in violation of it, one man started to capture him.

As our man approached this officer, he was Lt. Col. 5th Ills., as we afterwards learned, he began to fire on him.[15] I cried to the men about me, 'Save our man!' The officer watched as they aimed their muskets, and dodged behind a tree. One of our party, seeing this, stepped off to one side. So, while the foe was sheltering himself from the squad, he became exposed

---

[14] Acting Adj. Gen. Adam M. Hughes and Lt. Col. W. S. Swarthout of the 50th Illinois Infantry.

[15] The 5th Illinois Infantry was not at Shiloh, but the 50th Illinois Infantry was present and facing Jackson's brigade. Lt. Col. William S. Swarthout of the 50th Illinois was wounded fighting the 17th Alabama. Chaplain Milton L. Haney was the chaplain of the 55th Illinois Infantry and left a memoir of this fight.

to the fire of this man in his new position. The first shot produced no effect. At the second shot he fell to the ground, threw down his pistol, and cried, 'I Surrender.'

Meantime, the battle opened in our front. The gun I carried that day was a Colt's rifle which would shoot five times. As I found I had nearly exhausted all of the chambers, I sat down under the shelter of the ridge and reloaded my gun. When the battle opened in front of our line, I had been too much interested in the foe on our flank to know of the army on our front. I was entirely ignorant of the situation. The sudden heavy volley was a great surprise. I said to myself, I must see the condition of affairs. So I resolved that as soon as my gun was loaded I would go around to the point of the ridge until I could see the foe's line on the other side, take the safest position I could find, and make the desired observation.

When I reached the opposite side I found no object big enough to shelter me. However, there were a number of small trees close by. Throwing myself down beside a white hickory which was too small for the protection needed, yet the best I could find, I began my observation.

I went up on the parade ground of the Federals' camp—I crept up behind the trees and then moved forward to the rear of the camp. I saw a large trunk in the rear of the Officers' Quarters. It was open and I discovered that it belonged to Colonel B. Allen, of Michigan.[16] In it were many clothes, and there was a beaded purse in the top part of the trunk, containing $20.00 in gold. You can imagine how I felt. It would be mean to take it, for myself; yet there it was. I was for a time uncertain as to what to do. Finally I decided to keep the purse which I finally gave to Mrs. Ellsworth, my sister-in-law. I gave the $20.00 to the Hospital. I went forward and found a large shawl in front of the camp, with a bullet hole in it. I hung it over my shoulders, planning to give it to major Burwell.

I went further on into the camp and found all in order for Sunday inspection. The officer's [sic] breakfast was still on the table. Evidently they had been interrupted by the gunfire and were afraid to wait to eat, what with bullets whizzing through the camp. The complete surprise must have been frightening.

---

[16] Col. Benjamin Allen of the 16th Wisconsin Infantry, in Peabody's brigade of Brig. Gen. Benjamin Prentiss's division.

Chancellorsville and Gettysburg

Chaplain Francis Milton Kennedy, D.D.
28th North Carolina Regiment, Army of Northern Virginia

Francis Milton Kennedy was born on 13 January 1834 to the Reverend and Mrs. William M. Kennedy of the South Carolina Conference, Methodist Episcopal Church. Educated first in his father's parsonage, the young Kennedy was admitted to the South Carolina Conference when he was twenty years old and subsequently served pastorates mainly in the northern part of the state. From March to July of 1862 he was a transportation and tract agent for the Confederate Army, taking supplies and church tracts from Charlotte to Richmond for distribution to soldiers. On 3 January 1863, James A. Sedden, Confederate secretary of war, appointed F. Milton Kennedy the chaplain of the 28th North Carolina Infantry. He reported for duty a week later.[1]

Sunday, January 11th, 1863

I commenced my duties regularly as Chaplain today.[2] Preached to the regiment this morning at 11 o'clock. My Bible and Hymn Book lying on an old goods box and the men gathered in a semi-circle around me. My text was from *Romans 12th Ch., 1st Verse*.[3] The day was very raw and unpleasant, so that I felt cramped for time. The men were standing up and the ground was very wet and cold so that I felt I ought not to keep them long. They were very respectful and attentive and I sincerely pray that they may be profited by the Word. Sunday as it is, Gen'l Lane sent me over my appointment as Chaplain which he had just rec'd from the Secretary of

---

[1] Excerpts from Chaplain Kennedy's diary were given by his daughter to the United Daughters of the Confederacy in 1940 to be publicized and shared with the public. The Georgia State Department of Archives and History, Morrow GA, owns a typescript under the title, "Confederate Diaries of the War: Soldiers and Citizens, 1860–1865," donated by the UDC and compiled and copied with the authority of John B. Wilson, secretary of state, WPA. project no. 5993.

[2] The 28th North Carolina Infantry Regiment, in Lane's brigade of Maj. Gen. A. P. Hill's division, "Stonewall" Jackson's corps, was encamped along the Rappahannock River in the vicinity of Fredericksburg VA. Lane's brigade was composed of the 7th, 18th, 28th, 33rd, and 37th North Carolina infantry regiments.

[3] Romans 12:1: "I beseech you therefore, brethren, by the mercies of God, that you present your bodies a living sacrifice, holy, acceptable unto God, which is your reasonable service" (KJV).

War.[4] Just after roll call, I had the drum beaten at my quarter and held evening prayer with the Regt. which is to be a permanent arrangement.

Tuesday, January 13th

This being my 29th birthday we had a sort of dining at my tent. Gen'l Lane and his brother Lieut. Lane and Capt. Oates came over and dined with me.[5] We had a very good dinner and a very pleasant time.

Wednesday, January 14th

Today I rode over to the camp of the 23rd N. C. Regt in D. H. Hill's Division and made a visit to Col. Lehman and his brother, a captain in the same regiment. Thence I rode to the camp of the 14th N.C. in the same Division. Saw and dined with Bro. W. C. Power, the Chaplain.[6] Also met a number of friends in the Am. Guard, besides Col. Bennett and Adjut. Marshall of the staff.[7] Saw a large number of regiments in dress parade in an old field as I returned to my camp. Also had my first view of "Old Stonewall Jackson" who rode along the road.[8]

Thursday, January 15th

Spent today in camp visiting the sick and going among the tents getting acquainted with the men and talking with them. The wind is blowing a perfect gale and has been doing so for twenty-four hours. Several tents have gone over and several more will doubtless fall before morning. Can't have fire in our tent.

Saturday, January 17th

The orders having been issued for the Regiment to go out on Picket tomorrow, I anticipated the Sabbath Service and preached today from Romans 14th Ch., 7th Verse. Later in the day, the order to go on Picket was countermanded and an order issued to be ready to march at a moment's notice.

Sunday, January 18th

---

[4] Brig. Gen. James Henry Lane, brigade commander, former commander of the 1st North Carolina Regiment.

[5] Lt. John Lane, Sumter Artillery, and Asst. Qm. Robert Oates of the 37th North Carolina Infantry Regiment.

[6] William Carr Power (1831–1916), Methodist chaplain of the 14th North Carolina Infantry Regiment.

[7] Col. Risden T. Bennett and 1st Lt. James C. Marshall of the 14th North Carolina, "the American Guard" regiment. Both Bennett and Marshall were captured near Winchester VA, by Union forces in September 1864.

[8] Lt. Gen. "Stonewall" Jackson, Second Corps commander, Army of Northern Virginia.

We have been all day in a state of expectancy waiting instructions. Capt. Davidson of the 37th N.C. came over today to preaching, but was informed that the service was held on yesterday.[9] Just before nightfall we rec'd an order from Hd. Quarters to be ready to march by daylight in the morning. So I suppose we will be off.

Monday, January 19th

Rose before day this morning, packed my valice [*sic*], strapped up my bed clothes and had everything ready to start when the Sgt. Major came round to inform us that the "march was suspended until further order." Assisted Capt. Thompson with his report.[10]

Tuesday, January 20th

Continued today to help Capt. Thompson. No orders yet to move. Probability of getting off considerably diminished. Orders rec'd. for captains of companies to see that their men were furnished immediately with 40 rounds of ammunition. Looks like we are to get into a fight in this vicinity. Yankees reported crossing the Rappahannock above and below Fredericksburg.

Wednesday, January 21st

It snowed for a few minutes last night and then blew and poured down rain the balance of the night. This morning it continues without cessation to pour rain, so that military operations in the line of the Rappahannock will necessarily be suspended for a time. Weather so bad we could not have prayer tonight. No new orders relative to moving.

Thursday, January 22nd

Weather still quite bad though not so much as yesterday. No news in the way of "orders", but a considerable degree of suspense. Had prayer tonight notwithstanding the bad weather and had a good turn-out.

Friday, January 23rd

Orders today to discharge all loaded guns and have them put in order. Looks like a fight or as some of our men say—"it looks bilious".

Monday, January 26th

The regiment went on the River to Picket today. I rode down to the Picket Line and saw several Yankee Pickets on the opposite bank sitting on

---

[9] Capt. William Lee Davidson of Company K, 37th North Carolina Infantry Regiment.

[10] Capt. Elijah T. Thompson, wounded at the Battle of Second Manassas, wounded and captured at Gettysburg, paroled at Fort Delaware on 14 September 1864, and retired for disability.

their horses. They picket entirely with cavalry. Nick Gibbon and I rode back to Camp about twilight.

Tuesday, January 27th

An order came from Gen'l Jackson last night to be ready to break camp and march immediately to any point on our front threatened by the enemy. The Reg't. returned from Picket this morning. A fight is expected soon. Has rained a good deal all day.

Thursday, January 29th

Snowed all last night until about dawn this morning. The snow is about 12 inches deep and very, very cold. A poor fellow in Co. H is lying in a dying condition, with nothing between his body and the ground but a single blanket. Such is war.

Saturday, January 31st

Had rather a bad night. Moved to my new tent. Doubled my blankets and found in a bad plan, too narrow to cover me so that I slept cold, or rather passed the night for I slept but little. Bob Oates and Miles Pegram from the 37th came over to see me this afternoon.[11] The disposition of the men to spend their money for something to eat is amazing—$19 3/4 was paid in camp this morning for 1/2 gallon of honey.

Tuesday, February 3rd

Commenced to snow very briskly this morning and kept it up for an hour or two but soon cleared off. It is *desperately* cold. Can't sleep much tonight, I fear, from the cold.

Thursday, February 5th

Snowing hard this morning. Kept it up until afternoon when it changed to rain, which continues. Reg't. ordered out to build a road. To be done three days. Terrible weather for it.

Tuesday, February 17th

It has snowed hard all day, commencing an hour or two before light this morning, continuing uninterruptedly until nightfall. Our boys "charged" with snow balls this afternoon upon the 18th and drove them out of their camp. The excitement of witnessing the fight has helped me. I feel much improved.

Wednesday, February 18th

---

[11] Asst. Qms. Robert Oates and Miles P. Pegram of the 37th North Carolina.

We had a real battle-royal this morning with the 13th Reg't. with snowballs.[12] I am ashamed to say though, that they drove us back and held the field. It commenced raining about 11 o'clock and has continued since.

Friday, February 20th

Had a letter today from my friend, Mrs. A. E. Robinson. She is the victim of deep grief from the loss of a brother, E. H. Darby, killed in the 2nd battle of Manassas.[13] Weather very pretty.

Sunday, February 22nd

This is the anniversary of Washington's birthday, of the Birthday of our Confederacy, and of my Father's death. It snowed most of last night and all of today. No preaching in consequence. The elements seemed opposed to my duties, this is the third Sabbath I have been unable to hold service.

Saturday, February 28th

Col. Lowe and Capt. Thompson left this morning on furlough.[14] Received my box of good things today—Cake, ham, potatoes, rice, butter, etc. We will have a nice time while they last.

Monday, March 2nd

Walked about 300 yards to witness the execution of a deserter from 33rd Va. Regiment. Fortunately the poor fellow was reprieved. *Applied for a five day furlough to go to Richmond. *

(*A copy of the furlough referred to is attached to these pages. It is signed by W. H. A. Speer, Major Commanding, 28th N.C., Col. Barbour, Lane's Brigade, Major General A. P. Hill, M. Gen'l. T. J. Jackson (Stonewall) and by W. W. Taylor, A. A. E. By order of Gen'l. Lee.)[15]

Saturday, March 7th

Received a leave of absence today from Hd. Qts. A. N. V. [16]—Will leave Monday. Regiment received orders to go on Picket tomorrow. Rained and blew all day. Busy receiving orders from officers and men for things from Richmond.

Monday, March 9th

---

[12] The 13th North Carolina Regiment in Scales's brigade.

[13] E. H. Darby was a sergeant in Co. L, 1st South Carolina Infantry Regiment commanded by Col. Maxey Gregg.

[14] Col. Samuel D. Lowe, wounded later at Gettysburg and retired for disability.

[15] Chaplain Kennedy's note. Both Col. William H. Asbury Speer and Col. William M. Barbour were wounded three times in 1863–1864, and both died in Petersburg hospitals. Lt. Gen. A. P. Hill died from wounds in 1864, and "Stonewall" Jackson died in 1863.

[16] Army of Northern Virginia.

Rode over to Guinea today. Took the train and went to Richmond. Stopped at the Spottswood.[17]

Tuesday, March 10th

Saddle $50—Bridle 12—Halter 11—Cloth for suit 31.50—Essence of Coffee 1.25—Advocate Fund 10—Allspice .50—Cap 10—Martingale and Breast Strap 10—Havasack 1.25—Canteen 1—Saw Brother William tonight and called with him to see Johnny and Amy DeRossett.[18]

Wednesday, March 11th

Charity .50. Today I had lunch and other articles purchased for the Reg't. packed in a box and prepared for transportation.

Thursday, March 12th

Board Bill $23—Watch Keys $1.00—Paid my bill at the Spottswood Hotel, $8.00 per day! Met Bishop Early, Dr. Hurton, G. W. Langhorn and George Nolly, all prominent preachers today.[19] Dropped in the Congress Halls today and saw the Congregated wisdom of the Confederacy. Senators and Representatives. Heard a Lecture tonight on the "The Women of the South"—Lecture .50—Servant $1.00.

Friday, March 13th

Traveled in company with Dave Miller from Richmond to Guinea. Frank met me there with a horse and I rode over to camp.[20] Found things about as I left them. Officers refunded me the amount paid out for my expenses.

Monday, March 16th

Today the meeting of Chaplains was held at the Baptist Church in this neighborhood. There were about 25 present. In the Corps are 91

---

[17] Guiney Station was the railroad supply point south of Fredericksburg. The Spotswood Hotel in Richmond, built in 1857, was the home for Jefferson Davis's family when he first arrived as president of the Confederate States in 1861. Other guests who stayed there—at different times—included Generals Robert E. Lee, U. S. Grant, William T. Sherman, and Philip Sheridan.

[18] William Kennedy was Chaplain Kennedy's brother, both sons of Rev. William M. Kennedy of the South Carolina Conference, Methodist Episcopal Church, South.

[19] Bishop John Early (1786–1873) was one of the founders of Randolph-Macon College in Virginia; Dr. Robert O. Burton; Rev. G. W. Langhorn, presiding elder of the Richmond district; and Rev. George W. Nolley were the preachers Chaplain Kennedy met in Richmond.

[20] Pvt. David E. Miller, C Co., 28th North Carolina Regiment. Frank appears in a number of places as Chaplain Kennedy's assistant, but without further identification.

Regiments, 44 with and 47 without Chaplains. The meeting was eminently pleasant and profitable. I found some very pleasant acquaintances.[21]

Wednesday, March 18th

Walked out this morning to a neighboring "Old Field" and saw Major Speer, visited the regiment for a while. We rec'd. information today that the enemy was crossing the Rappahannock above us. We have not been ordered to move. Distributed tracts through the Regiment today. Had a larger crowd than ever at Prayer tonight. Talked to them with great freedom of utterance.

Thursday, March 19th

Visited sick and distributed some Testaments and Hymn Books. Col. Lowe returned to the Regiment today from home. During his absence he married, and after staying one short week with his wife started back to camp. It snowed for two or three hours this afternoon.

Saturday, March 21st

Snow, snow, snow—all last night and all today until 6 o'clock in the afternoon. But it has not attained to any great depth. The Regiment is ordered on Picket tomorrow. I think I shall go out with them, and preach in a church situated right at the Fort for the Picket Review.

Sunday, March 22nd

Went out on Picket today. The Church has been so mutilated and abused by the soldiers that Gen'l A. P. Hill has ordered it to be nailed up and not opened again, so I could not get the use of it for preaching. The morning was very dark and unpleasant so I preached to the Regiment in the open air from Hosea 4th Ch. 9th Verse.[22] Walked to the river and viewed the Yankee Pickets through my glass.

Monday, March 23rd

An old gentlemen in whose home I slept last night gave me a very nice breakfast this morning and would have no pay for it though he made all the other officers pay $1 for simply sleeping on his floor upon their own blanket. Called at the 37th as I returned from Picket. Cloudy again this morning and looks like rain.

Tuesday, March 24th

Today I attended the 2nd meeting of the Chaplains of Jackson's Corps. We had a pretty full meeting and everything passed off very pleasantly and profitably I hope. We were honored with the presence of Col. Charles J.

---

[21] Chaplain J. William Jones documents this meeting in *Christ in the Camp*, 514.

[22] Hosea 4:9: "And there shall be like people, like priest, and I will punish them for their ways, and reward them for their doings."

Faulkner, Chief of Gen'l. Jackson's Staff and former Minister to France from the U.S. who made us an encouraging speech. We also had a speech from Col. Battle of the 3rd Alabama.[23] We are to meet again on next Friday. It rained hard as I was returning to camp and dampened me a good deal.

Wednesday, March 25th

I walked with Dr. Gibbon this afternoon to the 37th Reg't. Saw Oates, Pegram and Col. Barbour, also Charlie Worsham who has lately come on from Charlotte to act as Q.M. for Oates.[24] The attendance upon Prayer these nights is very fine. The men attend in large numbers and seem interested.

Thursday, March 26th

By invitation I enjoyed a very fine *Shad* breakfast with Capt. Oates this morning. Called at the 13th S.C. on my return and saw Capt. Duncan and Lieuts. Carlisle, Douglas and Petty.[25] It rained for a while this morning then changed to the most beautiful snow I ever saw, then cleared.

Friday, March 27th

"day of Fasting, Humiliation and Prayer"—I preached this morning from Psalms 8th Ch., 3—4 Verses, to the largest audience I have ever addressed in camp—nearly the entire Regiment was out and quite a number from neighboring Regiment. In the afternoon at 5 o'clock and again at night I held Prayers which were well attended. The men seem to appreciate the importance of a proper observance of the day, and have kept it with the solemnity of a Sabbath—indeed more solemnity than any Sabbath I have spent in the Army. Pretty nearly all the men too *fasted*, this observed with comparatively few exceptions. God grant His blessing. The day also was a beautiful one and struck me in the morning as presenting a good omen. For a long time have been having snow, sleet, and rain and not one whole, fair day for weeks. Today it was clear, calm and pleasant. Just such a day as

---

[23] Charles James Faulkner was a former Virginia state senator, a four-term US congressman, and ambassador to France. He was fifty-six years old when he offered his services to Lt. Gen. "Stonewall" Jackson. Col. Cullen A. Battle was the commander of the 3rd Alabama Infantry Regiment in O'Neal's brigade of Rodes's division.

[24] Surgeon Robert Gibbon of Mecklenburg County, North Carolina, promoted to brigade surgeon in January, 1864. Four members of the Worsham family from Mecklenburg County served in the 37th North Carolina Infantry Regiment.

[25] Capt. David R. Duncan; Lt. John W Carlisle, Lt. Alexander S. Douglas, and Lt. Charles Petty of C Co.

Patriots and Christians could have selected had it been left to their choice. If feel hopeful of the influence of the day's work in the Confederacy.

Monday, March 30th

A beautiful, bright, sunshiny day, though rather soft under foot. The ground was frozen hard this morning and it continued to be cold until 10 or 11 o'clock when the general influence of the sun made itself felt. The officers of the Brigade made up a purse with which they purchased a sword, Sash and Belt, also a fine Saddle and Bridle for General Lane. I walked over into an old field adjoining the Hd. Qts. to witness the "presentation". Col. Barbour of the 37th made the presentation speech and General Lane responded. Everything passed off gently and without the least enthusiasm.

Tuesday, April 7th

I walked about 3 1/2 miles to the Baptist Church this morning to attend Chaplain Meeting. Brother Betts preached a sermon on the text, "He went on his way rejoicing."[26] We had then a very pleasant meeting, discussing many matters connected with the spiritual interest of the soldiers of the Corps. Special prayer was offered for General Lee who was reported ill from an attack of Pneumonia. Brother Power and I took a recess and dispatched a snack which I had prudently taken along with me. We got through our meeting about 5 o'clock and in company with several Chaplains, I walked back.

Thursday, April 9th

Brother Power came over and spent most of today with me. He is a noble fellow! A man whom I admire and love more and more as I see and know more of him.

Tuesday, April 14th

Attended a very delightful "Meeting of the Chaplains" today. We had a full meeting and a very pleasant time. Dr. Pendleton, an Episcopal Minister, and Brig. Gen'l. of Artillery C.S.A.[27]

Tuesday, April 21st

Walked out to Round Oak Church today and attended "Chaplain's Meeting". Brother Lacy preached a most admiral sermon from the text, "While thy servant was busy here and there, he was gone." I was elected

---

[26] Alexander D. Betts (1832–1918), Methodist chaplain of the 30th North Carolina Infantry Regiment.

[27] Brig. Gen. William Pendleton, Episcopal minister from Lexington VA, and General J. E. Johnston's chief of artillery in 1862, spoke at the meeting.

Chairman and presided over the meeting. Had a good meeting at night, quite a number of penitent. Buried Tacket of Co. F. this afternoon.[28]

Saturday, April 25th

General Pendleton was to preach for the Chaplains today at Round Oak Church but failed to come, and I having been chairman of the last meeting had to supply the failure as best I could. I preached to a crowded house from Rom.14th Ch., 7th Verse. We had a very pleasant meeting after the sermon.[29] I promised Mr. Hardee, Chaplain 2nd La. Reg't. to visit a man in his Reg't. condemned to be shot on next Friday.[30]

Wednesday, April 29th

Rec'd. orders this morning to be ready to move at a moment's notice and very shortly afterward the order to "fall in" came along and we started off. Reached Hamilton's Crossing in due time, and the Reg't. was immediately drawn up in the 2nd line of battle.[31] I had prayer with the boys and kept the trenches without shelter in a beating rain all night.

Thursday, April 30th

Went over to the Hospital about 1 1/2 miles from the line of battle this morning. Passed the morning without special incident. In the afternoon started over to the Reg't. to have service, and found myself just before reaching it and for an hour or two afterwards under a shower of shells which the enemy was hailing at a battery immediately in front of our Brigade. Held service.

Friday, May 1st

Started off before daylight this morning to meet the enemy some 12 miles higher up the River, the demonstration before Fredericksburg being a—[32]Some fighting, but our Division not engaged. Located hospital in the rear. Met a number of Chaplains today with their several commands.

Saturday, May 2nd

---

[28] The Rev. B. Tucker Lacy, Presbyterian chaplain of Jackson's Second Corps; Pvt. B. Frank Tackett, died at Camp Gregg VA on 19 April 1863, of pneumonia. Tackett was eighteen years old.

[29] J. William Jones, Baptist chaplain of the 13th Virginia Infantry, mentions this meeting in his book, *Christ in the Camp*, 521.

[30] Robert Hardie, Jr., Methodist chaplain of the 2nd Louisiana Infantry Regiment.

[31] Hamilton's Crossing is just southeast of Fredericksburg VA.

[32] Unknown word missing here may be "ruse."

Jackson's Corps started off this morning in a Flank movement.[33] As we passed a road with the Medical and Ordnance train, we were severely shelled by the enemy, and as they advanced on the road we had to put our horses on their mettle to escape capture. About an hour before dark our forces came upon the enemy's flank and drove him several miles with great slaughter. About 12 o'clock he made a desperate attack upon us but was repulsed. I was up all night with the wounded who were being constantly brought in to the hospital from the bloody field.

Sunday, May 3rd

This morning the fight was renewed and the bloodiest battle of the war was fought. Our Brigade has been fearfully decimated, and all day the wounded were being brought in. Oh! How fearful the scenes around a "Field Hospital" during a bloody battle. All day I have been incessantly employed in trying to mitigate their suffering and ministering to the spiritual wants of the sufferers. General Jackson was wounded last night by our own men through mistake![34]

Monday, May 4th

Heavy skirmishes have been going on between the advance forces of the two armies today but no general battle on this wing. We have pretty well all our wounded in, and sent off a large number of slightly wounded to Richmond. This afternoon there fell one of the heaviest rains I have ever witnessed. Our poor sufferers now almost covered with mud and water. We ripped off the planks from some houses and gathered pine tops, which saved them only from the mud but did not improve their comfort much.

Tuesday, May 5th

Rained hard all day. We were confounded and somewhat alarmed by learning that our Brigade was entrenched, *facing toward our Hospital* in anticipation of a flank movement of the enemy, which would expose the hospital and all in it to capture. Fortunately the precaution was unnecessary. Our wounded are in sad condition—wet, cold and hunger to be endured in addition to their wounds. Some heavy picket firing tonight.

Wednesday, May 6th

---

[33] The Battle of Chancellorsville. Lane's brigade was in the attack as part of Maj. Gen. A. P. Hill's division.

[34] Chaplain Kennedy meant by "our own men" that Lt. Gen. Jackson was mortally wounded by fire from soldiers of the 18th North Carolina, part of Lane's brigade. See James I. Robertson, Jr., *Stonewall Jackson: The Man, The Soldier, The Legend* (New York: Macmillan Publishing, 1997) 728–29.

This morning it was discovered by pressing our skirmishers forwards that the enemy had deserted his powerful works and under cover of the darkness and storm of last night had recrossed his shattered columns to the north side of the Rappahannock. Then the " 6th on to Richmond" had terminated in disaster and ignominious defeat.[35] We have gained another great victory but "Chancellorsville" is inscribed upon our banners with the blood of the best and bravest of the Confederacy. Oh! God, how long? Before this fearful war is over?

Thursday, May 7th

The fighting being over, the Regiment was yesterday afternoon ordered back to their respective camps. Still busy with the wounded. I shall remain at the Hospital until they are returned.

Friday, May 8th

We got off some of our wounded today, but still have a number left.

Saturday, May 9th

Breakfasted with Capt. Oates, Hughes and C.[36] The Division Wagon and Ambulance Train came in last night and we got off all our wounded to Hamilton's Crossing where they will be taken by train to Richmond.[37] Rode over the battlefield which is crowded with fearful sights. Proceeded toward the old camp to which we were all ordered back. Stopped several hours in Fredericksburg, and looked over the desolation wrought by the enemy. Many houses have been completely demolished and many more perforated and battered with ball and shell. Reached camp.

Sunday, May 10th

General Lee has by a general order set apart this as a day of Thanksgiving for the great victory. The Regiment returned from Picket this morning very much jaded so I deferred services until afternoon. I then preached with a considerable degree of freedom from the 2nd Verse of the 103rd Ch. of Psalms. The Lt. Colonel of the Reg't., 2 Captains and 1 Private joined the church at the close of the service. Tom Smith came over to see me today. Held service again at night.

Monday, May 11th

---

[35] Probably a reference to the defeat of Maj. Gen. John Sedgwick's VI Corps at Salem Church, east of Chancellorsville, on 3–4 May 1863.

[36] Capt. Robert Oates, Cpl. James W. Hughes of Co. B and probably Charles Worsham, acting quartermaster, all of the 37th North Carolina.

[37] Hamilton's Crossing was on the railroad south of Fredericksburg.

Completely prostrated. I have scarcely moved out of my tent today except to my meals and to distribute a number of religious papers which have come during my absence. My service tonight was very interesting and quite a large number knelt for prayer.

Thursday, May 14th

Called to see the sick this morning. A very happy rain fell about two o'clock and a tall tree right in the middle of our camp was struck by lightning. One man stunned but not seriously hurt. Thinking the rain was over, as the cloud had passed and the sun came out, I started over to the 12th S.C. but had not gone more than half way before another cloud came up and poured down. I got quite wet. Saw Bro. Anderson, Chaplain 12th S.C., Capt. Duncan, Carlisle, Petty and Douglas of the 13th S.C.[38]

Sunday, May 17th

I preached this morning from Eccl. 8th Ch., 11th Verse. Rather too long a sermon for the holiday, most of the men exposed to the sun. At night ten (10) joined the Church and a larger number presented themselves for prayer.

Thursday, May 21st

Called at Hd. Qts. to inquire after the health of Gen'l. Lane who had been quite sick. Rode down to Picket station and spent part of the day in *fruitless* fishing. Held service at night. Slept on the grass.

Monday, June 1st

I was set for today to visit some men who are condemned to be shot on Wednesday and Friday respectively. They seem to be perfectly prostrated with distress at the prospect of meeting such an end, yet, both profess to feel that their sins are pardoned.

Tuesday, June 2nd

Called again today to see the convicts of the 37th Reg't. Tried to talk searchingly to them. They seemed more resigned to their fate. Just after I left them an order came from the Secretary of War suspending the execution of the sentence and bringing them to Richmond. Attended Chaplains' meeting.

Wednesday, June 3rd

---

[38] The Rev. John Monroe Anderson (1821–1879), Presbyterian chaplain of the 12th South Carolina.

Changed our camp today and got into a delightfully cool place. Rode round to the Hd. Qts. of all the generals yesterday and had a furlough signed for Capt. Bohannan.[39]

Tuesday, June 4th

We are enjoying our new camp hugely. It is a most delightful place but I fear we will not enjoy it long as we have orders tonight to be ready to move at any moment. Our Prayer meeting was very interesting tonight.

Friday, June 5th

Rev. Mr. Watson, an Army Missionary, of the Presbyterian Church, preached for us tonight, a very good sermon from the text, "They that are led by the Spirit of God, are the Sons of God."[40] Just after the service we were ordered to march, and have to fix up as rapidly as possible and take the road.

Saturday, June 6th

Traveled all last night and reached Hamilton's Crossing just after daylight. Division found in line of battle and an established hospital.

Sunday, June 7th

Right in the trenches. Too windy to preach. Some shelling and skirmishing, otherwise all quite. Held service tonight.

Tuesday, June 9th

Still in line of battle. Shelling but no fight.

Wednesday, June 10th

Programme same as yesterday. I fear the enemy is holding us here with an inferior force while he is massing his troops at some other point. But Gen'l. Lee will be in time to check with any movement Hooker can make!

Thursday, June 11th

Met an old friend today, Dr. Leo V. Huot from Columbia, S.C.[41] Shelling in the afternoon and light skirmishing. Our Brigade ordered up and men ordered to pitch their tents along the entrenchment and make themselves as comfortable as possible.

Friday, June 12th

---

[39] Capt. Neal Bohannon of Yadkin County, North Carolina, wounded at Gettysburg in 1863 and captured at Spotsylvania Court House in 1864. He remained a prisoner at Hilton Head SC, and later at Fort Delaware until 16 June 1865.

[40] John Franklin Watson (1839–1870), Presbyterian chaplain of the 16th North Carolina Regiment.

[41] Dr. L. V. Huot, surgeon of the 14th South Carolina Regiment.

We are literally camped in line of battle. The enemy has entrenched himself on this side of the River but makes no offensive demonstration. We hear that Stuart has been surprised above and suffered considerably.[42]

Tuesday, June 16th

Received orders to march and started at 4 o'clock A.M. We traveled very well and crossed the Rapidan before sunset. The fording of the River by the troops was to me a very novel and beautiful scene. The day was warm, and later in the evening, I took a bath in the River.

Wednesday, June 17th

Today starting at 4 1/2 o'clock, we marched 14 miles to Stephensburg. The day was oppressively hot and a large number of men fell exhausted from the heat. The march was badly conducted, a whole day's march being accomplished by 12 o'clock.

Thursday, June 18th

We left Stephensburg and marched 14 miles to a point beyond Culpepper. Men fell by scores and several died in the road from exhaustion. Placing Dr. McCauley on my horse I walked several miles and came near being completely prostrated.[43]

Friday, June 19th

Marched a distance of 12 miles to Gaines Cross Roads. We bivouacked in large clover field. It poured down rain nearly all night, and having no tent I was completely drenched and lay in a stream of water the whole night.

Saturday, June 20th

No bad effect from my duckling last night. Marched 12 miles and bivouacked on the top of the Blue Ridge. I breakfasted and dined with a very nice family of English folks named Johnson near a little village called Flint Mill. I was very kindly treated without any charge. The gap at which we crossed the Ridge is called Chester Gap. It has rained incessantly all day.

Sunday, June 21st

Descended the Ridge and passed through a very pretty town called Front Royal, memorable for the castigation inflicted upon Banks by the immortal Stonewall Jackson.[44] Here we were regaled by the vision of some very beautiful ladies who waved their welcome to us as we passed.

---

[42] At the Battle of Brandy Station on 9 June, the largest cavalry battle of the war, the Federal cavalry sustained 866 casualties to Stuart's 523.

[43] Dr. James McCauley, a contract physician.

[44] Maj. Gen. Nathaniel P. Banks (1816–1894) defeated by Jackson in the Valley Campaign of 1862.

Bivouacked in a grass and clover field and had a fine night's rest. The men are now standing the march very well.

Monday, June 22nd

Marched to within 3 miles of Berryville and camped in a most beautiful oak grove which furnished us a dense shade. I had services this evening with the Reg't. for the first time since we left Hamilton's Crossing.

Tuesday, June 23rd

We rested today until 1 o'clock. I rode out with Dr. Moffett to Mr. Briggs' and ate a delicious dinner.[45] The entertainment was greatly enhanced by the presence at the head of the table of a beautiful lady. When we returned to camp we found the Division had moved. We followed on. Passed through Berryville, a pretty little town which the Yankees had forfeited handsomely, but the fate of Milroy's force at Winchester induced them to abandon their works without a fight.[46] We camped 1 mile from a little settlement called "Summit Point."

Wednesday, June 24th

Passed this morning through a very pretty little village called Smithfield. The patriotism of the ladies (who were numerous and pretty) was quite demonstrative as we passed. They surrounded Gen'l. Lee and must have worried the old gentleman with shaking his hand. Camped 3 miles from Shepherdstown. I breakfasted this morning at the home of a widow named "Timberlake". She is a Methodist and I found her and her daughters very pleasant.

Thursday, June 25th

Marched this morning through Shepherdstown memorable for the wholesale slaughter and drowning of Yankees when they attempted to follow our forces after the battle of "Sharpsburg". Notwithstanding their near proximity to the enemy, and having been under Yankee rule for two years, they were in ecstasies over our having advanced toward the enemy's country. Large numbers of beautiful ladies cheered us by their presence and marks of approval as we passed. Crossed the Potomac about 12 o'clock. The ford was up and the current swift but the entire Division crossed without accident save the drowning of one mule. Two miles from the River we passed Sharpsburg, which though in Maryland is a miserable Union hole. The

---

[45] Dr. George B. Moffett of Virginia, surgeon to the 37th North Carolina Regiment at this time.

[46] Maj. Gen. Robert H. Milroy, USA (1816–1890) defeated by Ewell's corps at Winchester in June 1863.

people, men and women, looked as though vinegar had been their only beverage since the Battle in their neighborhood. Camped near village called Tilmantown.[47]

Friday, June 26th

Rained hard nearly all day. Got perfectly wet. One of the Pioneers of our Brigade cut down a Union flagstaff which stood impudently in the streets of Sharpsburg. Tilmantown is a small place whose only distinguishing peculiarities are log houses and rank Unionism. Marched this morning through Hagerstown, a place of considerable size. One lady had the independence to wave a Confederate Flag which was heartily cheered by the boys as they passed. Otherwise, there was nothing to indicate a "in for the Marylanders". After leaving Hagerstown we passed a little place called "Leitersburg". Camped near by this place. Dr. Mayo and I rode out to a house and got supper for ourselves and horses.[48] The man of the house seemed to be frightened almost to death and though we could see he was for the Union, when Yankees were about, he seemed desperately afraid. This is a magnificent country, a perfect Goshen.

Saturday, June 27th

Passed the Pennsylvania line about 1 mile from last night's camps. Policy prevents many of these people from looking as sour as they did in Maryland. Passed through Waynesboro and purchased with Confederate money a number of things I needed. I felt like they were taking the money more as a "military necessity" then [sic] because they liked to. The next village we passed was Quincy, then Funkstown. This country abounds in villages, in fact we seem to be passing through one continuous village all the time. The farms are in a perfect state of cultivation, and the wheat which seems to be the main crop, is vastly superior to any I have ever seen before. Timothy grass and clover grow luxuriantly and our horses are indeed "in clover". I have gotten my horse's back sore and I fear I will have trouble with it. We are camped about 1 1/2 miles from Funkstown near a fine clover field in a large oak grove.

Sunday, June 28th

The orders are that we remain where we are today and that the men wash their clothes and clean their guns. We learned this morning that the

---

[47] Tilghmanton, five miles north of the Antietam Battlefield.

[48] Dr. M. Lewis Mayo, assistant surgeon in the 28th North Carolina. Dr. Mayo transferred to the hospital at Charlotte NC in January 1865. He was paroled there in May of the same year.

men committed many depredations yesterday afternoon and last night, going to houses and taking whatever they could lay their hands upon. Such practice, intrinsically wrong and indefensible will, I fear, unless promptly stopped, so demoralize the army as to bring disaster upon it. Stringent orders from Gen[']l. Lee have just been published which it is to be hoped will arrest the evil. Most of our men were on Picket this morning, and those left in camp were busy washing, cleaning their guns so that I could not preach until afternoon, when I addressed a pretty good congregation from I John 2nd Ch., 17th Verse. I took occasion to talk plainly to them on the subject to taking what did not belong to them from unarmed inhabitants of the country. A mail came to the Brigade today and almost everybody got a letter but me.

Monday, June 29th

We had orders to march at 5 o'clock this morning, and ate our breakfast about 4 o'clock, when we were instructed to wait for further orders before moving. In the afternoon we were ordered to be ready to move at a moment's warning, send cooking utensils back to the wagon, return rations, etc., and then about the time this order was complied with, another came revoking it and ordering the rations for three days to be cooked. There is some excitement, but none of us know what it is. Bennick held service for me this evening.[49] Our foraging parties do very well getting provisions, but are very unsuccessful about horses. The people have driven off their valuable stock to distant and secret places, and thus far the horses that have been gotten are in the main very inferior. Yesterday we learned "Bushwhackers" captured a party of 20 Artillery-men with their horses, who were out searching for horses—this was rather a losing trip on our side.

Tuesday, June 30th

We left our camp near Funkstown at 5 o'clock this morning and marched 12 miles, turning off from the road to Chambersburg which we thought was our destination, and taking the turnpike toward Gettysburg. On the road we passed the smoldering ruins of extensive iron works, the property of the notorious Abolitionist Thaddeus Stephens, which had been totally destroyed by order of Gen'l. Ewell.[50] This man Stephens was the author of "Yankees' Confiscation Bill" and preparer of the plan of

---

[49] Augustus R. Bennick, Methodist chaplain of the 34th North Carolina Regiment.

[50] Thaddeus Stevens (1792–1868), US congressman from 1858–1868; Lt. Gen. Richard Ewell, CSA, (1817–1872).

colonizing the South with free Negroes, illustrating his theory, I believe by a practical experiment in that portion of Florida which is held by the Yankees. The only unpleasant feature about the destruction of the property is that a considerable number of operators are left without employment. But upon inquiry among them I learned there was no danger of women and children suffering. We have today crossed the Blue Ridge Mountains.

Wednesday, July 1st, 1963

Left our camp in the mountainside and marched towards Gettysburg. Passed Graffenburg Springs, Cashtown and New Salem. When we reached the last named place we could hear the sound of battle. Cannonading and musketry. In the course of a few miles we came in sight of the battle, and from a commanding position, I for the first time, *saw* a battle in actual process. Our division was at once formed in line of battle and advanced. Only two Brigades of Pender's Division became engaged during today—Scales['s] and McGowan's—and they suffered severely. Heth's Division first encountered the enemy, and bore the brunt of the fight, so far as our part of the field was concerned.[51] Our Reg't. had six or eight men wounded, two of them severely. We have driven the enemy several miles and the City of Gettysburg which was stoutly defended by the enemy is occupied tonight by Rhodes' Division of Ewell's Corps.

Thursday, July 2nd

Rode over the battle-field and witnessed some hideous scenes, the most revolting of which were two men torn in two by a shell with their heads turned completely back upon their heels. The morning passed off quietly, save continual firing between the skirmishers and an occasional shell. I rode into town and saw some of my friends of Ramseur's Brigade.[52]

About 3 o'clock or 4 the most fearful cannonading of which I ever conceived commenced. The earth fairly shook with the explosions of the guns. The enemy occupied a position of great strength. Longstreet attacked their left about 4 o'clock and Ewell their right. Hill attacked them in the center.[53] The fighting has been fearful, and we have no means of ascertaining tonight the result of the conflict, but we all feel confident of success. Gen'l. Pender was disabled this afternoon by a shell wound on the

---

[51] The first units from Lt. Gen. A. P. Hill's corps to enter the fields at Gettysburg.

[52] Brig. Gen. S. D. Ramseur's brigade in Ewell's corps.

[53] General R. E. Lee's three corps commanders: Lt. Generals James Longstreet, Richard Ewell, and A. P. Hill.

thigh, not serious. Gen'l. Lane is now commanding Pender's Division, and Col. Avery our Brigade.[54]

Friday, July 3rd, 1863

We learned this morning that our success would have been complete but for the bad conduct of Posey's Brigade last night, which gave way, causing a panic, which resulted in the falling back of the whole line.[55] Today a general attack was made on the enemy's position, resulting in a failure to dislodge them and a fearful loss on our side, what it was on the side of the enemy, we don't know.[56] Our Brigade suffered very heavily, my Regiment losing a great many in killed and wounded. I occupied an eminence upon which Gen'l. Lee was stationed, from which I had a very good view of the battle.[57] The cannonading was fearful—the scene terribly sublime. I rode my horse this afternoon trying to find a new hospital which was established today. By some means the Medical Department was badly managed today causing a good deal of unnecessary pain and trouble to the wounded.

Saturday, July 4th

I slept but little last night being very busy with the wounded who were brought in by scores. Our Brigade suffered heavily, as indeed did the entire army. The enemy had an impregnable position, and we attempted to storm it, charging *one mile and a half* over an open field right in the face of scores of cannons. The men came within a few yards of the enemy's entrenchment but had to fall back for want of men enough to hold them. This day's work is *the mistake* of the campaign and it will be well for us if our repulse does not grow into our disaster. Our wounded were all moved 3 miles back and, while there was no fighting, everything looked like a retrograde movement. This afternoon all the slightly wounded, and such others as transportation could be provided for were started back in the direction of Cashtown. The Division Commissary and Quartermaster trains have also gone that way. About sundown we received orders to start with the medical train in an hour by another road.

Sunday, July 5th

---

[54] Maj. Gen. Dorsey Pender, Brig. Gen. James H. Lane, and Col. C. M. Avery.

[55] Brig. Gen. Carnot Posey from Wilkinson County, Mississippi, wounded at Bristoe Station in October 1863, and died in Charlottesville VA on 13 November 1863.

[56] Popularly known as Pickett's Charge.

[57] Seminary Ridge at Gettysburg.

I was in the saddle all last night, and in a pouring rain, thoroughly wet all night. Our progress was greatly impeded by the multitude of troops, artillery and wagons along the road, so that when we stopped about 8 o'clock this morning, on this side of a little village called Fairfield, we had only traveled about 8 miles.[58] I was quite sick when we started last night, the road was exceedingly rocky and muddy, my horse had one shoe off, and everything conspired to render it the most *disagreeable night* I ever spent. I had my feelings sorely tried when telling the officers and other men good-bye who were so seriously wounded as to disqualify them for traveling. They will necessarily fall into the hands of the enemy and they dreaded it, oh; so much. We rested near Fairfield until about 1 o'clock and then started forward on our backward course. It has rained on us most of the day. Late this evening we heard cannonading, front and rear, indicating that the enemy has discovered our withdrawal from their front and were also disputing our passage through the Blue Ridge.

Monday, July 6th

Passed a very unpleasant night. Didn't travel very far, but was in the saddle nearly the whole night, not knowing when the train stopped, but it would be in motion again in a moment. We were crossing the Blue Ridge and the road was, I think, the most rugged I ever passed over. My horse's bare foot made it extremely unpleasant riding. We reached the top of the Ridge this morning about 7 1/2 o'clock and got a very good breakfast at a mountain farm. One of the girls was quite spicy in her chat with some of the boys, indicating pretty plainly that she thought we had been badly whipped and were afraid of meeting Yankees again. In company with Drs. Holt, Higginbotham and Mayo, I rode on to the camping ground of the troops.[59] Found our Regiment with *100 men*. At 3 o'clock we commenced marching in company with the troops, passed through Waynesboro and camped within a mile or two of Hagerstown. But few of the people showed themselves as we went *forward* through Waynesboro. As we came *back*, we saw the whole population.

Tuesday, July 7th

Started early this morning and marched a few miles, going into camp about 1 1/2 miles this side of Hagerstown. I understand that we stopped so soon for the fact that the recent rains have made the Potomac *too deep for*

---

[58] Southwest of Gettysburg toward Waynesboro.
[59] Dr. L. V. Huot, Dr. Edward G. Higgenbotham of the 33rd North Carolina, and Dr. Lewis Mayo.

fording. I rode into Hagerstown hoping to make some purchases[,] but the place was crowded with soldiers and the stores all guarded by sentinels. I am informed that stores were broken open this morning and robbed. Gen'l. Lee is trying hard to prevent incidents of that sort[,] but I am sorry to say he has not been successful. If we meet with disaster before getting back upon our own soil, it will be a Providential visitation for the misconduct of the men. I have tried to do my duty in preventing such misdemeanors, and I think in our Reg't. there was less of it than in most commands. I held services tonight with the small remnant of the 28th which is left. It was a melancholy service to me, and the men seemed to feel very sad.

Wednesday, July 8th

Had a delightful night's rest, notwithstanding it poured down rain during the whole night. After daylight this morning, however, the water rose under me and I got pretty wet. We will doubtless remain here several days as the Potomac has risen 10 feet and is still rising. The topography of the country is favorable for us, and Gen'l. Lee, I think, would be rather pleased than otherwise for the enemy to attack him. Held service with the Regiment this evening.

Thursday, July 9th

We are still quiet. The river is falling slightly today, but is still many feet above the fording point. Not having a change of underclothes, I pulled off these I have on and made Frank wash them, going without in the meantime. While in this plight, I preached to Scales' Brigade from Romans 12th Ch., 1st Verse.[60] Bennick preached for me to our Brigade at 6 o'clock and had a very good congregation. Our wounded have all gotten safely across the Potomac.

Friday, July 10th

Today we are ordered 3 miles to the rear with the medical train and are camped within two or three miles of Williamsport. The river is still too deep for fording and everything indicates that we may have a battle in Maryland.

Saturday, July 11th

Slept without any shelter last night and got pretty damp with the heavy dew. I have been feeling for some cause very much depressed today. I feel unutterably anxious to get home. Rode down to the Reg't. and found them thoroughly entrenched. Some Picket firing on our right this afternoon. I had prayer with the Reg't. and felt unusually comforted in prayers.

---

[60] Brig. Gen. Alfred M. Scales (1827–1892), wounded at Gettysburg, post-war governor of North Carolina.

Sunday, July 12th

Slept with Dr. Mayo in a wheat field last night and rested very well. Changed our camp today. Held service this afternoon in a tent at the regiment of Col. Davis' of the 12th S.C.[61] Heavy rain this afternoon. I fear it will be sometime yet before we can cross the Potomac.

Monday, July 13th

Rec'd. orders about 3 o'clock to pack up and cross the Potomac as soon as possible. The ford was quite deep and a good many mules have been drowned and ambulances and wagons washed down the river, but before reaching the River we passed through the town of Williamsport, a place of some size. The effects of the proximity of any army are plainly visible.

Tuesday, July 14th

Passed a dreadfully disagreeable night. Poured down rain—in the saddle until about 1 o'clock. Bivouacked in a field which was ankle deep all over in mud and water, so that there was no possibility of lying down. I secured a place on the driver's seat of one of the wagons after standing for a long time, and was very fortunate in being thus relived from standing on my feet the balance of the night. Started this morning and traveled to within 4 miles of Martinsburg. Rested until 1 o'clock. Ordered to move. Order countermanded. Very hard rain.

Wednesday, July 15th

We fell in with our Brigade as it passed this morning and marched about 15 miles to Bunker Hill. Passed through Martinsburg, a town of considerable size, and strong Unionism. I remained there several hours hoping to get a shoe on my horse's foot but in vain. A poor fellow was lying on the side of the street as I passed dying from an accidental shot cutting the femoral artery. 13th S.C. Reg't. Bunker Hill near which we are camped is a place of 4 houses. We hope to remain here several days and recruit. Had a shoe nailed on my horse's foot.

Thursday, July 16th

Rested today. Took a delicious bath and scouring in a creek nearby. Received a note today from Brother William written on the *1st of June.*

Saturday, July 18th

The prospect seems to be for us to rest and remain here for some time to come. Held service with the Reg't. this afternoon and spoke with some considerable degree of satisfaction. Received a letter from Kate informing

---

[61] Lt. Col. Henry C. Davis, 12th South Carolina Regiment.

me that Brother William was declining rapidly and urging me to come to him.

Sunday, July 19th

Preached to our Brigade this morning from John 5th Ch., 39th Verse. Had a good attendance. I made application for 40 days leave, but am very much afraid I shall not succeed with it.

Monday, July 20th

Changed camp today and secured a beautiful place, clean and shady. If the troops can only stay here a few weeks, it will help them greatly. Our Hd. Qts. are established under a magnificent oak.

Tuesday, July 21st

Rode two or three miles into the country and got a very good breakfast. Thought we could remain in our new camp for several weeks, but the order to "march at 11 o'clock" disappointed the hopes of the men. The day was hot and the march severe. Passed through Winchester, which is a noble old town. The fortifications from which Ewell drove Milroy's forces were very formidable. I felt sorry for the good people of this glorious old town as we passed thorough, leaving them to the tender mercies of another incursion of Yankees. We camped about 1 1/2 miles from Winchester in an old field. Had no dinner or supper.

Wednesday, July 22nd

Left about 5 o'clock this morning, and had a long, weary march. The sun beamed down intensely and the dust was choking. We crossed the Shenandoah on a pontoon bridge which the boys thought was much better than wading. We marched about 19 miles and camped near Front Royal. Corp'l. Biles of Co. K, 28th Regiment, married in the place as we passed through going north. Poor girl; [t]he battle of Gettysburg made her a widow. He was killed in the unsuccessful charge on the enemy's works.[62]

Thursday, July 23rd

Started at the usual hour this morning. Made an all day's march of it, but only came 11 miles, our column being very much impeded by wagon trains. Crossed the Ridge at Chester's Gap. Had my horse well fed at old friend Johnston's. Our Brigade was detached to throw out skirmishes and protect the train from a threatened band of cavalry. Camped near Flint Hills. The people seem to regret our leaving them outside of our lines.

---

[62] Actually Cpl. William C. Biles was wounded and captured at Gettysburg, but survived to be paroled at City Point VA, on 20 March 1864. He was retired to the Invalid Corps on 21 December 1864.

Friday, July 24th

Today has been desperately hot. Frank having been sick for several days and vary [sic] feeble. I put him on my horse and marched the whole distance 15 miles. Crossed two Rivers, Thornton's and Hazel Rivers. Camped near the residence of a Mr. Rixy 9 miles from Culpepper, C. H. The Yankee Cavalry planted a battery and shelled the road for awhile, but our men soon drove them away capturing some prisoners and killing several. We lost 2 men killed and 9 wounded.

Saturday, July 25th

I rode several miles off the road and had my horse well shod. We are in camp 1 1/2 miles from Culpepper with the promise of resting for a day or two. Feel pretty sore from my walk of yesterday.

Sunday, July 26th

Preached this morning from Eccl.9th Ch., 18th Verse, rather a poor sermon but I trust good will result from it. It has been dreadfully hot all day and our camp is very ineligibly selected. The ground has been burned off, making it very disagreeable and the shade is very thin. It is rumored we will move tomorrow and I sincerely hope it may be so. Nothing from my furlough yet.

Tuesday, July 28th

Had a very hard rain last night and am put to it to keep dry. Received another letter from Kate bringing the painful news that Bro. William was still growing weaker daily. My furlough came back tonight approved for 30 days instead of 40 for which I asked. I shall get off in the morning, God willing. Another very hard rain this afternoon and tonight. Everybody seemed glad that I got my leave.

Tuesday, July 30th

Left Lynchburg at 4 1/2 o'clock this morning by the Virginia and Tennessee R.R. Breakfasted at Blue Ridge Springs. R.R. Fare $5.00. Breakfast 2.00, Hack 3.00, Papers .15. Stopped at Christianburg and took a hack to Blacksburg. Passed the Yellow Sulphur Springs and took a drink of the water. Walked from Blacksburg to Col. Preston's and was very cordially welcomed. Found Brother William *very feeble* but better than he had been.

Friday, July 31st

Had a delightful sleep last night. That climate here is delightfully exhilarating. We are right on the top of the Allegheny Mountains and in a short distance of all the famous Virginia Springs. Mrs. Preston is a noble woman, and despite his incessant swearing which seem s to be involuntary,

Col. Preston is an elegant man.[63] Everything is in the greatest abundance and their happiness seems to be to gratify an enlarged hospitality. Their kindness to Brother William is unbounded, notwithstanding his fretfulness, induced by disease. May God reward them for their kindness.

Saturday, August 1st

Spent the day in the room with my poor brother who is rapidly wasting away. Col. and Mrs. Preston are so devoted to him, as though he were their own son and the entire neighborhood seem deeply interested in him, and vie with each others in efforts to contribute to his comfort.

Tuesday, August 4th

Left Col. Preston's this morning and felt when I told Brother William good-bye that I would never see him in this world again. R.R. fare to Lynchburg $2.70, L. to Petersburg $3.70, Sundries $.25. The Virginia and Tennessee R.R. is a splendid work of art running through a rugged but beautiful country. I reached Lynchburg about 4 o'clock and in half an hour took the South Side Road for Petersburg. Shall have to travel all night to get there.

Thursday, August 6th

R.R. fare to Charlotte $5.00. Peaches $1.00, Eggs .50. Traveled all last night and today until 5 P.M. It was very hot. One of the cars ran off producing quite a stir in the ladies [sic] car where I had my seat, but doing no damage. I met with a terrible misfortune this afternoon—losing my pocketbook containing 6 or 7 hundred dollars—some mine—most the property of others, which of course I feel bound to make good to them. Spent the night at the home of my friend, Capt. E. H. Barnes.[64]

Tuesday, August 18th

Tonight I received a letter from my niece Anne Hart informing me of the death of Brother William. He calmly fell asleep a week ago today expressing his resignation to the will of God. "We are passing away". Of seven children but two remain. God grant that we may be re-united in the better land.

Friday, August 21st

This being National Fast Day, I rode to a Baptist Church a few miles off and attended service. Mr. Fincher, the Pastor, preached a very good sermon on the Text, "Oh Israel thou hast destroyed thyself, but in Me is thy

---

[63] Most likely Col. John Smith Preston (1809–1881), former South Carolina state senator .

[64] Capt. E. H. Barnes, Co. C, 50th North Carolina Infantry.

help." I made some remarks after the sermon. Much feeling in the congregation.

Monday, August 24th

Cousin Susan Little came down this morning bringing all sorts of good things, peaches, apples, figs, grapes, fruit, butter, etc. I packed up my things today preparatory to an early start tomorrow morning. John and Will Tillman and Jack witnessed my signature this morning to my "Last Will and Testament" and I sent it up to Mr. George W. Little to take care of.

Tuesday, August 25th

With a heavy heart I started for Charlotte about sunrise this morning. It is *dreadful* but duty demands the sacrifice and I must try and make it cheerfully. Oh! that this miserable war would end! Had a hot ride of 50 miles and reached Charlotte about sunset. Stopped at the Parsonage with Bro. Simmons.[65] After tea walked out and saw several friends.

Wednesday, August 26th

I spent most of the day in moving about among my old friends and found the time all too short to gratify my desire to see them. Mr. M. L. Minton handed me $700 to reimburse me for what I lost and a *splendid* overcoat. My friends hearing of my misfortune, made the handsome subscription mentioned above. Coffee 22.50, saddle bags 5.00, Pins 1.00, R.R. fare 9.50, Mending Saddle bags .50, postage 1.80, Richmond to pay expense back home 3.00, Peaches .25. Left Charlotte at 6 P.M. and traveled all night.

Friday, August 28th

Reached Petersburg about 3 1/2 A.M. Started at 5 for Richmond but had only gotten a few hundred yards when the train was stopped by order of Gen'l. Lee to take Jenkins's Brigade.[66] Through the kindness of Col. Kilpatrick commanding the train, I was allowed to go in the train to Richmond while the other passengers had to "vacate."[67] I left Frank but he came on in the evening. Reached Richmond about 11 o'clock. Stopped at the Spottswood. Busy all day.

Saturday, August 29th

Left on the Central Road at 6 1/2, reached Orange, C. H. about 3 o'clock. Traveled on an open flat car in company with Capt. Duncan 13th

---

[65] The Rev. Dennis J. Simmons of Charlotte, Methodist pastor from the South Carolina Conference.

[66] Part of Maj. Gen. J. E. B. Stuart's cavalry division.

[67] Colonel F. Whitner Kilpatrick, 1st (Haygood's) South Carolina Regiment.

S.C. Found our camp about 1 mile from the C. H. All well and glad to see me back. Postage stamps $15.00, Hotel Bill $12.00, Fruit .50, R.R. Fare $5.00.

Tuesday, September 1st

This morning I attended Chaplain's Meeting at Orange, C. H. And in the afternoon appeared in review with the Reg't. before Gen'l. A. P. Hill. Rev. Mr. King of the 18th Reg't. preached tonight.

Thursday, September 10th

Rode in company with Mr. Alexander to Montpelier this morning, the mansion and burial place of James Madison, Pres. of U.S. The tomb of granite 20 ft. high has the simple inscription "Madison, Born March 16th, 1751–Died June 28th, 1836." The iron gate at the entrance of the graveyard has the inscription "Madison,1720." The mansion is old-fashioned and massive. Mr. Peoples of the Associate Reform Presbyterian Church preached a fine sermon.[68]

Friday, September 11th

I rode over to the camp of Thomas' Brigade for the purpose of going with Bro. Morris to preach to Davis' Mississippi Brigade, but the service had been called off. I took charge of the wives of Drs. Mayo and Young who rode in an Ambulance and attended the Review of Hill's Corps.[69] The display was very fine, the troops being reviewed by Gen'l. Lee. We got back to camp late and held no service in consequence. I took tea at Mrs. Stephen's.

Sunday, September 13th

I preached this morning from "If any man preach any *other* gospel, etc." For the first time since my connection with the Army I saw Gen'l. Lane at service. At 2 o'clock P.M. Rev. Mr. Peoples preached on the Resurrection of Christ and at night Rev. Mr. Pritchard, a Baptist preached.[70]

Monday, September 14th

Cannonading and musketry in the direction of Rapidan Station distinctly audible. Orders to cook rations and prepare to move. An old

---

[68] The Rev. James Harvey Peoples, born in Mecklenburg County, North Carolina, in 1834, graduated from Erskine College in South Carolina, and preached to Confederate soldiers in camps from North Carolina to Virginia.

[69] Dr. Peter Wesley Young of the 38th North Carolina Regiment, surrendered with his soldiers at Appomattox.

[70] Thomas H. Prichard (1836–1914) Baptist chaplain of Brig. Gen. John B. Gordon's Georgia brigade.

Baptist minister from Newton, N.C. preached this morning. I rode over to town not knowing there would be any service. Bro. Eastman, Chaplain 33rd N.C. of this Brigade preached tonight.[71] Large number of penitent came forward for prayer.

Tuesday, September 15th

Rode over to town for the purpose of attending Chaplain's Meeting but the troops have been moved and there was no meeting. We are all ready to move but have had no orders yet. Being in the left of our line of defense it is probable we will remain where we are. I preached tonight—"How long halt ye between two opinions, etc." Very good meeting.

Wednesday, September 16th

Still quiet. The affair near Rapidan seems about blown over. And I hope we may be able to carry on our meeting without interruption. The old Baptist preacher from Newton, N.C. preached tonight—"Expect ye be converted and become as little children, etc." Very interesting meeting.

Friday, September 18th

Visited two men from the 33rd Regiment who are condemned to be shot for desertion tomorrow morning. They professed to feel prepared for their change. Service tonight. Distribution to them of a number of Gospels, Hymn Books and Tracts.

Saturday, September 19th

Witnessed the execution this morning of the two men from the 33rd Regiment. They met their fate with unflinching fortitude[,] but it was a very revolting sight. They died almost instantly upon discharge of the guns. We had service tonight conducted by Rev. Mr. Pritchard. A very fine sermon—"Grieve not the Spirit, etc."

Monday, September 21st

For the first time in my life I administered the ordinance of Baptism *by immersion* this afternoon in the Rapidan River. On the back of the River I baptized seven (7), then entering the stream I immersed eight (8). On my way back, I stopped at the camp of Thomas' Brigade and baptized one who was too unwell to walk to the River. Among the number baptized were Col. Folsom of the 14th Ga. And Lt. Col. McCullough of the 35th Ga.[72] Brother Eastman preached tonight but I did not get out. By the way, he was a

---

[71] Thomas J. Eatman, Methodist chaplain of the 33rd North Carolina Regiment.

[72] Col. Robert W. Folsom was wounded at the Battle of the Wilderness and died in Richmond 24 May 1864; Lt. Col. William H. McCullohs was medically furloughed out of the service on 28 February 1865.

Methodist until Sunday when he changed his colors and was ordained a Baptist Preacher.

Tuesday, September 22nd

Eight more men from our Brigade sentenced to be shot next Saturday—among them Charles McSwain (Brother of M. A. McSwain of our Corp) and J. M. Luther from my Reg't.[73] Luther's case was referred for final decision to President Davis and I go down with him today bearing a Petition from the officers of the Reg't. for his pardon. Rode to Richmond in company with Brother A. W. Moore of the 14th Ga.[74] and met Washington Stevens of S.C. one of the earliest converts to my ministry. Stopped at the American Hotel. Paper .50—R.R. 4.00.

Wednesday, September 23rd

Laid my petition before the President or rather placed it in the hands of one of his aides. Got a letter of introduction from Dr. Minnegerode, but did not see the President.[75] Met Mr. J. J. Blackwood. Called and saw Luther. Saddle cloth 10.00—Army comb and brush 3.50—Tobacco 7.50—Hotel bill 15.00—Met E. W. Thompson, 43rd N.C.[76]

Thursday, September 24th

Returned to Orange, C. H., in company with Brother Thompson. Found when I reached Orange that the Brigade had moved to the vicinity of Liberty Mills some five or six miles off, and have had a turn with the enemy in my absence. Frank met me at the cars with my horse and I reached Camp by late dinner. R.R. fare 4.00—Paper, etc. .75.

Friday, September 25th

Learned today that Gen'l. Lane was very much outraged at my leaving camp on the *Lt. Col.'s* permit and would prefer charges against me and bring me before the Gen'l. Provost Martial. I have no objection. Our prisoners who were lodged with the Provost Marshal when the Brigade moved, for safe-keeping, were brought down this evening. I called and spent some time

---

[73] Pvt. Charles J. McSwain, Co. K, 28th North Carolina, had served honorably for two years. He was shot near Liberty Mills VA, on 26 September 1863; Pvt. Jesse M. Luther, Co. E, escaped execution but was captured on 28 July 1864, taken to Elmira prison in New York, and exchanged 21 March 1865.

[74] Alexander W. Moore, Methodist chaplain of the 14th Georgia Infantry.

[75] The Rev. Dr. Charles Minnigerode (1814–1894), rector of St. Paul's Episcopal Church in Richmond and President Jefferson Davis's wartime pastor.

[76] Eugene W. Thompson (1833–1877), Methodist chaplain of the 43rd North Carolina Regiment.

with them in prayer and conversation. These are seven of the poor fellows who will die at the stake tomorrow. God have mercy on their souls!

Saturday, September 26th

The condemned men were shot this morning about 11 o'clock. I baptized two of them just before the execution. All professed to have obtained peace with God save one poor fellow who did not seem satisfied with his condition. Their names were Lanier (two brothers), McSwain, Lee, Greer, Collins, and Ford.[77] I don't think I shall ever forget the scene.

Thursday, October 1st

My Reg't. is beyond the Rapidan today on Picket. In company with Dr. Mayo I rode over the River to the station this afternoon to see how they were getting along, and to see some of the fortifications that have been recently erected. It looked so much like rain tonight that we did not sound the trumpet for service, but a number of the men assembled and commenced singing, so I went out and preached.

Wednesday, October 7th

Raining this evening. Orders to Quarter Masters concerning their teams and wagons, and to the doctors, to have their sick all moved to Orange, C. H., in time for tomorrow's train, indicates an early move. The probability is that we will be in a forward movement against the Army of the Potomac about day after tomorrow. We are just getting comfortable here, and I hate terribly to pull up stakes and go out into the weather, but I reckon it is for the best.

Thursday, October 8th

Everything indicates that we will get off tomorrow. Rations for several days have been issued and the men ordered to cook them. Had a visit from Dr. Trescott, 37th N.C.[78] I held service tonight. Eleven joined the church.

Friday, October 9th

Moved at 5 o'clock this morning and marched 8 miles reaching camp about 2 o'clock. We learn this evening that we are to take a different route

---

[77] Pvt. Elkana Lanier, age thirty, Co. C, 18th North Carolina; Pvt. Jacob Lanier, age nineteen, Co. A, 18th North Carolina; Pvt. Robert B. Lee, Co. K, 28th North Carolina; Pvt. James S. Greer, age twenty-eight, Co. B, 37th North Carolina; Pvt. Sam Collins, age twenty-two, Co. D, 37th North Carolina; Pvt. Green W. Ford, age twenty, Co. H, 37th North Carolina.

[78] Dr. George E. Trescott of Charleston SC, surgeon, 37th North Carolina Regiment.

from the balance of the corp, to guard the wagon trains. Our camp tonight is three miles from Madison, C. H. The weather is very cool and frosty.

Saturday, October 10th

Started this morning at 7 o'clock. Passed through Madison, C. H., a small village of diminutive pretension. Saw a Yankee signal flag on the summit of Thoroughfare Mountain. Marched today over a rough road and got into camp late. Got a little wet as we were marching this evening. Passed through a little town called ....lersville.[79] Crossed Roberson River.

Sunday, October 11th

Resumed our march early this morning and prosecuted it over a horribly rough route. We traveled no road, but made way through fields and forest as best we could. Passed over one little river 6 or 8 times, the Hughes River. Camp within a mile or two of the balance of the Corp and went into camp about 5 o'clock.

Monday, October 12th

Learned this morning that the enemy had discovered our movement, evacuated Culpepper and were falling back. We started at 8 o'clock and took another circuitous and dreadfully rough route. Camped near a little place called Amosville.[80] Several of us sent out and got a very nice supper. Got some corn for our horses from a field. Slept without any tent and had a good night's rest.

Tuesday, October 13th

Left camp this morning about 5 o'clock. Marched about 12 miles. Delayed some time in the crossing the Rappahannock River. Went into camp in the vicinity of Warrenton, about 2 o'clock[,] and the men proceeded to the preparation of two days' rations. Gibbon, Mayo and I rode over to town but were turned back by a guard who informed us that a Major Gen'l's pass was necessary to pass the lines. Being very anxious to have a shoe fastened on my horse, Gibbon and I flanked the guard and passed into town. Warrenton, the county site of Farquier is a very pretty place, and thoroughly loyal. Though the enemy has had possession of it a great part of the war, not a single man or woman has ever taken the oath. This whole country is desolated. Not a single panel of fence is left, and very little forest.

Wednesday, October 14th

We were ordered to move at 5 o'clock but did not get off until 8. Cannonading and small arms could be heard very distinctly to the right of

---

[79] Criglersville VA.
[80] Amissville VA.

our column. We marched very rapidly. Passed through a little place called Greenwich where we were greeted with the cheers and "God Speeds" of a number of ladies. Marched 18 miles to Bristow Station, when the head of our column struck the Yankees. Cook's and Kirkland's Brigades of Heth's Division, charged the Yankees who were behind the railroad, and were repulsed. We lost 7 pieces of artillery and about 500 men in killed and wounded. This affair was very badly managed and seems to be but another of the blunders which characterizes the military career of Major Gen'l. Heth.[81] One man from our Reg't. and the only one I believe from our Division was wounded by a round shot.

Thursday, October 15th

Had a very comfortable night's rest until about a half hour before day, when having no tent we were aroused from sleep by the rain. The Yankees left our front during last night. In the engagement of yesterday afternoon, Gen'l. Cook and Kirkland were wounded.[82] Having accomplished the object of the campaign, the main body of the Army received orders to march back—the cavalry pursuing and harassing the retreating army. We marched about sunset and took our course for some five or six miles along the Orange and Alexandria R. Road and went into camp about 11 o'clock—in the rain. I have had nothing to eat since morning—except a few biscuit I put in my pocket.

Friday, October 16th

Started this morning in the rain, without breakfast and marched several miles when we went to work tearing up the Rail Road. It was pouring rain but the men went at it with a will, ripping up the rails, making piles with the ties and firing them. We finished our last section for today a little before sunset and went into camp nearby. The rain poured down and the ground upon which we have to sleep is all afloat with water. The prospect is rather unpromising for much rest tonight.

Saturday, October 17th

Notwithstanding the condition of the ground, we slept soundly last night and did not rise until a late hour this morning. Moved out about 9

---

[81] Maj. Gen. Henry Heth (1825–1899), West Point class of 1847, division commander at Gettysburg, surrendered at Appomattox.

[82] Brig. Gen. John R. Cook (1833–1891), Harvard graduate, former colonel of the 27th North Carolina Regiment ; Brig. Gen. William W. Kirkland (1833–1915), West Point class of 1852, former colonel of the 21st North Carolina Regiment.

o'clock and resumed operations upon the Rail Road. By 3 o'clock P.M. the Road was destroyed to Rappahannock Bridge. We went into camp.

Sunday, October 18th

Ordered to prepare to cross the River about 6 o'clock this morning, and stood ready for some time. Pontooniers laying a bridge across the River. Have waited all day, ready to move at any moment, and in consequence of the state of things have been unable to preach as I would have liked to have done. Started to move about 7 P.M. when intelligence reached us that the bridge had broken in and that 5 men and two teams were drowned. Men ordered to go to bed and rest until morning.

Monday, October 19th

Roused this morning before day by the pelting in my face of heavy rain. It rained and hailed furiously for several hours. In the midst of the storm we commenced to march. Several ditches between our camp and the Bridge were filled by the rain waist deep in water, and though very cold had to be waded by the men. I crossed the bridge ahead of the troops, and catching up with the wagon train, partook of an elegant breakfast with Maj. Thompson, Brigade Quartermaster. I was soaked to the skin but the good breakfast made me comfortable. The troops came on after awhile, and I joined them. We are camped now in a very pretty piece of woods[,] and it is probable that we will remain here for several days, as the whole Army is encamped in this vicinity. We are about 1 1/2 miles from Brandy Station on County farm.

Thursday, October 22nd

Still quiet. Men very much crowded. A change of camp eminently desirable. I conducted service again tonight. Air very cold. Made the service short.

Friday, October 23rd

Nothing of interest today. I commenced to read "My Novel" by Bulver. A book that was recommended to me by Dr. Whiteford Smith [*sic*], when I was stationed in Greenville, S.C. several years ago.[83] Raining this evening and very unpleasant. Unable to have any service in consequence of the weather.

Sunday, October 25th

Morning clear, beautiful, but very cold. We changed camp today, moving about 1 1/2 miles and securing a vastly preferable place. Prevented

---

[83] The Rev. Whitefoord Smith, D. D. (1812–1893), Methodist professor at Wofford College, South Carolina.

by our move from holding service until late in the afternoon. The weather was very cold and the attendance small.

Tuesday, October 27th

Had a first rate chimney built and now everything promises comfort if we stay where we are. The men are working with a will at their "winter quarters", and while huts and chimneys are rapidly going up, the frost is as rapidly disappearing. Service again this evening.

Wednesday, November 4th

Called to see two men of the 18th Reg't. who are condemned to be shot tomorrow, and were just brought to camp today. They are both members of the Lutheran Church and profess to feel prepared for death. They desire the Sacrament of the Lord's Supper and I rode through the neighborhood trying to get wine, but have failed so far.

Thursday, November 5th

Succeeded this morning in getting some wine from my friend, Capt. Oates. In company with Rev. A. W. Morris, administered the Sacrament to the two convicts. Held service with them, and then walked with them to the place of execution. At the stake I read the burial service, Bro. Morris prayed, they were tied to the stakes, the word was given, and one of them was killed, but the other had to be shot a second time. A most revolting spectacle. Their names were Hook and Sigman from Co. A. 18th N.C. Reg't.[84] I witnessed in the latter part of the day, a grand review of the Calvary of the Army by Gen'l. Lee. It was certainly the grandest show in the way of a military display I have ever witnessed. I held service upon my return to camp in the afternoon.

Saturday, November 7th

Heavy cannonading audible this afternoon, and the indications all point to an early move. Should we remain where we are, Mr. Johnson is to preach for my Reg't.[85] Called on Gen'l Lane.

Sunday, November 8th

Received orders about 11 o'clock last night to cook one day's rations and be prepared to move as soon as they were done. Left camp a little before day this morning and marched some six miles when we overtook the balance of the Division and went into line of battle. In the course of two or three hours, our Brigade was ordered about one mile to the left to repel cavalry.

[84] Pvt. John Shook and Pvt. M. D. Sigman, both of Catawba County, North Carolina, executed on 5 November 1863.

[85] B. J. Johnson, chaplain of the 8th Alabama Regiment.

Heavy skirmishing when we charged and drove the Yankees back. Our loss was two (2) killed and about twelve (12) wounded. I got into a shower of minnie balls, but escaped without injury. Our hospital was established at Culpepper, C. H. about 3 1/2 miles from the Battlefield. The weather is extremely cold, and the house we have is a judicious selection for a hospital if we should have many wounded.

Monday, November 9th

Drew in our skirmishers after dark last night and commenced falling back. Marched the whole night, dark and bitter cold as it was until 5 o'clock this morning, rested one hour and resumed the march which was kept up until about 1 o'clock today when we entered our old camp near Liberty Mills. Last night was almost as disagreeable and comfortless as the night we left Gettysburg and the night we crossed the Potomac. The fences for miles along the line of march were all ablaze and such straggling I have never witnessed. Thousands were gathered around the fires. If the Yankee Cavalry followed us closely, they would have captured many of them. It has been snowing today. Very cold as it is, the men had to wade the Rapidan River. I brought a number over behind me on my horse.

Tuesday, November 10th

Busy today fixing up our old quarters and preparing to be comfortable. Someone has pushed off most of the tops of our chimneys but we can soon replace them.

Wednesday, November 11th

Still quiet. Men busy fixing up winter quarters. Weather so cold have not attempted to have service yet. Had a call today from Rev. Mr. Patterson, Baptist Preacher from Orange. Called to see condemned men in 37th Regiment.

Thursday, November 12th

Visited convict. Lent my horse to Miss Luther who goes to Gen'l. Lee to intercede for her brother who is under sentence of death, the same man for whom I took a petition to the President. Mr. Patterson preached for me tonight: "As Moses lifted up the serpent, etc."

Friday, November 13th

Received orders this morning to cook two days' rations and be ready to move at any moment, but the day has passed off, and no further orders have been received. I handed in an application for "leave" yesterday afternoon but withdrew it this morning in consequence of the order. I held service tonight, and a fine congregation and a good deal of feeling.

Saturday, November 14th

Attended the execution of Private James Holman, Co. F. 37th Reg't., Wilkes Co.[,] shot for desertion and misbehavior in the presence of the enemy.[86] Poor fellow; his nerves were terribly unstrung, and I fear he was not prepared for his change. Just before the guard was ready, he asked that I should request them not to shoot him in the face. His wish was respected and he died from the first volley, pierced with three balls in the heart and one in the thigh. Rode with Dr. Mayo to the Picket line where our Reg't. is on post. Got wet.

Thursday, November 26th

Weather cold, clear and frosty. Nothing of special interest this morning. Bad news from Bragg this afternoon.[87] Mr. Davis will doubtless have to give up his favorite General—his defeat, supplementing the popular clamor will be too much for even Mr. Davis' tenacity of purpose and poor Bragg will have to go by the Board. Meade is said to be moving. Hard bread was issued this afternoon and orders to be ready to move at any moment.

Friday, November 27th

Received orders last night about 11 1/2 o'clock and marched out of our comfortable quarters at 2 1/2 A.M. The morning was bitterly cold, the breath congealing upon my whiskers as I breathed, and yet many of the men were trudging along ragged, blanketless and barefooted. The scenes of suffering at Valley Forge in the old Revolution which are so historically famous, are surpassed in the present war. We made a long march, some twenty-two or three miles and went immediately into line of battle. The enemy it is said has crossed into heave force at Germana Ford and are between our forces and their old formidable works at Chancellorsville which is about 5 or 6 miles distant. We are camped tonight in an abominable place—an old field pine thicket with nothing for fuel but green pines and some old dry boughs.

Saturday, November 28th

Slept gloriously last night. Roused about 3 o'clock this morning by orders to move back two or three miles to a little village called Vidurville and establish a hospital. Our lines are now formed about 2 miles in front of the hospital and our troops are entrenching themselves thoroughly. No

---

[86] Pvt. James Holman, Co. F, 37th North Carolina Regiment. Holman, a farmer from Wilkes County, North Carolina, had served honorably for almost two years.

[87] Gen. Braxton Bragg's Army of Tennessee had been driven from Missionary Ridge in Tennessee. Thursday, 26 November 1863, was the first national Thanksgiving Day proclaimed by President Lincoln.

firing on our front today. Some on the left of our lines. It poured down rain all the morning.

Sunday, November 29th

Wind very high and terribly cold. The enemy is on our front and entrenching. I rode down to the lines this morning, but just as I got to the—,[88] the skirmishers became heavily engaged and the cannoneers took their position at their guns, so I rode back. The troops suffer in the ditches with the intense cold. If the enemy will only attack us where we are, they will be most awfully cut to pieces.

Monday, November 30th

Weather still desperately cold. The enemy feels our lines occasionally but hesitates to make an attack. I rode down to the lines, and could see the Yankee's line of battery and artillery very distinctly. Our skirmishers were hotly engaged for awhile [sic] and killed six or eight Yankees, whose new blankets and clothes they furnished themselves with. We have one (1) man from Co. A. wounded.

Tuesday, December 1st

Another quiet day. One or two guns from our extreme left were heard today, but no firing of any consequence. Our position is a very strong one and Meade seems to be very loath to attack it. We have bad news still from the West.

Wednesday, December 2nd

Found out this morning that the enemy had disappeared from our front during the night. We are ordered this morning to follow the Brigade "down the plank road". Pursued the enemy for several miles, but when the head of our column reached the River, the enemy had crossed. We returned to the vicinity of the Hospital...I saw an old schoolmate and friend today. Bill Timmerman of Darlington, S.C.

Thursday, December 3rd

Started before daylight this morning and marched hard making the distance of 22 miles by 3 o'clock when we marched into our old camp at Liberty Mills. This is the second campaign we have made, returning to this same camp. I hope now we will remain here during the balance of the winter.

Friday, December 4th, 1863

---

[88] Illegible, presumably to the rear of the lines since the artillery would be there.

Spent the time quietly in camp, fixing up and trying to make ourselves comfortable. We are on rations of crackers which makes the living pretty hard. Held service tonight, preaching a short sermon from the text, "Bow and pray unto the Lord your God."

Monday, December 7th

In company with Dr. Prescott I rode over this morning to the camp of McGowan's Brigade. Made inquiry of Capt. Kelly concerning Eddy Darby's body, who was killed at Manassas No. 2. Dined with Capt. Duncan, Lieuts, Carlisle, Petty and Douglas.[89] Held service tonight and had quite a pleasant meeting.

Monday, December 28th

Rose at 2 o'clock this morning and left at 4. Poured down rain. Broke carriage tongue near Monroe, borrowed another from J. C. McLaughlin [sic], roads very muddy.[90] Reached Charlotte between sunset and dark. Stopped with my friend, M. L. Minton, Esqr.

Wednesday, December 30th

Travelled all night and reached Raleigh this morning about 10 1/2 o'clock. Started in 15 minutes for Weldon, which point I reached at 6 P.M. and am now waiting for the Petersburg train which leaves at 9 o'clock.

Thursday, December 31st

Reached Petersburg this morning at 3 o'clock. Richmond at 7. Poured down rain all day. Saw Messrs. Davis and Ashe—the former C.S. Senator, the latter Representative from N.C.[91] Met quite a number of officers from my Brigade on their way home on furlough. Am stopping at the Spottswood Hotel.

Friday, January 1st, 1864

Bill at Spottswood $19.00! Left at 6 1/2 o'clock. Pleasant this morning but turned desperately cold before mid-day. Reached G. at 1 o'clock.[92] Found Frank there with my horse and Capt. Parker with a wagon. Had a fearfully cold ride 6 miles to camp.

Saturday, January 2nd

---

[89] All from Co. C, 13th South Carolina Infantry.

[90] J. C. McLauchlin, Co. K, 26th North Carolina Infantry.

[91] George Davis (1820–1896), Confederate senator and attorney general; Thomas Samuel Ashe (1812–1887), later associate justice of the Supreme Court of North Carolina.

[92] Presumably Guiney Station.

Reg't. out picketing and building and corduroy road. Cooked my turkey and had several of my friends to dine with me. Otherwise, the day passed without incident. Reg't. returned to camp this evening.

Tuesday, January 5th

Attended a Military Board near Gen'l. Power's. Hd. Qts. to testify as to Col. Lane's competence for a Post position commensurate with his military rank. Called on Dr. and Mrs. John F. Miller who occupy a room in the house where the Court met. In company with Dr. Gibbon, rode a mile or two farther and called on Mrs. Scales. Weather mild and pleasant.

Wednesday, January 6th

Several men very sick with pneumonia. One of them, Mr. Holyfield, an old citizen from North Carolina who came over to visit two sons, and taking pneumonia, will doubtless die before morning.[93] No service tonight in consequence of the severity of the weather.

Thursday, January 7th, 1864.

I took a dreadfully cold ride today, visiting the Hd. Qts. of all the Generals in our "regular channel" to get their approval of a furlough for Sgt. Holyfield to take the body of his father home.[94] The old gentlemen died last night, a very melancholy case. He told me he was totally *unprepared* for death. My trip today was one of considerable suffering from cold—otherwise pleasant enough, as the officers were very respectful and granted my request without hesitation.

Wednesday, January 13th, 1864

Today I attain my 30th year. I feel deeply grateful to God for sparing my life worthless as it has been, so long, and I humbly pray that the year upon which I enter today many be signalized by greater usefulness and zeal, and more rapid growth in grace than any previous year of my life.

Friday, January 29th

Rec'd. orders today to keep three days' rations on hand, one day's rations cooked, and be ready to march at any moment. Rev. Mr. Ross of the Associate-Reformed Presbyterian Church preached a fine sermon for me this afternoon.[95] No services tonight—men busy cooking.

---

[93] Four members of the Holyfield family of Surry County served in A Co., 28th North Carolina.

[94] 1st Sergeant Watson B. Holyfield, twice wounded in 1864 and retired from service 22 February 1865.

[95] The Rev. Robert A. Ross, D. D. (1817–1903), from York County, South Carolina.

Saturday, January 30th

No news yet. Some Yankee cavalry stirring across the River. Weather threatening. Held service tonight. Rained before we got through.

Sunday, January 31st

Cloudy and threatening rain, but I preached nevertheless to a tolerable congregation from Hebrews 4th Ch., 1st Verse. Had great liberty in preaching. Half of the Reg't. on Picket. Cavalry advancing on the other side of the River. Balance of our Reg't. and half of the 63rd ordered out. The rest of the Brigade ordered to be ready to go immediately to their support should firing be heard.

Monday, February 1st, 1864

Reg't. returned from Picket this morning. Enemy gone back over the Robison and all quiet again.[96] No service tonight in consequence or rain.

Thursday, February 4th

The 28th Regiment re-enlisted today for the war. The vote was put and nine-tenths stood firmly by their colors while one tenth who were unwilling to re-enlist marched forward and dressed on some guides who had been thrown out for the purpose.[97] Service tonight more than usually animated.

Saturday, February 6th

Quite an excitement in consequence of the re-appearance and threatened advanced of the enemy. Half of our Reg't. on Picket, the balance together with 33rd ordered to their support. Had a very pleasant visit today from Rev. B. F. Lacy who dined with me.[98]

Sunday, February 7th

No service today. Our Brigade all on the line awaiting an attack from the enemy. Heavy cannonading and musketry at Barnettsford 3 miles below us. J. E. B. Stuart took command of our Brigade and marched several miles to get in rear of the Yanks but they go away before he could make the trip.

Tuesday, February 9th

Attended Chaplains' Meeting in Presbyterian Church at Orange, C. H. Shook hands and conversed with *Gen'l. R. E. Lee* who was present at our

---

[96] The Rapidan, not Robison, River.

[97] "Dress on" means to line up on soldiers (guides) who run ahead and establish the right flank of a line. Then the command to get everyone in a straight line is "Dress right, dress!"

[98] Rev. Dr. B. Tucker Lacy, 2nd Corps, Army of Northern Virginia, and Stonewall Jackson's personal chaplain before the general's death in May 1862.

meeting. Returned to camp. Mr. Abill preached at night, congregation quite small. Weather very cold.

Friday, February 12th

Rode over to 7th and 18th Regiments to notify several gentlemen of result of application to Grand Lodge of Virginia for dispensation for military lodge in the Brigade. Held service tonight, good congregation.

Thursday, February 18th

Walked out a half mile to Mr. Ammon's pond and saw some very handsome skating.

Friday, February 19th

Rode out to the Pond and witnesses the performance of the skaters—a large number of men and some ladies present. Weather moderating a little.

Saturday, February 20th

Quite a pretty day, large skating party on the Rapidan today but I did not go out. Went down to the 33rd Reg't. and heard Bro. Eastman preached from the text, "What do ye more than others."

Monday, February 29th

Rode over with Power to call on Gen'l. McGowan and as far as Orange, C. H. Orders to march by daylight in the morning.[99]

Tuesday, March 1st

Marched all day in the rain, freezing to the trees as it fell. A most horrible day on men and horses. Advanced to within two (2) miles of Madison, C. H. where the enemy is said to be in strong force. Halted for an hour, about faced, marched a mile and have gone into camp. It is now snowing and the prospect for the night is most unpromising.

Wednesday, March 2nd

Tried to sleep in the Medical Wagon with Dr. Prescott, Brigade Surgeon, but it was dreadfully cold, and I passed a horrible night.[100] Snowed and sleeted most of the night. Clear this morning and very cold. Marched back to camp, the enemy having retired from Madison during the night.

Friday, March 18th

---

[99] Chaplain William C. Power, 14th North Carolina Infantry; Brig. Gen. Samuel McGowan (1819–1897), commanding Gregg's South Carolina brigade.

[100] Dr. George E. Trescott of Charleston, surgeon for the 37th North Carolina Infantry.

Called to see Private Murphy of the 7th Regiment who was shot at 11 o'clock this morning for desertion.[101] Rode to Major Field's Qts. and funded $2200. for men in my Regiment. Dined at Dr. Taliaferro's in Orange, C. H. Very pleasant family, into which Johnny Boatright married. Returning to camp in the afternoon. Very windy and unpleasant.

Tuesday, March 22nd

Attended Chaplain's Meeting. Heard a delightful sermon from J. C. Granberry [sic]—"Let patience have her perfect work, etc."[102] Gen'l. Lee and J. E. B. Stuart both present. Rode home in a very heavy snow which still continues at 11 o'clock P.M.

Saturday, March 26th

Nothing worthy of note has transpired today. Governor Vance spoke today in Faniel's Brigade; will address us some time next week.[103]

Monday, March 28th

This morning I sent up an application which I received last night from Surgeon in charge Gen'l. Hospital, Charlotte, N.C., for my transfer to that post. It was approved by the Regimental and Brigade commanders.[104]

Thursday, March 31st

I rode over to Scales' Brigade today and heard a very fine speech from Governor Vance of N.C.[105] He speaks for us on tomorrow.

Friday, April 1st

A tremendous number of people, soldiers, citizens, ladies and gentlemen assembled today to hear the Governor. Before the hour for speaking arrived it commenced to rain, and he being very hoarse anyhow sent word that he would have to postpone. The men cried "April Fool" and dispersed. Rained all day.

Saturday, April 2nd

---

[101] Pvt. George W. Murphy of Alexander County, North Carolina, assigned to Co. K, 7th North Carolina Infantry.

[102] John C. Granbery (1829–1907), chaplain of the 11th Virginia Infantry, missionary to the Army of Northern Virginia after he was wounded, later professor at Vanderbilt University and a Methodist bishop.

[103] North Carolina Governor Zebulon B. Vance (1830–1894), colonel of the 26th North Carolina Infantry in 1862, elected governor on 8 September 1862, served as a US senator from 1879–1894.

[104] Dr. Lewis Mayo, surgeon of the 28th North Carolina Infantry transferred to the same hospital in January 1865.

[105] Brigade of Brig. Gen. Alfred M. Scales (1827–1892), governor of North Carolina from 1884–1888.

Poured down rain all the morning. Cleared only partially about 1 o'clock and the Governor addressed the Brigade. A taking speech, but not near so good as his effort at Scales.' The wind was high and the ground very wet so that all the circumstances were unfavorable.

Tuesday, April 5th

Sleeted all night, and with occasional changes to rain, all day today. Military operations will certainly be blocked for some time to come. No prospect tonight of a cessation of the storm which has continued so long.

Wednesday, April 6th

Had a visit today from A. D. Betts, Chaplain 30th N.C. Reg't. and C. W. Westbrook, N.C. Conf. Missionary to this Brigade.[106] I am afraid the latter will have a hard time as he can't buy rations and nobody is allowed to draw more than one ration which is scarcely enough for one man. This afternoon I rode over to McGowan's Brigade to see Dr. Hart of the 14th S.C. Regiment about re-considering Lt. Lowe's rejected application for Relief from field service.[107] Very pleasant and kind, but no chance for re-consideration. Weather quite pretty today.

Thursday, April 7th

Bro. Power of the 14th N.C. Reg't. came to see me and spent a little while this morning. I am very busy in the preparations of a sermon for tomorrow which is set apart by Congress and the President as a day of "Fasting, Humiliation and Prayer."

Friday, April 8th

Sky cloudless and the air still and balmy. I had a tremendous congregation and preached with unusual freedom for an hour in the morning from 2nd Chronicles 15th Chapter, 2nd Verse. In the afternoon we assembled again and I delivered a lecture on "Our relation as individuals to the moral character of the nation." The day has been, so far as I could see, very strictly observed, and I sincerely trust God will be propitiated and will manifest His favor toward us in the coming campaign. Chancellorsville followed the First day of last spring, may a greater victory succeed this.

Sunday, April 10th

I received orders this morning from the Secretary of War, relieving me from duty with the 28th Reg't. and to report to the Commandant of the Post at Charlotte, N.C. for assignment. Preached my last sermon to the

---

[106] Missionaries were not in the army, so they had to depend on their own resources for subsistence.

[107] Dr. Louis V. Huot, surgeon of the 14th South Carolina Infantry.

Reg't. in the morning from Eccl. 8th Ch., 11th Verse. Rained hard this afternoon.

Tuesday, April 12th

Very busy getting things ready to leave. Rode at the invitation of my friends, Drs. Mayo, Trescott and Graham to Mr. Kite's at Liberty Mills and had supper.[108]

Wednesday, April 13th

Bade my friends Good-Bye and rode in John Brinkley's wagon to G. Took the train for Richmond having in charge Mrs. Dr. Gaston. Reached Richmond in good time, Delivered Mrs. G. over to her brother, Lt. Terrence, and stopped at S.C. Soldiers' Home. A very nice place.

Thursday, April 14th

Applied and received a leave of absence for 30 days from the Secretary of War. Could not draw any pay, and sold a $7.50 note for par in new issue. Called at N.C. Soldiers' Home and saw Dr. John Bennett. In the afternoon took a long walk around the city with Capt. Nicholson and Lt. Oates.[109] Met a good many old acquaintances from South Carolina at the "Home". Board at the hotels in Richmond is $40 per day!! At the Home $12 per day. When I called for my bill tonight, was told that they made no charge for Chaplains.

Friday, April 15th

Left Richmond at 5:45. Arrived at Petersburg in time. Left P. and at the rate of 10 miles per hour reached Weldon about 5 P.M. Met Col. Barry 18th N.C. Reg't.[110]

Saturday, April 16th

Traveled all night and reached Raleigh about 4 A.M. in the morning. Got a good seat in the Ladies' Car and after very slow, tedious traveling reached Charlotte tonight about 9 o'clock. Had a very interesting traveling companion in the person of Capt. Cunningham an Adjt. Gen'l. to one of Gen'l. Morgan's Brigades.[111] Mr. Minton and John Springs met me at the depot.

Monday, May 17th

---

[108] Drs. Louis Mayo of the 28th North Carolina; George Trescott and Daniel M. Graham of the 37th North Carolina.

[109] Captain Edward A. T. Nicholson, adj., and Lt. Robert Oates, qm., 37th North Carolina Infantry.

[110] Colonel John Decatur Barry, commanding the 18th North Carolina Infantry.

[111] Brig. Gen. John Hunt Morgan, commanding the Department of Southwestern Virginia in the spring of 1864.

Reported for duty this morning as Chaplain of the Hospital, Charlotte, N.C.

Chaplain Kennedy remained in Charlotte until the end of the war and was in that city for the 80th Session of the South Carolina Methodist Conference, which opened 1 November 1865. Bishop George F. Pierce appointed him to be the Presiding Elder of the Wadesboro District. He subsequently served as Secretary to the South Carolina Conference and as Editor of the Southern Christian Advocate *from 1872 through 1878. He was a delegate to three General Conferences of the Methodist Episcopal Church, South, in 1870, 1874, and 1878. When he died on 5 February 1880, his body was interred at Macon, Georgia, where he had resided while the* Advocate *was published in that city.*

Field Hospital at Chancellorsville

Chaplain James B. Sheeran
14th Louisiana Infantry Regiment,
Army of Northern Virginia

Father James B. Sheeran was born in County Longford, Ireland, in 1819. At the age of twelve he emigrated to Canada, then to New York City, McConnellsville, Pennsylvania, and Monroe, Michigan. At Monroe he taught in a boys' school operated by the Redemptorist Fathers. In 1849 his wife died, so he devoted himself completely to his teaching. In 1855 he joined the Redemptorist Congregation, and after three years was ordained a priest in the Roman Catholic order. In 1861 he was stationed at the Redemptorist Church in New Orleans. When his Father Provincial asked for volunteers to act as chaplains for the Confederate Army, he leaped at the opportunity. On 2 September 1861, he was assigned to the Army of Northern Virginia. The following brief account of his ministry to Union prisoners after the battle of Chancellorsville in May of 1863 is taken from his journal.

May 4—Across the road from our hospital was one full of Yankees. As usual having attended to the wants of our own men I visited the wounded of the enemy and offered my services. I found a good number of Catholics, some of whom were severely wounded. Having administered the sacraments to some[,] I enquired if they had no surgeon of their own or any person to dress their wounds. They told me that they had several surgeons over there (pointing to an adjacent building), but they had paid no attention to them, did not even come to see them. I repaired to the house, enquired for the surgeons, told them of the painful condition of the wounded and requested them as a matter of humanity not to neglect them so, adding that we had now as much as we could do with our own wounded. They told me that they had no bandages to dress the wounds, no instruments to operate with, and that they were fatigued from the labors of the night. I remarked it would be some consolation to their wounded, if they would but visit them and wash the wounds of those who were bathed in their own blood. I next went to their men paroled to attend the wounded, asked why they did not wait on their companions, many of whom were suffering for a drink of water. They told me that they had no one to direct them, that their surgeons seemed to take no interest in the men.

I became somewhat indignant to hear the excuses of these worthless nurses, and putting on an air of authority ordered them to go to the rifle pits filled with the dead bodies of their companions and they would find hundreds of knapsacks filled with shirts, handkerchiefs and other articles that would make excellent bandages. They obeyed my orders with the utmost alacrity and soon returned with their arms full of excellent bandage material, and bringing them to me asked: "Now, sir, what shall we do with them?" "Go and tell your surgeons that you have bandages enough now." Off they went to the surgeons and I to our hospital. In about two hours I returned and was pleased to find the surgeons and nurses all at work attending to their wounded.

May 6—I have passed over many a battlefield but this perhaps was the most revolting scene I had ever witnessed. Our line of battle extended over some eight miles and for that distance you see the dead bodies of the enemy lying in every direction, some with their heads shot off, some with their brains oozing out, some pierced through the head with musket balls, some with their noses shot away, some with their mouths smashed, some wounded in the neck, some with broken arms or legs, some shot through the breast and some cut in two with shells. But what was most shocking of all: the underbrush on one part of the battlefield took fire and for nearly half a mile burned the dead bodies and many of the wounded to a crisp.

After the war, Father Sheeran became a pastor in Morristown, New Jersey. The two-volume journal of his experiences in the Army of Northern Virginia, and the support he received from General Robert E. Lee for his ministry, remained unpublished during his lifetime. He died of a stroke on 3 April 1881.[1]

---

[1] Joseph T. Durkin, S. J., ed., *Confederate Chaplain: A War Journal of Rev. James B. Sheeran, c.ss.r. 14th Louisiana, CSA* (Milwaukee: The Bruce Publishing Co., 1960).

Spotsylvania, 1864

Chaplain Charles J. Oliver,
Cabell's Artillery Battalion, Army of Northern Virginia

The Reverend Charles James Oliver was born 16 May 1831 in Warwick, England. He emigrated with his parents to Brooklyn, New York, and at age nine, to Athens, Georgia. Shortly before the war he became a local Methodist preacher, pursuing studies for ordination in the Methodist Episcopal Church, South. On 6 August 1862 he enlisted in Athens as a private in the Troup Artillery, Cobb's Georgia Legion. Subsequently the Troup Artillery was transferred to become one of four artillery companies in Colonel Henry C. Cabell's artillery battalion, Army of Northern Virginia. Oliver served as an artillery crew member in numerous battles including Antietam, Fredericksburg, Chancellorsville, and Gettysburg where he was slightly wounded. During the battles around Spotsylvania Court House in Virginia, he was assigned ambulance duty and worked with the surgeons to care for the wounded and bury the dead.

On 25 March 1864 while in camp at Raccoon Ford near Chancellorsville, Oliver applied for a commission as chaplain of Cabell's artillery battalion with a letter of endorsement from 1st Lieutenant Columbus W. Motes, also of the Troup Artillery. His first request was denied because there was no position for a chaplain in the artillery unit, but with the backing of Brigadier General William N. Pendleton, an Episcopal minister and Lee's nominal chief of artillery, Oliver was appointed chaplain of Cabell's artillery battalion on 12 September 1864. Oliver served as a chaplain with his unit until December 1864, when he received a furlough to return home to Athens. His wartime journal ceases in Athens on 13 December 1864. The following selection highlights his service at Spotsylvania and at Richmond, Virginia, as a chaplain in 1864.[1]

Property of Charles J. Oliver[2]

---

[1] Charles J. Oliver, journal, microfilm, mss #444, Special Collections department, Robert W. Woodruff Library, Emory University, Atlanta GA. Included in the journal are some of Oliver's pencil sketches of camp life in the Confederate Army. Chaplain Oliver's original spelling and punctuation have been preserved except in cases that might be confusing. Editorial insertions are in brackets.

[2] Pvt. Charles J. Oliver was thirty-three years old in May 1864.

Which, should I ever lose it, the finder will please return to The Troup Artillery, formerly of Cobb's Georgia Legion or convey to C. S. Oliver,[3] Athens, GA

New Hope Church May 6th 1864

We got under weigh This morning before daylight[.][4] Heavy firing began on our left very early[.] We supposed that we were going to the right coming into the Catherfield Road [, but] we turned to the left our men were driving the enemy before them—There was nothing for us to do. we were ordered to this place don't know why[.] Have been assisting to take of[f] the arm of J. F. Agner Co. B 46 N. C. T.[5] Gen Longstreet is reported mortally wounded.[6]

[May] 7th[.] About noon—half a mile from camp—The weather is sultry[;] cannonading has began again pretty heavily in front—The artillery has ceased[,] but I can hear the musketry like the hum of a distant city or the sound of a gentle waterfall. It has [been] a lazy, luxurious day[.] We had a large p.m. conducted by Let. Callaway[.][7]

---

[3] Charles Samuel Oliver (1805–1871), his father, a painter and member of the Masonic Order in Athens.

[4] Oliver's unit, Cabell's artillery battalion, Longstreet's corps, Army of Northern Virginia, was at New Hope Church on the Orange Plank Road southwest of Chancellorsville VA. The battalion was composed of four artillery companies: the Troup Artillery from Athens, the Pulasaki (Fraser's) Artillery from Savannah, the First Richmond Howitzers from North Carolina, and Manly's artillery from North Carolina.

[5] The 46th North Carolina was in Hill's Third Corps. As a member of the medical and ambulance team, Oliver was assisting with the amputation.

[6] Lt. Gen. James Longstreet (1821–1904) was accidentally wounded by his own soldiers on 6 May and remained on medical furlough for five months. He survived the war and eventually moved to Gainesville, Georgia. When he died in 1904, he was buried in the Gainesville cemetery.

[7] In Oliver's journal the abbreviation p.m. stands for prayer meeting; 1st Lt. Morgan Callaway had served as acting chaplain while assigned to the 11th Georgia Battalion, Sumter Artillery, before being detailed to the Pulaski Artillery. Callaway became a Methodist minister after the war and was ordained by Bishop George F. Pierce at Macon GA on 15 November 1865, in a group of new deacons that also included Charles J. Oliver. Dr. Morgan Callaway became the vice president of Emory College at Oxford GA, and served there with President Atticus Haygood in 1880.

Sun [May] 8th[.] Rose early, had a hot march down the Catharpin road.[8] The short range guns went into position some where on the right (on the Block road) near Spotsylvania C. H. Here I assumed control of the ambulance corps—The fight did not last more than 20 minutes but it was pretty sharp[.] Two of our men were shot down[:] J. H. Belcher, Thigh broken (doing well)[9] J. W. Ledbetter shot through the lungs.[10] The Howitzers lost one man shot in the thigh.[11]

From this position we mooved To another on the right which proved To be a foolish one. When we discovered that[,] we took hasty leave[,] selected another position & fortified[.] Many of the boys worked all night.[12]

M[ay]. 9th[.] I enjoyed a good nights rest[.] This morning we completed our breastworks including one for the Am[bulance] Corps. This being done we mooved away[.] I am ordered by the Adjutant to take charge of the ambulances.[13] We are waiting for the fray. Mooved late in The evening To a new position, a more accessible—looking one than some I have seen. Our skirmishers were driven in & The minnies[14] came pretty thick, by one of them Let Murray lost his toe[15]—Threw up breastworks at night.

[May] 10th[.] Slept well & late on the litter—We are having a pretty lively time of it now—I must go up & see Let Motes[16]—I may not live to finish this—

1 P.M. Well the fight (that is our fight) is over[.] Twas an awful one but I felt so happy for I thought God would hear my prayers[,] but it did not

---

[8] Catharpin Road intersected Brock Road north of Spotsylvania Court House.

[9] Pvt. John H. Belcher, Troup Artillery.

[10] Pvt. James W. Ledbetter, enlisted at Athens GA.

[11] The First Richmond (VA) Howitzers, Cabell's artillery battalion.

[12] Maj. Gen. Richard H. Anderson, commanding Longstreet's corps, moved his troops southeast to defend Spotsylvania Court House.

[13] 1st Lt. John O. Waddell enlisted in Athens GA on 24 April 1861. He was appointed adj. on 26 June 1863. He was wounded and captured on 14 September 1862, and paroled at Fortress Monroe VA, by Maj. Gen. John A. Dix on 11 October 1862.

[14] Minnie balls, i.e., .58 caliber rifled bullets.

[15] 1st Lt. Thomas A. Murray, Troup Artillery. Oliver sometimes abbreviated lieutenant as "Let."

[16] 1st Lt. Columbus W. Motes from Athens GA.

please Him to answer my petitions to their fullest extent for I am sitting now by poor Ab. Lee, watching him draw his struggling breath[.] I saw him hit & heard the fatal thing—poor fellow!—he is dead.[17]

Heavy firing on the right[;] at one point as many as 17 charges was made so they say[.] certainly the Yankees are very pertinacious.

[May] 11th[.] I can't read knowing that the enemy are advancing & a fearful battle must begin in a few minutes, but perhaps I can write the events of yesterday.

Another charge was made about 2 P.M. I left the grave, lay down in a little gully & watched with great interest[.][18] The shells passing over my head[,] my pleasant cogitations were suddenly interrupted by the appearance of Dr. Carter in the scene bringing down Egglestone of the Howitzers with a broken arm[.][19] We made a bungling job of bandaging his arm but the H. [Howitzers'] Litter Corps were in a great hurry to be off & off they went—he lost a good deal of blood & There was some confusion about the ambulances. E. Porter was brought down, dec'ed, Just as I started to go, back of his head knocked off by a piece of shell.

I had returned & was in the (now) somber grave when the minnies began to fly again. Thus I went to the hospital & This was a battle indeed = [*sic*]

The Yankees[,] excited with ardent spirits & probably The promise of a bonus made a desperate charge on Gregg & Anderson[.][20] They ran over the 1st Texas in an angle of the works when the 9th Ga colly[21] opened a cross fire on them killing 9 wounding 2 in the trenches. This was[,] while it lasted[,] such a battle as you read of in the story books. Stiles and I ran up there directly after the *repulse we uttered a brief prayer over* one poor fellow at his earnest request & Then ran back. The only effect produced upon my nerves by the excitement of the day was a desire for quiet at my *fire* & *I had* it.

---

[17] Pvt. Absalom E. Lee of Watkinsville GA, killed in action 10 May 1864.

[18] Oliver dug a trench grave in which he and others slept at night, with the dead, as protection from enemy fire.

[19] Dr. Charles S. Carter from Longstreet's corps was appointed to Hospital Number 8 in Richmond on 12 May 1864.

[20] Brig. Gen. John Gregg commanded Gregg's Brigade (formerly Hood's Texas brigade); Brig. Gen. George T. Anderson commanded Anderson's Brigade composed of the 7th, 8th, 9th, 11th, and 59th Georgia infantry regiments.

[21] Coolly

I enjoyed my supper & That being over[,] I assembled as many of our poor worn down fellows as I could & we laid in this grave & covered from our sight the bodies of our two comrades. It was now midnight & Major Gibbs and I laid down together and slept soundly the balance of the fight. (A. E. Lee was buried five hundred yards W.S.W.[22] of Mr. _____ house in the corner of the pines in a double grave on the left as you face the pines[.]) The anticipated fight did not come off. The afternoon has worn wearily away. The weather became very bad & I became thoroughly disgusted. Went over & slept at the house where The other section is & slept There. The enemy are supposed to have mooved.

[May] 12th[.] We tumbled out sans ceremonie a little after daylight This morning to the music of a lively charge on our lines. It proved a small affair to us[,] but the fighting continued on the right all day, at least, till 2 P.M. The sharp shooters annoyed us all day. Coil of the Howitzers was shot in the thigh. After Gen Bryan mooved away & saw on[e] of the Arkansas men shot & heard that peculiar *thug* again as the bullet went through his heart.[23] It appears The other sections have been into it on the right. H. Conyer had his arm broken.[24] Tom Hughes shot through the ear[,][25] others slightly. slept in our little hospital *soundly*.
On The lines near Spotsylvania C. H.

Fri. [May] 13th[.] A dull day plenty of mud & rain and fighting.

Sat [May] 14th[.] Equally so. Yankees left from our front this afternoon. we went out & got plenty of flys & ect.[26]

Sun [May] 15th[.] We were drying our flys & blankets last night till 11 P.M. The major insisted upon our lying down[.] about 12 we were aroused by orders to repair to the S. C. H. road.[27] it was near daylight when we got

---

[22] West-southwest

[23] Brig. Gen. Goode Bryan commanded Bryan's Georgia Brigade in Brig. Gen. Joseph B. Kershaw's division.

[24] Cpl. Hedges B. Conger was admitted to the Jackson Hospital in Richmond on 18 May 1864.

[25] Pvt. Thomas M. Hughes of Athens was also wounded at Chancellorsville on 3 May 1863.

[26] Flys were pieces of canvas used as flaps or reinforcement for tents.

[27] Spotsylvania Court House.

there & we marched on without any more sleep. The mud so deep and terrible[,] but fortunately we marched only a little way beyond S. C. H. I went in the afternoon to visit The hospital. The boys all seemed to be doing well. Then went over to see Rev. W. B. Owens[28] who was shot through the elbow while near the lines on the 10th. He is a remarkable instance of Christian fortitude. returning to the hospital I read a chapter to them[.] Too wet for p.m.

Mon [May] 16th[.]We mooved before daylight this morning a mile further to the right & were resting[.] no sound of war today. I have washed up & feel better. We had a small prayer meeting Tonight.

Tues [May] 17th[.] A quite day The infantry (Wrights brigade) are industriously Throwing up the new line of breastworks in front of us.[29] I have been reading Lara & etc & since washing
& so forth. The weather is delightful. Mooved back.

Wed [May] 18th[.] This morning I have an indistinct recollection of hearing The bugle blown[,] but a very distinct recollection of being fully awaked by heavy firing on The line to our left. Ewell was charged it seems about daylight but the Yankees could not be induced to stick.[30] The serious part of the duel is going on in sight. Mailed a letter to father. We had a large prayer meeting Tonight[.] All quiet.

Near Spotsylvania C. H.
May 19th[.] Weather delightful—have been washing today visited the hospital and paid a visit to Bro. Owens.

Fri [May] 20th[.] Another pleasant day—have written to Eliza[31] & I learn Dr. B. is superceeded I must go over and see him—Poor Dr. B. has certainly been much outraged & greatly mortified—I have had a petition by

---

[28] Chaplain William B. Owen, 17th Mississippi Infantry.

[29] Brig. Gen. Ambrose R. Wright's brigade, composed of the 3rd, 22nd, and 48th Georgia infantry regiments and the 2nd Georgia Battalion, in Lt. Gen. A. P. Hill's Third Corps.

[30] Lt. Gen. Richard S. Ewell's Second Corps, Army of Northern Virginia.

[31] Probably his cousin in Athens, Elizabeth J. Richards (1827–1891).

all of the company officers but the colonel refuses to sign it for reasons best known to himself.[32]

Sat [May] 21st[.] Six of us went over to the hospital today to moove Belcher to the Corps hospital.[33] We got all the wounded there in safety. put up The tents—made the pine brush pallets & removed the wounded to them. (The new surgeon did not condescend to put his hand to anything.) The battalion rec'd orders in the meantime & fortunate for us passed The hospital just as we got through. We marched to Waller's church & camped there.

Sun [May] 22nd[.] Resumed our march toward Hanover Junction[,] passed Through Childsburg and soon found that we were in the immediate vicinity of our old friend Mr. Adams. Some set off 7 A.M. E. E & I were cordially received by the girls & by each member of the old gentleman's family.[34] A couple of hours were passed very pleasantly. Then we had a good dinner—held prayers with the family & pushed on[,] highly delighted with our visit. We soon overtook the battery & had an hour remaining for a nap. The whole army seemed to be in motion. The wagon trains extend for miles. We resumed our march—crossed the North Anna at Butler's Mills, The C. R. R.[,] & camped a little lower down.[35]

May 23rd[,] Hanover Junction 9 pm[.] The case being so urgent we were roused at 2 o clock this morning and marched down here (3 miles) where we are now lying waiting like "micawber for something to turn up." Well something did turn up. I wrote to G. & went down to the Junction—got a Negro boy to take it[36] up[,] at least promise to do so—returned to the camp & found them hitched up. I missed seeing Dr. B.

---

[32] Dr. William C. Brown of Tarboro NC was the assistant surgeon in Cabell's artillery battalion. He was ill when he was relieved and admitted to the hospital on 28 May 1864, with a fever and given a thirty-day furlough. Dr. Brown was re-admitted to General Hospital Number 9 in Richmond VA, on 10 June 1864. Oliver mentions in his diary that Dr. Brown was back on duty in October 1864.

[33] Pvt. John H. Belcher was eventually transported to Hospital Number 9 in Richmond.

[34] Pvt. Eli England of Athens GA

[35] The Virginia Central Railroad. Lee's Army of Northern Virginia was withdrawing toward Richmond.

[36] His letter.

We then went down the road and took up position in Fox's farm near the F. R. R. Bridge.[37] The enemy had come up rather suddenly & the citizens were flying in great confusion. 5 o' clock P.M. However familiar a man may become with the sound of rushing & bursting shells now shrieking through the air[,] now crashing through the timber, no thinking & feeling man can but opine[,] but as I now sit, ocupied only with a book & listen unmoved to the deafening sound of these missiles pregnant with death. They moove me especially because I know the wood through which they bear their way so fearfully is full of men & because I hear, even now[,] the fainter & fainter sounds of suffering from some poor maimed or mangled fellow soldier—God shield them—

As evening drew on the fight became very exciting. I became very interested & watched The bursting of shells untill night spread her mantle over the contending hosts & long after marked their fire-fly flashings of their muskets at the R.R. bridge.[38]

About midnight they got off a practical joke on us without intending it. I put my knapsack on the caisson & laid down by it to guard it late in the night they brot the horses in the wood hitched them to the caisson & drew it off without my waking.

We were all roused & marched back to the Junction.

Tu [May] 24th[.] I slept late this morning. We mooved back a little[.] I have rested all day very pleasantly[.] The fight is going in front. Heavy thunder from the enemy.

Wed [May] 25th[.] Mooved back across the River this evening. Another rain storm came up as we started[.] Found shelter under a very dirty dischiviled overcoat[.] stopped at the hospital & helped to moove poor L. H. McElhenny who was shot this morning thru the bowells.* Camped near the river[.]

*died, 27th on the cars going to Richmond.

May 31st[.] The infantry ran their works so close to us that we were fairly united. We therefore went up to the guns & hastily dug another

---

[37] Richmond, Fredericksburg, and Potomac Railroad.
[38] Battle of the North Anna River, twenty miles from Richmond.

trench immediately behind them. We scarcely had got it completed when the enemy opened on us. The firing was splendid but we were secure. The day was pleasantly passed in fighting, sleeping, eating, etc. I met in going to the spring today Cap. Elms & Lets Oats & Wriggler from C. N. C. They are with the 37th Regt Learner's Brigade.[39] Corp B Mosely of the Howitzers killed today.

June 1st[.] We mooved out about 1 o clock this morning. 9 A.M. Have been taking a good nap. Waiting for the ball to open. Meanwhile Pickets division in on us & The battery mooved off without our knowledge.[40] We soon found it, however, & are now watching the exciting preparations making for a fight on this part of the line. In the evening we mooved up again & got up behind The division in time to hear the sharp action in which Wofford was driven temporarily from his lines.[41] It was quite an exciting time but we couldn't get into it. Some stragglers came by but they were very few. Our lines were retaken & toward night the Howitzers went into position.

Thurs [June] 2nd[.] More than half the battalion are on the line today. They have been under a severe fire of sharpshooters still they have had but one mortally (Campbell) & one slightly wounded; Callaway's battery.[42]

Sat [June] 4th[.] The first section mooved to the lines this morning about daylight. We have had a lively time all day with the sharpshooters[,] a man dropping here and there. Just before dark Cap McCarthy was shot through the head by a sharpshooter.[43] There was a considerable skirmish about 9 P.M. I stood on the hill in camp watching the flash of the Yankee guns along the horizon or the bursting of their shells as they emerged from the pines in front[.] The minnies sounded like bees passing & one shell exploded in The camp[.]

Lt Dunn lost a leg this morning[.]

---

[39] The 37th North Carolina Infantry was in Lane's brigade, Wilcox's division. "Lets" is an abbreviation for Lieutenants.

[40] Pickett's division was the third division in Longstreet's corps.

[41] Wofford's brigade, commanded by Brig. Gen. William T. Wofford, was made up of Georgia troops: the 16th, 18th, and 24th Georgia infantry regiments, Cobb's Legion, Phillips's legion, and the 3rd Battalion of Georgia sharpshooters.

[42] Cpl. Alexander Campbell, Fraser's battery, Cabell's artillery battalion.

[43] Capt. McCarthy commanded the Richmond Howitzer Battery.

Sun [June] 5th[.] R. R. Stiles was severely wounded this morning. I did not go to the front till afternoon. preached to part of my companions this morning remained in the works late at night[.] There was a spirited attack on our right in which our division took part[.] It was sublime.

Gaines Mill June 7th 1864
Spent a dull day in the lines today. The enemy are working away in our front. Their sharpshooters picking of[f] a man here and there. The other section goes in tonight.

Wed [June] 8th[.] Red letter from father & Sue—have written to S.[44] I must get dinner & return to the line. Very sad news came up the line soon after my return. Cap. C's gun was fired about dusk & Allen Moore was just sighting the gun again to fire it after dark when the bullet of a sharpshooter struck him in the forehead & he dropped dead across the trail. We buried him soon after dark[.] I exhorted the few comrades assembled around the grave "not to let the feigning of death & The presence of danger harden their hearts." But I must confess this is an influence hard to resist.

Thurs [June] 9th[.] Walked up to the other section this morning. Lt. Bartow was shot through the head just before I reached there. Our men, though uncomfortably situated, are in rather a good health & very good spirits. The Minnie practice continues pretty sharply—no artillery firing from the enemy's liens for two or three days—Have been doing guard duty tonight for J. W.[45] We have been firing at intervals the last two night. There has been less working parties on the works tonight including our own[,] but the Yankees have not fired a gun.

Fri [June] 10th[.] Rec'd a letter from Liza today.[46] Rose late, went immediately down to the spring, washed, a good breakfast[.] Returned in time to witness a tragedy. A young South Carolinian near the battery a

---

[44] Oliver's younger sister, Susannah Caroline Oliver (1849–1908). Another sister, Selina Jane Oliver, who was born in 1843, died in August 1863.

[45] Pvt. James J. Williams, ambulance driver in the Troup Artillery.

[46] Probably his cousin, Elizabeth Richards.

whitworth bullet[47] passed thru his face & into the heart of another poor fellow who had rose in his pit to stretch himself. They have opened on us today. They have contained their fire up to a late hour tonight. Doing a little hospital tonight. Sleeping.

Sun 21 August 1864[.] Our Bible Class & courses were more prolonged than usual today[,] if not more interesting[.] I preached with tolerable freedom upon the observance of the Sabbath.

Sun 4th Sept[.] Very much to my surprise a large audience assembled this morning[,] something for which I was wholly unprepared[.] among them were Cap Carlton, Bro Callaway, Bro Hyman, the Let led by Major L—with a great many of the privates & co. officers, of the 49th Ga Regt.[48] I managed, however, from the subject selected[,] to weane a discourse with which moast of the congregation seemed to be pretty well satisfied[.] p. meeting conducted by the adjutant tonight.

Swift Creek Sep. 7th/64
Beautiful day cool night and clear[.] And therefore we are not dead yet. I am made exceedingly happy by a written communication from G. T. Bennett to the effect that he believes "God has forgiven his sins & that he desires to connect himself with the people of God[.]"[49] Have just sent a note to Gen Pendleton requesting him to preach for us next Sunday.

Sat [Sept.] 10th[.] The days glide so rapidly by now that I don't have time to rewrite my diary[,] nor is there much vanity[,] but they are alike busy but peaceful & happy[.] I have filled all my appointments this week but that of Thursday night when it rained. The meeting last night at Manley's was very encouraging for the first time I invited the anxious forward but noone responded. Gen. Pendleton has consented to preach for us tomorrow.[50]

---

[47] Elongated bullet of English manufacture with smaller diameter than a minnie ball.

[48] Capt. Henry Carlton, Lt. Morgan Callaway, Baptist chaplain John James Hyman (1833–1906) of the 49th Georgia Infantry, and a lieutenant and major unnamed.

[49] Pvt. George T. Bennett, Troup Artillery.

[50] Brig. Gen. William Nelson Pendleton (1809–1883) graduated from West Point in 1830 and was ordained an Episcopal priest in 1838. He was the rector of Grace Episcopal Church in Lexington VA, until he accepted a captain's commission

Mailed letter to L—

Sun [Sept.] 11th[.] Gen P met us this morning according to appointment & found waiting for him a large congregation. He addressed us from the miracle in Nain[51]at large. Held service again, in the Episcopal manner, at headquarters[,] but unfortunately a shower broke up the meeting before he began to preach. I addressed the Howitzers in an exceedingly lovin[g] manner on the love of God[.] The p.m. well attended[.] I enjoyed exercised freedom in more than one sense—words of Paul "when I am weak then am I strong."[52]

Swift Creek Sep 13th/64

Tues 13th[.] I am sitting in my rural study where I kindled a fire this morning where I came down to pray[.] Here I wrote yesterday letters to J. W. Burke, Georg F. Pierce[53] & one to Bessie which the major with whom I had a long & pleasant talk last night promised to have forwarded for me by way of Charleston—and now I must write some more letters.

Wed [Sept.]14th[.] Today I dissolved partnership with my old friend C. C. K. & Tharmone & I have set to work to build a cabin. Prayer meeting largely attended[.] Rec'd letters from Father & Miss P.

Fri [Sept.] 16[.] The Col sends me word my commission has been forwarded.[54] Cabin covered. The Adjutant led [prayer meeting] tonight at Manly's, address admirable.

---

in the Rockbridge Artillery on 1 May 1861. He rose rapidly in rank to Brig. Gen., and became Lee's nominal chief of artillery in the spring of 1862. His son, Col. Alexander "Sandy" Pendleton was killed in action in 1864. After the war Rev. Pendleton returned to his ministry in Lexington.

[51] Luke 7:11.

[52] Oliver had applied for a commission as a chaplain on 25 March. Secretary of War James Seddon approved his commission on 12 September 1864.

[53] Rev. John W. Burke of Macon, book agent for the Georgia Conference, and Rev. George Foster Pierce (1811–1884), bishop of the Georgia Conference of the Methodist Episcopal Church, South, who would ordain Charles Oliver as a deacon at Macon in 1865.

[54] Oliver's appointment as a chaplain made him a commissioned officer. He was directed to report to Brig. Gen. William Pendleton for further orders.

Sept 1864

Sun 18[.] At 11 A.M. I went down to the stand & found Bro Caly preaching—made an appointment for myself at 7 P.M. Went to dine with Bro. C.[,] had an excellent dinner but rain came up & no congregation assembled[,] so we went down with Dr. Carter & participated in the Episcopal service. Then I went over to the Hospital & preached there to an attentive table[.] Called at headquarters on my way back & had a long & pleasing talk with the Col & Majors.

Mon [Sept.] 19th[.] Did not get to Richmond till Tuesday evening. Had a busy but pleasant time there untill Thursday morning when I came off in the rain having some appointments[.] I had[,] while there[,] the pleasure of hearing Dr. Duncan preach twice.[55] It is my misfortune to be thrown in contact with some very stupid people in R[ichmond]—but the circumstances under which I made the acquaintance of Young Cap McMillan will outweigh all that.

Oliver
Sept 24, 1864
Swift Creek Sat Sep 24, 1864

Rec'd yesterday a long letter from Sallie more intellectual than any I have had the pleasure of reading from her pen. The Dear Girl certainly sheds a halo light around me. May God reward her! The p.m. at Manly's was large attended last night.[56] They gave me some money to buy stationary for them next week. We had a brisk little shelling here this morning which caught me at the spring but didn't last long. We have had two or three days of damp weather[,] but the skies are brightening now as if it would clear up. I have written to S. I did not succeed while in R. [Richmond] in getting my English letter off.

Sun [Sept.] 25th[.] Preached this morning at the "stand,"[57] from which place I went immediately To the hospital—dined there[,] preached there a sermon which did not seem to be without effect. four of our company,

---

[55] James Armstrong Duncan (1830–1877), Methodist hospital chaplain in Richmond.

[56] The prayer meeting at Manly's (North Carolina) artillery company.

[57] Typically the soldiers built a platform for the preachers to stand on, so all could see them.

officers being present Sunday night[,] I preached tonight at "The stand[.]" God gave me free & earnest utterance[.] I should not have called mourners up for I have ever felt a dread of this new responsibility[,] but Bro. Callaway relieved me of this duty & Oh! how my head thrilled with the sight that followed[.] They poured forth faster than we could grasp their hands[,] sobbing[,] eager[,] broken hearted men inquiring the way of life[.] Blessed be God[,] but I feel keenly my own unworthiness.

Mon [Sept.] 26th[.] Went to Richmond today—had a most unfortunate experience at The Hospital[.] upon the whole tho[,] the trip was a pleasant one as I discharged moast of my little commissions[.] I had not time To eat dinner and got back very hungry & having a slight headache[.] a cup of coffee, however, sent me right. I went down rather late to the "stand" & we had a good meeting.

Tu [Sept.] 27th[.] Another good meeting, Bro Barrett preached.[58]

Swift Creek Sep 28th/64
I have mailed Today letters to Mrs. Wm. Harris, Monroe, Ga. Miss Pauline Thomas Secy L. V. A.[59] a paper to Miss S—We received today a package of "The Army & Navy Herald[.]"[60] Preached tonight with freedom, many fresh mourners including the captain[.] Heavy shelling of the lines near P. tonight. In the letter to J. W. B.[61] enclosed the remaining 20 [dollars] of Col. Cabell's present.

Thurs [Sept.] 29th[.] I have written a letter to Bro. John Burke intended for publication. I have done my washing—It is noon & I seem to be at leisure for the balance of the day, Many little things have as usual, arisen to fill up that leisure[.] The meeting was well attended Tonight[,] notwithstanding The fact that a great many out of the battalion were engaged all night on the bombproof. I felt like my discourse was rather a belabored one or That I labored at it[.] Nevertheless it pleased God to pour out His spirit upon us—a large number came forward for prayer. I thought it prudent to break out all the obstacles real & imaginary[.] That seemed to

---

[58] Chaplain Edward B. Barrett, Baptist chaplain of the 45th Georgia Infantry.
[59] Ladies Veil Association
[60] Oliver took newspaper subscriptions for the soldiers at $1.00 each issue.
[61] Rev. John W. Burke.

interfere with such a step & open The door of the church which I did & four came forward besides Let. H. Jennings[.][62]

At night after our return I had a long conversation with Cap. C. & Lt. M. very satisfactory & assuring in both cases.

Well! I must moralize a little[.] I am really conducting a revival[.] I long looked forward To the possibility of such a thing with peculiar dread[.] I would, sinner as I am, have postponed it indefinitely if I could & did not myself take the step which developed The works of God in Those hearts[.] But God has forced me into the work & now like each additional duty it sits lightly upon me—Tho it has made me more prayerful & The pastoral duties which seemed so foreign To my taste and talents I seem to discharge acceptably and successfully.

Tu [Sept.] 30th[.] Barry & Culp returned today.[63] I visited The works this morning & distributed tracts. The captain urges me to join The officer's mess[.] dined with them today A rainy night[,] no change for either meeting.

Swift Creek Sat Oct 1st 1864

A rainy day[.] I have been all day engaged on some reflections upon the "relation of Christ to us" but have been so much interrupted That I have not completed it. My little cabin is paying me handsomely Today Tho unfinished. The Hymn Books which Bro Burke sent are the little kind & of no value to me.

Sun [Oct.] 2nd[.] Preached at the "stand" This morning, did not enjoy much freedom. Went to the hospital to see Dr Brown. Was shocked by what I saw Alas! Is there neither constancy nor consistency in man? We beguiled Dr B down to the meeting with us[.] Bro C preached[.] after the sermon we invited to the front seat, Those who desired to find Their way to Jesus[.] a larger number than ever came forward. Then, under peculiarly solemn circumstances, I opened The door of the church; eight came forward including Cap. Carlton.[64] We had a very interesting little meeting here after my return. May God confirm His blessing!

---

[62] 2nd Lieutenant Henry Jennings, Troup Artillery.

[63] Privates Joseph M. Barry and Benjamin F. Culp of Athens, Troup Artillery.

[64] Capt. Henry H. Carlton commanded the Troup Artillery.

Mon [Oct.] 3rd[.] Rainy day, I have spent the whole day in my cabin, wrote & mailed a letter to Sue[.] No meeting tonight enjoyed some "sweet hours of prayer."

Tu [Oct.] 4th[.] Have made out a church book[.] Today have spent The day indoors—have enjoyed interesting conversation with the Captain, Lieutenent M & others. Rec'd The package from home containing Calico Shirt, socks & soap. Rec'd another letter from S. full of fine sentiment.

Wed [Oct.] 5th[.] Dr. Stiles[65] reached here Today—preached for us Tonight, a fine discourse. He is a wonderful old man (74!) makes one think of Moses on Nebo.[66] The congregation was large & mourners as numerous as ever.

Mailed a kind letter to S. today.

Thurs [Oct.] 6th We buried Tom the Major's boy This morning & I improved the time by resolving to Bring the Negroes of the battalion Together & address myself particularly to Them[.] God grant That it may not be without effect[.] we are so apt To neglect This part of The Work. The attendance upon The meeting was good & encouraging.

Swift Creek Oct 13th 1864

I am advised To go to Gordonsville which is quite a disappointment but I dare not risk my furlough home. The weather is pleasantly cold & windy Today but I have spent a portion of the day in The woods rather pleasantly, perhaps not unprofitably.

Oct 19th[.] The past few days have not been remarkable for anything. The meetings have gradually waned in interest Tho pretty regularly kept up. A new project[,] To build a church & school house[,] has been much interfered with [by] The building of stables & other details but will

---

[65] Rev. Joseph C. Stiles, D. D., Presbyterian evangelist. Dr. Stiles was in his seventies, yet frequently preached three times a day to soldiers. Chaplain J. William Jones, 13th Virginia Infantry, wrote that "the beginning of the great revivals which swept through our camps was due, under God, more to Dr. Stiles than any other man," *Christ in the Camp*, 524–25.

[66] Deuteronomy 32:49.

doubtless yet be put into execution. I rode over to see Bro Ware[67] Today in the 8th Va. had a pleasant canter on the Captain's old black horse.

Thurs [Oct.] 20th[.] Went out to the horse camp, ours & Manlys, Think They will have to build a chapel There too[.] brought back with me The cloth Col. Cabell Kindly presented me with.

Sat [Oct.] 22nd[.] Started the foundation of the church yesterday amidst the usual amount of ridicule & fault finding & with the usual insult. Today I have been cutting logs all day[.] Rec'd a letter from S. of great interest & beauty which aroused me from a fit of sleepiness & enabled to make some preparation for the contingencies of tomorrow.

Sun [Oct.] 23rd[.] Bro T. A. Ware[,] chaplain of 8th Va Regt[,] preached for me this morning and then baptized 6 members of the battalion. I went over at night and preached for him. The congregation was large & The visit was delightful To me.

Swift Creek Nov 1st 1864
Dr. Stiles held a little meeting in our chapel this morning[.] Took dinner with us. large prayer meeting at the Howitzers this evening where the doctor talked to us again.

Wed [Nov.] 2nd[.] The weather has become inclement[.] I have been working on my cabin—hung the door, closed the end & etc. Dr S. came agreeable to appointment but rather to our surprise The church was soon crowded & he preached us a stirring & enlightening discourse & spent the night with us.

Thurs [Nov.] 3rd[.] Cold & wet. Red letters last night from Father, Rev. A. Wright & Rev. R. T. Bingham.[68] have written Rev. D. Kelsey

---

[67] Chaplain Thomas A. Ware (1810–1897), Methodist chaplain of the 8th Virginia Infantry.

[68] Rev. A. Wright was the presiding elder of the Columbus (GA) district of the Georgia Methodist Conference in 1864; Rev. R. W. Bigham was a Methodist pastor in Eatonton GA.

recommending W. F. Lane[.][69] Will mail[,] that is hand ones[,] To The major my long delayed letter for sister Anna.

Fri [Nov.] 4th[.] The adjutant consented to lead the meeting for me at Manly's Tonight & I am waiting the arrival of Brother Granberry[70]

Sat [Nov.] 5th[.] Brother Granberry, who according To appointment came over & preached us an excellent sermon, he remained all night—is a very pleasant man. I walked out to the Horse camp & Took dinner out there—The wind very high.

Sun. [Nov.] 6. Preached at The stand, again at night in our little chapel. Dr. Stiles was with us. We had a very interesting class meeting.

Swift Creek Nov 8th 1864

[Nov.] 9th[.] Spent yesterday in Richmond very busily but rather pleasantly except that[,] in hurrying to get to the train in Time[,] I made my head ache severely and reached The Depot a tad late, having been missing former [train] as to the time of its departure. Slept at the Ga. Wayside Home—all who are connected with it seem to be as stupid as ever. I found my way perfectly clear at the Hospital & They tried to make it so at The 2nd Auditor's Office. Procured the stationary I wanted & returned in This morning's Train. Have been down To see Bro. Fraser all night about the barn, his regt. The battalion, & etc. The masons are to occupy it conjointly. Bro. Aldridge[71] preached for us tonight.

Pleasant letter rec'd from Miss S.

[Nov.] 10th[.] Rec'd a letter from J. Calvin Johnson by Bennett. Red a note from Father This morning by H. Conyer. I have passed half The day working round my cabin. Now I will study a little if I can. We held a little meeting in the open air at Let Callaway's battery. The major was present & we had a good meeting.

---

[69] The Rev. Daniel Kelsey was the Methodist pastor at Monroe GA; Wesley Lane was elected an elder in the Methodist Conference in 1864.

[70] Chaplain John C. Granbery (1829–1907), 11th Virginia Infantry, later a bishop in the Methodist Episcopal Church, South.

[71] Chaplain William A. Aldrich, Episcopalian, 1st Virginia Infantry.

Fri [Nov.] 11th[.] Have written letters This morning to Ga. Relief & To A&N [Army and Navy] Herald have done a little sewing & etc.

Sun [Nov.] 13th[.] This morning the dedicatory sermon in the barn which is a large commodious place of worship. I preached to a small congregation in the chapel. To night the class meeting was large.

Mon [Nov.] 14th[.] Went this morning to the chaplains meeting. The Methodist chaplains had many gone to conference. Made some pleasant acquaintances.

[Nov.] 15th[.] The girls came out to camp today according To appointment[;] it was really a cheery sight. The meeting in the barn of the Christian Association was thinly attended. The p.m. tonight pretty well attended. After the meeting was over The adjutant told me that he was ordered away which is very bad news but by way of compensation gave me my furlough. I deem it my duty to get home by the 20th so I am busy making preparation *Good night.*

Hd Qtrs Post
Athens, Ga Dec 13th/64
The A. C. S. will issue thirty-day rations C. J. Oliver chaplain Cabells Batt Arty army of Nothern Virginia[72]
Wm J. Magill[73]
Col Comg Post

Chaplain Oliver's wartime journal does not resume after his furlough to Athens, Georgia, except for a collection of his sermons, meditations, and reflections on scriptural passages that seem to go back at least to Sunday, 5 April 1863, when he wrote on the 13th chapter of 1st Corinthians, "The Greatest of These is Love." Other topics were "Jesus of Nazareth," from Luke 11:20, written 29 May 1864,

---

[72] Evidently, Chaplain Oliver preserved this generous authorization for rations as an addition to his journal. Confederate chaplains rarely received a thirty-day supply of food, especially while on furlough.

[73] Col. William Joseph Magill (1828–1890), formerly capt. of A Company, 1st Regiment Georgia Regulars. Wounded and arm amputated at Sharpsburg MD, 17 September 1862.

and "Who are They?" from Revelation 7:13 written in November 1864. One of the last passages he wrote in praise of God, based on the Book of Revelation 7:9–12, was recorded in his journal as follows:

Nov 1864

"When the Thrones are set & the Lamb of God in the midst of the Throne see in the mild effulgence That streams from the sun of righteousness The gathering of the heavenly hosts from East & West & North & South of all lands & lineage of each age & Tongue clad in those snow white robes of purity waving their blood bought palms of victory, filling heaven with The glad refrain "Alleluia, Glory in the highest" casting their glittering crowns before Their Savior as they cry "Amen: Blessing & glory & wisdom & thanksgiving & honor & power & might—be unto our God forever & ever[.]"

Charles James Oliver returned to the Georgia Conference of the Methodist Episcopal Church, South, after the war. He was ordained a deacon at Macon, Georgia, on 15 November 1865, and an elder two years later. He served as an associate pastor at Waynesboro in 1865, pastor for the Sailor's Mission in Savannah in 1866, and 1867–68 as minister to the City Mission in Atlanta where his wife, Nannie, and child died. Thereafter he served pastorates in Augusta, Ringgold, and Athens, where he located in 1873. In 1911 he died in East Point, a suburb of Atlanta, and was buried in Athens. His obituary contained his brief summary of his experience as a minister, "With me, to Live is Christ."

The Fall of Atlanta

Chaplain Thomas H. Deavenport,
3rd Tennessee Infantry Regiment
Army of Tennessee

Thomas H. Deavenport was born in Giles County near Pulaski, Tennessee, in 1835. His mother was a member of the Primitive Baptist Church, but she allowed her son to attend a Methodist Sunday school. Thomas determined to study for the ministry and was received into the Memphis Conference of the Methodist Episcopal Church, South, while still in his early twenties. He served as pastor of the Cageville Circuit and then, in 1860, as pastor of the Pototoc Church in the Aberdeen District. Leaving his church, he enlisted as a private in Company A, 3rd Tennessee Infantry Regiment, in September of 1861. He was captured at Fort Donelson, Tennessee, in February of 1862. After he was exchanged, he was appointed chaplain of the 3rd Tennessee Infantry Regiment with an effective date of 18 November 1862. He resigned on 7 April 1863 and was furloughed four days later. Deavenport returned to the regiment on 25 January 1864 at Dalton, Georgia. His report of the fall of Atlanta reflected great personal anguish, yet also admiration for the barefoot Confederate soldiers who were his companions. Chaplain Deavenport remained with his regiment until it surrendered at Greensboro, North Carolina, in 1865.[1]

We remained near Atlanta till 31st Aug. Around that city we lost many brave men. It was a dreadful time and yet our boys held up bravely. At last we had to leave, marched down to Jones Borough, twenty-two miles, and fought a battle the same day. There we lost Lt. Col. C. J. Clack, and many more.[2] We gained nothing. Early next morning we started back, bivouacked for the night in a few miles of Atlanta. It became necessary to evacuate the place and at daylight we began the march, and on the 3rd Sept. bivouacked near Lovejoy. Hardee's Corps in the meantime had another desperate

---

[1] The unpublished diary of Thomas H. Deavenport (1835–1888) is in the Tennessee State Library and Archives in Nashville, Tennessee. A partial service record for Thomas H. Davenport, 3rd Tennessee Infantry, may be found in the National Archives Compiled Service Records of Confederate and General Staff Officers, microfilm M331, CW 0998, at the South Carolina State Archives in Columbia.

[2] Commanding the 3rd Tennessee Regiment when he was killed at Jonesboro GA.

engagement which resulted in a drawn battle though the enemy's loss was much heavier than ours. On the night of the 4th the enemy began to fall back, which they continued till they reached Atlanta. Thus ended the Summer Campaign. An Armistice of ten days was agreed upon that the citizens of Atlanta might be sent through the lines. Here was a piece of Heartless cruelty. There seems to be no deed too base or cruel for a Yankee. Gen. Sherman had without warning shelled the city more than a month destroying a vast amount of property and many lives[,] and when he gained possession of it immediately ordered every man woman and child to leave, and also all living in five miles of the R.R. in the rear[;] thus several thousand women and children were turned out of their homes, driven away from all they possessed and cast upon the charities of the world. How shall that base man answer for all his dark deeds. The campaign just closed has been the most arduous of the war. For four months we listened daily to the roar of cannon and rattle of musketry. All day, all night the leaden messengers were flying around us. It seems incredible that men could endure so much. Cheerfully each labor was performed, each danger met. True many looked worn and haggard but still their spirit was unbroken. We rested a few days and again took up the line of march and are now fortifying near Palmetto on the W. P. R. R.[3]

A new campaign has been inaugurated, how it will end God only knows. We have been compelled to give up much of our country at this point. It has cost the enemy much. At other points we have been successful. I am not discouraged, though there is some discontent in the Army. Oh God, how long will this cruel war last[?] My heart yearns for the society of home. I count each day and ask when will the last come? Poor weak human nature is ready to complain and say my burden is too heavy. Cease thy murmuring, God is wise and good. He doeth all things well. Health is yet mine. Through many dangers I have been led, have just escaped death time and again. It seems that I have led a charmed life. God be praised for his goodness. I see around me much distress and my heart sickens at the destruction of life and property on every hand, in the army and out of it. I see grey hairs and helpless infancy driven from home, penniless almost friendless. I see the strong men cut down without a moment's warning, or left a cripple for life. I see the poor soldier as he toils on, sustained by the hope of better days and by the love he bears for those far away. I saw but

---

[3] The West Point Railroad that ran from Atlanta to West Point GA.

yesterday the Captain commanding his regiment barefoot. Such men will not be conquered. I cannot give the history of this campaign language to describe its suffering. It has been long and bloody, many of our noblest have fallen. 'Requiescant in pace.' They live in our hearts.

Thomas Deavenport returned to the parish ministry after the war. He joined the Tennessee Conference in 1865 and then transferred to the North Alabama Conference of the Methodist Episcopal Church, South, in 1870. For the next eighteen years he served churches in Jacksonville, Birmingham, Tuscumbia, and Anniston. Described as a man "small of stature, sinewy, nervously constructed, and richly endowed with the power of endurance," he was also remembered as a brave soldier and a spiritual preacher.[4] He died in 1888 at the age of fifty-three while serving, appropriately perhaps, as pastor of the Warrior Church in the Gadsden District of the North Alabama Conference. He was buried in Birmingham.

---

[4] *Minutes of the Annual Conferences of the Methodist Episcopal Church, South, 1888* (Nashville: Publishing House of the M. E. Church, South, 1889) 132. Copy in the Pitts Library, Candler School of Theology, Emory University, Atlanta GA.

Chapter 4

Ministries of Revival and Encouragement

Create in me a clean heart, O God, and put a new and steadfast
spirit within me...then will I teach transgressors thy ways...
Psalm 51

During the war, in addition to weekly Bible studies and Sunday (or Sabbath) worship services, some Confederate chaplains offered week long revival meetings for soldiers. Many of these, especially during the summer of 1862, enjoyed modest success in the Army of Northern Virginia.[1] A much greater interest in religion began to be seen, however, after the battle of Antietam, fought on 17 September 1862. Antietam marked the first major defeat of the Army of Northern Virginia under the leadership of Lee, Longstreet, Jackson, and Stuart. But more cogently, for the mindset of the average soldier, were the monumental casualties—approximately 13,724 killed, wounded, or missing—30 percent of Lee's original force of 45,000.[2] Union casualties were almost as great—12,410 or 25 percent of those who went into action. It was and remains the bloodiest single day in American military history.

On 19 and 20 September after the battle, Lee retreated across the Potomac east of Winchester, to the vicinity of Bunker Hill, Virginia, near the Opequon River. There during a few weeks of rest, chaplains went from tent to tent to inquire about the health and mental condition of the soldiers. Many, if not all, had lost friends, camp mates, and even relatives at

---

[1] Jones, *Christ in the Camp*, 278–79.
[2] Burke Davis, *Our Incredible Civil War* (New York: Ballantine Books, 1960) 145; John W. Chambers II, ed., *The Oxford Companion to American Military History* (New York: Oxford University Press, 1999) 32.

Antietam. The soldiers were a long way from home and free from distractions, another way to describe loneliness and grief.

Two Baptist chaplains, Asa M. Marshall, a former private before receiving his commission in the 12th Georgia, and James Nelson of the 44th Virginia, announced a series of services in Trimble's brigade of Jackson's corps the second week in October. Chaplain J. William Jones of the 13th Virginia and Dr. Joseph C. Stiles, Presbyterian evangelist, volunteered to preach at least once a day. Some 1,500 soldiers attended Stiles's first service.[3] Chaplain Jones wrote to the *Religious Herald* in Richmond:

> There is a very interesting revival in our corps. Soon after the return of our army from Maryland, Brother Marshall, chaplain of the Twelfth Georgia Regiment, assisted by Brother Nelson of the Forty-fourth Virginia and other brethren, began a series of meetings which soon became very interesting—attendance from the entire brigade being very large, and many coming forward for prayer. There has also been, under the same efficient labors, an interesting revival in Jackson's old brigade ("Stonewall"), and in Taliaferro's. Brethren, pray for us that the word of the Lord may have free course in our midst.[4]

On the 13 October, Lieutenant General "Stonewall" Jackson wrote from his headquarters at Bunker Hill to his wife: "I heard an excellent sermon from the Reverend Dr. S——[Stiles]. His text was I Timothy, chap. ii, 5th and 6th verses. ('For there is one God, and one Mediator between God and men, the man Jesus Christ, who gave himself a ransom for all, to be testified in due time.') It was a powerful exposition of the word of God. He is a great revival minister."[5] Soon other brigades began requesting services. In Jackson's corps, Winder's Stonewall brigade, Early's brigade, and Lawton's brigade (and Pryor's brigade from Longstreet's corps) followed Trimble's brigade in meeting for worship a week or more at a time.

Chaplains conducted revival services early in the morning, at mid-day, or before tattoo, that is, before the soldiers retired to their tents or blankets for the night. On the Sunday, services might go on any time there was a group assembled if there was no fighting. Services would be held outside or

---

[3] Jones, *Christ in the Camp*, 283.

[4] Ibid., 285.

[5] R. L. Dabney, *Life and Campaigns of Lt. Gen. Thomas J. Jackson, (Stonewall Jackson)* (Harrisonburg VA: Sprinkle Publications, 1983) 585.

in a barn or in a makeshift chapel. If available, split log benches, wooden crates, or boxes were used for seats and barrels for pulpits. If the temperature dropped, the soldiers would build a fire around which the congregation gathered.

After a few hymns, the preachers would read scriptures and deliver sermons calling sinners to repent and rededicate their lives to Christ. Another hymn might be sung and then the minister called upon all those who felt a special need for prayer to come to the front. Some locations had mourners' benches for soldiers who had been convicted by the sermon. Other soldiers might kneel or prostrate themselves before an altar, or just on the ground, seeking forgiveness for their sins. It was not unusual to have 100 soldiers kneeling or sitting in front on the mourners' bench during the service.[6] One of the familiar refrains from the services seems to have been,

> How know you but that ere tomorrow's sun shall rise the long roll may beat and this brigade be called to meet the enemy? It may be that some brave men *are hearing now their last message of salvation*! Accept Christ as your personal Savior here and now. Know where you will spend eternity—in a hell of fire with miserable sinners, or with your wives, mothers, fathers, and sisters in the Father's house prepared for you. He gave of himself for you, why will you remain in sin and die alone and without hope, when you may turn to your Heavenly Father and live?[7]

Although circumstances varied, there are accounts of revivals that lasted for several weeks. In one meeting of thirty days in Featherston's Mississippi brigade of Longstreet's corps, 140 men professed their faith and 100 men of Barksdale's brigade did likewise during a meeting of 21 days.[8] The records may have been established by Chaplain Robert E. Cooper of Cobb's Georgia Legion who preached every night save one for four months and five days, and by Chaplain G. R. Talley of the 6th Alabama Regiment in

---

[6] Sidney J. Romero, *Religion in the Rebel Ranks* (Lanham MD: University Press of America, 1983) 117.

[7] Jones, *Christ in the Camp*, 301.

[8] Romero, *Religion in the Rebel Ranks*, 119.

Rodes's brigade, who claimed an average of 500 converts per week for the chaplains in his services.[9]

Soldiers who wished to be baptized could choose their mode and denomination. Baptist chaplains baptized by immersion, Methodists and Presbyterians mainly by pouring. Baptist Chaplain John J. Hyman of the 49th Georgia reportedly baptized 260 soldiers; Chaplain J. E. King of the 14th Tennessee some 90 in 75 days; and Chaplain J. William Jones baptized 410. To accommodate some soldiers from Davis's Mississippi brigade, Jones cut a hole in the ice at a mill pond in Orange County, Virginia, and reportedly immersed fourteen in ice water.[10] Chaplain A. D. Betts, a Methodist in the 30th North Carolina, baptized by pouring, but he noted later that one of his converts had whiskey on his breath, so he wasn't sure that one "took."[11]

Stonewall Jackson and the Revival of Religion

In December of 1862, the Army of Northern Virginia defeated Major General Burnside and the Army of the Potomac at Fredericksburg and settled into winter quarters between Moss Neck and Hamilton's Crossing, south of the town. While at Hamilton's Crossing, Lieutenant General "Stonewall" Jackson took a strong personal interest in the spiritual fitness of his corps and of his chaplains. Chaplain A. D. Betts of the 30th North Carolina, who was with Jackson's corps, said that Jackson knew the next battle would be hard, and he wanted all of his regiments to have a chaplain to minister to the wounded and dying.[12] In Jackson's Second Corps, Chaplain Betts counted forty-four regiments with chaplains, and forty-seven regiments without.[13] Clearly, recruiting forty-seven additional chaplains would be challenging, if not impossible in the winter of 1862–1863.

---

[9] Herman Norton, *Struggling for Recognition: The United States Army Chaplaincy* (Washington DC: Office of the Chief of Chaplains, Department of the Army, 1977) 152.

[10] Ibid., 150; Jones, *Christ in the Camp*, 224; Frank L. Hieronymus, "For Now and Forever: The Chaplains of the Confederate States Army" (PhD diss., University of California at Los Angeles, 1964) 260.

[11] William A. Betts, ed., *Experience of a Confederate Chaplain 1861–1864* (Greenville SC: privately printed, 1864) 38. There is a copy in the Emory University Library, Atlanta GA.

[12] Ibid., 31.

[13] Ibid., 29.

In a letter to the Reverend William S. White, pastor of the Presbyterian Church in Lexington where he was a member, Lieutenant General Jackson suggested some guidelines for organizing a more effective Christian ministry in the army:

> My views are summed up in a few words, which are these: Each Christian branch of the church should send into the army some of its most prominent ministers, who are distinguished for their piety, talents, and zeal; and such ministers should labor to produce concert of action among chaplains and Christians in the army. These ministers should give special attention to preaching to regiments which are without chaplains, and induce them to take steps to get chaplains, to let the regiments name the denomination from which they desire chaplains selected; and then to see that suitable chaplains are secured. A bad selection of a chaplain may prove a curse instead of a blessing...Denominational distinctions should be kept out of view, and not touched upon; and as a general rule, I do not think that a chaplain who would preach denominational sermons, should be in the army.[14]

The Reverend Dr. R. L. Dabney, who had served as chaplain of the 18th Virginia Infantry before becoming Jackson's chief of staff during the Valley Campaign, recorded further decisions and suggestions Jackson made in March of 1863 to make the ministry of chaplains more efficient: "First, General Jackson requested that the Reverend B. T. Lacy from the Presbyterian Church in Fredericksburg serve as his Corps Chaplain to help the other chaplains coordinate their ministries. Normally chaplains were appointed to regiments or brigades. In this case the Secretary of War commissioned Lacy without assignment as a courtesy to Jackson who, in turn, appointed him Corps Chaplain-at-large."[15] Second, Jackson urged chaplains to adopt an itinerant schedule to serve regiments destitute of chaplains and to communicate their needs to their denominational leaders at

---

[14] R. L. Dabney, *Life and Campaigns of Lt. Gen. Thomas J. Jackson, (Stonewall Jackson)* (Harrisonburg VA: Sprinkle Publications, 1983) 647.

[15] Jones, *Christ in the Camp*, 530. Ironically, two months after his appointment, Lacy ministered to the first of his mortally wounded soldiers—General Jackson himself.

home. Jackson wanted all churches to be in "vital sympathy with the army."[16]

Third, Jackson directed that worship services would be conducted at his own headquarters at Hamilton's Crossing as encouragement to other units. The younger members of his staff formed a choir. The services began in an open field, but soon several regiments of the Stonewall Brigade built a chapel of logs and clapboard. Benches were made of split logs and heat furnished from clay-plastered chimneys.[17] Chaplain Abner Hopkins of the 2nd Virginia Infantry wrote later that the Stonewall Brigade had built the first chapel in the Army of Northern Virginia.[18]

Fourth, Jackson urged chaplains to conduct weekly meetings, usually on Tuesdays, and to form ecumenical associations of chaplains from throughout the army. This measure was designed to further coordinate religious education and preaching services. Chaplain Hopkins reported that the first chaplains' meeting was held 16 March 1863, at the nearby Round Oak Baptist Church, announced by circular to all the chaplains in Jones's and Winder's brigades. Chaplain Lacy presided.

Fifth, Jackson applied to the Military Committee of Congress to provide chaplains with horses, fuel, tents, and forage. Most of these requests were adopted piecemeal over the next year, but by 1863 many chaplains were already living in captured tents and riding captured "Yankee" horses.

Soon the chaplains of the Second Corps had spread the news of Jackson's evangelical initiatives among their colleagues throughout the army, and regular Chaplains' Associations appeared among most of the Protestant clergy. Roman Catholic chaplains did not traditionally attend, though there was a cooperative relationship between Protestant and Catholic clergy in hospital ministries.

Other cooperative efforts of the chaplains included the formation of "army churches" which seemed to have originated in the West before being adopted by some of the chaplains in the Army of Northern Virginia.[19] Army churches were very much like those of evangelical Protestants throughout the South except that they were nondenominational. There were articles of faith which usually included the reliability and inspiration of Scripture and the acceptance of Christ as Savior. The 8th Texas Cavalry, also known as

---

[16] Dabney, *Life and Campaigns of Lt. Gen. Thomas J. Jackson*, 648.
[17] Ibid., 650.
[18] Jones, *Christ in the Camp*, 468.
[19] Hieronymus, "For Now and Forever," 201.

"The Texas Rangers," formed their own church and promised to study the Bible, write the family of any soldier who died, and meet at least once a week.[20] There were regular "soldier members" who could transfer their membership "back home" whenever they wished. The Charleston Synod of the Presbyterian Church in South Carolina voted affirmatively to recognize such church memberships provided the soldiers wished to be Presbyterians when they returned home.[21]

Many Chaplains' Associations and army churches kept exact records of attendance at Bible study, prayer meetings, and church membership. Chaplain Thomas R. Markham of the 1st Mississippi Light Artillery counted 790 members on the "Consolidated List of Members of the Protestant Church in the 3rd Miss. Regiment." Of those on Markham's list, 443 were Baptist, 259 were Methodist, 75 were Presbyterian, 7 were Campbellites, 3 were Episcopalian, and 3 were Roman Catholic.[22] Chaplain A. D. Betts of the 30th North Carolina Infantry listed 228 members of his soldiers' church from nine companies in 1862, but he did not list them by denomination.[23]

The Chaplains' Associations and army churches were closely allied to a third organization that ministered to both the soldiers' spiritual and physical needs—the Young Men's Christian Association (YMCA). YMCAs were formed in the army and organized in Richmond as early as 1862. Chaplain Nicholas Davis of the 4th Texas Infantry in Hood's brigade praised the YMCA for distributing clothes, food, gloves, shoes, and 410 pairs of socks for his men. The YMCA also held prayer meetings, Sabbath schools, and Bible classes for the soldiers.[24]

A General Revival in Georgia and the Results

You will seek me and find me when you seek me with
all your heart...
Jeremiah 29

Although there had been some scattered revival meetings in the western theater, most witnesses agreed that the major revivals in the Army

---

[20] Ibid., 203.
[21] Ibid., 202.
[22] Ibid., 204.
[23] Ibid.
[24] Ibid., 210.

of Tennessee did not begin until the winter of 1862–1863.[25] Chaplain A. S. Worrell of the 34th Georgia Infantry, Cumming's brigade, wrote that after the battle of Stone's River, "the signs of that wonderful revival in the army of the West began to appear."[26] Chaplain William H. Browning of the 154th Tennessee Infantry recalled, "I shall never forget the look of astonishment in the Association of Chaplains in January, 1863, when Brother Winchester, a chaplain and a minister in the Cumberland Presbyterian Church, announced a conversion in his command, and stated that he believed we were on the eve of one of the most glorious revivals ever witnessed on the American continent...."[27] Certainly many others besides Brother George Winchester were surprised as well. The army was supposed to be a den of iniquity where guzzling whiskey, gambling away pitiful pay, and swearing were among the minor sins. In the minds of the pious, a revival in a saloon, racetrack, or bordello was as likely as a revival in the army.

However, many of the same conditions that favored a revival in the Army of Northern Virginia were also present in the Army of Tennessee. Both armies had gone through some hard campaigns, both had sustained severe casualties, both had influential leaders who supported the revivalists' efforts to create "a converted army," and both had visiting missionaries and assigned chaplains who were dedicated to evangelical preaching. Division and brigade commanders in the Army of Tennessee not only gave permission for the meetings to take place, but some also preached and led prayer meetings with the chaplains. For example, Brigadier General M. P. Lowry of Mississippi, an ordained Baptist minister, preached to his brigade frequently from a rostrum Major General Patrick Cleburne had constructed in the middle of his division specifically for worship services. Lieutenant General A. P. Stewart, a Presbyterian elder, assisted in the administration of the Lord's Supper, and Brigadier General Finley of the Florida Brigade, led in audible prayers.[28]

Chaplains and missionaries left many accounts of the revival meetings in 1863 and in 1864. The Reverend L. R. Redding, an army missionary from the Georgia Conference of the Methodist Episcopal Church, South,

---

[25] Herman Norton, "The Organization and Function of the Confederate Military Chaplaincy, 1861–1865" (Ph.D. diss., Vanderbilt University, 1956) 183–84; Hieronymus, "For Now and Forever," 250–53.

[26] Jones, *Christ in the Camp*, 542.

[27] Ibid.

[28] Ibid., 555.

reported that beginning in Gist's brigade, soldiers built chapels for the daily worship services in their camps. The Reverend J. B. McFerrin of Nashville, a charismatic preacher, gathered "an immense congregation" which eventually included soldiers from thirteen brigades.[29] Chaplain John J. D. Renfroe of the 10th Alabama Infantry described mass meetings outside with rails, logs, and rocks to serve as seats. By one account, fourteen miles of such revival services were taking place in the Army of Tennessee while they were bivouacked in Georgia in 1864.[30]

The mass revivals in the Army of Tennessee may not have lasted quite as long as did the evangelical fervor in Virginia, but the results were just as impressive. At Dalton, Georgia, where General Joe Johnston quartered the army in the winter of 1863–1864, forty-seven chaplains, evangelists, and missionaries held services in every church and in the open fields for thirty-three regiments and brigades for five months.[31] The Reverend S. M. Cherry, chaplain and colporter, recalled that at Dalton, the Chester House was the distribution center for "army papers, tracts, Bibles, Testaments, hymn books, and other religious literature" and the Methodist, Baptist, and Presbyterian churches were the favorite sites for evening meetings.[32] In 15 brigades, Reverend Cherry counted 321 conversions and 728 soldiers asking to join the Church in 1 month, an average of 35 conversions or professions of faith each night for 30 days. Over the course of five months, the chaplains added an estimated 13 percent of the Army of Tennessee to those who already identified themselves as Christians.

These revivals, which eventually encompassed an area from Virginia to Arkansas and Georgia to Texas, tended to feature strong evangelical preaching by Methodists, Baptists, and Presbyterians. Yet there was also a spiritual rebirth among the Episcopalians and other liturgical faith groups as well. Lieutenant General Leonidas Polk, Brigadier General William Pendleton, and Chaplain Charles T. Quintard of the 1st Tennessee Infantry were all ordained Episcopal priests; and Polk was, of course, also an Episcopal bishop. On 8 May 1864, when the Army of Tennessee was in winter quarters at Dalton, General John B. Hood, General Joseph E. Johnston, and Lieutenant General William Hardee all asked Polk to baptize them. In addition, Chaplain Quintard baptized Major General B. F.

---

[29] Hieronymus, "For Now and Forever," 245.
[30] Ibid.
[31] Cherry's report as cited in Jones, *Christ in the Camp*, 580–81.
[32] Jones, *Christ in the Camp*, 580.

Cheatham and Brigadier General O. F. Strahl of Cheatham's division in Atlanta at about the same time.[33] The other national leaders who joined churches in 1863–1864 included General Braxton Bragg, Lieutenant General Richard Ewell, and President Jefferson Davis.[34]

There is no question that the revivals in the Confederate armies from 1862 to 1864 were significant events. Chaplain J. William Jones and Chaplain L. C. Vass estimated that at least 15,000 soldiers in the Army of Northern Virginia made professions of faith during the war. The Reverend W. W. Bennett, post chaplain at Richmond and future president of Randolph-Macon College, believed that 150,000 soldiers in all the Confederate armies, East and West, had been converted and that one-third of all Confederate soldiers in the field were members of some branch of the Christian church at the end of the war.[35] Chaplain Jones, moreover, discovered after the war was over that "four-fifths of the Christian students of our colleges had been in the army, and that a large proportion of them had found Christ in the camp—and nearly all of the army converts were maintaining their profession, many of them pillars in the Churches."[36]

If Chaplain Bennett was even close in his estimates, it means that the revivals and other evangelical work in 1862–1864 produced an army which was significantly more religious than the society which originally produced it. In 1860, approximately 25 percent of the Southern people were church members, whereas in 1865 some 33 percent of the soldiers supposedly had made a Christian commitment. Professor R. L. Dabney of the Union Theological Seminary in Virginia, who had once been chaplain to the 18th Virginia Infantry in Pickett's brigade, wrote after the war:

> In short, the conversions in the various Confederate armies within the ensuing year were counted…The strange spectacle was now presented, of a people among whom the *active religious life seemed to be transferred from the churches at home—the customary seats of piety—to the army*; which, among other nations, has always been dreaded as the school of vice and infidelity. Thus the grief and fears of the good, lest this gigantic war should arrest the religious training

---

[33] Arthur Howard Noll, ed., *Doctor Quintard, Chaplain CSA* (Sewanee TN: The University Press, 1905) 96.

[34] Henry Steele Commager, ed., *The Blue and the Gray*, vol. 1 (Indianapolis: The Bobbs Merrill Company, 1950) 302.

[35] Jones, *Christ in the Camp*, 390.

[36] Ibid., 463.

of the whole youth of the land, cut off the supply of young preachers for its pulpits, and rear up for the country a generation of men profane and unchristian, were happily consoled; they accepted this new marvel, of *an army made the home and source of the religious life of a nation....*[37]

Not since the Great Awakening under the Reverend George Whitefield, Dabney proposed, had there been a more imposing display of "the power of the truth" upon such a great congregation.[38] Most chaplains who left records agreed that it was the most amazing display of spiritual power ever witnessed among fighting men on the American continent.[39]

---

[37] Dabney, *Life and Campaigns of Lt. Gen. Thomas J. Jackson*, 657.

[38] Ibid., 649.

[39] Charles Pitts, *Chaplains in Gray* (Nashville: Broadman Press, 1957) 2; W. W. Bennett, *A Narrative of The Great Revival Which Prevailed in the Southern Armies* (Philadelphia: Claxton, Remsen and Haffelfinger, 1877) 365–66.

Memoirs, 1862-1863

Chaplain J. William Jones
13th Virginia Infantry,
Army of Northern Virginia

John William Jones was born at Louisa Court House, Virginia, on 25 September 1836. He was educated at the University of Virginia and at the Southern Baptist Theological Seminary. He was ordained at Charlottesville in 1860 and accepted a call to be the pastor of the Little River Baptist Church in his home county.

In May of 1861 Jones enlisted as a private in the Confederate Army. A year later he was commissioned as chaplain for the 13th Virginia Infantry, and in 1863 as a Baptist missionary to Lieutenant General A. P. Hill's Corps.

In his ministry of three and a half years in the Army of Northern Virginia, Jones baptized 520 soldiers and preached in meetings that resulted in the conversion of at least 2,000. He documented much of the work of the revivals in the Confederate armies from 1862 to 1864.

Revivals in the Lower Valley and around Fredericksburg

Even in the brief season of comparative quiet which we enjoyed in the Lower Valley of Virginia, after our return from the first Maryland campaign, developed very decided indications of revivals in a number of the brigades.[1]

So far as I have been able to learn, the first revival of much interest which occurred in the army at this time was in Trimble's Brigade, and especially in the Twelfth and Forty-fourth Georgia Regiments.[2] Rev. A. M. Marshall, who had been a gallant private in the Twelfth Georgia, had been a

---

[1] In the Shenandoah Valley and parts of Northern Virginia after the Antietam Campaign. See also W. W. Bennett, *The Great Revival in the Confederate Armies* (Harrison VA: Sprinkle Publications, 1976) 204.

[2] In "Stonewall" Jackson's Second Corps.

short time before commissioned chaplain in his regiment, and, like other chaplains promoted from the ranks, proved himself as faithful in the chaplaincy as he had been as a soldier.

As soon as the army went into camp, near Bunker Hill, in the Lower Valley of Virginia, Mr. Marshall began a series of special services, which at once developed decided interest. He called Rev. James Nelson, of the Forty-fourth Virginia, and myself to his aid, and was especially fortunate in having Dr. Joseph C. Stiles, who was then preaching in Lawton's Georgia Brigade, to preach for him once every day. Large crowds attended the meetings, numbers presented themselves for prayer, there were a number of professions of conversion, and the work had developed into a revival of increasing power, when it was interrupted by the active campaign which culminated in the great victory of First Fredericksburg.

Dr. Stiles thus wrote of his labors at this time:

"At his earnest request, I preached to General Pryor's Brigade last Sabbath. Upon one hour's notice, he marched up 1,500 men, who listened with so much interest to a long sermon that I was not surprised to hear of such a beginning of religious interest in various regiments of the brigade as issued in a half-way promise on my part to fall in with the proposal of the general to preach very early to his soldiers for a succession of nights. In General Lawton's Brigade there is a more decided state of religious excitement. The great body of the soldiers in some of the regiments meet for prayer and exhortation every night, exhibit the deepest solemnity, and present themselves numerously for the prayers of the chaplains and the Church. Quite a number express hope in Christ. In all other portions of Early's Division a similar religious sensibility prevails.

"In General Trimble's, and the immediately neighboring brigades, there is in progress, at this hour, one of the most glorious revivals I ever witnessed. Some days ago a young chaplain took a long ride to solicit my co-operation, stating that a promising seriousness had sprung up within their diocese. I have now been with him three days and nights, preaching and laboring constantly with the soldiers when not on drill.

"The audiences and the interest have grown to glorious dimensions. It would rejoice you over-deeply to glance for one instant on our night-meeting in the wildwoods, under a full moon, aided by the light of our side-stands. You would behold a mass of men seated on the earth all around you (I was going to say for the space of half an acre), fringed in all its circumference by a line of standing officers and soldiers—two or three deep—all exhibiting the most solemn and respectful earnestness that a Christian assembly ever displayed. An officer said to me, last night, on returning from worship, he never had witnessed such a scene, though a Presbyterian elder; especially such an abiding solemnity and delight in the services as prevented all whisperings in the outskirts, leaving of the congregation, or restless changes of position.

"I suppose at the close of the service we had about sixty or seventy men and officers come forward and publicly solicit an interest in our prayers, and there may have been as many more who, from the press, could not reach the stand. I have already conversed with quite a number, who seem to give pleasant evidence of return to God, and all things seem to be rapidly developing for the best.

"The officers, especially Generals Jackson and Early, have modified military rules for our accommodation. I have just learned that General A. P. Hill's Division enjoys as rich a dispensation of God's Spirit as General Early's. In General Pickett's Division, also, there are said to be revivals of religion."

In 1865 Reverend Jones became the pastor of the Goshen and Lexington Baptist churches in the Shenandoah Valley. He also served as one of the chaplains at Washington College during the presidency of Robert E. Lee and held prayer meetings at neighboring Virginia Military Institute.

Beginning in 1874 Reverend Jones began writing biographies of Generals Robert E. Lee and Stonewall Jackson as well as a history of the revivals in the Confederate Army, published under the title, Christ in the Camp. *That same year Washington and Lee University conferred upon him the Doctor of Divinity degree. Dr. Jones then became the secretary of the Southern Historical Society and editor of their monthly paper. He died in 1909, still a passionate witness to the presence of the Holy Spirit in the great revivals of his time.*

"By the aid of the Spirit they preached with power..."

Chaplain Asa M. Marshall
12th Georgia Infantry Regiment, Doles's Brigade,
Army of Northern Virginia

Asa Monroe Marshall was born 26 December 1832 in Jones County, Georgia. He enlisted as a private in Company G, "The Putnam Light Infantry," of the 12th Georgia Infantry Regiment at Eatonton, Georgia, on 15 June 1861. He was wounded at Alleghany, Virginia, in December of 1861. He was commissioned chaplain of the 12th Georgia Infantry in the fall of 1862 and served in that capacity during the Antietam, Chancellorsville, and Gettysburg campaigns. Marshall was one of three Baptist chaplains who began the Great Revival in the Army of Northern Virginia in the fall of 1862. In December, 1863 he was wounded again and resigned his commission to return to Putnam County.

Letter from the Reverend Asa M. Marshall, Pastor of the Eatonton Baptist Church, Eatonton, Georgia, to the Reverend J. William Jones, former chaplain of the 13th Virginia Infantry Regiment, Army of Northern Virginia:[3]

Eatonton, Georgia, March 22, 1867

Dear Brother Jones: I was, as you know, chaplain Twelfth Georgia Regiment, Doles' Brigade, but did not get my appointment until just before the battle of Sharpsburg.[4] As soon as the army crossed back on the Virginia side, I commenced a meeting in the regiment, which increased in interest until several regiments and battalions became interested. I called to my assistance Dr. Stiles, Brother Nelson and yourself.[5] The meeting was one of

---

[3] J. William Jones, *Christ in the Camp or Religion in the Confederate Army* (Harrisonburg VA: Sprinkle Publications, 1986) 506–507.

[4] At the Battle of Antietam (or Sharpsburg) the 12th Georgia Infantry was part of Trimble's brigade, Ewell's division, in Lt. Gen. "Stonewall" Jackson's Second Corps. In 1863 the 12th Georgia became part of Brig. Gen. George Doles's brigade in Rodes's division of the Second Corps, commanded by Lt. Gen. Richard Ewell at Gettysburg.

[5] Rev. Dr. Joseph C. Stiles, Presbyterian evangelist in the army; Rev. James Nelson, Baptist chaplain of the Second Corps Artillery; and Rev. J. William Jones, Baptist chaplain of the 13th Virginia Infantry. These four preachers, including Chaplain Marshall of the 12th Georgia, were instrumental in beginning the "Great Revival" in the Army of Northern Virginia in 1862–1864, which they credited not to one another but to the intervention of the Holy Spirit in the lives of soldiers.

great interest, and promised to result in many conversions, but was suddenly broken up one night by the order to get ready to move. General Jackson attended this meeting several times, and remarked after hearing Dr. Stiles preach one night, that he was 'more convinced than ever, that if sinners had justice they would all be damned.'[6]

There was no opportunity given for persons to join the Church; but there was every reason to suppose that a number were converted. This was one of the first revivals of religion that I heard of in the army. And I learned at that meeting *how* to conduct services in camp. I was for a long time the only chaplain in Doles' Brigade, and on that account had a great deal to do. I never kept any account of the number of sermons I preached, nor of prayer meetings. It was our practice to hold prayer meetings every night when in camp, and frequently of a night when on the march. We had Bible-classes composed, I think, of men in all the regiments of the brigade—Twelfth, Fourth, Twenty-first and Forty-fourth, Georgia. I supplied these regiments as well as I could with Testaments, religious papers and tracts, but have no idea how many were distributed.

The most remarkable revivals in this brigade were at Guinea's Station, Orange Court House, and Morton's Ford. The first was during the winter of 1862, and the others during the summer of 1863.

At Orange Court House we made such arrangements as would accommodate the whole brigade, and I wrote to Brother Geo. B. Taylor,[7] who came and preached very acceptably for several days; other brothers preached frequently, and the meeting increased in interest until we moved to Morton's Ford. I think there were twenty-five or thirty conversions in the meeting. At the ford the meeting was more interesting than before. Here I was assisted by Brother A. T. Spalding of Alabama, and W. N. Chaudoin, of Georgia.[8] These brethren did most of the preaching, and by the aid of the Spirit they preached with power. There were forty or fifty conversions in this meeting.

---

[6] Lt. Gen. "Stonewall" Jackson as cited in Jones, *Christ in the Camp*, 506.

[7] George B. Taylor (1832–1907), Baptist chaplain of the 25th Virginia Infantry Regiment.

[8] Rev. Albert Theodore Spalding, pastor of the Baptist church in Selma AL, and in 1871, pastor of the Second Baptist Church in Atlanta GA, and the Rev. William Nowell Chaudoin, pastor and missionary to the Army, later in 1872 a member of the Southern Baptist Convention's Domestic Mission Board in Florida.

As far as I am able to judge, those who professed religion in the army are as sincere as those who professed at home. Of the officers of the Twelfth Georgia, it affords me pleasure to speak of Colonel Willis,[9] who always rendered me every assistance he could, and gave every encouragement to the men to attend meeting. He was one of the best officers in the army, one of the best friends I ever had, one of the most promising men I ever knew. He was killed while in command of Early's old brigade, at Bethesda Church, in June, 1864. His earnest request was, that if he was ever wounded he wanted the surgeon to tell him his true condition. Dr. Ethridge told him that he was mortally wounded. He said: ' I am no more afraid to die than I am to fight for my country.' Lieutenant-Colonel Hardeman, Major Carson and Dr. Ethridge,[10] were all professors of religion, and were always ready to do all they could for the cause of Christ. There were several captains and subordinate officers of whom I would like to speak if I had time.

I am yours, etc., A. M. Marshall

In the winter of 1863, Chaplain Marshall returned to his home at Rudden in Putnam County, Georgia. For the next fifty years Reverend Marshall ministered to the people of three congregations, as pastor of the Eatonton, Harmony, and Ramoth Baptist churches. His wife was often ill, but together they raised seven children, five to adulthood. He was elected chaplain of the Doles-Cook Brigade Survivors Association at their meeting in Macon, Georgia, in September of 1900 and attended numerous Confederate veterans' meetings throughout the state. The Reverend Asa M. Marshall died on 7 October 1914, after a ministry of fifty-five years, and was buried next to his wife, Rebecca, in the Harmony Baptist Church cemetery in Putnam County.

---

[9] Col. Edward Willis, 12th Georgia Infantry Regiment. He died of wounds suffered during the fighting at the North Anna River near Richmond.

[10] Lt. Col. Isaac Hardeman, formerly of Company B, 12th Georgia Infantry, was captured at Spotsylvania VA on 10 May 1864, and released by Federal authorities from Ft. Delaware prison camp on 24 July 1865; Maj. John T. Carson died on 30 September 1864 of wounds received at Winchester VA; 1st Lt. James A. Ethridge was appointed assistant surgeon on 1 March 1862, wounded at McDowell VA, seven days later, and recovered sufficiently to be appointed surgeon on 15 May 1862.

"The Lord poured out His Spirit..."

Chaplain John James Hyman
49th Georgia Infantry Regiment,
Army of Northern Virginia

John James Hyman enlisted at age twenty-nine as a private in Company I of the 49th Georgia Infantry, " The Pierce Guards," in Hancock County, Georgia, on 4 March 1862. His family had moved to Hancock County from North Carolina sometime prior to 1850. A devout Baptist, he was commissioned as the chaplain of his regiment on 5 July 1862, with a retroactive date of rank of 1 May in the same year. He served as chaplain of the 49th Georgia Infantry during the Peninsula, Fredericksburg, Chancellorsville, Gettysburg, and Petersburg campaigns. On 30 October 1864, while at Petersburg, he was granted a furlough by General Robert E. Lee. He rejoined his unit and was present at the surrender of the Army of Northern Virginia at Appomattox Court House on 9 April 1865. Chaplain Hyman's memoir, written in 1867, is focused on his evangelistic work from December of 1862 until April of 1865.

I left my home on the 10th day of March, 1862; joined the Forty-ninth Georgia Regiment as a private soldier on the 1st day of May. I was commissioned chaplain of the Forty-ninth Georgia Regiment. The battles around Richmond prevented us from having regular Divine service. After the battles were over, the Forty-ninth Georgia Regiment was attached to General J. R. Anderson's Brigade, afterwards General E. L. Thomas's.[11] At this time I was the only chaplain in the brigade (four regiments). I, being young, knew but little about the duties of a chaplain, but was willing to do anything in my Master's cause. Being in the command of General Jackson, we had but little time for religious service during the whole of 1862.[12] On the 16th of December, 1862, we went into quarters at Camp Gregg, six miles south of Fredericksburg, Virginia, where I opened regular night service; sometimes in the open air, at other times (when the weather was

---

[11] Brig. Gen. Joseph Reid Anderson (1813–1892), a West Point graduate, was wounded in the Seven Days' fighting near Richmond in 1862; Brig. Gen. Edward L. Thomas (1825–1898), a graduate of Emory College, Oxford GA, was wounded in 1862 at Mechanicsville VA, but recovered to command the brigade at Gettysburg.

[12] Lt. Gen. "Stonewall" Jackson (1824–1863).

bad) in tents. Congregations were very good; often I have seen large numbers leave the door of the tent, being unable to get in, when the snow was all over the ground. Finding that we had gone into winter-quarters, I commenced preaching regularly three times a week to each regiment in the brigade. About the 1st of February, 1863, the good Lord poured out His Spirit upon us; hundreds were seeking the Lord for pardon of sins; almost daily there were some going down into the water, being buried with Christ in baptism. At this time our brigade was so scattered that I had to preach to each regiment separately; the interest was so great that I preached for weeks from four to six times in a day. Just as I was about to break down, Brother E. B. Barrett came from Georgia as a missionary and gave me much assistance.[13] He joined himself to the Forty-fifth Georgia Regiment as chaplain, and at once entered upon the faithful discharge of his duties; about the same time Brother A. W. Moore came on as chaplain of the Fourteenth Georgia Regiment.[14] The battle of Chancellorsville broke into our service for a few days; when we went back into camp Brother Moore left for Georgia, leaving Brother Barrett and myself in the brigade. We preached night and day, baptizing daily in a pool we prepared for the purpose.

In the month of May, 1863, I divided my labors with Thomas's and Wright's Georgia Brigades.[15] I baptized during the month fifteen in Forty-ninth Georgia and sixty-five in Wright's Brigade. The day that the army was ordered to march on the Pennsylvania campaign, yes, while regiments were being ordered to fall in, I was baptizing near Wright's Brigade. Baptized forty-eight, all in twenty minutes. At another time, near the same place, Brother Marshall and I baptized twenty-six.[16] The long-roll being beat, we left our pleasant camp; was in active campaign until about the 1st of August, when we camped near Orange Court House. Here again we met in Christ's name and He met with us. Never before have I seen the like; often we would meet in worship, having only the dim candle-light; hundreds would be there. When the invitation was given for prayers there would come so many I knew not what to do with them. At this time Brother Barrett was at home,

---

[13] Edward Benjamin Barrett, Baptist chaplain of the 45th Georgia Infantry.

[14] Alexander W. Moore, Methodist chaplain of the 14th Georgia Infantry from 5 August 1862, later appointed post chaplain for Greenville SC.

[15] Brig. Gen. A. R. Wright's brigade, in Maj. Gen. R. H. Anderson's division, was composed of the 3rd, 22nd, and 48th Georgia infantry regiments and the 2nd Georgia Infantry Battalion.

[16] Asa M. Marshall, Baptist chaplain of the 12th Georgia Infantry Regiment.

but Brother Moore was present. I did all of the preaching that I could. At this time kept my command supplied with tracts, papers, etc.

In August and September I spent some time with General Walker's Virginia Brigade, where souls were being converted.[17] On one occasion, in August, 1863, I went down to Rapidan river with Brother Anderson, chaplain in General Walker's Virginia Brigade, to baptize.[18] We met about 2,000 soldiers, besides many citizens. He (Brother Anderson) went down into the water and baptized twelve. After he came out I opened service in our usual way by singing and prayer. Such music I never before heard. It sounded as though the heavenly host had come down to take part in our earthly worship. I went down into the water and baptized twenty-three. This state of feeling continued with but little change until about the 1st of December, 1863, at which time Thomas's Brigade was ordered to the Valley, below Staunton, Virginia, where we were in active campaign during the whole of the winter. While in the Valley, Brother J. H. Taylor became chaplain of Thirty-fifth Georgia Regiment; Brother Moore resigned as chaplain of Fourteenth Georgia Regiment.[19]

About the 1st of April, 1864, we left the Valley and returned to Orange Court House. Just as we had arranged for and were having regular Divine service the battle-cry was again heard and we hurried off to meet the enemy. We halted not until we stopped near Petersburg, Virginia.

During the months of July and August, 1864, our meetings were truly interesting. I was the only chaplain present in our brigade, preaching both night and day; I visited almost daily Scales's North Carolina Brigade,[20] also Third and Fourth Virginia Regiments, preaching as I went, seemingly with much effect. I preached from three to five times per day all during July and August, besides baptizing almost daily. The labors of these months broke me down and I was forced to leave my command on sick furlough. From this time I was not of much service to the brigade until winter. During my absence the prayer-meetings were kept up by the private members.

---

[17] Brig. Gen. James A. Walker's brigade was composed of the 2nd, 4th, 5th, 27th, and 33rd Virginia infantry regiments and was also known as "The Stonewall Brigade" from its stand at First Manassas.

[18] James Madison Anderson (1837–1906), Methodist, later chaplain of the 40th Virginia Infantry Regiment.

[19] John H. Taylor, Baptist chaplain of the 35th Georgia Infantry Regiment.

[20] Brig. Gen. Alfred M. Scales, later governor of North Carolina, commanded five North Carolina regiments: the 13th, 16th, 22nd, 34th, and 38th.

February, 1865, we built us a large chapel near the line of works around Petersburg. We organized a Sabbath-school of 120 pupils. At this time religious services were truly interesting. We baptized a great many. From here we marched on the 2d of April, 1865, leaving our beautiful camp behind. We halted at Appomattox Court House, Virginia, and 'yielded to overwhelming numbers and resources.'

Here I leave the field of blood (ever looking back upon many sacred spots where the Lord blessed us) with mingled grief and joy. I baptized while in the army 238 soldiers. Number professing conversion, 500. Preached about 500 sermons, besides exhortations, lectures, etc.

Yours fraternally, John J. Hyman

After the war, Chaplain Hyman returned to Georgia to serve as Principal of the Mount Vernon Institute in Riddleville and eventually as moderator of the Mount Vernon Baptist Association. One of his colleagues in the Army of Northern Virginia wrote that Hyman "was one of the most laborious, self-denying, and successful Chaplains in the army, and he probably preached as many sermons, baptized as many men, and accomplished as much good as any other chaplain during his period of service."[21] John J. Hyman died in 1906.

Chaplain Robert L. Dabney
18th Virginia Infantry and Assistant Adjutant General,
Lieutenant General "Stonewall" Jackson's Staff,
Valley District of Northern Virginia

Robert Lewis Dabney was born in Louisa County, Virginia, on 5 March 1820. He was educated at Hampden Sidney College, the University of Virginia, and Union Theological Seminary in Richmond. From 1853 to 1883 Professor Dabney taught at Union Theological Seminary and Hampden-Sidney College. Even though he initially opposed secession, he accepted a commission as the chaplain for the 18th Virginia Infantry in 1861. In 1862 he was invited by Lieutenant General "Stonewall" Jackson to accept the position of assistant adjutant general on his staff with the rank of major. In this position Dabney functioned as Jackson's chief of staff for the Valley Campaign of 1862. His account of the organization of

---

[21] Jones, *Christ in the Camp*, 375.

religious work in Jackson's command pays high tribute to the personal initiative and Christian commitment of his commanding general.

On the first of March, Rev. Mr. Lacy, a minister of the Presbyterian church, came on General Jackson's invitation, to his headquarters.[22] The Government, after a time, commissioned him as an army chaplain, without assigning him to a particular regiment; an exceptional act of courtesy accorded to General Jackson's high character and express request. In his letter to his other friends, General Jackson had modestly expressed his inexperience of ecclesiastical affairs, and his intention to commit the details of the plan of evangelical labors in the army to the advice of the clergyman, after Mr. Lacy had examined his ground.

His objects were three: to supply regiments destitute of chaplains with a partial substitute in the shape of the itinerant labors of efficient ministers; to supply a channel of intercourse between the army and the bodies of clergy of different denominations, through which the latter might learn the wants of the former, and to give to the labors of the chaplains and other ministers in the army, the unity and impulse of an ecclesiastical organization within their own peculiar field. His chaplain was intended by him to be an exemplar, who, he hoped, would be followed by many others from among the most efficient preachers of all churches, until they should be brought into vital sympathy with the army.

One of the measures adopted was the preaching of the gospel at the head-quarters of General Jackson, and under his immediate countenance, every Sabbath, while the troops were in their camps. For this end, a place in the open field was prepared, near Hamilton's crossing, (to which General Jackson removed his quarters soon after), with rude seats and a temporary pulpit, where public worship was held in the open air. The example of so famous a warrior, always potent among soldiers when sustained by official rank, the curiosity to see him and the galaxy of celebrities who came to worship with him, the eloquence of the preachers, and the purer motives which the great religious-awakening now began to propagate far and wide, soon drew a vast congregation to this spot on the Sabbath days. From hundreds it grew to thousands, until the assemblage surrounded the preacher in a compact mass, as far as his voice could be distinctly heard.

---

[22] R. L. Dabney, *Life and Campaigns of Lt. Gen. Thomas J. Jackson* (Harrisonburg VA: Sprinkle Publications, 1983) 648. Chaplain Beverly Tucker Lacy (1819–1900) was Jackson's pastor and corps chaplain.

Here, on a bright Sabbath in the spring, might be seen the stately head of the Commander-in-Chief,[23] with a crowd of Generals, whose names had been borne by fame across the ocean, and of legislators and statesmen, bowed along with the multitude of private soldiers, in divine worship; while the solemn and tender wave of sacred emotion subdued the great and the unknown alike before it. At these scenes, which were so directly produced by his instrumentality, General Jackson was the most unobtrusive assistant. Seated in some retired spot amidst the private soldiers, he listened to the worship and the preaching with an edifying attention, and watched the power of the truth upon the great congregation, with a glow of elevated and tender delight. Never, since the days when Whitefield preached to the mingled crows of peers and beggars in Moorfields, has the sky looked down upon a more imposing worship.[24]

Another enterprise which marked the evangelical labors of this winter was the building of temporary chapels by the men for their own worship. Two or three contiguous regiments usually concurred in the work. Tall trees were cut down, and brought to the spot by the teams of the Quartermasters, and build into walls of logs. Chimneys were built of the same rude material, and plastered with clay, whence the huge fires, and the torches of resinous pine, diffused a ruddy glow of warmth and light. The structure was roofed with clapboards and seated with rude benches formed from the split bodies of trees. The Stonewall Brigade was the first to begin this work, to General Jackson's great delight. No sooner had they completed their own huts, than they set to work, and by a multitude of willing hands, completed their church in a few days. The next Sabbath it was formally dedicated to the worship of God; and during the winter, was constantly occupied in turn by the chaplains of the several regiments. During the week, frequent meetings for prayer, and bible [sic] classes, were held here by torchlight, and the men were encouraged to expend their leisure in the study of the scriptures, and in sacred music, instead of the degrading amusements of the card-table. As this chapel was near the quarters of General Jackson, he often came to worship in it with his favorite brigade. Instead of affecting the chief seat in the synagogue, he delighted to sit among the rough, weather-beaten privates, and lay aside all official dignity to accompany them to the throne of grace on the common footing of worshippers. Their reverence for

---

[23] Gen. Robert E. Lee.
[24] Rev. George Whitefield (1714–1770) set up a chapel in Moorfields near Bristol, England, in 1741, as a focal point for his evangelical preaching.

his person sometimes led them to leave a respectful distance between themselves and the seat he occupied; but he would never consent that any space should be thus lost, where so many were crowding to hear the word. As he saw them seeking seats elsewhere, he was accustomed to rise, and invite them by gesture to the vacancies near him; and was never so well satisfied as when he had an unkempt soldier touching his elbow on either hand, and all the room about him compactly filled. Then he was ready to address himself with usual fixed attention to the services.

The most important measure which he introduced was the weekly chaplains' meeting. This was temporary association of all the chaplains and evangelists of his *corps*, who, on meeting, appointed one of their own number to preside as a chairman or moderator, and another as their secretary, and after joining in public worship, proceeded to consult upon the spiritual interests of their charges, to arrange and concert their labors, and to devise means for supplying the destitutions of the army. These counsels were a true evangelical union. By a common and silent consent, which bears high testimony to the cultivation and honor of these laborious men, all subjects of sectarian debate, were effectually excluded, and their deliberations were confined to the interests of our common Christianity. But it was also a high evidence of the general soundness of religious opinion in the Confederate States, that there was not a single regiment in the army, which showed a disposition to introduce a minister who did not belong to an evangelical and orthodox communion, as their chaplain, except one or two priests of the Romish Church. On the other hand, the office in the Federal army was as frequently filled by Universalists, and other erratic heretics, or by laymen who never preached, as by regular ministers of the gospel....

The stated meetings of the chaplains were the means of awakening them to a greatly increased zeal and fidelity, as well as for adding system and concert to their labors. So that this service, which, while adorned by the fidelity of a number of truly apostolic men, had yet fallen, in general, into no little disfavor, was now thoroughly renovated. Thus the energy of General Jackson's will, though so modestly exerted, made itself felt among his chaplains, just as among his staff and field officers, in communicating efficiency and vigor to all their performance of duty.

The Government had never made any provision for the support of the chaplains in their work, other than a very inadequate salary. The General now applied to the Military Committee of Congress, to bring in a law enabling Quartermasters to provide chaplains, like other officers, with tents, fuel, and forage for horses. This just measure was indeed neglected amidst the hurry of the closing session, but was finally adopted by a subsequent Congress....

One more favorite project remains to be mentioned, in which about this time, he sought to interest those who met him. This was the establishment of a Christian Daily Newspaper, which should honor God by refraining from all Sabbath work. He argued that their issue of Monday should contain nothing printed after Saturday evening; and that Christians should be willing to receive their news later by one day, once during the week, in order to honor God's law. If this delay should diminish the circulation of such a journal, and make it less remunerative than others, he declared that he was willing to repay a part of this loss out of his own means.

As soon as his quarters were established at Hamilton's Crossing, he began the custom of regular domestic worship in his mess, each morning.[25] These services were willingly attended by all his staff, out of respect for his Christian character, or from their own interest in them. He, who was of all men least obtrusive in his religion, carefully forbore from commanding their attendance, although his beaming face indicated plainly enough the pleasure he felt in seeing them present. Whenever his chaplain was not there, he always conducted these services himself, with his customary unction and humility. On Wednesday and Sunday nights, there was also a prayer meeting observed at his quarters, where he was always a worshipper, and led the devotions of his brethren, when desired to do so by a minister. A few of the young men upon his Staff had cultivated the delightful art of sacred music. On the afternoon of the Sabbaths, when the necessary business, which he always reduced within the narrowest limits, was dispatched, it was his favorite occupation to have singing; and frequently, as the little choir was concluding, he said; "Now let us have the hymn;"

"How happy are they
Who their Saviour obey."

On every intelligent Christian who approached him at this time, he made the impressions of the most eminent sanctity. They all left him with this testimony: that he was the holiest man they had ever seen. The effort thus begun in General Jackson's *corps*, was imitated in the others. The movement was not limited to the army of Virginia; but was also propagated in the South and West. Soon the General Assembly of the Presbyterian

---

[25] Hamilton's Crossing was just southeast of Fredericksburg VA.

Church, and the other ecclesiastical authorities, encouraged by the advice which the friends of General Jackson were permitted to quote from him, began to take action on behalf of the army; and a number of the most distinguished ministers were sent to the different *corps* to labor with the chaplains as itinerants, and to communicate the wants of the army to the churches. The speedy fall of the originator of the work rather gave new *impetus* to it, than retarded it; and the result was, that general revival of religion in the Confederate armies, which has been even more astonishing to the world, than the herculean exertions of the Confederate States. A wide-spread reform of morals was wrought which was obvious to every spectator, in the repressions of profanity and drunkenness, the increase of order and discipline, and the good conduct of the troops in battle. It was just those commands in which this work of grace was most powerful, that became the most trustworthy in the post of danger. The brigade of Barksdale, for instance, which had held its ground in Fredericksburg with almost incredible resolution under the great bombardment, was equally noted for its religious zeal. Returning to their post of honor in the city, they occupied one of the deserted churches as their chapel, and maintained a constant series of nightly meetings, attended by numerous conversions, for many weeks. In short, the conversions in the various Confederate armies within the ensuing year were counted, by the most sober estimate, at twelve thousand men. The strange spectacle was now presented, of a people among whom the active religious life seemed to be transferred from the churches at home—the customary seats of piety—to the army; which, among other nations, has always been dreaded as the school of vice and infidelity. Thus, the grief and fears of the good, lest this gigantic war should arrest the religious training of the whole youth of the land, cut off the supply of young preachers for its pulpits, and rear up for the country a generation of men profane and unchristian, were happily consoled; they accepted this new marvel, of an army made the home and source of the religious life of a nation, with grateful joy, as another evidence of the favor of God to the afflicted people.

After the war Professor Dabney taught philosophy at the University of Texas for eleven years and was instrumental in establishing the Austin School of Theology. His most famous historical work, The Life and Campaigns of Lt. Gen. Thomas J. Jackson, (Stonewall Jackson) *was published in 1866. In 1870 he was elected moderator of the General Assembly of the Presbyterian Church in the United States. Dabney wrote seven other books on theology and philosophy before becoming blind in 1890. In spite of his disability, he continued to lecture on Christology in Texas and in the Carolinas until the fall of 1897. He died in Victoria, Texas, on 3 January 1898, at the age of seventy-eight.*

Fast Day Sermon

Chaplain Isaac T. Tichenor
17th Alabama Infantry

After the Confederate defeats at Vicksburg and at Gettysburg, President Jefferson Davis proclaimed 21 August 1863 a day of fasting for the people and churches of the Confederacy. The Reverend Isaac Tichenor, pastor of the First Baptist Church in Montgomery, Alabama, was asked to preach the Fast-Day sermon for the Alabama Legislature. His sermon was later published by resolution of that body. In this sermon Tichenor reminded the legislators of God's sovereignty and also chastised slave owners for their mistreatment of slaves.

Fast-Day Sermon
By Rev. I. T. Tichenor, Pastor of the First Baptist Church of Montgomery
August 21, 1863

> *"He maketh wars to cease unto the end of the earth; He breaketh the bow and cutteth the spear in sunder; he burneth the chariot in the fire." Psalms 46; 9th verse*[26]

"When shall we have peace?" Two weary years of war have wrung this question from the agonized heart of our bleeding country. "Oh! that we could have peace," exclaims the statesman, as he ponders the problems which demand solution at his hands.

"Peace!" sighs the soldier, as he wraps his blanket around him and lies down to sleep upon the open field.

"Peace!" moans the widow as she reads the sad intelligence of her husband fallen on some bloody field, and bitterly thinks of the future in store for herself and her orphaned children. The prayer of the land is for

---

[26] Isaac Taylor Tichenor, diary and unpublished papers, microfilm #0336, Southern Baptist Historical Library and Archives, Nashville TN.

peace. You may hear it in the sanctuary, at the fireside, around the family altar, in the silent chamber on the tented field. *When will it come?*

I propose to respond to this inquiry today, and to tell you when peace will come. In attempting this task, it would be manifest folly to pretend to penetrate the future, or to claim superior wisdom in state affairs. I have no cabinet secrets to disclose, no prophetic visions to announce, no revelation to make. I have only to tell you, and to insist upon the truth of the declaration that God alone can give us peace, for "He maketh wars to cease unto the end of the earth; He breaketh the bow, and cutteth the spear in sunder; He burneth the chariot in the fire."

The continuance of this war does not depend upon the result of battles, upon the skill of our generals, the valor of our soldiers, the wisdom of our statesmen, the resources of our country, or the mad determination of our foes; but *upon the will of our God.* He who hath said "the wrath of man shall praise Him, and the remainder of wrath He will restrain," will give us peace when we are prepared to receive it.[27] If any one here today hesitates to adopt this opinion, I ask his patient attention to the argument by which I shall seek to establish its truth.

I. *God governs the world.* No truth is more plainly taught in His word. "The Lord reigneth; let the earth rejoice; let the multitude of isles be glad thereof," is the language of inspiration.[28] The Savior teaches us a most beautiful and impressive lesson on this subject. When urging His disciples to place an unfaltering trust in the protection and providence of God, He says, "Consider the lilies of the field, how they grow; they toil not, neither do they spin, yet I say unto you, Solomon, in all his glory was not arrayed like unto one of these. Wherefore, if God so clothe the grass of the field, which today is, and tomorrow is cast into the oven, shall He not much more clothe you, oh ye of little faith?[29] Behold the fowls of the air, for they sow not, neither do they reap, nor gather unto barns, yet your Heavenly Father feedeth them."[30] "Are not two sparrows sold for a farthing, and one of them shall fall on the ground without your Father."[31] "The very hairs of your head

---

[27] Psalm 76:10. All scripture references in the sermon are to the King James Version.

[28] Psalm 97:1.

[29] Matthew 6:28–30.

[30] Matthew 6:26.

[31] Matthew 10:29.

are all numbered."[32] If God clothe the grass of the field with more than royal beauty, watch the sparrows fall, listen to the young raven's cry, number the hairs of our head, who can resist the conclusion that such a pervading presence and power governs the world?

The fulfilled prophecies of His word teach us the same lesson. Many of the predictions of Isaiah, Jeremiah, Ezekiel and Daniel have become history of the past. The minuteness with which they have been fulfilled forces upon us the conviction that He who inspired the prophecy rules the world. Jerusalem sitting in her lonely and desolate widowhood, Tyre, upon whose bald rocks the fisherman spreads his net, Babylon and Nineveh, mothers of empires, lying entombed in the reins of their former greatness; Edom, in whose stronghold reign perpetual desolation, are witnesses that rise up from the "dim and shadowy past," to testify to us that God reigns over the earth!

God has declared in His word, that He will give His Son the dominion of the world. "He will overturn, overturn, overturn, until He shall come whose right it is, and He will give it to Him."[33] "Ask of me," says he, "and I will give you the heathen for thine inheritance, and the uttermost parts of the earth for thy possession."[34] If God exercised no directing, controlling, restraining power over the world, how could He pledge Himself to give it to His Son, or what confidence could be felt by that Son, or by His people, that the promise would ever be redeemed? If God be not the Sovereign Ruler of the universe, then the sacrifice of His Son may have been almost in vain; then the day of deliverance for which the earth "groans and travails in pain until now,"[35] may never come; then the rich promises of His word and the bright anticipations they have inspired, with reference to the coming glories of the Millennial Day, are not certainties of future years, but the chilling shadows of doubt spreads over all. Who that believes the Bible is true can adopt such a conclusion?

An opinion, the offspring rather of the heart than the intellect, has been adopted by some, which would deprive the world of its Ruler, and place all things under the control of nature. They seek to trace back all things to what they term natural causes; they attribute every event to natural laws. But these men only "darken counsel by words without knowledge."[36]

---

[32] Matthew 10:30.
[33] Ezekiel 21:27.
[34] Psalm 2:8.
[35] Romans 8:22.
[36] Job 38:2.

Laws of nature! What are they? Or how can they set to produce any result? Law is not and *cannot* be *an actor*. It is but a *rule* of action. Behind these laws, which are but principles of His government, there sits enthroned in inscrutable majesty the Power that moves and governs the world, and that Power is God. The literal import of our Savior's words is true, "God clothes the grass of the field."[37] God expands every leaf, opens every flower, breathes in every wind, sends the genial shower, fertilizes the earth, and

> "scatters plenty over a smiling land"—
> "Warms in the sun, refreshes in the breeze,
> Glows in the stars, and blossoms in the trees,
> Lives through all life, extends through all extent,
> Spreads undivided, operates unspent."

That religion, if such it may be called, which deifies nature, is worse than heathenism.

The nations of antiquity worshiped gods whom their imaginations invested with life and powers of action. They were believed to interest themselves in the affairs of men, and preside over the destinies of nations. They were worshiped under the idea that they had power to assist the suppliant. But the man who trusts to nature has a dull, blind, dead god, which can "neither see, nor hear, nor deliver."[38]

If God governs the world then His hand is in this war in which we are engaged. It matters not that the wickedness of man brought it upon us, that it was caused by the mad attempts of fanaticism to deprive us of our rights, overthrow our institutions, and impose upon us a yoke which, as freemen, we had resolved *never to bear*. This fact is by no means inconsistent with the truth asserted. Speaking of the crucifixion of the Son of God, Peter says: "Him being delivered by the determinate counsel and fore-knowledge of God, ye have taken, and by wicked hands have crucified and slain."[39] God avows himself the author of calamities that befall nations. "Shall there be evil in a city" (evil in the sense of affliction,) and the Lord hath not done it?"[40] "I make peace and create evil," says the Lord.[41] "Come, behold the

---

[37] Matthew 6:30.
[38] Revelation 9:20.
[39] Acts 2:23.
[40] Amos 3:6.
[41] Isaiah 45:7.

works of the Lord," says the Psalmist, "what desolation He hath made in the earth."[42]

The eye of the Omniscient and the arm of the Almighty are over the earth. He makes these swelling waves of sinful pride and passion the tide on which rides the great ark of His mercy and his truth to that Ararat around which shall spread a new world, wherein dwelleth righteousness. "Revolutions never go backwards."[43] This sentiment was contained in the Bible long before it was clothed in his language by its author. Forward, along the track of ages, over the ruins of empires, steadily through scenes of revolution and blood, triumphing over the wickedness of men, and "making the wrath of man to praise Him,"[44] moves the grand design of Jehovah to its glorious consummation—that consummation which gives eternal peace and freedom to a regenerated world. While the storm cloud sweeps over our land, let us remember that God rides upon the wings of the tempest, and subjects it to His will.[45]

II. The Scriptures disclose two purposes for which God visits suffering upon the nations of the earth: first—punishment for sin. Second—development of national character and resources, so as to qualify a people for some high and holy mission which he designs to give them in charge.

On the first of these I need not enlarge. The Bible and the history of the world are too full of evidences of its truth to have permitted you to overlook it. The other, though not so apparent a truth, is as much a lesson of the past.

When God wanted a man for the Ruler of Egypt, that the patriarch and his family might find there a refuge from famine, He led Joseph to the seat of power, not with the pomp of princes, or the triumphs of a conqueror, but in the chains of a slave, and through the depths of a dungeon. When God wanted a king for Israel, "a man after his own heart,"[46] He brought David to the throne, through those long years of exile, when he was "hunted by Saul as a partridge upon the mountains."[47] In those dark and dreary days, David learned lessons of the wickedness of oppression, of the necessity of

---

[42] Psalm 46:8.

[43] Not scripture, but a quote from a speech by Wendell Phillips (1811–1884) given on 12 February 1861 in Boston. Phillips was a lawyer and a strong advocate for the abolition of slavery.

[44] Psalm 76:10.

[45] Psalm 104:3.

[46] Acts 13:22.

[47] 1 Samuel 26:20.

justice in a ruler, of sympathy with the suffering, which all the splendors of royalty, nor triumphs of his arms ever eradicated from his heart. When God gave the world a Savior, though it was His own Son, yet "learned He obedience by the things which He suffered,"[48] and the All-Wise "made the Captain of our salvation perfect, through suffering."[49] God's mercy gave His Son a ransom for guilty men, but God's wisdom brings them to His promised glory through "great tribulation."[50] One of the strangest announcements contained in the Bible, is made in God's promise to Abraham, "know of a surety that thy seed shall be a stranger in the land that is not theirs, and shall serve them, and they shall afflict them four hundred years, and also that nation whom they shall serve I will judge; and afterwards shall they come out with great substance."[51] This was said of those whom God had promised to make a blessing to all the nations of the earth. By slavery, the Israelites were elevated from the condition of wandering herdsmen to be nation possessed of all the arts and sciences known to the most civilized people of that day, and were fitted to receive the oracles of God, and be the light-bearers of the world.

One or both of these purposes God has in view in permitting the calamities of war to scourge this people. Peace will not come until His design shall have been fully accomplished. Taking this view of the subject, I ask are we *prepared for peace?* Have we yet repented of our sins and reformed our lives, so that God, as Judge of the nations, can turn away from us the rod of His anger?

One of the most crying of our national sins is the covetousness of our people. In the view of many, covetousness is associated only with extortion, niggardly avarice, or miserly practices[,] but the Savior teaches us a different doctrine. "Take heed," said He, "and beware of covetousness."[52] To enforce this doctrine He speaks a parable to His audience: "The ground of a certain rich man brought forth plentifully, and he thought within himself, saying, What shall I do because I have no room where to bestow my fruits? And he said, *this* will I do: I will pull down my barns and build greater, and there will I bestow all my fruits and my goods, and I will say to my soul, soul then has much goods laid up for many years, take thine ease, eat drink and be merry;

---

[48] Hebrews 5:8.
[49] Hebrews 2:10.
[50] Revelation 2:22.
[51] Genesis 15:13.
[52] Luke 12:15.

but God said unto him, Thou fool, this night shall thy soul be required of thee."[53]

Observe, my hearers, his riches were not the result of fraud or dishonesty. They were not obtained by some questionable speculation; nothing dishonest or dishonorable is laid to his charge. The blessing of God upon his labor the ample yield of his harvest brought him his abundance. His covetousness manifests itself not in the manner in which he obtained his wealth, but in the use he proposed to make of it. He had obtained his competency, and proposed to retire from business and enjoy the cool shadows of the evening life. Are no the vast majority of our people as obnoxious to the charge of covetousness as he? Nay, is not the man who indulges the purpose of ceasing to derive and toil for money regarded as an example of moderation by his fellow men? Yet this is the man selected by the Savior as an illustration of His meaning, and pronounced a fool by the Judge of the earth.

What change has the war produced on our people in this respect? Have we grown less covetous, less selfish, less grasping? Who does not know that it had developed a thirst for gain, a spirit of speculation and extortion which is the reproach of our land. Men have bought to monopolize articles of prime necessity, and by withholding them from market to enhance their price, and fatten themselves upon the sufferings of their country. They have attempted to coin into money the groans and tears of the wives and children of your soldiers, and of the widows and orphans of those who have died in freedom's holy cause.

If God chastises us for our covetousness, surely we are not yet prepared for the blessings of peace.

Another of our national sins has been our proud and boastful self-reliance. At the commencement of this struggle, we had a vain confidence in our national strength, we placed a high estimate on the valor of our people, and held in contempt the martial qualities of our foes. We expected no defeat; we thought nothing but victory awaited us. We confidently believed that our agricultural products in which the world is so largely interested, would bring us recognition by the nations of our earth, defeat the purpose of our enemies to blockade our coasts, and insure our independence. Cotton was our hope, enthroned the god of our confidence, and almost worshiped

---

[53] Luke 12:18.

as our national deliverer. Our trust has been disappointed, our idol has fallen like Dagon before the ark of the Lord.[54]

After two years of war, in which the sword has vindicated the justice of our claim, we have yet to receive the first hand of welcome to a place among the nations of the earth. Our ports have been blockaded in a manner contrary to the law of nations. Our enemies have been permitted to wage a brutal warfare against unarmed citizens and helpless women and children. Burning and plunder, and outrages of every character, even to the murder of helpless innocence, have marked the track of their vandal hordes. The *people* of the civilized world denounce the tyranny of Butler as atrocious to the last degree, but the *governments* of the world have uttered no word of remonstrance.[55] We have been shut up to the necessity of relying upon our own resources. "An appeal to arms, and to the God of Hosts, is all that is left us"!

It needs only the proper spirit on the part of our people to make this a blessing rather than an evil. The day is past when God will permit the nations of the earth to ignore Him. For centuries the governments of Christendom have been more godless, more atheistic than the heathen empires of antiquity. They consulted the will of their imaginary gods in affairs of state. Egypt, Babylon, Greece and Rome sent forth their thronging legions in obedience to the will of their gods, or refrained from their enterprises of conquest and blood when that will seemed averse. But nations professing to be Christians have made war for the most unholy purposes, and without the slightest reference to the will of Jehovah. Europe has again and again been deluged with blood by kings professing Christianity, when "God was not in all their thoughts." England made war upon China because she would not consent to be drugged and brutalized with her opium. The United States formed a Constitution, after a war in which God's hand had been almost as manifest in their deliverance as though He had led them with a pillar of cloud by day and a pillar of fire by night,[56] made no mention of the name of God, had no recognition of His existence. The times of this ignorance God may have winked at, but the day has come when He will vindicate His long ignored right as Sovereign of the world. It is an evidence

---

[54] 1 Samuel 5:3.

[55] Maj. Gen. Benjamin Franklin Butler (1818–1893), USA, commanded the Department of the Gulf in 1862. He was denounced by many in the South for insulting the women of New Orleans and for recruiting black soldiers.

[56] Exodus 13:21.

of His merciful designs towards us, that He is breaking down the bulwarks of self-confidence, and saying to us in thunder tones; "put not your trust in princes."[57] Are we ready to turn out hearts to Him? I fear we are not. When Vicksburg surrendered; and the campaign into Pennsylvania disappointed our hopes, what was the effect upon our people? There was universal gloom, despondency in the hearts of many, a feeling that all was lost with some; but was there more prayer, greater reliance on the Most High? As dangers thickened around us, was there a nearer approach to Him who can save by many or by few, and who can make the very successes of our foes the means of our triumph? Alas! we looked for these things in vain.

Other sins of our people demand consideration, and call for repentance, but time permits only to mention, not to dwell upon them. We have failed to discharge our duties to our slaves. I entertain no doubt that slavery is right, morally, socially, politically, religiously right. But there are abuses of it which ought to be corrected.

Marriage is a divine institution, and yet marriage exists among our slaves dependent upon the will of the master. "What God has joined together, let no man put asunder,"[58] yet this tie is subject to the passion, caprice or avarice of their owners. The law gives the husband and the father no protection in this relation. Nay, the remorseless creditor may avail himself of the power of the law to separate husband and wife, parent and child. This is an evil of no minor magnitude, and one which demands an immediate remedy.

Too little attention has been paid to their moral and religious culture. By their labor our fields have been made white with abundant harvests. The wealth they have produced has been spent with lavish hands, while scarcely a pittance has been given to furnish them with the Bread of Life.

It is a significant fact that those parts of our country which have suffered most, in the loss of property, have been the very localities where these abuses have been greatest.

We have sinned by abusing our liberties. In the extent and bitterness of party spirit once so rife in our land, in the choice of men to be our rulers, "availability" constituting the grand qualification for office, in the manner in which our popular elections have been conducted[,] pandering to the lowest passions and appetites of depraved humanity, to succeed in electing the

---

[57] Psalm 146:3.

[58] Traditional language from the wedding ceremony in the Episcopal Book of Common Prayer, Ephesians 5:31, Matthew 5:32.

candidates of our party; in our Sabbath-breaking, setting our business or our pleasures above the law of God. In all these ways we have sinned against the Most High. Until He shall see penitence in our hearts, and reformation in our lives, we cannot hope for the removal of the scourge, or for the dawning of the day of peace.

III. But it may be that God intends, but suffering, to purify, develop and elevate this people, and commit to their charge a mission for the world. This I firmly believe to be an end which He has in view.

We stand, in one respect, almost alone among the nations. They are a unit in their opposition to our social system. They have declared it the "sum of all villainies."[59] The very people with whom we were associated in the Government of the United States regarded us as their inferiors because involuntary servitude existed in our midst. When we sought to reason with them, they denounced the very authority from which we derived our arguments, and in the madness of their fanaticism, they demanded an "anti-slavery Constitution, an anti-slavery Bible and an anti-slavery God"!

That slavery is sanctioned by the Bible seems scarcely to admit of a doubt. Founded on the divine decree that "Canaan should be a servant of servants unto his brethren,"[60] existing in the days of the patriarch, twice spoken of in the ten commandments, with laws written in the New Testament for its regulation, it stands as an institution of God. The Apostle says of the man who opposes it, that he is "blinded with pride, and understands nothing, but is filled with a sickly appetite for disputations and contentions about words, whence arise envy, strife, reproaches, evil suspicion, violent collision of men whose mind is corrupted and who are destitute of the truth; who think that godliness is a gainful trade."[61] What a portraiture of modern abolitionists! The picture, in every feature, and lineament, and shade, is true to the very life. We cannot but believe that God will vindicate the honor of His word, the rectitude of His institution and the wisdom of His providence, by overwhelming these impious attempts to destroy what He has established, and will confound those men who seek to be more wise and more righteous than their Maker.

---

[59] Referring to slavery. In 1790, Rev. John Wesley wrote to William Wilberforce, a member of the British Parliament, that slavery in America was an "execrable villany." See Umphrey Lee, *The Lord's Horseman* (Nashville: Abingdon Press, 1954) 212.

[60] Genesis 9:25.

[61] 1 Timothy 6:4.

For this purpose He has cut us off from all political association with them, and held us back from all entangling alliances with other nations, so that guided by His hand we may rise up to future greatness, and show to the world in all coming time that God was right when He instituted slavery among men; that it is the best form of human society, that it consists with the true happiness of both master and servant, that in it He has solved the great problem which had baffled the wisdom of man—reconciled the long conflict of capital and labor, thus giving social order and peace to the world, never again to be disturbed by the insane fanaticism of men. For such a mission I confidently believe God is preparing us. This preparation requires purity among our people; a proper understanding and regard for the rights of both master and servant, confidence in Him as our God, and above all a desire not so much for national glory as for the honor of God and the good of our race. Not yet I fear are we prepared for so great a distinction. God grant that we soon may be.

IV. If these things be true, we ought this day to bow ourselves in deep humiliation before our Maker, and for ourselves and our people ask of Him who is exalted a prince and a Savior, repentance and forgiveness for all our sins. While the cloud of His wrath impends over us we ought never to cease to pray. While our enemies are invading our territory, enslaving our people, destroying our property and threatening our subjugation, we ought never to forget that our only hope of deliverance lies in the interposition of His hand, "to whom belongeth all the shields of the earth."[62] Let prayer continually ascend from all our sanctuaries, and from the temple of every heart, until "he shall make our wars to cease, breaking the bow, cutting the spear in sunder, and burning the chariots in the fire."[63]

Some men will tell you that prayer will avail little against the hosts of our enemies, and sneering at its power, assert that "Providence always favors the heavy battalions."[64] It is an infidel opinion, branded with falsehood both by the word of God and the history of the past. God says, "The horse is prepared against the day of battle, but victory is of the Lord."[65] God says, "the race is not to the swift nor the battle to the strong."[66] Who so impious

---

[62] Psalm 47:9.

[63] Psalm 46:9.

[64] Attributed to Napoleon Bonaparte by the English historian Edward Gibbon (1737–1794).

[65] Proverbs 21:31.

[66] Ecclesiastes 9:11.

as to rise up and contradict his Maker? History confirms the word of the Most High. Was the battle to the strong when Cyrus overthrew the proud city and empire of Babylon, and established his throne upon its ruins? Was the battle to the strong when Xerxes invaded Greece, and met with overwhelming defeat? Did Providence "favor the heavy battalions" when Bonaparte invaded Russia, and breaking its power, was himself broken by the hand of God? Did Providence favor "the heavy battalions" in the revolution of our fathers, when the ships of the strongest power of the world shaded our coasts, and when, from the St. Lawrence to the Savannah, the continent trembled under the tread of his legions? Has Providence "favored the heavy battalions" during this struggle for independence? Let Bethel and Manassas, Shiloh and Chancellorsville answer, and confound him who dares to make so impious an assertion. I rejoice to know that many of those who control our civil and military affairs believe in prayer. From our assemblage here today, at the request of the Chief Magistrate of our Confederacy, it is evident that he trusts in that God who "heareth prayer."[67] The gallant and noble General who leads our army in Virginia is a man of prayer.[68] He whose name was a tower of strength, the watchword of victory, who fought but to conquer, and over whose fall the heart of this people still bleeds in sorrow, was pre-eminently a man of prayer. Nor are many of our soldiers less imbued with the spirit which relies upon God for victory. Pardon me for relating an incident which illustrates this point. During one of the bloodiest battles of the war, in a change of position incident to great conflicts, a regiment from our own State was thrown forward upon the masses of the enemy into a position which it was victory to hold, a defeat to lose. Soon the converging fire of five times their number poured its leaden storm upon them. Those untried soldiers, never before upon a field of battle, staggered for a moment, as the strong ship staggers when smitten by the first breath of the tempest. Then there arose upon one who reminded them that it was Sunday, that at that very hour their fathers and mothers, and wives, and brothers and sisters were gathered in the sanctuaries of our land praying to God for them. They caught the inspiration of the thought, every eye brightened, every bosom heaved with emotion, and closing up their thinned and bleeding ranks, they stood like a wall of adamant against the surging masses of the foe, until the broken tide of war rolled back before them, and

---

[67] Pres. Jefferson Davis.
[68] Gen. Robert E. Lee.

victory was won! It was the thought that prayer was then ascending for them that nerved their arms, and made them heroes in that fearful hour.

Gentlemen, members of the Legislature of the State of Alabama, it well becomes you to cultivate this spirit of prayer, and to bow this day before the Lord of Hosts with reverence and godly fear. Your position gives you influence over the minds of the people. They will listen to your words and follow your example; let that example lead them in paths of piety and uprightness. You are convened by the Executive at a crisis in the affairs of our State and of our country. Much of the future history of Alabama, of the security and happiness of our people, depends upon your acts. It is no disparagement of your intelligence to urge you in this perilous hour to seek wisdom of Him who "giveth liberally to all men, and upbraideth not,"[69] to seek, by fervent prayer, for Divine guidance in the discharge of your responsible duties. The influence of your actions will live through all coming generations. You will meet it at the bar of God! Ask His aid that you may not blush to confront it before the "Judge of the quick and dead."[70]

With this spirit of reliance upon God cherished in your hearts, and having discharged your duty to your country, you can return home with the approval of your consciences, and calmly await that hour when the sun of peace shall rise upon a land of freedom, "like another morn risen on mid-noon"![71]

May you live long and enjoy the blessing of that day.

After the war, Reverend Isaac Tichenor resigned his position in Montgomery and spent three years at his plantation in Shelby County, Alabama. In 1871 he accepted a call to be the pastor at First Baptist Church in Memphis, Tennessee, but the following year returned to Alabama to be the first president of the State Agricultural and Mechanical College at Auburn. For ten years he was at the head of the college that became Auburn University. In 1878 his wife, Eppie, died. In 1882 he resigned his collegiate position to become the Secretary of the Home Missionary Board of the Southern Baptist Convention located in Atlanta, Georgia.

---

[69] James 1:5.

[70] 1 Peter 4:5.

[71] From John Milton's *Paradise Lost*, Book V, line 310.

For eighteen years he served in that position, helping to establish, it was said, some 10,000 churches in Texas and other states west of the Mississippi. In 1899 he retired as secretary emeritus. After a protracted illness, he died on 2 December 1902 in Atlanta.

Chapter 5

Ministry at the End

*I beat them fine as dust before the wind...*Psalm 18

Although the revivals in the Confederate armies did not cease during the last year of the war, the coordinated offensives in Virginia and in Georgia by the Union generals beginning in May of 1864 tended to limit the time chaplains and soldiers had to spend in church services.[1] During the Atlanta Campaign in June of 1864, Lieutenant General Hardee admonished the officers and soldiers not to meet in large groups lest they draw artillery fire.[2] Missionaries L. B. Payne, L. R. Redding, and J. B. McFerrin, marching with the troops from Dalton to Atlanta, recorded prayer meetings in the breastworks and in wood lines behind the trenches. Redding wrote on 18 July that twenty-five soldiers in Gist's brigade had joined the church and "notwithstanding the booming of cannon and bursting of shell, the good work goes bravely on."[3]

The total or "hard" war policies of the United States Government against civilians who would not take a loyalty oath, including clergy serving churches, was in full effect in 1864. These policies, inaugurated and endorsed by the War Department and implemented by Generals Grant, Sherman, and Sheridan among others, resulted not only in the destruction of war materiel and food supplies of potential use by the Confederate

---

[1] Herman Norton, *Struggling for Recognition: The United States Army Chaplaincy* (Washington DC: Office of the Chief of Chaplains, Department of the Army, 1977) 153–54.

[2] T. Conn Bryan, *Confederate Georgia* (Athens: University of Georgia Press, 1964) 241.

[3] Jones, *Christ in the Camp*, 556.

armies, but also in the disruption and disintegration of the social, educational, and religious infrastructure of the South. Public buildings, colleges, libraries, churches, farm buildings, and private homes were subject to immediate destruction if they lay in the path of contending armies.[4]

The arrest and imprisonment of "disloyal" church leaders as war measures were well known in Tennessee and Virginia in 1862, but some of the more famous applications occurred during the 1863 Vicksburg Campaign in Mississippi. When Natchez was captured in the summer of 1863, Federal Brigadier General James M. Tuttle ordered the Most Reverend William Henry Elder, the Roman Catholic bishop of Natchez, to pray for the President of the United States. Bishop Elder refused to have his ecclesiastical authority subjected to army control and declined to offer a forced prayer. He was, after some discussion, detained for twenty days as a prisoner at Vidalia, Louisiana, while St. Mary's Cathedral was administered at the pleasure of the provost marshal.[5]

Bishop Elder was more fortunate than his colleague, Episcopal Bishop William Mercer Green. In 1863 Bishop Green was forced out of Jackson, Mississippi, during the battle for that city. When he returned, he found every room in his home looted and both the Episcopal and Catholic church buildings burned to the ground. All church schools were closed but one.[6]

In December of the same year, Major General James B. McPherson expelled four ladies and one gentleman from Vicksburg for leaving the Episcopal Church before prayers for the president of the United States.[7] These civilians were allowed forty-eight hours to gather their baggage and prepare for departure from the city.

A Baptist writer from Georgia summarized the plight of the churches under the subjugation of the Federal armies: "They refuse to let us have Bibles…They drag our preachers from our pulpits, and send them to prison. They deprive us of our churches, and burn them or use them as stables or store-houses. They send preachers of their own to preach wherever they have taken…our towns, and if they conquer us they will take away all our

---

[4] Jefferson Davis, *The Rise and Fall of the Confederate Government*, vol. 2 (New York: Appleton and Co., 1881) 709.

[5] John K. Bettersworth, ed., *Mississippi in the Confederacy: As They Saw It* (Baton Rouge: Louisiana State University Press, 1961) 226–27.

[6] Ibid., 235.

[7] Ibid., 341.

churches...and not even let us pray in our families as we wish..."[8] Indeed one could trace the progress of the Union armies across Mississippi, Alabama, Tennessee, and Georgia by the desecrated and burned church and church school buildings.

In some cases there was considerable resistance, even from unarmed clergy. When Major General Sherman's three armies occupied Atlanta in the fall of 1864, the churches of the city were viewed as suitable for quartering horses or for any other military necessity. However, the Reverend Thomas O'Reilly, an Irish Catholic priest thirty-one years of age, refused to allow the Federal officers to take his rectory or his Church of the Immaculate Conception for their use. Father O'Reilly had ministered to both Confederate and Union wounded both at Chickamauga and in the Atlanta hospitals. Indeed he held a commission as a Confederate hospital chaplain dated 16 March 1864, a detail that he forgot to mention to Major General William T. Sherman and Major General Henry W. Slocum. Moreover, Father O'Reilly served Mass regularly to the Union soldiers who requested it. Father O'Reilly informed General Slocum that he had the authority to send all the Catholic soldiers home and that seizing his church would surely cause a riot among those loyal Catholics in Sherman's army.

General Sherman's wife, Ellen, was a devout Catholic who had just buried their son at Notre Dame. Sherman himself was an Episcopalian with Catholic leanings. General Slocum had been educated partly at a Methodist seminary in upstate New York before he received an appointment to West Point. Neither General could see any benefit in quarreling with a priest. Father O'Reilly not only saved his own church during the burning of the city, but he also saved the Methodist, Baptist, Presbyterian, and Episcopal churches.[9] He could not, however, protect St. Luke's Episcopal Church where Lieutenant General Polk's funeral had been held four months before. St. Luke's was burned to the ground in the general firing of the city.

There were many other instances of churches destroyed during Sherman's march through Georgia and the Carolinas. In Columbia, South Carolina, the Reverend John Bachman, a Lutheran pastor, stated that Union soldiers deliberately burned five churches, including his Lutheran church

---

[8] Bryan, *Confederate Georgia*, 240.

[9] Dumas Malone, ed., *Dictionary of American Biography*, vol. 17 (New York: Charles Scribner's Sons, 1946) 216; Elizabeth H. McCallie, *The Atlanta Campaign* (Atlanta: Atlanta Historical Society, 1939) 26.

and a school belonging to the Sisters of Charity.[10] Sherman stated that the fire was accidental.[11]

Yet these isolated instances are trivial when compared to the dispersed congregations, scattered and missing ministers, absent church members, and financial ruin that characterized Southern churches across the entire region at the end of the war. Based on actual membership rolls, the Methodist Episcopal Church, South, had 113,256 fewer members and 342 fewer ordained ministers in 1866 than in 1860.[12] Four state conferences of 117,000 members and the General Conference representing 2,615 ministers and lay representatives had been prevented from meeting for three years of the war. Only three bishops could be located in 1865.

The Southern Baptist Convention could not count all of its losses for several years. The Georgia Baptist Convention alone had 700 fewer churches, 322 fewer ministers, and 46,182 fewer members in 1869 than in 1859.[13]

In 1864 the Charleston Presbytery in South Carolina reported that all but four of its fifteen churches had been closed by the calamities of war, and only one had retained its own pastor.[14] In Mississippi, of thirty-three Episcopal priests in Bishop Green's diocese at the beginning of the war, twenty-one were absent in 1867.[15] In Nashville, Tennessee, a Union officer reported that "The citizens of Nashville—25,000 to 30,000 in number—are without gospel privileges. They have no houses of worship and no pastors, and if they had both, with Southern proclivities they would find it difficult to hold religious services here now."[16]

At Appomattox, Virginia, some forty-nine Confederate chaplains and one missionary surrendered and were paroled with Lee's Army of Northern Virginia. They walked, rode horses, or took trains, when available, back to their homes. Twenty-six other chaplains surrendered at the Bennett House

[10] Davis, *Rise and Fall of the Confederate Government*, 709–11.

[11] William T. Sherman, *Memoirs of General William T. Sherman*, vol. 2 (New York: Da Capo Press, 1984) 287.

[12] Holland N. McTyeire, *A History of Methodism* (Nashville: Southern Methodist Publishing House, 1885) 665.

[13] James Adams Lester, *A History of the Georgia Baptist Convention 1822–1972* (Atlanta: Baptist Convention of the State of Georgia, 1972) 179.

[14] Ernest Trice Thompson, *Presbyterians in the South* vol. 2 (Richmond: John Knox Press, 1973) 54.

[15] Bettersworth, ed., *Mississippi in the Confederacy*, 235.

[16] Ernest Trice Thompson, *Presbyterians in the South*, 66.

near Durham Station, North Carolina, with General Joseph E. Johnston's Army of Tennessee. Chaplain A. D. Betts of the 17th North Carolina Infantry rode his horse to his home at Chapel Hill and applied for a parole. The Reverend John B. McFerrin, who had served as a missionary and a chaplain for three years, surrendered in North Carolina. When he arrived at his home site outside Nashville, he found his family and livestock gone, his house burned, and his timber cut. Chaplain Charles James Oliver was on furlough from the Troup Artillery in Athens, Georgia. He simply waited for the Federal soldiers to arrive. Soon their religious denominations would call upon these former chaplains to help reconstitute the decimated churches, publishing houses and colleges of the South.

Memoirs, 1864-1865

"We are building shanties…"

Chaplain Atticus G. Haygood
15th Georgia Infantry, Army of Northern Virginia

Atticus Greene Haygood was born in Watkinsville, Georgia, on 19 November 1839. In 1852 the Haygood family moved to Atlanta where his father, Greene B. Haygood, practiced law. Atticus Haygood received his elementary education from his mother who operated a private school near Trinity Methodist Church in that city. In 1856 he entered the sophomore class at Emory College in Oxford, Georgia. Haygood graduated from Emory College and was admitted on trial at the Georgia Conference of the Methodist Episcopal Church, South, in December of 1859. In 1861 he was commissioned as chaplain of the 15th Georgia Infantry in Brigadier General Henry L. Benning's Brigade. In 1863–1864 he served as a missionary chaplain with Longstreet's Corps, providing aid and comfort to the wounded after the battle of Chickamauga. During his trips to Confederate field hospitals, he often traveled with Father J. F. O'Neal from the Church of the Immaculate Conception in Atlanta.[1] In 1865 Haygood reported on the condition of Atlanta's churches after Sherman left.

---

[1] "A Wartime Sketch. An Interesting Incident in Bishop Haygood's Life," *The Constitution* (Atlanta GA), 27 Jan. 1896, 8. Mr. Frank T. Ryan, who was wounded at Chickamauga in the fall of 1863, reported that "ministering angels" appeared on the battlefield, Rev. Haygood and Father O'Neal, bringing fried chicken, buttermilk biscuits, turkey, cakes, jellies, and pies out to the wounded. "There they were," Ryan wrote in wonder, "Methodist minister and Catholic priest—joining their forces on an errand of love and mercy, roaming around through the dead, dying and wounded, where death for two whole days had been holding a high carnival, with a prayer for the dying, a word of cheer and comfort for the badly wounded, and contributing from their baskets to those who needed nutritious diet."

Letter from the Reverend Atticus Haygood[2]

Atlanta, April 13, 1865

Dear Brother Harp[3]: the ensign of tyranny, the modern 'abomination that maketh desolate,' has for a while, at least—God grant that it may be forever!—passed away from us.[4] Nearly all of our noble houses of business have been destroyed: many, very many of our 'pleasant places' have had the beauty, and music, and life, crushed and burnt out of them, but for an old resident like myself, I assure you 'it is good to be here.'

Except the few who found special friends and near relatives, Atlanta refugees and exiles were not specially overwhelmed with kindness. But, my good friend, we forget all the sorrows of the way in our joy that we have got back home, or to the place where home was. The attachment of the old citizens of our war-scathed city to this place of former business and happiness is almost romantic. Women and children cry for joy when they get back, and the men are not proof against tender and grateful emotions. Our people have the quick, springy step of the olden time; nearly everybody is cheerful and hopeful, and I do not know a single reconstructionist among us. If such a one should visit us, these sad ruins would shame him out of his cowardice. Of course we cannot build fine houses, but we are building shanties, that will serve, in the want of something better, for shelter and for trade.

As to our churches, we are getting along better than any despondent man can believe. I have alluded to the energy of our people. Why, our negro Methodists set themselves to the work (as zealously as the returned Jews at Jerusalem), of rebuilding their temple. They have rebuilt their church, and are having regular services.[5]

---

[2] J. William Jones, *Christ in the Camp or Religion in the Confederate Army* (Harrisonburg VA: Sprinkle Publications, 1986) 604–605.

[3] Robert James Harp, former Methodist chaplain of the 52nd Georgia Infantry, Stovall's Georgia brigade, Army of Tennessee; Editor of the *Army and Navy Herald*, 1864–1865.

[4] Presumably Haygood meant the flags of Maj. Gen. William T. Sherman's army.

[5] The African Methodist Episcopal Church on Gilmer Street was one of four churches in Atlanta destroyed by fire. The others were St. Luke's Episcopal on Walton Street, the Methodist Protestant Church on Forsyth Street, and the Christian Church on Decatur Street. The Atlanta Medical College was saved by a ruse. Dr. P. P. Noel D'Alvigny, a French-born physician on the faculty, passed out

Rev. A. M. Thigpen, an old Army Chaplain and Missionary, is at Wesley Chapel, doing good work.[6] Rev. Mr. Hornady serves the Baptist, and the venerable Dr. Wilson the Presbyterian congregation.[7] Your correspondent 'holds forth' at Trinity, his 'nursing mother.'[8] Fathers O'Reilley and O'Neal minister to the Catholic membership.[9] Sunday-schools are flourishing, congregations steadily improving. We have an 'itinerant' weekly union prayer-meeting. We devoutly hope for a glorious revival of religion.

Our first communion was a blessed time we will never forget. 'Brethren, pray for us!'

A constant stream of paroled prisoners flows through our city daily. 'Still they come.' These from Missouri, those from Arkansas, others from Louisiana, and from all the States west of the Savannah. No reconstructionists among *them*. And there will be no such monstrous

---

whiskey to his hospital assistants and had them pose as wounded soldiers in a ward of the college. The Federal officers were unwilling to burn the building with soldiers still inside. They gave the doctor twelve hours to move them. By the time the deadline expired, the Union army was on the march and the Medical College was saved. See Franklin M. Garrett, *Atlanta and Environs*, vol. 1 (New York: Lewis Historical Publishing Company, 1954) 651, 654.

[6] Alexander M. Thigpen (1832–1889), Methodist, former chaplain of the 6th Georgia Infantry.

[7] Henry Carr Hornady, born 22 February 1822 in Jones County, Georgia. Ordained in 1848, Hornady had been pastor of the Baptist church in Americus, an agent for Mercer University, and editor of the *Cherokee Baptist*. Dr. John S. Wilson (1796–1873) was born in the Pendleton District of South Carolina and preached the first sermon in Marthasville, later Atlanta. He received a Doctor of Divinity degree from Oglethorpe University and organized the First Presbyterian Church in Atlanta where he served as pastor until his death in 1873.

[8] Trinity Methodist Church then located on Mitchell Street.

[9] At the Catholic Church of the Immaculate Conception at Hunter and Lloyd Streets. Father J. F. O'Neal and Father Thomas O'Reilly (1831–1872) were the pastors. O'Reilly was commissioned a Confederate chaplain in 1864 for the post and hospitals of Atlanta. He was credited with saving five churches from the torches of Sherman's soldiers. O'Reilly appealed to the Roman Catholic soldiers in the 2nd Massachusetts Infantry camped on the site of the present Georgia State Capitol to help protect his church. He also appealed to Maj. Gen. Henry W. Slocum, commander of the XX Corps, to preserve the churches. Slocum, educated at a Methodist seminary in New York, granted Father O'Reilly's request.

growths among them so long as they remember Rock Island, Point Lookout, Elmira, and those other places of torture, and hunger, and oppression.[10]

God bless these brave fighters, these long-enduring sufferers! Let the people receive them as such heroic sons of the South deserve to be received.

We sigh and weep over the evils of war, and we wonder what is to become of the county and the Church. The All-Seeing Eye is upon us, and all will be well.

Hundreds of these brave boys have been born again, even in so dreary a place as a prison. Hundreds have learned to read and to write, have added to their stock of information, and are preparing under a strange tuition to do good service to their country and race. When Stephen was stoned, the Church wept one of her strongest pillars broken. She saw no good in that fierce Saul of Tarsus standing by.[11] But the Master did. I am informed by reliable Christian men, among them Rev. Robert W. Ayres, of the Memphis Conference, that a large number of young men in those dreary prisons have been *'studying for the ministry.'*[12] We read about God's making the 'wrath of man to praise Him.' Now, here is an instance. 'He that keepeth Israel neither slumbereth nor sleepeth.' What earnest preachers these theological students of the army and the prison will make.

The Church and the country will need them every one. 'Pray ye therefore the Lord of the harvest.'

Very truly yours in the faith, etc.

Atticus G. Haygood

After the war Atticus G. Haygood was elected Sunday school secretary and first editor of Sunday school publications for the southeastern jurisdiction of the Methodist Episcopal Church, South. He was a member of the boards of trustees of the Wesleyan Female College at Macon and of Emory College at Oxford. In 1875 he was elected the eighth president of Emory College. Along with many other duties, Haygood spent three weeks in New England in 1881 speaking in fifteen towns and cities on "The New South from a Southern Standpoint." In 1890 Atticus Haygood was elected a bishop of the Methodist Episcopal Church, South. He died on 19 January 1896.

---

[10] Locations of Union prison camps for Confederate soldiers.

[11] Acts 7

[12] Robert W. Ayers was ordained at the Memphis Conference in 1858.

"Have you burned all our towns?"

The Reverend James D. Anthony
Methodist Episcopal Church, South
Sandersville, Georgia

James D. Anthony was not a chaplain, although he was offered a chaplain's commission several times. He was pastor of the Methodist church in Sandersville, Georgia, when General William T. Sherman's soldiers camped there on 26 November 1864.[13] Reverend Anthony was credited with saving most of the private homes from destruction by interceding with General Sherman. This account from his autobiography provides a rare glimpse of life on the home front and survival in the path of contending armies during Sherman's "March to the Sea."[14]

James D. Anthony was born in Abbeville County, South Carolina, on 12 October 1825. His father, the Reverend Whitfield Anthony, moved his family in 1843 to Vann's Valley, eight miles from Rome, Georgia. James was educated at a country school but managed to learn some Latin and Greek. He studied for the ministry at home and was admitted to the Georgia Conference in December of 1846. After serving several circuits in Gwinnett and Hall counties, he was appointed to the Methodist church in Sandersville in 1862. Reverend Anthony, his invalid wife, and his small children were living there when the war came to his parsonage.

Why I Did Not Go To the Front

Perhaps it would be well for me to say here, that I was offered a chaplaincy in each of three regiments, and in one battalion of artillery. Owing, however, to my wife's helpless physical condition, I felt it to be my duty to remain at home and take care of and help her. I also realized the great necessity of the pastorate to those at home; especially did the poor

---

[13] William T. Sherman, *Memoirs of General William T. Sherman*, vol. 2 (New York: Da Capo Press, 1984) 191.

[14] James D. Anthony. *Life and Times of Rev. J. D. Anthony: An Autobiography with a Few Original Sermons* (Atlanta: C. P. Byrd, Printer, 1896). There is a copy in the Georgia State Department of Archives and History, Morrow GA.

good women need the counsel and the prayers of the pastor.[15] Many of them lost husbands, others sons. The burying of the dead, going to the army to carry food and clothing, visiting the sick, etc.[,] occupied all the pastor's time.

The fearful war, through which we were passing, grew more and more terrible in its effects upon all the interests of our people. The continued call for men to go to the front gradually reduced the white male population, at home mainly, to men over fifty years of age and boys under sixteen.

True, there was a large army, so to speak, engaged as enrolling officers, marshals, etc.[,] whose business it was to see that all except themselves and the few permitted by law to stay at home, were rushed to the front. Practicing physicians, ministers of the Gospel in charge of churches, school teachers and overseers in charge of twenty or more hands, were exempt from army service.

The reduction of the male population at home, in many respects, crippled the operations of the church. Yet every faithful pastor had his hands full—yea, all he could possibly do.

I remained in my assigned fields of labor during those awful years of heartrending grief and dreadful carnage. I can truthfully affirm that those four years demanded and received at my hands more labor than double that length of time before or since. The bereaved were to be visited and comforted, the sick nursed and the dead buried. At one of my churches in Washington County, Bayspring, I did not for two years preach any other than funeral sermons—sometimes two or more in one sermon. Long journeys were to be made by the pastor, to the armies at different points, sometimes to be the bearer of articles of food, clothing, etc., at others to accompany the wife or mother of some sick or dying husband or son.

Atlanta had fallen into the hands of the invading foe. General Sherman was on his almost uninterrupted "march to the sea." Governor Brown had, with his state officers, abandoned Milledgeville, then the capital of Georgia. The enemy took possession without opposition. The Federals, on leaving Milledgeville, blew up the magazine, the report of which was distinctly heard and the shock unmistakably felt by us in Sandersville, twenty-seven miles distant!

---

[15] It was also true that when he was fourteen years old, James D. Anthony lost the sight in his right eye as a result of a powder horn that blew up during a July 4th celebration.

All kinds of rumors of the cruelty and vandalism of the approaching army preceded its advance.

Our town authorities called a meeting of all the white males. This meeting was presided over by Judge Hook. The best course to pursue was the subject of discussion. It was resolved that the proper plan would be, for a committee of citizens to meet the army and turn over the town to the tender mercies of the commanding general, but when the chairman began to name the committee he was informed by each man, as his name was called, that particular committeeman had decided to take his horse, or horses, etc., and go to the woods, to save himself and his horses if possible! Finally my name was called. I informed his honor that I had decided to remain with my invalid wife and helpless children. Perhaps I should say, that it was not sheer bravery nor foolhardy daring that caused me to come to this conclusion, but the fact that my poor wife was unable to feed herself or turn herself in bed. Then I also had a precious daughter just budding into womanhood, and others, helpless little children. I decided that it was my duty to remain with them, protect and care for them as far as possible, and, if need be, die for or with them, which decision I have never regretted!

On stating my purpose to his honor, Judge Hook, appointed me a committee of one to meet General Sherman, and, having fixed up the necessary papers to show that I represented the town's wishes, they left me and three old men and one of the descendants of Abraham, a Mr. H, the sole male population among the whites.[16] A few hours later a portion of the Confederate cavalry, under General Wheeler, came into town.[17] They went out that afternoon and met the advance cavalry of the enemy, had a skirmish, three miles from town and camped on a vacant lot with the prisoners, near the parsonage. These prisoners were under the care of Captain Harlow, with whom I was at one time intimately acquainted in North Georgia.[18] Early next morning I went out to Captain H's camp and found all in a hurry to leave. All the prisoners had disappeared during the night except one, a lieutenant of cavalry, who was badly wounded in the left forearm. Both bones were broken by a mine ball. On inquiry, I learned that the twelve who were not wounded had been sent off during the night. I

---

[16] Purcus Happ, a Jewish cotton merchant, stayed behind. His son later settled in Macon GA.

[17] Maj. Gen. Joseph Wheeler (1836–1906), Confederate cavalry commander, was born in Augusta GA.

[18] Captain James Harlow, Co. H, 6th Georgia Cavalry.

asked the Captain what they were going to do with the wounded man, and was informed by him in these words: "We'll shoot him, as soon as we get out of town." Finding that this was almost certain to be the fate of the poor man, I began to plead for his life, and finally, after the poor fellow had been placed in the ambulance, the surgeon, with an oath, told me to take him. The wounded man sprang from the wagon and came to me. I conducted him into the parsonage. Just at that moment Dr. S., and old gentleman and practicing physician, passed my door, came in and removed the bandage and tried to relieve the man's sufferings. About the same moment Wheeler's Cavalry formed in line, about 2,000 strong, near the parsonage, fired and galloped away.[19] In a minute or two more the Yankee infantry fired. The deadly missiles flew thick. The parsonage was struck in several places. I and family and the wounded Yankee were not hit by any of the flying shots. In a moment or two more the Yankees were as thick as blackbirds in and around the house. As soon as the Yankee soldiers entered, the wounded man told his friends not to allow me or mine or anything we had to be injured. He sent for his colonel of cavalry, who soon came in, placed a guard around the house and protected my family from all insult and injury. It was soon spread pretty extensively over the army that there was a rebel Methodist preacher who had remained at home and, better still, this rebel preacher had saved the life of a wounded enemy. A large number of their officers and privates came to see me and professed faith in a religion that prompted such a deed. Among them an old chaplain in one of the Western regiments, came and talked with me for some time. He said his name was Thomas A. Morris.[20] I remarked that he had the name of a former Methodist bishop. He replied, "Yes, he was my cousin and we were both named for the same man." This incident taught me clearly that it always pays to do right. I never thought of benefit accruing to me. I was actuated entirely by what I regarded as Christian and philanthropic principles. The good Lord blessed that act to the good of myself and family—indeed to the interests of our town.

I certainly would have carried out the instructions given me by the citizens' meeting and turned over all to be the tender care of General Sherman had opportunity been given, but, as may be seen in the foregoing statements, there was no opportunity afforded. The unexpected early

---

[19] Brig. Gen. Samuel W. Ferguson's brigade of Wheeler's cavalry.

[20] There was a soldier named Thomas A. Morris serving in the 38th Indiana Infantry Regiment, but no evidence available that he was commissioned as a chaplain.

advance of the Federals, the hasty fire of the Confederates, then their instant flight and the immediate occupation of the town by the Federals, the confusion and noise caused by the knocking down of fences, out-houses, and, indeed, every obstacle in the way of the advancing army, together with the cries of the alarmed women and children, the shouts and oaths of the Federals, etc., all united to demand and keep me in my house for two or three hours.

Later in the afternoon I was informed by the general who commanded the division of cavalry to which my guest, the wounded lieutenant, belonged—and who, by the way, had come with the surgeon to carry the injured man to their camp hospital—that General Sherman had issued an order to reduce the town to ashes next morning at sunrise. The Federals had remained in and around town all day and were to move forward next morning, firing the town as they left. This general of cavalry suggested that I go to General Sherman's headquarters and intercede in behalf of the town. Said he, "Your house won't be burned because you saved Lieutenant Deason."[21] He continued, "From what you tell me, General Sherman is wrongly informed. He has been told that it was the citizens of the town who fired on us."

I parted with the wounded man. He earnestly grasped my hand assuring me that he would ever hold me in grateful remembrance. Said he "If I live until this cruel war is over you'll hear from me." I presume he died from the effects of his wound, and was probably buried somewhere between that point and Savannah—otherwise, I am persuaded I would have heard from him. He belonged to an Illinois regiment.

This general of cavalry sent me as a guide and escort one of his subaltern officers, who conducted me to near General Sherman's headquarters. We met the General a hundred yards or more from his tent, in company with two of his generals, viz. Logan and Davis.[22] The guide saluted the General and introduced me to him as "the Rebel parson who had saved one of our men from being shot."

---

[21] 2nd Lt. William M. Deason, 9th Illinois Mounted Infantry, and Brig. Gen. Judson Kilpatrick.

[22] Maj. Gen. John A. Logan, who had been absent since October, and Maj. Gen. Jefferson C. Davis, commander of the XIV Corps. See William R. Scaife, *Order of Battle: Federal and Confederate Forces* (Atlanta: McNaughton and Gunn, Inc., 1992) 5.

The Interview

I then showed him my credentials as a minister of the Gospel. He looked over them and replied that he knew nothing about such matters. I explained that I only used them to show him that I was really a minister of the Gospel in the Methodist Episcopal Church, South. I then handed him the papers given me by the authorities of our town meeting, turning over to him a muchly surrendered town! On reading these he replied, "Why did you not hand me this before we reached the town? I would have marched my men through town and nothing should have been injured." I explained to him the utter impossibility of delivering the papers then. I continued, "General, I have been informed by some of your men that you have issued an order to burn our town tomorrow morning. Is this true?" He replied, "Yes, it is true." Said I, "Have you burned all the towns and villages in your rear?" He replied, "No, I have not." "Then," said I, "Why treat us more severely than others?" The reply was, "I haven been I informed that it was your citizens that fired on my men." I replied, "Well, General, I must say, sir, that your information is untrue, false—not one word of truth in the statement. I certainly know whereof I speak. Here are only, beside myself, four adult white males in town. Three of the others are old men. All our males left before you came. They were gone, sir, hours before your advance came into town." I never had a man to look so long and so intently into my face. I determined to keep my eye on his. He was evidently trying to read me through and through. I was trying to see if I could find a tender spot in his heart. I began to fear that it was a fruitless attempt. I then drew a picture of the terrible hardships to which the poor innocent women and children would be reduced. Said I, "General, no man can divine the fortunes of wars. Suppose, while you are here marching through Georgia, that a body of our cavalry should go to the town or city where your family is and burn your dwellings and turn your helpless ones out, without food or shelter, to come in contact with the pelting storms and freezing blasts of winter." To this he replied, "There is no danger of that. General Thomas will take care of Hood, General Grant is in Lee's front and I'll take Savannah and Charleston by a flank movement. Then, when I move up in Lee's rear, Grant in his front, what will become of Lee? You preachers ought to be out preaching peace and submission to the best government in the world." I felt our chances truly were slim. I gave the "grand hailing sign of distress," used by Master Masons when all else fails, without using the accompanying words, and with all my powers made the final appeal. Said I, "My dear sir, we preachers down South let politics alone. We preach Christ Jesus and the Gospel of peace, and leave to Caesar the things of state. Besides, it would cost me or any other preacher his life to preach as you suggest now. Moreover, General, I have heard it said, 'tis not best to shout until one gets out of the woods.' The fortunes of war may yet place you and your splendid army in the hands of those whom you seek to conquer, but, sir, 'tis not my business now to discuss these questions. I am here, General, to plead for the shelters over the heads of these innocent women and children, whose husbands and fathers are either in the field or have fallen in battle. Your soldiers have already taken all we have to eat. Now, if you burn our houses, what can save these people from starvation and death? This, sir, is my final appeal!"

The Order Revoked

What effect my Masonic appeal may have had, I can't say, nor whether any one of the three or all three were Masons, [23]—only this I do know; the trio held a short conversation in an undertone; then General Sherman said; "Sir, upon your assurance that your citizens did not fire on my men, I will revoke the order to burn the town; but will burn these two public buildings," viz, the court house and jail. I thanked him, saying, "I can say no more if you think that the burning of those buildings will promote your cause. Since you spare our dwellings I ask no more," and left him.

Early next morning the army began the forward movement. About the same time the court house and jail were fired. In the stillness of early morning their flames shot far up into the heavens, especially the former. All the inmates of the jail were set at liberty. Other buildings near the jail caught fire from the failing sparks. It was with great difficulty that the buildings were prevented from burning down. Had it not been that we were helped by an Irish Federal, who kindly gave valuable aid, all that portion of town would haven been reduced to ashes.

Added Woes

If possible, it was a worse trial to our little city to stand the consequences of the next twenty-four hours than the twenty-four that the Federal army was with us.

---

[23] All Masons were supposed to honor "the grand hailing sign of distress" if given by a brother Mason. The sign is a Masonic secret.

The report came in, soon after the rear of the army left that the negroes, together with stragglers from the army, were following, taking what the Yankees had left, murdering all indiscriminately and burning everything before them! We had no one to send forward to reconnoiter, inspect and bring back a true report. The buried guns were dug up. The five men of us armed ourselves and also the ten[-] and twelve[-]year[-]old boys and formed ourselves into a little army. Somewhere between a dozen and twenty guns of different kinds were made ready for action. We patrolled he streets and watched for the approaching enemy through the entire night. Our constant watching gave a degree of quiet to the minds of the women and children, who surely needed rest. Next morning we learned that some negroes had shot a man by the name of Strange and had also burned his dwelling. This shooting and burning occurred twelve or fifteen miles from town. This was the foundation out of which all the alarming reports had grown. It was a trying night to us all. I had not slept any for two nights previous.

Mr. Happ and the Federals

Mr. Purcus Happ, a former merchant and one of our best citizens, remained at home with his family. He was an Israelite, both by descent and faith. He did not feel that it was necessary for him to leave his home. He was not fighting the Federals,—was born in the old world—hence he felt that he and his would be safe in the hands of the Federals.

It was told the Yankees by someone—I suppose likely, by somebody who was of the colored persuasion—that Mr. Happ had, at his own expense, equipped a company for the Confederate service. Mr. H. had a large amount of cotton on hand. This the Federals threatened to burn. In this extremity Mr. H. sent for me. He introduced me to the Federals as "our pastor, one that everybody loves and all know will tell the truth. Let him tell you all about me." Then, addressing me, he said, "They are trying to make me a terrible Rebel." I said, "Gentlemen, Mr. Happ, as you can readily perceive, was born in the old world. He is a good citizen,—was opposed to secession, but with all the rest of us he had to go with his adopted State. Being a foreigner by birth, he was closely watched by his neighbors. It became him to be liberal. Had he not been he would have been branded as an enemy. He has done nothing more than either of you would have done, situated as he was. I hope that you will not burn his cotton. Near all the earnings of his life are in that cotton."

They listened to me attentively and then ordered a guard to be placed around him and his property.

I feel sure that I never had a truer friend than was Mr. Happ. He often afterwards told me that he owed his life and his property to my true friendship. When the war closed he had a large amount of cotton on hand, which he converted into gold at a high price. This capital, under his fine business qualifications, continued to grow. Since his death his son, Mr. M. Happ, now of Macon, Georgia, has continued to increase in worldly prosperity.

Questionable Liberality

During the stay of the Federals, after having taken all our people had on the line of eatables, they became quite liberal. They sent a piece of beef to, I suppose, every family in town. Perhaps they felt that they could afford to do so, as the cattle from which the beef was taken was the property of our citizens. Liberality is a commendable virtue—and was appreciated by us in this particular instance!

A Gloomy Time

It was a dark hour. Many had to go to the camps that the Federals had just vacated to pick up pieces of meat, potatoes, etc. Most of these scraps were but the leavings of what the enemy had taken from our citizens. Hungry people can enjoy coarse food. Hunger is said to be the richest sauce!

We all felt, as our country had been devastated over a space forty miles in width, reaching all the way from Atlanta to Savannah, that the ghost of famine would haunt the habitations of all alike. True, we all had to live hard—subsist on the coarsest and simplest fare—yet I did not learn of any actual suffering, even among the poorest of the poor.

'Tis said, "Kindred sufferings cause us to feel wondrous kind." Our people seemed to forget all former distinctions and all met upon the plane of humanity and true Christianity. All denominational bigotry was buried for the time—Jew and Gentile, Christians of all persuasions, all, all met on one common level! It is said, "'Tis an ill wind that blows good to none." I felt at home among all our people—preached in very nearly all the churches of all denominations in our county. It was a foretaste of the millennial glory that is yet to come!

I do most devoutly pray the Great Head of the Church to hasten the glad, happy hour when all strife, bigotry, yea, sin in all its varied shapes, shall be banished from our earth! When good will toward all mankind shall abound and true peace be the universal heritage of our race!

In 1865 Reverend Anthony became the presiding elder of the Sandersville District and editor of The Central Georgian, *one of the few newspapers in middle Georgia. For this additional job he was paid $100 a month. In the following years he preached in the Mobile Conference in Alabama before returning to Georgia. It was said that he personally led 30,000 people to Christ. He wrote his autobiography in Statesboro, Georgia, in 1896. He died three years later.*

"Lee Had Surrendered!"

Chaplain Alexander D. Betts
17th North Carolina Infantry, Army of Tennessee

Alexander Davis Betts was born in Cumberland County, North Carolina on 25 August 1832. At age seventeen he was thrown while riding a steer, and thereafter was unable to do farm work. Consequently he turned his attention to academic studies, first at a school at Summerville and later at the University of North Carolina from which he graduated in 1855. He entered the ministry of the Methodist Episcopal Church, South, in 1856, and served four circuit appointments until 1861.

Many of the officers of the 30th North Carolina Infantry had known Reverend Betts or heard him preach before the war, so they asked him to be their chaplain. On 25 October 1861, Betts accepted a commission as chaplain of the 30th North Carolina Infantry. He was present with his regiment at Antietam, Gettysburg, and Winchester. On 25 March 1865 he went home to Chapel Hill on leave where he received the news that General Lee had surrendered the Army of Northern Virginia.

Virginia
Regiment near Petersburg.
Sunday, Dec. 25—I preach from the song of the angels, "Glory to God, in the highest!"
This was the last Christmas of the war. It was Sunday, too.
Dec. 26—In camp. No mail for three days.

Dec. 29—Get into my winter quarters—a wall of poles covered with cloth. Chimney of mud and sticks.

Dec. 30—Visit my brother, Allen Betts, in Co. C. 56th Regiment, just beyond Petersburg, near the enemy. Hear from my wife. Sick. God be with her!

Dec. 31—Last day of the year. Where shall we be the last day of '65?

Some of us were at home with our loved ones, others in Heaven, and others—dreadful thought! A man may fight and die for his country and lose his soul! Mohammed taught that all who died for his cause would be saved and some men in this day seem to think that all who are killed in defense of their country are saved; but the Bible assures us "the pure in heart" shall "see God."

Jan. 1, 1865—Snow! Snow! Preach four times in the cabins of my Regiment.

Jan. 2—Spend day with my brother Allen. Prayer meeting nearly every night. Build stable for pony.

Jan. 17—Meet Chaplains in Tabb Street Presbyterian Church, Petersburg.

Jan. 18—Go to Richmond. Spend night with my father-in-law. Meet Mr. Mullins of Henry county, Va.

Jan. 19—Hear Dr. W. A. Smith on "Oath" in First Baptist Church.

Jan. 20—Return to Regiment with boxes.

BOXES FOR THE SOLDIERS.

Families at home sent thousands of boxes to husbands, fathers, sons and brothers during the war. Some contained pieces of clothing that the soldier would fall and be buried in. We had no chance to wash and dress those who fell in battle. Some of those boxes contained the last food the mother ever cooked for her soldier boy. The soldier seldom could go to the station to claim his box. The Chaplain was often a convenient, cheerful agent. It sometimes involved a great deal of care and fatigue to take boxes from home in N.C. to the army in Va. To hunt them up and get them to the soldiers after they had reached Va. was no light task. But, thank God, "Love lightens labor."

Jan. 21—Rain and sleet. Brigade goes on picket.

Jan. 22—In camp. Rain.

Jan. 23—Hear from wife. In trouble. God help her! Terrible cannonade on our lines till nine at night.

Saturday, ride to McRae's Brigade to see Coin, Jim and A. Davis.

Preach on Sunday A.M. and pray with prisoners in P.M.

Feb. 7, 1865—Rain and sleet. Our Division is ordered off. Three men in my Regiment had to leave their wives in camp. As the troops were ordered to "fall in" I saw the situation and made haste to tell the brave men that I would take their wives to the depot and see them start for their homes in N.C. The men may have lived to go to their homes. I wish I knew. That was a touching scene. The wife thought she might never see her husband again. She heard the men were in camp around Richmond. She got Grandma or some one to take care of the other children while she took the babe to see its father in camp. They reached the camp. Both were so happy for two or three days. Now! That drum calls the man to give his babe a hasty kiss (it may be the last one) and turn away from his wife, and go out to fight and face death. I secured an ambulance and took the three good women to the depot. I wish I now had their names.

Feb. 8—"Peace Commission" fails.[24]

Feb. 9—Regiment get away.

Feb. 10—Fast and pray.

Feb. 11—After prayermeeting in Co. B. I am taken suddenly and seriously ill and stay in bed three days and nights.

Feb. 14—Revs. Ira T. Wyche and J. A. Cunninggim arrive in our Brigade. Bro. W. stops with me; Bro. C. with Rev. B. F. Lacy.[25] Each preaches at night.

Feb. 20—Brigade goes on picket.

Feb. 21—Division moves to Sullivan's depot. I attend Chaplain's meeting.

Feb. 25—Brigade returns to camp. I carry John (Capt. Allen's negro servant) to hospital with typhoid fever.

Feb. 26 (Sunday)—I preach.

Feb. 27—Visit my brother, Allen Betts.

March 3, 1865—Regiment goes on picket. Revs. O. J. Brent and W. H. Moore arrive from N.C. and stop with me.

---

[24] On 30 January 1865, three commissioners from Richmond, Alexander H. Stephens, R. M. T. Hunter, and John A. Campbell, met with President Lincoln and Secretary of State Seward at Hampton Roads VA, to discuss terms of peace. The conference was a failure in part because Lincoln would not recognize the Confederate States as a separate power. See Jefferson Davis, *The Rise and Fall of the Confederate Government*, vol. 2 (New York: Appleton and Co., 1881) 619.

[25] Beverly T. Lacy (1819–1900), Presbyterian chaplain for the Second Corps of the Army of Northern Virginia.

March 4—Brother Brent goes to Richmond. Brother Moore remains with me.

March 5 (Sunday)—I walk nine miles and preach to my Regiment in picket camp.

March 10 (Friday)—I fast and pray. Preach to my Regiment six times in their quarters. Rain all day. God help our nation in this sore extremity!

March 12 (Sunday)—Preach to my Regiment. Hold prayers at night.

March 13—Brother Power preaches at night.

March 14—Hear from wife and Brother Willson. Preach at night. Brother Power and I alternate in our chapel, preaching every day and night.[26]

March 18—Go to Petersburg to see John (negro servant) nearly dead. Get him into hospital.

March 19 (Sunday)—Preach to Weiseger's Brigade in A.M. and ours in P.M.

March 20—Brigade moves near Dunlap's and relieves Thomas' Ga. Brigade.

March 21—Meet Chaplains in Petersburg, and see John and Capt. Allen.

March 23—Go by 11th N.C. Regiment and spend night in 56th with my brother. Preach to R.'s Brigade.

March 24—Meet Cousin Grey Utley in P. He raised three daughters. Two became wives of Rev. L. S. Burkhead, D.D. One Sunday night in October, 1853, Rev. J. L. F. opened the doors of his church in Chapel Hill to receive members. Just as I started forward, that good man, Grey Utley, began to sing "Jesus, I my cross have taken." That soft, sweet, voice and the sentiment of that hymn stir my heart to-night in October, 1897, as I write these lines—44 years after that solemn scene.

Jim Davis, of Chapel Hill, my wife's cousin, comes to see me.

March 25—Brigade moves and I start home on "leave." It was my last furlough, though I had no idea that I was to see the soldiers and Chaplains no more. How tender would have been the leave-taking, if I had known it was my last sight of those with whom I had been so long associated.

March 26 (Sunday)—Heard Rev. Christian preach at Clay Street in Richmond in A.M., and start to N.C. at 6 P.M. It was the last sermon I was to hear in Va. during the war. All night on the railroad.

---

[26] William Carr Power (1831–1916), Methodist chaplain of the 14th North Carolina Infantry.

March 27—Get to Durham and spend night.

March 28—Reach home and find all well. How happy to be with my wife and little ones. My oldest son had but lately given his heart to God and joined the Church.

March 31—Ride thirty miles horseback and spend night with my brother, A. N. Betts.

April 1, '65—Walk five miles to see my mother in the home of Allen Betts. Visited sister Jane Betts, widow of my brother, Andrew, who was captured as captain of his company on R. Island in 1862, and reached home on parole to die. He took his eldest son with him. He died in prison. Spent night with C. H. Cofield, who was my guardian for ten years of my boyhood.

April 2 (Sunday)—Preach at Myatt's schoolhouse. Spend night with my youngest brother, Archibald. "When shall I see my mother again?" Those words were written with the expectation of returning to Lee's Army in a short time.

April 3—Return to Chapel Hill with sick horse. Spent week at home gardening. Receive bacon and lard I had bought on the Harnett line, thirty miles away. Hurrying up to be ready to return to the Army.

April 9 (Sunday) During this week heard that Lee had surrendered! Sad news. Johnston's Army passed through Chapel Hill. We knew Sherman would soon be in. I did not wish to meet him. I told some of my friends I was going with Gen. Johnson's Army. Rev. Dr. Charles Phillips tenderly told me to go on and my friends would take care of my family.[27] After midnight I kissed my wife and children and mounted a mule and rode away, thinking I might not see them in months or years. I rode all night, crossing the Haw River, overtook Johnston's Army, and reported to Brig. Gen. Hoke, who assigned me to duty as Chaplain to 17th N.C. Regt.[28] We camped a few miles from Greensboro for two or three days till we heard we were to be surrendered. I rode to Greensboro one day and met Rev. Dr. John B. McFerrin of Nashville, Tenn., at the home of good Mrs. F. M. Bumpass.[29] The night following the tidings of our contemplated surrender

---

[27] Rev. Charles H. Phillips, Methodist pastor at Franklinsville NC.

[28] Maj. Gen. R. F. Hoke, commanding Hoke's division, Hardee's corps, Army of Tennessee.

[29] Rev. Dr. John B. McFerrin of the Tennessee Conference, Methodist Episcopal Church, South. Dr. McFerrin had served as a missionary with the Army of Tennessee, but surrendered as chaplain of the 2nd Tennessee Infantry with Gen.

was a still, sad night in our camp. Rev. W. C. Willson, the Chapel Hill pastor, was with us.[30] We had preached a few times in that camp; but that night we made no effort to get the men together. In little, sad groups they softly talked of the past, the present and the future. Old men were there, who would have cheerfully gone on, enduring the hardship of war, and protracted absence from their families, for the freedom of their country. Middle aged men were there, who had been away from wives and children for years, had gone through many battles, had lost much on their farms or stores or factories or professional business; but would that night have been glad to shoulder the gun and march forward for the defense of their "native land." Young men and boys were there, who loved their country and were unspeakably sad at the thought of the failure to secure Southern Independence.

Rev. W. C. Willson and I walked out of the camp and talked and wept together. As I started back to my tent—to my mule and saddle, I should say, for I had no tent—I passed three lads sitting close together, talking softly and sadly. I paused and listened. One said, "It makes me very sad to think of our surrendering." Another said, "It hurts me worse than the thought of battle ever did." The third raised his arm, clinched his fist and seemed to grate his teeth as he said, "I would rather know we had to go into battle tomorrow morning." There was patriotism! There may have been in that camp that night generals, colonels and other officers who had been moved by a desire for worldly honor. Owners of slaves and of lands may have hoped for financial benefit from Confederate success. But these boys felt they had a country that ought to be free! I wish I had taken their names. And I wonder if they still live. They are good citizens, I am sure.

Next day I mounted my mule and started to Chapel Hill, intending to surrender there. I took along a Negro servant and horse for a friend. At sunset we met an old man at his spring near his house. I politely asked to be permitted to spend the night on his land. He objected. I said, "Boy, take off our saddles and halter our horses." The farmer quickly said, "If you will stay, come up to the house." I slept on his porch.

My First Interview with a Federal Soldier on Duty.

Johnston's army. After the war McFerrin became editor of the *Nashville Christian Advocate* and author of *Methodism in Tennessee*.

[30] Rev. William C. Wilson was appointed to the Methodist church in Chapel Hill in 1864.

I had seen many of them dead, wounded, or prisoners. Near Chapel Hill one rode up to my side. The Blue Coat and the Grey chatted softly and sparingly. He kindly offered to show me the way to headquarters. I thanked him and told him I would ride to my house and see my family and report myself later. The town was full of Federals. Each home had a guard detailed by the commanding General. My guard was a faithful, modest fellow. In due time I called at headquarters and was paroled.[31]

After the war Reverend A. D. Betts served Methodist churches and circuits in nineteen towns and counties in North Carolina. His son, W. A. Betts, followed in his father's footsteps and became a Methodist minister at Greenville, among other places, in the South Carolina Conference. In 1904 he had his father's memoirs privately printed. The Reverend Alexander D. Betts died in Greensboro, North Carolina, in 1919.

"The sound of the last cannon has died..."

Chaplain Thomas W. Caskey
18th Mississippi Infantry Regiment and Hospital Chaplain,
Meridian, Mississippi

Thomas W. Caskey was one of the most colorful Southern preachers in the nineteenth century. He worked as a cotton farmer, a blacksmith, a preacher, a chaplain, a hospital administrator, a lawyer, and "a powerful orator" all with barely a grammar school education. He was born in Maury County, Tennessee, on 12 January 1816 to Thomas and Mary Caskey, active members of the Cumberland Presbyterian Church for more than forty years. Thomas W. Caskey probably spent no more than two years in the local elementary school where one acre of cotton per family paid the tuition for the teacher. At the age of sixteen, he was apprenticed to a local blacksmith who taught him a trade he could use whenever money was scarce—which was most of the time.

At the age of nineteen, when Caskey had finished his apprenticeship, he tied up his belongings in a little bundle and walked to Mississippi to seek his fortune. He

---

[31] William A. Betts, ed., *Experience of a Confederate Chaplain 1861–1864* (Greenville SC: privately printed, 1904) 77–79. Copy in the Pitts Theological Library at Emory University, Atlanta GA.

arrived in Holly Springs in August of 1835. For the next two years Caskey worked as an ox driver, blacksmith, overseer for slaves. In 1837 he married Lucy Jones, a devout Methodist. Caskey decided to study for the Methodist ministry. He read grammar, logic, rhetoric, natural and moral philosophy, and ancient and modern history, but decided that he did not agree with the Methodist discipline. Accordingly in 1840 he joined the Christian Church and for fifty-six years was one of the leading ministers in that denomination.

During the Civil War, Caskey served as chaplain for the 18th Mississippi Infantry Regiment, the 16th Mississippi Cavalry Regiment, and later, when his health failed, as chaplain for the Confederate hospital at Meridian, Mississippi. In this excerpt from his biographical memoirs, titled Caskey's Book: Lectures on Great Subjects, *he discussed his feelings at the end of the war.*[32]

The sound of the last cannon has died away in the distance. The smoke and dust of the battle have been wafted away by the flying winds of heaven. Victory has perched on the banner of the starts and stripes. And now, palsied be the hand that shall ever be upraised to pluck one of those stars from its place in the blue field of the glorious sisterhood. Long, long may those striped folds wave in peace triumphant over a united people, a nation blessed of God! The flag of the Confederacy is furled and folded; laid forever in the dust, where her heroic dead sleep. For four long years of the unequal internal conflict, their strong right hands vainly upheld it. The glad shouts of the victors and the groans of the vanquished together to heaven ascend! Angels, perhaps, rejoiced in the joyous shouts of the victors, but sighted for the sorrows of the vanquished. The dead, who periled all that man holds dear this side of heaven, quietly sleep side by side. They sleep their last sleep. They have fought their last battle. No sound shall awake them to conflict again; and blistered be the tongue that utters one word of reproach, standing over the graves of our great-hearted dead who fell on either side; I mean those who went into the struggle on the great principles involved; who believed they were right.

I have anticipated and must turn back to Meridian, not as it now is, but as it then was; and when I say that it was the dirtiest, most filthy and villainous hole in all the Confederate States I do not use the language of exaggeration, but of simple truth. Nice people lived there, of course, but the general public part of it was abominable. The gathering place for the

---

[32] G. G. Mullins, ed., *Caskey's Book: Lectures on Great Subjects* (St. Louis: John Burns Publishing Co., 1884) 329.

soldiers, Confederate and Federal; the stockade for the poor prisoners; the crowded and badly-kept hotels for the traveling masses of soldiers and citizens who were able to pay for poor beef, badly cooked; a biscuit out of third-class flour, and any quantity of saleratus, bad lard, and half baked; with a dirty cup of dirty slop, made of a quart of water, a few grains of rye, badly parched, and burned molasses; and then catch a few hours of restless sleep, provided you were so fortunate as to get to tumble into a bed, to which clean sheets were utter strangers, and which was yet warm from an occupant who had just tumbled out and was almost half way to the depot, to catch the up or down train. To give to the reader, unacquainted with the place and the time, some idea of the estimation in which the place was held by our soldiers, and the feeling was universal with them, although our hospitals were not really so very bad, but things suffered in their estimation from the general character of the place, so that the sick soldier dreaded the hospitals then little less than the cold grave; and if they could have had their own way many of them would have risked the grave to avoid the hospital. Just above Meridian is Lauderdale Springs, a cool, well shaded and finely watered village, a delightful place for hospitals, and they were well kept, which made them very popular. They would get crowded, and under a barbarous order of red tape, prohibiting letting the sick be sent except to the next nearest hospital. Lauderdale was daily sending her excess of sick down to Meridian. My health having failed, I had been transferred from field to post duty, and was then hospital chaplain. One morning I walked down to the depot with one of the surgeons, expecting as usual a lot of sick on the train. They were sent, as we expected, from Lauderdale. About an average lot of sick, some not much sick, and able to walk; others could walk with some help; others on litters which had to be borne by men from depot to hospital. Among these there was a youth, perhaps twenty years old, who was very sick. He was beyond doubt the most ghostly, ghastly, haggard and emaciated specimen of a dirt and persimmon eating North Carolinian that ever left the tar-heel State for tented field. There was not much of him left except eyes and stomach, and these were out of all proportion to the rest of his fever-smitten body. A crowd gathered round his litter and showed their sympathy, while in pity they looked upon his skeleton form and pallid face. I thought I caught a slight gleam of humor twinkling in the corner of his enormously large eyes. The surgeon stepped up to the litter, and with considerable irritation in his voice, said, "In God's name, what could the surgeons have been thinking of to ship you down here? They are a disgrace to their profession." I give his reply in his own words, which showed his and the estimate of others in regard to the place. He spoke very low, for his voice was feeble. Very earnestly he said, "Don't blame the good doctors; they did it in kindness. They held a consultation on my case, and decided that I was bound to die, that in three days I was gwine ter leave these low grounds of sin and sorrer." Here he paused, apparently for want of breath. The surgeon said, "Why, then, did they send you?" He replied "They knew that when I died I was gwine straight to hell, and that three days in this cussed place would make me glad to swap, and throw in my old clothes ter boot!" The crowd fairly yelled, while a grim smile played around the corners of his mouth. I said to the surgeon, "He is not going to die," and die he did not, but got well, and was quite a pet at the hospital; but he vowed that if neither the doctors or the disease, nor both together, could kill him, that he would make the swap, if he had to do it by suicide, for in that place he would not stay.

The reflections that crowded upon my mind on that the gloomiest day in my life's history were not calculated to make a man shout as loud as a Methodist at a first-class camp meeting. County devastated; real estate all converted into Confederate bonds, and no Confederacy! Stock eat up; negroes fled; the toils and cares of two-thirds of a life's struggle with poverty—crowned at last with success—now, when the sun of life had passed its meridian height, an hastening on to its setting, all gone! And I standing amidst its blighted and pitiful wreck... All vanished like mist before the rising sun—flat broke; nothing to do; nothing to do it with, and an abundance of help to do it! Indeed, I might venture to say, without indulging in hyperbole, surplus help. Wife, two negro women, and eight children; and about everybody else; one bovine, and fifteen dollars; short inventory of available assets; not much trouble to count—no skill in bookkeeping needed.[33] Standing under the dark clouds, listening to the deep-toned, distant thunder, gazing on the streaked lightning flashes, the rush and roar of the howling storm as it whirled the debris of a wrecked fortune beyond the range of vision. I turned my disturbed thoughts for consolation to the part of a quarter of a century actively spent in trying to do good; preaching day and night, through sunshine and showers, clouds and storms; laborious days, months and years of mental, moral and physical toil. I had, I trust, turned many from darkness to light. But the outlook was gloom, darkness, tempest, and widespread desolation. Oh, how many of my

---

[33] Caskey was left with his wife, two former female slaves, and eight children, but with no ready income.

fondly-loved spiritual children quietly slept, without coffins or shrouds, in far-distant and unvisited graves! How many had lost faith in God, when the cause whey they believed was right, and which they fondly loved, went down in a sea of blood. Our chaplains prophesied success as among the certainties, since our cause was right, and God was on the side of right; therefore, the right was bound to triumph. I told them that they were sowing the seeds from which an abundant harvest of infidelity would be garnered in the event that our cause went under; that I did not believe that God had anything to do with the accursed thing from beginning to end on either side; that final victory would depend on courage, skill, numbers, and the heaviest guns best handled; that right and wrong would not weigh as much as a feather in the scale. It turned out as I knew it must, and many for whom I had toiled had been hopelessly demoralized by the influences thrown around them in camp and field, and for the time being were religious wrecks. The plow-share of ruin had run its furrows as deep in this field as the others, and as bitter a pang was felt as that produced by those was from the thought that the cause was lost—the cause I then believed to be right, and yet believe it; the cause on which I had periled all, and to which I had given the love of my heart, strong as the love of woman. All lost! What had I let to cheer my poor sad heart? Nothing but a consciousness of what to me was sacred—duty faithfully discharged. I had done the very best I could. During the whole struggle I had sang, prayed, preached, exhorted, and occasionally got pugnacious and shouldered a Colt's sixteen-shooter, and pitched into the fight; and now I am afraid somebody got hurt![34] This, an item of experience, not after but during the war, that I would gladly blot from memory's page, I hope with Uncle Toby, in "*Tristram Shandy*," that when the recording angel set down the charge against me he dropped a tear of pity on the page and blotted it out.[35]

I had served the sick and wounded on both sides, protected prisoners from insult and wrong, administered to their wants, living, and dying so far as I could. I had saved thousands of the lives of our men by good nursing and the best of medical attention. My noble state furnished the money—one hundred thousand dollars; the aid societies poured in their thousands; patriotic men, who could not mingle in the strife, and who desired to aid their cause, flocked to the hospitals, of which I had four, and nursed day and

---

[34] He fought at the Battle of First Manassas in 1861.

[35] *Tristram Shandy* was a novel written by Laurence Sterne (1713–1768), English clergyman and writer.

night without money and without price. I had given the enemy the best fight I had on hand, and came out badly whipped, so badly that I have not felt like fighting since. If ever I fight any more it will be personal, and under protest at that, and with pretty near a certainty that I come out best. But I find I am rather inclined to advance backwards and linger over my experience during the war. Some forward movements are not as pleasant to take as backward ones; but pleasant or unpleasant I must leave Meridian, for a number of good and substantial reasons, only one of which need here be given, and that is I had nothing to stay there on, and could not find anybody in all the place whose heart and purse was sufficiently expanded to take us all in and take good care of us; so I sold my only cow, that gave an abundance of milk for her own calf, and for mine both white and black; gathered up what little household furniture we had brought from our country home on my partner's farm; borrowed a little money and took passage on a miserable poor car for Jackson. I believe the first relief to my pent up feelings was experienced by getting up a big mad. It created a diversion, produced a sensation. I got gloriously mad; that is, if there is any such a mad as that. I got mad all over, inside and outside, right side and wrong side, top side and bottom side; had I been blind in one eye, I doubt not I would have been mad on the blind side and seeing side, too. Oh! I did get terribly mad; mad at every thing, and every body; mad at the Yankee Nation, and at every thing that began or ended with a "y," or even had a "y" in the middle; mad at our people who skulked in the hour of trial; mad at the poor dead Confederate Congress, because they did not do as I begged them to do—*set free! three hundred thousand of our slave men* in 1863, put guns in their hands, manly pride in their hearts and put them into the fight! Well, I could not think of anything but that it made me madder! I verily believe that if I had thought of the angel Gabriel, I would have gotten mad at the length of his wings. I am glad I did not; and right here I am going to stop for fear the old mad come back again! Poor, stumbling, foolish mortal; God help, guide and save us all!

After the war Thomas W. Caskey moved with his family to Fort Worth, Texas, where he accepted the call to be the pastor of the Fort Worth Christian Church. He supplemented his salary as a criminal lawyer in 1878 but returned to the pulpit when his salary was increased. He published Caskey's Book *in 1884, edited by Chaplain G. G. Mullins of the US Army. Caskey offered to refund the price of his book to anyone who decided that it was not worth the money.*

Thomas W. Caskey died in 1896.

Chapter 6

Building a New South

And many of those who sleep in the dust shall awake...And those who
are wise shall shine like the brightness of the firmament; and those
who turn many to righteousness like the stars forever and ever...
Daniel 12

As the ex-chaplains of the Confederacy arrived back in their home counties, many found that although the war between the states had ended, "the war between the churches" had not. The states in the lower South were divided into military districts and governed by Union generals and newly-formed Republican legislatures. President Andrew Johnson, the former military governor of Tennessee during the war, was just as determined to prevent the influence of disloyal preachers throughout the Deep South in 1866 as he had in Tennessee in 1862. The requirements for Southern clergy to take a loyalty oath to the United States Government, approved during the war by Secretary of War Stanton, were therefore resurrected and reformulated. In several of the Southern states army-backed Republican legislators enacted laws forbidding any minister to preach unless he repeated under oath that he had in no way assisted the Confederacy nor even offered to it his sympathies.[1] In others, including President Johnson's home state of Tennessee, ministers like other citizens, could be barred from voting for fifteen years unless they took an "iron-clad oath" of allegiance to the United States.[2] The penalties for breaking these laws were strict and severe.

---

[1] Charles Pitts, *Chaplains in Gray* (Nashville: Broadman Press, 1957) 122.
[2] John T. Moore and Austin P. Foster, *Tennessee: The Volunteer State 1769–1923*, vol. 1 (Nashville: S. J. Clarke Publishing Co., 1923) 475.

The Southern Baptist Convention of 1866 opposed these violations of the principle of the separation of church and state in America by declaring "that all interference with these functions on the part of civil rulers transcends their legitimate authority, and is a usurpation of the rights of conscience; and that when the claims of civil ruler comes in conflict with those of Christ, it is our duty to 'obey God rather than men,' and endure the consequences."[3] The Baptists, joined quickly by many Presbyterians and Methodists, decided to preach openly and risk whatever fines, imprisonments, or other indignities the "carpetbaggers" could dream up.

The enforcement of these Reconstruction laws against the Southern clergy proved short lived and impossible to enforce. Tennessee had returned to the Union on 24 July1866, and would be soon followed by other states. Former Confederate chaplains could not be punished for disloyalty under state Reconstruction laws if those laws were repealed or ignored by new state legislatures. The Episcopal clergy who had ministered in the South during the war were reuniting unhindered with their Northern colleagues. The Roman Catholic Church had never split. Disrupting churches that had already reunited made no sense even to radical Republicans who had bigger national issues to consider. Moreover, most Southern clergy were busy helping to reconstruct the South on a new model of a free society as mandated by the Thirteenth Amendment to the Constitution, a major goal of the US Congress.

It is noteworthy, however, that for about five years there was a certain silence in the Southern churches about the part their spiritual leaders had played in the war. The chaplains were not separated from the rest of the clergy, but had simply formed an extension ministry to soldiers during the conflict—a ministry that was representative of the churches as a whole. Therefore from 1865 until about 1870, public mention of military service as a Confederate chaplain was risky at a time when such service could cause civil penalties not only against the ex-chaplains but against the churches themselves.[4]

---

[3] Pitts, *Chaplains in Gray*, 122–23.

[4] Noted in reading some 200 obituaries of Methodist chaplains in the *Minutes of the Annual Conferences of the Methodist Episcopal Church, South*, from 1865 to 1870. The minutes were published in Nashville (Methodist Publishing House), but there are multiple volumes, each by year. Copies of the published minutes for each annual conference are located in the reference section of Pitts Theological Library, Emory University, Atlanta GA.

Nevertheless, the spirit, courage, and leadership skills of the returned Confederate chaplains played a major role in the rapid reconstruction of Southern churches. In the years 1862–1864, when the Federal armies were expelling civilian ministers from their pulpits and seizing, transforming, or burning Southern churches, many of these chaplains had seen and helped lead the largest spiritual revival ever witnessed among American soldiers. As Professor Robert L. Dabney, formerly a chaplain and adjutant for Lieutenant General "Stonewall" Jackson, had observed, "the active religious life" in the South was transferred in those years from the churches at home to the army.[5] During the next thirty years after the war, the former chaplains would continue their leadership and organizational skills and their revival techniques, honed on a dozen battlefields, to build a New South with a new spirit and a new heart for God.

Born Again

Come up hither and I will show you what must take
place after this…
Revelation 4

The revivification of religious institutions in the South took place simultaneously in all of the major Christian denominations from 1865 to 1890. Immediately after the surrender of the last Confederate army, Southern bishops, moderators, and other denominational leaders who had survived the war sought to reunite their people and plan strategies for recovery. In August of 1865, six bishops of the Methodist Episcopal Church, South, met in Columbus, Georgia, and announced that "Southern Methodism still survived!"[6] They called for a meeting of their general conference, delayed since 1862, to be held at New Orleans the next summer. There, for four weeks in 1866, the Methodist delegates hammered out a plan for recovery and growth. Lay delegates were introduced into church conferences; the six-month probationary period for membership was abolished; pastoral appointments were extended to four years; the mission board, the publishing house, and the College of Bishops were reconstituted;

---

[5] R. L. Dabney, *Life and Campaigns of Lt. Gen. Thomas J. Jackson, (Stonewall Jackson)* (Harrisonburg VA: Sprinkle Publications, 1983) 657.

[6] Marion E. Lazenby, *History of Methodism in Alabama and West Florida* (Nashville: Parthenon Press, 1960) 343.

and four new bishops were elected.[7] For the black members of the church, plans were begun which would result in their own Colored Methodist Episcopal Church—with their own clergy. Former Confederate chaplains were welcomed home and given immediate, often very responsible, appointments.

Southern Baptist Associations throughout the South began to reorganize with special emphasis on the new role of the Domestic Mission Board to unite Baptists, to form and encourage plans for the revival of experimental and practical religion, to afford opportunities to form funds for education of "pious young men" who may be called to the ministry, and to promote "pious, useful education" throughout the Baptist denomination.[8] Eight former Confederate chaplains, including James P. Boyce, president of the Southern Baptist Convention for seven years; John Broadus, president of the Southern Baptist Theological Seminary; and J. William Jones, secretary of the Southern Historical Society, became leaders in Baptist evangelism, growth, and education.[9]

Charles Todd Quintard, formerly chaplain of the First Tennessee Infantry, pioneered the revival of the Episcopal Church in the South. Consecrated the second Episcopal bishop of Tennessee in Philadelphia in 1865, Quintard served for thirty-three years, reuniting the Church across sectional lines, and establishing The University of the South at Sewanee, Tennessee. For his work, he was invited to the University of Cambridge where the Doctor of Laws degree was conferred upon him.[10]

Dr. Benjamin M. Palmer, perhaps the leading voice of the Presbyterian Church in the Confederate States and a former evangelist in the Army of Tennessee, had been forced into exile during the war. As soon as he could leave Columbia, South Carolina, he returned to his First Presbyterian Church in New Orleans. From his old pulpit, Palmer championed the establishment of eight schools in New Orleans enrolling 800 students in the first session. Palmer was invited to speak in New York at the church of Dr.

---

[7] Halford E. Luccock, *The Story of Methodism* (New York: Abingdon Press, 1926) 344.

[8] *Minutes of the 44th Anniversary of the Georgia Baptist Convention, April 1866* (Macon GA: Burke, Boykin & Co., 1866) 28–29 in the Georgia State Department of Archives and History, Morrow GA

[9] Pitts, *Chaplains in Gray*, 132. Boyce was formerly chaplain of the 16th South Carolina Infantry; Broadus was chaplain of the 23rd South Carolina, and Jones of the 13th Virginia Infantry.

[10] Ibid., 131.

Henry Van Dyke where one Union Army veteran noted that "he preaches like an angel!"[11] Later in life he was offered the presidency of Southwestern University as well as a professorship at Columbia Presbyterian Seminary.[12] With Dr. Moses D. Hoge of Virginia, a former Confederate chaplain at Camp Lee outside Richmond, Palmer became a symbol of the new Presbyterian spirit.

In 1867 the Reverend J. William Jones took a census of college presidents "in order to ascertain how far our returned soldiers were maintaining their Christian profession."[13] Jones discovered that eighty percent of the Christian students in the colleges he surveyed had served in the Confederate Army and that "nine-tenths of the candidates for the ministry had determined to preach while in the army."[14] Clearly the emphasis on rebuilding the South's educational infrastructure was providing another generation of Christian ministers for the future—a generation inspired at least in part by the Great Revivals of 1862–1864.

Much of the leadership of the post-war churches also had come from the same source. By 1892 thirteen former Confederate chaplains and two army missionaries had been consecrated bishops in the Episcopal, Roman Catholic, and Methodist churches in every one of the former Confederate states except Mississippi.[15] Three ex-Confederate officers who did not serve

---

[11] Ibid., 124.

[12] Ibid.

[13] J. William Jones, *Christ in the Camp or Religion in the Confederate Army* (Harrisonburg VA: Sprinkle Publications, 1986) 463.

[14] Ibid.

[15] Chaplains Pellicer (Roman Catholic) in Texas, Marvin (Methodist) in Arkansas, Leray (Roman Catholic) and Keener (Methodist) in Louisiana, Hargrove (Methodist) and Manucy (Roman Catholic) in Alabama, Haygood (Methodist) and Beckwith (Episcopal) in Georgia, Gray (Episcopal) in Florida, Watson (Episcopal) in North Carolina, Duncan (Methodist) in South Carolina, Granbery (Methodist) and Randolph (Episcopal) in Virginia, Quintard (Episcopal) in Tennessee, and Ryan (RC) in Missouri. Bishops Marvin and Keener were missionaries in Arkansas and Louisiana during the war. The rest were commissioned chaplains. Compiled from Herman Norton, "The Organization and Function of the Confederate Military Chaplaincy, 1861–1865" (Ph.D. diss., Vanderbilt University, 1956) 77ff; Frank L. Hieronymus, "For Now and Forever: The Chaplains of the Confederate States Army" (PhD diss., University of California at Los Angeles, 1964) 308ff; Frederick DeLand Leete, *Methodist Bishops* (Nashville: Parthenon Press, 1948) 60ff.

as chaplains were also consecrated bishops in the South from 1874 to 1884—all three in the Episcopal Church.[16]

Another twelve former chaplains, at least, were presidents of major colleges or seminaries including W. W. Bennett, president of Randolph-Macon in Virginia; William Ryland, president of Bethel College in Kentucky; James Nelson, president of the University of Richmond; John L. Johnson, president of Mary Sharpe College in Tennessee; R. W. McDonald, president of Lebanon College in Tennessee; Isaac T. Tichenor, first president of the State Agricultural and Mechanical College at Auburn, Alabama; J. N. Waddell, former superintendent of Presbyterian Army Missions in the southwest, chancellor of the University of Mississippi; and Atticus G. Haygood, eighth president of Emory College in Oxford, Georgia. Crawford H. Toy, former chaplain of the 53rd Georgia, became professor and head of the department of Semetic languages at Harvard University; T. D. Witherspoon of the 2nd Mississippi became the chaplain of the University of Virginia; and L. B. Wharton of the 59th Virginia, a professor at the College of William and Mary in Williamsburg.

Although it is unknown exactly how many parishioners and students these eighteen bishops and scores of presidents, professors, and preachers may have influenced, the population of their denominations, taken as a whole in 1890, exceeded five million persons. This was almost twice the estimated total Protestant church membership in the South in 1860.[17]

As further evidence of the recovery of the churches, the value of church buildings and colleges increased dramatically. The value of church properties held by the Southern Methodists practically quadrupled from $10 million in 1860 to $38 million in 1890; that of the Southern Baptist Convention did the same from $7 million to $29 million; the Presbyterians increased from $6.9 million to $16 million; the Episcopalians from $5.1 million to $12 million; and the Roman Catholic Church's properties

---

[16] Charles C. Tiffany, *History of the Protestant Episcopal Church of the USA* (New York: Christian Literature Co., 1895) 506: The bishops were Robert Elliott of Texas (1874), John Galleher of Louisiana (1880), and Thomas Dudley of Kentucky (1884).

[17] Compiled from Hieronymus, "For Now and Forever," 3–5; Sydney E. Ahlstrom, *A Religious History of the American People* (New Haven: Yale University Press, 1972) 725; *Minutes of the Annual Conferences of the Methodist Episcopal Church, South: 1890* (Nashville: Southern Methodist Publishing House, 1891) 194; Robert T. Handy, *A History of the Churches in the United States and Canada* (New York: Oxford University Press, 1977) 270; and Robert E. Thompson, *A History of the Presbyterian Churches in the United States* (New York: Christian Literature Co., 1895) 193.

doubled in value in the Southern states from $7.3 million to $15 million.[18] Some of the increase in wealth came from Northern philanthropists such as Commodore Cornelius Vanderbilt of New York City who endowed Vanderbilt University in Nashville in 1873 "to strengthen the ties which should exist between all sections of our common country."[19] Vanderbilt's gift to Bishop Holland McTyeire incidentally set up the first seminary of the Methodist Episcopal Church, South, at Vanderbilt University, which became a premier training ground for preachers. Other gifts, of course reflected personal giving by those who benefited from the general prosperity of the decade of the 1880s.

Among the many former chaplains who made incredible contributions to the recovery of the churches, two might be mentioned as having had wide-ranging influence well beyond their local areas. Chaplain Isaac Tichenor, Baptist chaplain of the 17th Alabama, became not only president of Auburn, even though he had not attended college himself, but he was also elected secretary of the Baptist Home Mission Board in Atlanta. In that role, from 1882–1899, he inaugurated mission work throughout the South and especially west of the Mississippi. It has been estimated that as many as 10,000 Baptist churches were organized from the programs of evangelism he inaugurated. The Southern Baptist Convention credited him with "taking possession of Texas" for the Lord.[20] These 10,000 churches constituted 25 percent of the total 40,000 Southern Baptist congregations which had been formed in the South by 1906.[21]

Atticus G. Haygood, formerly chaplain of the 15th Georgia, President of Emory College and a bishop of the Methodist Episcopal Church, South, was a pioneer in many aspects of education and evangelism embracing his denomination and the South as a whole. He was secretary of the Sunday School Board in Nashville, associate secretary of the Board of Missions, a member of the Board of Trustees of the Wesleyan Female College at Macon, editor of the *Wesleyan Christian Advocate*, president of the Georgia Teachers Association, and delegate to the Ecumenical Conference of the

---

[18] William Warren Sweet, *The Story of Religion in America* (New York: Harper Brothers, 1950) 352.

[19] Pat Wilkinson, ed., *Vanderbilt Commodore* (Nashville: Benson Printing Co., 1966) 5.

[20] Pitts, *Chaplains in Gray*, 133.

[21] Ron Ellison, "An Overview of Southern Baptists' Ministry to Confederate Soldiers," unpublished manuscript, Southern Baptist Historical Library and Archives, Nashville TN.

Methodist Church held in London in 1881. But Haygood's Thanksgiving sermon of 1880 titled "The New South" was so influential that Henry Grady, publisher of the Atlanta *Constitution*, credited Haygood with being one of the sources of the philosophy that turned the South from a past of slavery and secession to a future of progress and productivity.[22]

Although there were many factors that contributed to the renaissance of the Southern churches after the war, the influence of the former Confederate chaplains must be weighed favorably with the rest. Most historians agree that although a number of Confederate generals favored "a converted army," the revivals of spirit and confidence among the soldiers would not have occurred without the intervention of the evangelical preachers who served as their chaplains.[23] Moreover, as has been demonstrated, many of the chaplains used the organizational and leadership skills they had learned in the army to help rebuild the churches after the war and perpetuate evangelical Christianity not only in the South, but also throughout the nation.

Lieutenant General A. P. Stewart, post-war chancellor of the University of Mississippi, remarked in 1874, "I do not know who was finally right or wrong in the last war. I do not even know whose side God was on. I do believe that in the end, God had need of a *United* States of America."[24]

When the last surviving Confederate chaplain, the Reverend George L. Petrie of Charlottesville, Virginia, died in 1931, the Southern churches counted more than 14 million members among their evangelical congregations.[25] However, the largest denominations were still definitively Southern and white. The Methodists did not reunite with their Northern brethren until 1939; the Presbyterians not until 1983. The Southern Baptist Convention remains autonomous to the present day. When the Confederate Congress proclaimed that "The clergy of the land have done more for the success of our cause than any other class; they have kept up the spirits of the

---

[22] Atticus G. Haygood, *The New South: Thanksgiving Sermon, 1880, by Atticus G. Haygood*, Judson C. Ward, ed. (Atlanta: Emory University Library, 1950) viii.

[23] Dabney, *Life and Campaigns of Lt. Gen. Thomas J. Jackson, (Stonewall Jackson)*, 654. Most of the chaplains who were involved in the revivals attributed them to an outpouring of the Holy Spirit, not to their sermons.

[24] Dumas Malone, ed., *Dictionary of American Biography*, vol. 18 (New York: Charles Scribner's Sons, 1946) 3.

[25] Winthrop Hudson, *Religion in America* (New York: Scribner, 1965) 354.

people," no one could have known what long, enduring memories "the war between the churches" would engender.[26]

---

[26] Ernest Trice Thompson, *Presbyterians in the South*, vol. 2 (Richmond: John Knox Press, 1973) 84.

Memoirs, 1871-1880

"Hold Your Ground!"

Chaplain John L. Girardeau
23rd South Carolina Infantry, Army of Northern Virginia

John Lafayette Girardeau was born 14 November 1825 on James Island near Charleston, South Carolina. He entered the College of Charleston at age fourteen and graduated four years later. From 1845 to 1848 he studied at the Columbia Theological Seminary in Columbia, South Carolina. Licensed to preach in 1848, he officiated at a number of small Presbyterian churches in the country until 1853 when he took charge of a mission for negroes in Charleston begun by the Second Presbyterian Church. In seven years the Zion Church, as the mission became known, grew from 48 to 600 members. Girardeau's eloquence, learning, and piety attracted a number of influential white members who built a new church in 1857 at the corner of Calhoun and Meeting Streets that would seat 1,500 black and white attendees and assumed the costs of its operation.

In June of 1862, at the age of thirty-nine, Girardeau accepted a commission as chaplain of the 23rd South Carolina Infantry. He remained with them throughout the war as performed exemplary ministry during the long siege of Petersburg from June of 1864 to April of 1865. Captured at Sailor's Creek, Virginia, on 6 April, Girardeau was confined in the Old Capitol Prison in Washington and then at Johnson's Island, Sandusky, Ohio, until he was released on 20 June 1865.

In April of 1866 he returned to Charleston to assume the pastorate of a new Zion Glebe Street Church. While serving in this capacity, he was asked to deliver an address at the Magnolia Cemetery when the bodies of Confederate soldiers killed at Gettysburg were brought home for interment. His remarks were printed in the Charleston newspaper.[1]

Address given by Reverend John L. Girardeau, D.D. at the
Reinterment Ceremony, Magnolia Cemetery in Charleston, of the South
Carolina Confederate Gettysburg Dead on Confederate Memorial Day
10 May 1871

In introducing what may be said, I beg leave to make two requests:

First, that in any utterances which may have a political complexion I may not be understood to assume to speak as a minister of the Gospel, and as delivering a message from the LORD, but as any citizen might express his sentiments who professes to fear God and to cherish the interests of his people;

Secondly, that as a special interest attaches to this occasion some indulgence as to time may be granted for the remarks which may be offered. And wilt Thou, Almighty Being, inspire what may be uttered with the spirit of wisdom, justice and truth.

The circumstances which assemble us in the streets of this City of the Dead are, in the last degree, solemn, tender and affecting. The bones of our brethren have for nearly eight years been sleeping in the graves in which they were laid on the bloody battle-field of Gettysburg. Their repose was unbroken by the roar of subsequent conflicts, by the wild wail of grief which broke forth at the fall of their beloved country, or by the triumphal honours paid to the memories of those who battled against the cause for which they died, and fell on the same field with them. The wounded who survived for a brief while the carnage of that day turned amid their last thoughts on earth to the State they had loved so well, even as dying children to a mother, and ere they yielded up their gallant spirits breathed the fervent entreaty: "Send our bodies to South Carolina to be buried there!"

Was it that in their latest moments of consciousness they recoiled from the thought that they would be interred in an enemy's soil, and that their graves would be designated as those of rebels and traitors? They did not mistake. The remains of their opponents have very naturally been carefully collected, and with distinguished funereal honours been laid side by side in a

---

[1] "Memorial Day," *Daily Courier* (Charleston SC), 11 May 1871, 1. There is a copy on microfilm in the South Caroliniana Library, Columbia SC, listed in the collection of Charleston newspapers.

place of sepulture decorated by the hand of affection. They were left to sleep apart. We could not have wished it otherwise. They had, as a peculiar people, contended for their rights, and, as a peculiar people, occupied graves by themselves—in death as in life adhering to a noble and sacred, though despised and execrated, Cause.

They were entitled to strangers' accommodations and they received them. But they will no longer sleep alone. They will now have a fellowship in death from which they have hitherto been excommunicated. Their dying wish is fulfilled. Their isolated repose has been interrupted by the gentle hands of their country women who have tenderly removed them from alien graves, and brought them hither for admission to the communion of kindred dead. They have come home at last; and we, their brethren, their comrades, bone of their bone and flesh of their flesh, are met with one accord to welcome them to their native soil. We receive them not as conquerors, else would a whole people in funeral procession and with military pageant have escorted them to their coveted repose; but none the less honour on that account shall be awarded them. Not one chaplet, not one laurel-wreath shall be withheld albeit twined with the willow and the cypress. Not the roll of drums, the blast of bugles and the thunder of cannon, but the throb of grief, the quick-flowing tear, the yearning of an unspeakable love, all that boundless admiration, undying gratitude and unconquered principles can give,—these, Heroes of a defeated but glorious Cause, are the tribute we offer you today.

Afflicted Carolina, rise in thy mourning weeds, and receive thy returning children to thy maternal breast! Pillow them softly there, for there they prayed to sleep their long and dreamless sleep! Here let men who never surrendered except to death find a fitting resting place in a spot overlooking the waters which were never parted by a hostile keel so long as an artillery-man remained with his port fire behind the guns which guarded them, and yonder battered and ragged fortress which though often assaulted was never carried by storm. Here let them sleep with those who never looked upon a conqueror's flag floating over the citadels of a sovereign State, but closed their eyes upon a still free and defiant Commonwealth. Shoulder to shoulder they stood; now let them lie side by side. Confederates in life, confederates let them be in death.

Deep as is the grief which this occasion calls forth we are not here simply as mourners for the dead. There are living issues which emerge from these graves—gigantic problems affecting our future, which starting up in the midst of these solemnities demand our earnest attention. The question which thrills every heart is, Did these men die in vain? Their death was but the logical conclusion of the principles which led to our great struggle, and furnished their highest and most significant illustration. It was the costliest sacrifice which an injured people could make for the maintenance of their fundamental liberties. Fathers and mothers gave up their children, wives their husbands, sisters their brothers, sovereign States their sons, and these men themselves, for the sake of a cause which involved every earthly interest and overshadowed every earthly relation. What sacrifice could for a moment be put into comparison with this? To have yielded up our fortunes, to have been ejected from our burning homes, to have witnessed the sacking of our cities, and the destruction of our harvests,—could all these have borne any analogy to the loss of these lives? The questions, therefore, force themselves upon us, Was this sacrifice a useless one? Was this precious blood spilt wholly in vain?

There are two senses in which it must be admitted that they lost their cause,—they failed to establish a Confederacy as an independent country, and they failed to preserve the relation of slavery. But there were fundamental principles of government, of social order, of civil and religious liberty, which underlay and pervaded that complex whole which we denominated our Cause. And the question whether those who fell in its support died in vain, as to those principles, must depend for its answer upon the course which will be pursued by the people of the South. What then shall be the nature of our answer? What [is] the course which we shall adopt? There is but one reply which deserves to be returned to these inquiries—our brethren will not have died in vain, if we cherish in our hearts, and as far as in us lies, practically maintain, the principles for which they gave their lives.

Either these men were rebels against lawful authority, or they were not. If they were, then the principles upon which they acted ought to be abandoned and the cause for which they contended ought to be consigned to oblivion. Dear as their memory is to us, we would have no warrant in being moved by personal relations to them to perpetuate a grievous wrong. If they were not, then every noble attribute of our nature, every sacred sentiment of justice, gratitude and consistency should impel us to justify their course, and to perpetuate their principles. And this is our position. In the face of the world we protest, that so far from having been rebels against legitimate authority and traitors to their country, they were lovers of liberty, combatants for constitutional rights, and as exemplars of heroic virtue benefactors of their race. This is not mere assertion dictated by sympathy or uttered in the spirit of bravado. It is susceptible of proof.

There are three great elements in the social constitution of man, involving corresponding necessities—the Domestic, the Political and the Religious. Answering to these fundamental features of our nature there are three Divinely ordained institutes, independent of, but related to, each other—the Family, the State, and the Church. Taken together they constitute the trinity of human relations. Each of them is indispensable to the wellbeing, if not the very preservation, of the race. They are the pillars on which rests the stability of society, as well as the prime motors in its catholic Progress—its organic nisus towards the great end for which it was originally ordained. To injure either of them is to strike a blow at the root of human happiness; and so intimate is the bond between them, so nice and delicate their action and re-action upon each other, that to impair one of them is to imperil the integrity of them all. Adverse to each and all of these beneficent ordinations, and consequently antagonistic to the vital interests which they suppose, there is a spirit abroad in the earth, almost universal in its operation, the measures of which are characterized by a subtlety and unity betokening the shaping influence of one master intelligence—that of the Arch-foe of God and man. Need it be said that this is Radicalism? Conceived in revolt from the sublime and harmonious order in which the different elements operate, it purposes to upturn the very ground-forms of society. Nothing that is sustained by the experience of the past, nothing that is venerable with age and consecrated by immemorial associations, nothing that descending through the ages has retained, in the midst of change and revolution, the fragrance of our primeval estate, or even of patriarchal dignity and simplicity, nothing just, true and pure, will be allowed to escape the sweep of this deluge. Montalbert has said, [2] in effect, that there is a force in Europe, set in motion, by radical agitators, and penetrating and impelling the sea-like masses; which, if unchecked, is destined erelong to obliterate every existing secular and ecclesiastical organization.

This ruthless, leveling Spirit wages war against the Family, the State and the Church. Hearth-stones, grave, altars, temples,—all are borne down under its tempestuous irruption. Nothing is safe from it. There is no sanctuary which it will not invade, no just, holy, time-honored sanction

---

[2] Charles le Comte de Montalembert (1810–1870), French author who championed liberty during the revolutions of 1830 and 1848.

which it will not violate. Contemning the ordinances of man, it swaggers, in its Titanic audacity, against the empire of the Eternal. A leader of Parisian Socialism is reported recently to have exclaimed, that if he could reach the Almighty he would poniard Him upon His throne! Breach after breach has it already opened through the barriers which limit and restrain it, and in its onward rush, should laws, constitutions and public sentiment fail to impede its course, can only be arrested, aside from immediate Divine intervention, by the iron power of imperial Absolutism. Plunged into the vortex of anarchy by this Genius of Lawlessness, swimming for life in the vast gulf of the miseries induced by it, men will in very despair turn for refuge to Autocratic Despotism. It has been said by a great writer on Government, that there are two cardinal wants of society—protection and liberty; and that of these the first in order is protection. Existence must be pre-supposed by happiness. In accordance with this principle it is but natural to judge that, when men have tried the desolating misrule of radical anarchy, they will recoil for protection under the sceptre of Despotism. But a selfish desire for safety will not have eradicated the prescriptive habits of democratic license, and the probable resultant of these conflicting forces will be a mechanical union between the imperial and popular element—between Consolidated Despotism and Democratic Absolutism. To this the indications in Europe and on this Continent seem to point. Extremes will meet on a principle shared by both—uncompromising hostility to regulated government and constitutional liberty. Apparently as far apart as the poles, they will be united by a common axis, on which the insane attempt will be made to drive the revolutions of the political world. And if an opinion might be ventured, suggested by a probable view of Inspired Prophecy, the day may not be far distant when this consummation will be reached. The body of iron will attached to feet of clay—significant symbol of a great Imperial Despotism resting on the uncertain masses of a fierce Democracy. When this climax of crime and folly shall have been attained, there will be one of two alternatives before a sickened and despairing world,—on the one hand the experience of a condition of things in which a social, political and religious Chaos will reign, in which star after star of hope will be quenched, the constellations of the great lights be blotted from the firmament, and the earth saturated with blood shall go down into a seething abyss of destruction; or, on the other hand, a supernatural interposition of God to rectify the otherwise remediless disorders of the world, and the re-establishment of a theocratic government no longer confining its sway to one favoured people, but assuming the diadem of universal dominion, healing the schisms of the race, collecting the struggling nations into one peaceful flock, and distributing with impartial hand the blessings of equal rule, regulated liberty and wide-spread domestic peace.

This somewhat extended portraiture of the spirit of Radicalism will not be deemed out of place, when it is remembered that it powerfully contributed to produce the evils under which we are now suffering. It was against its aggressions, in the particular forms in which they were directed upon the South, that these men whose memories we honour today and their compatriots contended unto death. It was this fell spirit which, aiming at the destruction of an institution peculiar to the South, overrode very moral and constitutional obstacle which opposed its progress, drenched a once peaceful land in fraternal blood, and has occasioned that disturbed condition of affairs which is now likely to be confined to no section, but threatens to agitate the whole country. It began by assuming the existence of a "higher law," growing out of what were denominated the instincts of human nature, which it held to be superior, in the sphere of morals, to Divine Revelation, and, in that of politics, to the provisions of the Federal Constitution. Which such a theory from which to derive its inspirations, it is not to be wondered at that it regarded neither the laws of God nor of man which were conceived to lie in the path to the attainment of its ends. Pushing out this baleful dogma to its legitimate results, it boldly invaded the political order, and the fundamental principles of that federative government, which we had inherited from our fathers. Resting not until it had destroyed the attitude of strict neutrality imparted to the Constitution by the wisdom of its framers, it perverted that instrument into an organ, and the government into an agent of a section, trampled under foot the rights of sovereign States, and utterly refused to the people of the South all claim to think and act for themselves. It was a case demanding resistance from freemen. It was in view of such subversions of their constitutional rights and liberties that the Southern States in their organic capacity, and by the solemn acts of conventions, determined to withdraw from a confederation in which it was plain as day that their hopes of justice and equal consideration were destroyed. This act of sovereignty they were refused the liberty of performing; and no choice was left but unconditionally to submit or meet force with force. They adopted the alternative of freemen. In the struggle which ensued the Sons of the South, feeble in numbers and in the apparatus of war, excluded from the fellowship of nations, cut off by a cordon of fire from access to the ports of the world, and overwhelmed by vast hordes representing almost every European nationality, failed to secure the Independence they sought. They lost the power to exercise certain rights and principles. But did they lose these rights and principles themselves? How could they? except in the case of any which, acting in their organic capacity since the close of the war, they may have deliberately relinquished. Lost them? Yes, as a weak man, overpowered by the superior physical strength of another, may be said to lose the right for which he has contended. He loses the exercise of it, until he has the power to recover it. Are the religious principles of the martyr destroyed because he is burnt for them? Does the freeman lose his natural or political rights because tyranny represses their exercise? The very struggle to maintain them, the blood that was shed for them, the lives that were sacrificed in their defense render their rights and principles all the dearer to men out of whom all love of liberty is not completely crushed. Our principles were defeated, not necessarily lost. It behooves us to cling to them as drowning men to the fragments of a wreck. They furnish the only hope for our political future—the only means of escape from anarchy on the one hand, or from despotism on the other, which are left to a once free and happy country. If the death of our brethren shall have the effect of enhancing these principles in our regard it will not have been in vain.

These men also contended for the existence and the purity of their social relations, particularly in the domestic form. They fought for their firesides as well as for their political rights. The same Radical spirit which disregarded the limitations of the Constitution, contemns the Divinely-instituted barriers which fence in the sanctities of the Family relation. Its triumph bodes for us no good. The danger is imminent of the introduction amongst us of novel social theories, born on another soil, and coming in as filthy camp-followers of a conquering host. Their first appearance may excite no alarm. They may even be derided; but they start tendencies, and tendencies, especially when seconded by the depraved instincts of nature, speedily become results if not arrested in their inception. It becomes us with all our might to resist that corruption of manners which is incompatible with the simplicity of free institutions, and the purity and integrity of moral character. The overwhelming affliction through which we have passed, the trials through which are still passing, and the memory of our dead, should lead us to a corresponding gravity of deportment. Who of us is there who does not sometimes weep over the glorious past? Is there one of us across whose soul there does not sometimes sweep the storm of an irrepressible grief? We are not yet done burying our dead. We are now standing by the open graves of those who died for liberty, who died for us. We cannot put off the signals of mourning yet. Shall we ever do it, while our liberties are prostrated? It is to be greatly feared that a temper of levity is growing upon us which ill befits the seriousness, the deep sadness of our condition. These are homely counsels. Would that they were not suggested by obvious dangers. O! my countrymen, if ever we are really, finally conquered, it will be by ourselves. The process of dissolution will commence from within. The history of the past indicates it to be an almost universal law. The most powerful nations have succumbed under their own deterioration of moral sentiment, and degeneracy of manners. As long as these causes of decay were inoperative no external force or internal agitations availed to destroy them. Look at the English people. While comparative simplicity and purity of manners prevailed, revolution followed revolution but the country stood. The fundamental law was perfected by fresh guarantees of freedom. Every conflict enhanced the vigour of their institutions; every storm settled the roots of the tree of liberty deeper and faster in the soil. It is said by observers the luxuriousness of living has greatly increased among them. If so, the checks and balances of their conservative government will be soon put to the strain; its noble embankments will not long stand against the sea of Radicalism which is beginning to dash in thunder against them.

We must resist the influence of Radicalism in its Socialistic aspects as we would oppose the progress of a plague. Socialism and Communism are developments of the same Radical spirit. They go hand in hand. When the relations of life are subverted, the rights which spring from them are destroyed. When the altars of the Family are overthrown, it is but a step to tear down the pillars of the State. The stability of political principle and the happiness of the people depend upon the preservation of the social system from the inroads of corruption. To poison this is to poison the fountain. Let us read in the fearful tragedy now enacting in Paris before the horrified gaze of the world the bitter end to which we, too, shall inevitably come unless we steadfastly maintain the principles which have been twice consecrated by patriotic blood—that of our ancestors in the first, and that of our brethren and fathers in the second, revolutionary war.

We have seen that in the complex constitution of our nature the religious element forms an integral part, and that provision is made for its exercise in the Divinely appointed institute of the Church. In contending against those influences which threaten to sap the foundations of every venerable institution, our slain brethren fought for their altars, as well as for their fire-sides and their political franchises. This is not an extravagant statement. The spirit of the Christian Religion pervaded the armies of the Confederacy. The vast majority of our soldiers were its nominal adherents, and thousands of them were professors of the faith. Its influence was felt in almost every regiment. In the quiet of camp, during the march and on the eve of battle its sacred services imparted fortitude under hardship and heroic courage for the day of conflict. From the Commander-in-chief to the humblest private in the ranks a reverent respect was paid to its ministers and its ordinances. We have seen Robert E. Lee, unattended by even a sergeant, go afoot through the mire to the soldiers' gathering for worship, and sitting in the midst of them devoutly listen with them to the preaching of God's Word, and mingle his prayers and praises with theirs. Jackson was proverbially a man of prayer. He led his fiery and resistless columns into the tempest of battle with hand uplifted to heaven in token of dependence on God, and supplication for His blessing. It deserves to be mentioned that that great soldier before the breaking out of hostilities taught a humble Sabbath-School at Lexington, the pupils of which when his remains were taken there for burial followed them with every mark of affection to their last, quiet resting-place. I desire to record it, amidst the affecting solemnities of this funereal occasion, that during an extended experience as chaplain I never encountered a sick, wounded or dying Southern soldier who rejected the Christian faith, or treated its proffered consolations with contempt. Let us then accept from them as in some sort martyrs for religion as well as for liberty the solemn obligation to maintain the Christianity which sustained them amid the privations of a soldier's life and the anguish of a soldier's death.

The relation between our people and the Gospel at once confers invaluable benefits and creates imperishable responsibilities. We cannot impair it without doing ourselves irreparable damage. Our civilization takes its dominant type from Christianity. All its distinctive moral features are derived from it. Ancient Pagan civilizations embodied the intellectual as well as our own. We can boast of no capacity of thought, no mental culture superior to that which distinguished the land of Homer and Aristotle, or the home of Virgil and Cicero. But the incompleteness and self-destructiveness inherent in a civilization merely intellectual are illustrated in the history of every great power, save one, of ancient times. The stability of a State, and of the institutions which it embraces and which go to make up its organic life, depend on the degree in which the principle moral obligation obtains, and the rules of virtue are practiced. But, as has been observed by a splendid writer on American Democracy, there can be no true morality without religion. It is incumbent on us, therefore, as possessing the only perfect religion which the world has known, to appreciate the responsibilities which flow from such an endowment. Apostasy from Christianity would be suicide. But may be asked, What special danger is there of such an event growing out of present circumstances? It may be said in reply that the danger is two-fold:

First, [t]he critical changes through which we have passed expose us to the invasion of theories and the pressure of influences which were excluded by the settled condition of the past. The violence of the revolution in our circumstances can scarcely be exaggerated. Not only has our political state been so altered as to reverse relations formerly existing, but one element has been torn by force, and torn suddenly out of the very fabric of our social system. Our domestic life is passing through a most extraordinary transition. We are therefore in a forming condition. Every month is settling precedents for the future. Old institutions, customs and sentiments are breaking up as by the upheaval of a deluge; and it is a question of the last importance, into what order, what type of thought, opinion and practice we shall finally crystallize. It is while we are passing through this transitional process that the peril is immanent that ideas, theories and usages may be imbedded in the yielding mass which, when it shall have consolidated, no power will avail to extract. Already does this danger threaten us in the sphere of religion; and it becomes us to watch against tendencies which carry in them the seeds of defection from a pure religious faith.

Secondly, [t]he prostration of our civil, forebodes injury to our religious, liberties. Civil Liberty and Religious Liberty are twin sisters. They stand or fall together. Here, however, a distinction is necessary. It is freely conceded that the essential liberty of the soul cannot be formed by human power. There are two prerogatives with which our Maker has endowed us which no tyranny can affect. They lie beyond the jurisdiction of human courts and the coercion of human executives. They are as free in the dungeon, at the stake and on the gibbet, as in the assemblies of an unconquered people, or in the issues of an unlicensed and unmuzzled press. They are the inalienable, indestructible powers of thought and language—the faculty by which we form our opinions, and that by which we express them. They body may be manacled in irons, while the mind in its limitless excursions mounts as on wings of fire above the stars. The tongue, the glory of our corporeal frame, the harp from the strings of which is evoked the spontaneous adoration of God, the trumpet which heralds forth to mankind the noble conceptions of the human intelligence, the tongue—the obedient organ of free thought—cannot be coerced. It may be cut out but cannot be compelled to speak. When, therefore, physical liberty is restrained, these essential, godlike prerogative of the soul are as untrammeled as ever. But the freedom to express positively our convictions, to embody in outward form our worship of the Diety, to maintain institutions significant of our faith—this freedom may be crushed by human power. The Church in its external manifestations may be suppressed. In this point of view the difference between civil and religious liberty becomes exceedingly thin. The one may to some extent survive the other, especially if the ruin of that other be not total; but the destruction of one originates the impulse to the subversion of the other, and supplies the motive to it. What has been done may be done; and when civil liberty has in fact been extinguished, the argument is a short one to the extinction of religious. It is the argument of triumphant power. Farther than this, the connection between these two complementary forms of liberty is so close—the fire on the one altar so readily communicates itself to the smouldering ashes on the other—that it is evident that as long as one is enjoyed, the other cannot be completely quenched. Their principles are akin; and the existence of one necessarily conduces to the maintenance of the other. Consequently, that a people should be thoroughly subdued, neither can be left intact. Both must be crushed. The people, therefore, which deliberately consents to the destruction of one form of liberty vainly dreams when it hopes that the other may escape. As surely as the law of contagion operates, so surely will one not long survive the contact with the corpse of the other. To this conclusion, then, must those come who abandon the last struggle for civil liberty—they must expect as a legitimate inference the loss of religious.

To sum up what has been said: Our brethren will not have died in vain if we their survivors adhere to the great principles for which they contended unto death; if we preserve an attitude of protest against those Radical influences which threaten to sweep away every vestige of constitutional rights and guarantees, to pollute the fountains of social life, and ultimately to whelm our civil and religious liberties in one common ruin.

Can this attitude be maintained? I presume not to speak of special political measures, but would earnestly urge the adoption of a course which will enable us to retain our hold upon our principles, and keep a posture of preparation for any relief which a gracious Providence may be pleased in answer to our prayers to grant us from the evils which now oppress us:

Let us cling to our identity as a people! The danger is upon us of losing it—of its being absorbed and swallowed up in that of a people which having despoiled us of the rights of freemen assumes to do our thinking, our legislating and our ruling for us. Influences are operating on us with every last breath we draw which, if we be not vigilant, will sooner or later wipe out every distinctive characteristic which has hitherto marked us. Are we prepared for it? In that event, nothing of the past will be left to the South but a history which will read like and elegiac poem, nothing for the present but a place on the maps which our children study, nothing for the future but a single element of existence—a geographical one.—But can we preserve our identity in the face of the difficulties which oppose it?

We may do it, by continuing to wear the badges of mourning befitting a deeply afflicted people; by consenting to undergo the trials which distinguish us from a people inflated with material prosperity rather than abate one jot or tittle of our adhesion to principle; and by transforming the sufferings endured for freedom's sake into a discipline which may save our virtues from decay, and our liberties from extinction. We may do it, by utterly refusing to participate in any measures, of however great apparent utility, which require the slightest compromise of our innermost convictions; by declining to acquiesce where only to submit is demanded of us; and by preserving a dignified silence by which we shall signify our resolution, if we may not act for truth, right and liberty, not to act at all. We may do it, by instituting peculiar customs and organizations which will discharge the office of monuments perpetuating the past; by forming associations of a memorial character like that whose call gathers us here today; by collecting and publishing materials for our own history; and by appointing anniversaries by which if we may not celebrate the attainment of independence we can at least commemorate the deeds of men who died for our fundamental liberties and constitutional rights. We may do it, by scrupulously adhering to the phraseology of the past—by making it the vehicle for transmitting to our posterity ideas which once true are true forever, all opposition to them by brute force to the contrary notwithstanding. We may do it, by the education we impart to the young; by making our nurseries, schools and colleges channels for conveying from generation to generation our own type of thought, sentiment and opinion;

by stamping on the minds of our children principles hallowed by the blood of patriots, and by leading them with uncovered heads to gaze upon the grandest monuments the South can rear to liberty—the headstones which mark the last resting-place of Southern Volunteers!

If we adopt not this course, what will be the consequences, which must ensue? One of the results will be that the only remaining representatives on this continent of free republican principles—especially in their federative form—will have ceased to exist, and the faintest, the last hope of a return to the noble, the glorious estate inherited from our patriotic ancestors will have gone out in the blackness of darkness. And then it must in all probability follow that the question of the possibility of republican institutions, or of the maintenance of the principle of free representation will have been negatived forever. The failure of the experiment on this continent instituted under conditions so favourable, under auspices so happy will discourage any similar attempt for the future in any country under heaven. It may without extravagance be said that we occupy a moral Thermopylae in the struggle for republican liberty, and if we go down it will buried in the same grave with us.

Another consequence of our refusal to take this course will be—and it deserves our solemn consideration—that our deliberate acquiescence in the criminal acts by which the liberties of the country are subverted will make us partakers in the condign punishment which must some day be visited on their perpetrators. It implies no ordinary crime to break the faith of compacts between people and people, to despoil sovereign States of rights won by sacrifice and independence purchased by blood, to disturb the balances of equitable government, and to threaten with ruin as fair a fabric of constitutional liberty as the sun ever shone upon. "The offense is rank and smells to heaven;" and if nations are punished for their sins in this world, the penalty of such acts must soon or late descend. It matters little that its approach is delayed, or is noiselessly made. It was a saying of the ancients that "the feet of the avenging Deity are shod with wool." The tread of the pursuing Nemesis may not be heard, but it presses with inevitable and tremendous certainty upon the track of national transgression. The demon of Radicalism has been invoked. It knows no law; and may yet turn upon those who have imagined it obedient to their will. And shall we elect to participate in these retributions? No, my countrymen; let us prefer to suffer present affliction for righteousness' sake rather than to incur the future punishments of national guilt. Let us keep our skirts clear. We can only do this by maintaining our identity as a people. And is this impossible? There is a race, which, coming down through the centuries enveloped with antagonistic influences and hostile nationalities, has stood out in perpetual protest against amalgamation with other peoples, and today preserves its characteristics, as the current of the great Western River flows into, without blending with, the multitudinous waters of the Gulf. Even so must we hold to our identity, or, as a people, we are undone. We may perish if we attempt it; perish we must, as a Southern race, if we do not. It is now almost the only hope that is left us. Conservation of our peculiar principles is our great, our paramount duty. We owe it our forefathers; we owe it to these our dead brethren; we owe it to ourselves; we owe it to our children; we owe it to the struggling, waning, almost expiring sense of constitutional liberty in this land. If we yield in the extremity, all is lost. If we tenaciously hold on to the fragments of a noble past, cling to the planks of a ship-wrecked Constitution, the very attitude we shall maintain may possibly inspire other lovers of liberty in this land to rally to a last, mighty effort to regain lost ground, or at least to arrest further strides to ruin, as the firm stand of a colour-bearer, in the crisis of battle and danger of rout, sometimes recalls a discomfited and retiring host. It is thought by some that there is a speck of hope—a gleam of light in the stormy horizon. The disregard of the limitations of the Federal Constitution, the disposition to make fresh inroads upon the provisions of that instrument, the seeming determination to be balked by no barriers of fundamental law in its march to permanent triumph—these features disclosed by the dominant party are awakening thought and exciting apprehension. It may please a merciful Providence by this means to restore to the people of this land some measure of respect for the guarantees of liberty enjoyed in the past. If so, it would be suicidal in us by any unfortunate concessions to relinquish the conservative position we have held. Whether this be so, or not, we must stand by our principles. When Stonewall Jackson had, on that fearful night at Chancellorsville, received his fatal wound, and the ground was swept by a storm of grapeshot, he was informed by an officer that it was thought necessary to retire. Faint from the loss of blood, and suffering from excruciating pain, he partly raised himself from his prostrate posture and in a tone of authority said: "Hold your ground, Sir!" The bleeding form of Liberty rises from the earth before us and utters the same command. We must, by God's help, hold our ground, or consent to be traitors to our ancestry, our dead, our trusts for posterity, to our fire-sides, our social order, and our civil and religious liberties.

Barring a certain fearful looking for of a retribution, which would be the end of such a policy, no doubt we might better our material condition by accommodating our principles to the demands of circumstances. But shall we come to that? Who of us holds Principle so cheap as to prefer to her his gold, his houses and his lands? Who of us will put her into the market, and barter her for so many pieces of silver? Who of us, gazing into these open graves and upon these coffins, will measure her value by even life itself? These men loved not their lives in comparison with her. They died for her. Who will cleave to material goods and sensual ease at the sacrifice of principle? Were there one here who would answer in the affirmative, every mouldering bone in these narrow houses would find a tongue of rebuke for him! Better, far better would it be to gain a bare subsistence with our principles retained than to revel in luxury with the consciousness of treachery in our souls and the welcome collar of servitude on our necks! Rather than surrender character, better would it be in the last extremity to leave a soil on which it would be no longer possible for freemen to live, to take with us all that would remain of a historic Carolina, and to seek in some happier clime liberty to enjoy a few natural rights without being menaced by those who were our equals for not acquiescing in the tyranny of those who were our inferiors. That was the issue to which Carolina's great Statesmen declared, in the Senate of the United States, it would come in case force measures should succeed when employed against a Southern State. But, whither could we go from the relentless, all-pervading Spirit of Radicalism? Could we ascend into heaven, it would not be there; but should we make our beds in hell, behold, it would be there. If we should take the wings of the morning and dwell in the uttermost parts of the sea, even there would not its hand pursue us, and its right hand hold us? If we should say, surely the darkness will cover us, would not the night be made light about us by its incendiary conflagrations? Whither could we turn? Where on earth could the last asylum of the oppressed be found? Merciful God, we lift our appeal to Thee! Thou hast been our dwelling-place in all generations; cover us with Thy feathers, and let our trust be in the shadow of Thy wings!

But enough! [T]he mournful office which has summoned us hither waits to be performed. Let us hasten to remove these relics of unconquered patriots from a strange atmosphere less free than the air of the sepulchre. And if we have abandoned the last hope of maintaining their principles, if we are prepared to give up everything for which they died, let us discharge this office for them with the feelings of those who are interring their principles with their bones—of those who are solemnizing the funeral-rites, and burying the corpse, of Liberty. Let us place no emblem of hope above their heads, but having in the silence of death struck the last stroke of the spade upon their graves, retire from the scene as men withdraw from a field on which all has been lost.

But if it be our determination that we will cease to cherish the sacred principles which these men consecrated with their blood only when we cease to live, then let us, comrades, fellow-citizens, lovers of liberty, with reverent mien and tender hands consign all that remains of our brethren to their coveted resting-place in the bosom of their beloved Carolina. And as we cover them for their last sleep let us bury with the every proposal to us to apostatize from their principles, every tendency even to compromise them, every desire to recover position, wealth or ease at the sacrifice of honour, virtue and truth. Let us lay them down in hope; and as each modest stone rears its head above them, inscribe upon it a Resurgam—the token of our faith that their principles now trodden into dust will rise again, the symbol of our invincible resolution that these men shall not altogether have died in vain.

Heroes of Gettysburg! Champions of constitutional rights! Martyrs for regulated liberty! Once again, farewell! Descend to your final sleep with a people's benedictions upon your names! Rest ye here, Soldiers of a defeated—God grant it may not be a wholly lost—Cause! We may not fire a soldier's salute over your dust, but the pulses of our hearts beat like muffled drums, and every deep-drawn sigh breathes a low and passionate requiem. Memory will keep her guard of honour over your graves; Love will bedew them with her tears; Faith will draw from them her inspiration for future sacrifices; and Hope, kindling her torch at the fires which glow in your ashes, will, in its light, look forward to a day when a people once more redeemed and enfranchised will confess that your death was not in vain.

In 1874 the Reverend J. L. Girardeau was elected moderator of the General Assembly of the Presbyterian Church in the United States then meeting in Columbus, Mississippi. The next year he became professor of didactic and polemic theology at the Columbia Theological Seminary, a position he held for twenty years. He wrote several books including The Will in its Theological Relations (1891), an exposition of his belief that Truth lies somewhere midway between free-will and predestination. Dr. Girardeau died on 23 June 1898.

"The New South"

Atticus G. Haygood
President of Emory College

The Reverend Dr. Atticus G. Haygood, former Confederate chaplain and missionary, was not the first to coin the phrase "The New South," but this sermon caught the attention of the public almost immediately. It was a call for new attitudes and new actions.[3]

The New South: Gratitude, Amendment, Hope.
A Thanksgiving Sermon*[4]
By Atticus G. Haygood, D.D.
President of Emory College, Oxford, Ga.
Text: Psalm cxvii.
"O praise the Lord, all ye nations: praise him, all ye people. For his merciful kindness is great toward us: and the truth of the Lord endureth forever. Praise ye the Lord."

Nearly all nations, in both ancient and modern times, have incorporated into their religious and social customs annual thanksgivings for the blessings that crown each year. Your classic literature, young gentlemen of the College, will tell you of many festivals, celebrated by the Greeks and Romans, that publicly recognized the gifts of the gods in the vintage and harvests of their fields. These festivals were a part of their social and religious life. I cannot conceive of anything more becoming than that a Christian nation should celebrate a day of universal thanksgiving to the God and Father of our Lord Jesus Christ, the Father, also, of all men, and the giver of all good. To me it is most inspiring to think that at this hour there are millions of our brethren and fellow-citizens in this heaven-favored land engaged, like ourselves, in songs of praise and in the worship of our ever-

---

[3] Used by permission of Ms. Ginger Cain, University Archivist for Emory University, Atlanta GA.

[4] "*Preached before the students of Emory College and the citizens of Oxford, Ga., Nov. 25, 1880. Its publication was requested by a unanimous vote of the congregation, on a motion by the Rev. Dr. Morgan Callaway, Vice-President of the College." [The same Morgan Callaway who served with Chaplain Oliver in the Troup Artillery.]

merciful God. From unnumbered hearts and voices goes up the song: "O praise the Lord, all ye nations: praise him, all ye people. For his merciful kindness is great toward us: and the truth of the Lord endureth forever. Praise ye the Lord."

Before considering some of our peculiar obligations to be grateful to God, let us first ask two questions:

Why should we observe this particular day, Thursday, November 25, 1880, as a day of thanksgiving? And why should we assemble in our accustomed place of worship for this purpose?

I answer, Because our rulers have commanded it. We are here in obedience to proclamations from the chief executives both of our nation and State—from his Excellency Rutherford B. Hayes, President of the United States, and from his Excellency Alfred H. Colquitt, Governor of Georgia. These proclamations make it not merely our privilege, but our duty also, to meet together on this particular day to unite in public thanksgiving to Almighty God for his manifold and great mercies. And the Scriptures—our only rule of faith and practice—sustain this proposition. In all things lawful, as tested by the greater law of God, it is a Christian man's duty to obey those in authority.

I have thought it well to examine with some care the scriptural basis of this doctrine. Why should we obey law? Why ought we to promote the efficiency and usefulness of the government under which we live—whether municipal, state, or national? Whether domestic, civil, or ecclesiastical? The subject is broad, and there are many passages which bear upon it; but two or three will answer our present purpose. St. Paul, in his Epistle to the Romans, gives us a remarkable and unmistakable passage upon this subject. I read Romans xiii, 1–7: "Let every soul be subject unto the higher powers. For there is no power but of God: the powers that be are ordained of God. Whosoever therefore resisteth the power, resisteth the ordinance of God: and they that resist shall receive to themselves damnation. For rules are not a terror to good works, but to the evil. Wilt thou then not be afraid of the power? Do that which is good, and thou shalt have praise of the same: for he is the minister of God to thee for good. But if thou do that which is evil, be afraid; for he beareth not the sword in vain: for he is the minister of God, a revenger to execute wrath upon him that doeth evil. Wherefore ye must needs be subject, not only for wrath, but also for conscience' sake. For, for this cause pay ye tribute also: for they are God's ministers, attending continually upon this very thing. Render therefore to all their dues: tribute to whom tribute is due; custom to whom custom; fear to whom fear; honor to whom honor." St. Peter gives us a statement no less distinct and emphatic. I read 1 Peter ii, 13–18: "Submit yourselves to every ordinance of man for the Lord's sake: whether it be to the king, as supreme; or unto governors, as unto them that are sent by him for the punishment of evil doers, and for the praise of them that do well. For so is the will of God, that with well doing ye may put to silence the ignorance of foolish men: as free, and not using your liberty for a cloak of maliciousness, but as the servants of God. Honor all men. Love the brotherhood. Fear God. Honor the king. Servants, be subject to your masters with all fear; not only to the good and gentle, but also to the froward."

On this whole subject there can be, I think, no doubt as to the general doctrine of the Bible. It may be briefly stated thus: 1. God is the source of all law and authority, as he is the fountain of all existence. 2. He ordains government; that is, the thing, not the form. The texts just read are as applicable to one form as to another. 3. Obedience to "the powers that be" is a duty, not only as to our rulers, but as to God, who is the Governor of all. 4. Let us observe further, for it is a matter of vital importance, it is not to the King, or President, or Governor we owe obedience, but to the ruler; not simply to the highest, "the King as supreme," but to all rulers; to "Governors" also, of every grade, as representing the highest—rather, as representing, under him, the law and government that are back of him and above him; that is, to push the thought further, but not too far—not merely the law and constitution of the State, but the divine law and constitution of the universe. Wherefore St. Paul says: "Render to all their dues: tribute to whom tribute is due; custom to whom custom; fear to whom fear; honor to whom honor." St. Peter teaches the same doctrine. So does Moses. So does our Lord himself.

The foundation truth of the whole doctrine is this: Whoever administers legitimate authority represents, in so far forth as his office and functions go, God. Men speak sometimes of God's vicar-general. He has none—neither in King, nor Pope, nor Democracies. God's vicar is government—all government. Just as the simplest, as well as the most complex, processes of nature show forth the power and providence of God, to the humblest office-bearer, enforcing the least of all laws that are in harmony with eternal righteousness, represents the majesty and authority of the divine government. The principle and the obligation are the same, whether it be the President, the Governor, the local magistrate, the town marshal, the college professor, the village school mistress, the employer. In a word, whoever bears rightful rule does, in his sphere, whether it be great or small, represent God. And "whoso resisteth the power," in things lawfully commanded, "resisteth God." Be it remembered, furthermore, the obligation does not depend upon the personal character of the rulers, but upon the fact of their authority. Nero was Emperor of Rome, yet Paul commands obedience.

The right of amending bad laws, of seeking, by right methods, to change unsatisfactory administrations, or even the right of revolution, if it come to that, all guaranteed to our race by both the Scriptures and sound reason, it is not needful to discuss at this time. But it may be remarked, that even revolution should have this basis—that it seeks obedience to that which is the real law, and which ought to be the rule of existing governments. Disobedience becomes a duty when literal obedience would be real disobedience. "Children, obey your parents in the Lord," expresses the principle. There is no authority more sacred than the parental, but it must be "in the Lord;" otherwise, authority is so perverted that obedience becomes disobedience.

The duty of thanksgiving to God needs no argument. It is summed up in the language of St. James: "Every good and every perfect gift is from above, and cometh down from the Father of lights, with whom is no variableness, neither shadow of turning." Our entire dependence is stated by St. Paul in his discourse to the Athenians: "In Him we live, and move, and have our being." A very large part of the Scriptures is made up of different statements of this truth. In every age inspiration has been at infinite pains to teach men the truth and reality of their entire dependence upon God for all things. Thousands of texts might be brought forward in confirmation of this statement and in illustration of this truth. Have we life, health, peace, food, raiment, homes, friends, civilization, grace, religion—any blessing of any kind for our bodies or our souls, for this world or the next? Then it is God's free and gracious gift. It is the expression of his fatherly love for us, his children. If our industry has been blessed, it is God's blessing; if our friends have done us good, they are God's providential ministers to us. The Old Testament writers recognize the divine hand in every blessing; the Psalms of David, and of every other good man of every nation, are full of it. Our Lord Jesus teaches it in discourse and parable—above all, in his mighty works and mightier life. He calls upon the lilies of the valley, and the sparrows of the house-tops and the fields, to make plain and sure to us the doctrine of the infinitely gracious, all-wise, and all-embracing providence of God.

Let us consider briefly our special obligations to be grateful to God.

I waive, at this time, any discussion of those obligations that are common to all men, as the gift of life; the constant providences that bring us blessings every day and hour; above all, the gift of Jesus Christ and his gospel, bringing life and immortality to light. This morning let me mention some considerations that should influence us, as citizens of these United States, at this time, to thanksgiving, and especially as residents of that section of the country that is known as "the South."

1.We should thank God that ours is a Christian nation. Granting all that may be said of the wickedness that is in the land, it is still true that in its institutions and overruling spirit this is a Christian nation.

2.That our country is at peace, and that it is not threatened with war.

3.That we have passed through the quadrennial convulsion incident to the election of President so quietly and safely.[5] And we should be thankful that the election is so pronounced that the country is saved from the strain of a six-months' debate and conflict, such as we had four years ago, to settle the question of the Presidency. Although nearly half the people have been disappointed in the results of the election, still no sane man can doubt whether General Garfield has been elected President of the United States.

4,That we have had so clean and able an administration during the last four years.

5.That the general business interests of the whole country are so prosperous.

I come now to mention some reasons why we of "the South" should both "thank God and take courage."

I may possibly (but I trust not) speak of some things that you may not relish, and advance some views that you may not approve. If so, I only ask a fair and reasonable reflection upon them. If you should condemn them, I have left me at least the satisfaction of being quite sure that I am right, and that, if you live long enough, you will agree with me. And first, we of the South have great reason to be thankful to God that we are in all respects so

---

[5] Perhaps referring to the political convulsions the South had experienced every four years since 1860 whenever there was an election of a U.S. President. Most recently, for Haygood's congregation, was the contested election of Rutherford B. Hayes as 19th president (1877–1881). Haygood hoped Garfield would bring more stability. Ironically, President Garfield was assassinated his first year in office.

well off; and that, too, so soon after so great a war, so complete an upturning of our institutions, so entire an overthrow of our industries, so absolute a defeat of our most cherished plans. Recall briefly the last twenty years. Think of what we were in 1860 and in 1865. Then look about you and see what we are in 1880. What was thought by our people after Appomattox and April, 1865, as to the prospect before us? Some of you can recall the forebodings of that time as to the return of business prosperity, the restoration and preservation of civil and social order among ourselves, and the restoration of our relations to the Union.

You know how many of our best and bravest left our section forever in sheer despair. Behold now what wonders have been wrought in fifteen years!

Firstly, considering where and what we were fifteen years ago, considering the financial convulsions and panics that have swept over our country during that time—I might say, that have disturbed the civilized world—our industrial and financial condition today is marvelously good. It is not true, as certain croakers and "Bourbons,"[6] floated from their moorings by the rising tides of new and better ideas, are so fond of saying, that the South is getting poorer every day. These croakings are not only unseemly; they are false in their statements, as they are ungrateful in their sentiment. A right study of our tax returns will show that there is life and progress in the South. But statistical tables are not the only witnesses in such a case. Let people use their own eyes. Here is this one fact—the cotton crop, as an exponent of the power of our industrial system. In 1879 we made nearly five million bales; in 1880 it is believed that we will make nearly six million bales. We never made so much under the old system. It is nonsense to talk of a country as ruined that can do such things. There are more people at work in the South today than were ever at work before; and they are raising not only more cotton, but more of everything else. And no wonder, for the farming of today is better than the farming of the old days; and in two grand particulars: first, better culture; second, the ever-increasing tendency to break up the great plantations into small farms. Our present system is more than restoring what the old system destroyed.

The great body of our people not only make more than they did before the war, but they make a better use of it—they get unspeakably more comfort out of it. I am willing to make the comparison on any line of things

---

[6] "Bourbons" are defined as those who cling to the social and political ideas of previous generations, as in the Bourbon rulers of Europe who resisted revolutionary change in France, Spain, and Italy.

that you may suggest, for I know both periods. Remember that I am speaking of the great mass of the people, and not of the few great slave-holders, some of whom lived like princes, not forgetting, meantime, that the majority of our people never owned slaves at all.

For one illustration, take, if you please, the home-life of our people. There is ten times the comfort there was twenty years ago. Travel through your own county—and it is rather below than above the average—by any public or private road. Compare the old and the new houses. The houses built recently are better every way than those built before the war. I do not speak of any occasional mansion, that in the old times lifted itself proudly among a score of cabins, but of the thousands of decent farm-houses, comely cottages that have been built in the last ten years. I know scores whose new barns are better than their old residences. Our people have better furniture. Good mattresses have largely driven out the old-time feathers. Cook-stoves, sewing-machines, with all such comforts and conveniences, may be seen in a dozen homes today where you could hardly have found them in one in 1860. Lamps that make reading agreeable have driven out tallow dips, by whose glimmering no eyes could long read and continue to see. Better taste asserts itself: the new houses are painted; they have not only glass, but blinds. There is more comfort inside. There are luxuries where once there were not conveniences. Carpets are getting to be common among the middle classes. There are parlor organs, pianos, and pictures, where we never saw them before. And so on, to the end of a long chapter.

Test the question of our better condition by the receipts of benevolent institutions, the support of the ministry, the building, improvement, and furnishing of churches, and we have the same answer—our people are better off now than in 1860.

In reply to all this someone will say: "But it costs more to live than in 1860." I answer, True enough; but there is more to live for.

Secondly, the social and civil order existing in the Southern States is itself wonderful, and an occasion of profound gratitude. For any wrongs that have been done in our section, for any acts of violence on any pretext, for any disobedience to law, I have not one word of defense. Admitting, for argument's sake, all that the bitterest of our censors have ever said upon these subjects, I still say, considering what were the conditions of life in the Southern States after April, 1865, the civil and social order that exists in the South is wonderful. Our critics and censors forget, we must believe, the history of other countries. They have never comprehended the problem we had given us to work out after the surrender. Only those who lived through that period can ever understand it. Why has not this whole Southern country repeated the scenes of Hayti [*sic*] and San Domingo? Not the repressive power of a strong Government only; not the fear of the stronger race only; not that suggestions have been lacking from fierce and narrow fanatics; but chiefly in this, the conservative power of the Protestant religion, which had taken such deep root in the hearts and lives of our people. The controlling sentiment of the Southern people, in city and hamlet, in camp and field, among the white and the black, has been religious.

Thirdly, the restoration of our relations to the general Government should excite our gratitude. Possibly some do not go with me here. Then I must go without them, but I shall not lack for company; and as the years pass, it will be an ever-increasing throng. We must distinguish between a party we have, for the most part, antagonized, and the Government it has so long a time controlled. Whatever may be the faults of the party in power, or of the party out of power, this is, nevertheless, so far as I know, altogether the most satisfactory and desirable Government in the world; and I am thankful to God, the disposer of the affairs of nations and of men, that our States are again in relations with the general Government.

Should we be surprised or discouraged because our section does not control the Government? History, if not reason, should teach us better. Is there a parallel to our history since 1860—war, bitter, continued, and destructive, defeat utter and overwhelming, and all followed so soon by so great political influence and consideration as we now enjoy? When did a defeated and conquered minority ever before, in the short space of fifteen years, regain such power and influence in any age or nation? And this is the more wonderful when we consider the immeasurable capacity for blundering which the leaders of the dominant party in our section have manifested during these years of political conflict. And it is the more wonderful still when we consider how ready the dominant party of the other section has been to receive, as the expression of the fixed though secret sentiment of the mass of the Southern people, the wild utterances of a few extreme impracticables, who have never forgotten and have never learned. I tell you today, the sober-minded people who had read history did not, in 1865, expect that our relations with the general Government would be, by 1880, as good as they are. But they would have been better than they are if the real sentiment of the masses on both sides could have gotten itself fairly expressed; for these masses wish to be friends, and before very long they will sweep from their way those who seek to hinder them. My congregation, looked at on all sides and measured by any tests, it is one of the wonders of history that our people have, in so short a time, (fifteen years is a very short time in the life-time of a nation,) so far overcome the evil effects of one of the most bloody and desolating and exasperating wars ever waged in this world! And the facts speak worlds for our Constitution, for our form of government, and, above all, for our Protestant religion—a religion which will yet show itself to be the best healer of national wounds and the best reconciler of estranged brethren.

Fourthly, there is one great historic fact which should, in my sober judgment, above all things, excite everywhere in the South profound gratitude to Almighty God: *I mean the abolition of African slavery.*

If I speak only for myself, (and I am persuaded that I do not,) then be it so. But I, for one, thank God that there is no longer slavery in these United States! I am persuaded that I only say what the vast majority of our people feel and believe. I do not forget the better characteristics of African slavery as it existed among us for so long a time under the sanction of national law and under the protection of the Constitution of the United States; I do not forget that its worst features were often cruelly exaggerated, and that its best were unfairly minified; more than all, I do not forget that, in the providence of God, a work that is without a parallel in history was done on the Southern plantations—a work that was begun by such men as Bishop Capers, of South Carolina, Lovick Pierce and Bishop Andrew, of Georgia, and by men like-minded with them—a work whose expenses were met by the slaveholders themselves—a work that resulted in the Christianizing of a full half-million of the African people, who became communicants of our Churches, and of nearly the whole four or five millions who were brought largely under the all-pervasive and redeeming influence of our holy religion.

I have nothing to say at this time of the particular "war measure" that brought about their immediate and unconditioned enfranchisement; only that it is history, and that it is done for once and for all. I am not called on, in order to justify my position, to approve the political unwisdom of suddenly placing the ballot in the hands of nearly a million of unqualified men—only that, since it is done, this also is history that we of the South should accept, and that our fellow-citizens of the North should never disturb. But all these things, bad as they may have been and unfortunate as they may yet be, are only incidental to the one great historic fact, that *slavery exists no more*. For this fact I devoutly thank God this day! And on many accounts:

1. For the negroes themselves. While they have suffered and will suffer many things in their struggle for existence, I do nevertheless believe that in the long run it is best for them. How soon they shall realize the possibilities of their new relations depends largely, perhaps most, on themselves. Much depends on those who, under God, set them free. By every token this whole nation should undertake the problem of their education. That problem will have to be worked out on the basis of co-operation; that is, they must be helped to help themselves. To make their education an absolute gratuity will perpetuate many of the misconceptions and weaknesses of character which now embarrass and hinder their progress. Much also depends upon the Southern white people, their sympathy, their justice, their wise and helpful co-operation. This we should give them, not reluctantly, but gladly, for their good and for the safety of all, for their elevation and for the glory of God. How we may do this may be matter for discussion hereafter.

2. I am grateful that slavery no longer exists, because it is better for the white people of the South. It is better for our industries and our business, as proved by the crops that free labor makes. But by eminence it is better for our social and ethical development. We will now begin to take our right place among both the conservative and aggressive forces of the civilized and Christian world.

3. I am grateful because it is unspeakably better for our children and children's children. It is better for them in a thousand ways. I have not time for discussion in detail now. But this, if nothing else, proves the truth of my position: there are more white children at work in the South today than ever before. And this goes far to account for the six million bales of cotton. Our children are growing up to believe that idleness is vagabondage. One other thing I wish to say before leaving this point. We hear much about the disadvantages of our children of leaving them among several millions of freedmen. I recognize them, and feel them; but I would rather leave my children among several millions of free negroes than among several millions of negroes in slavery.

But leaving out of view at this time all discussion of the various benefits that may come through the enfranchisement of the negroes, I am thankful on the broad and unqualified ground, that there *is now no slavery in all our land*.

Does anyone say to me this day: "You have got new light; you have changed 'the opinions you entertained twenty years ago.'" I answer humbly, but gratefully, and without qualification: I have got new light. I do now believe many things that I did not believe twenty years ago. Moreover, if it please God to spare me in this world twenty years longer, I hope to have, on many difficult problems, more new light. I expect, if I see the dawn of the year 1900, to believe some things that I now reject and to reject some things that I now believe. And I will not be alone.

In conclusion, I ask you to indulge me in a few reflections that are, I believe, appropriate to this occasion.

And first of all, *as a people, let us of the South frankly recognize some of our faults and lacks, and try to reform and improve.* I know this is a hard task. And it is all the harder because we are the subjects of so much denunciation and misrepresentation by our critics of the Northern States, and of other countries. Much of this comes through sincere ignorance; much of it through the necessities of party politics; some of it, I fear, through sinful hatred; and much of it through habit. Many have so long thrown stones at us that it has become a habit to do so. The rather Pharisaic attitude that many public men at the North have assumed toward us has greatly embarrassed and arrested our efforts to discover our faults and to amend them. But all this only furnishes a reason for beginning the sooner and trying the harder. What is really good—and there is much that is good—let us stand by, and make it better if we can.

There are some unpleasant things that ought to be said. They are on my conscience. Will you bear with me while I point out some of the weaker points in our social make-up—some of the more serious lacks in our development?

First, then, let us endeavor to overcome our intense provincialism. We are too well satisfied with ourselves. We think better of ourselves than the facts of our history and our present state of progress justify. Some of us are nearly of the opinion that the words "the South" is a synonym for universe. As a people we have not enough felt the heartbeat of the world outside of us. We have been largely shut off from that world. Slavery did this, and this suggests another reason for gratitude that it exists no more. On this point I will add only one word more. Had we been less provincial, less shut in by and with our own ideas, had we known the world better, we would have known ourselves better, and there would have been no war in 1861.

Secondly, there is a vast mass of illiteracy among us. There is white as well as black illiteracy. There are multiplied thousands who can neither read nor write. They must be taught.

Thirdly, let us recognize our want of a literature. We have not done much in this line of things. It is too obvious to dispute about, it is too painful to dwell upon.

Fourthly, let us wake up to our want of educational facilities. Our public school system is painfully inadequate. Our colleges and universities are unendowed, and they struggle against fearful odds in their effort to do their work. We are one hundred years behind the Eastern and Middle States. We are also behind many of the new States of the West.

Fifthly, consider how behindhand we are with our manufacturing interests. And remember that nature never did more to furnish a people with the conditions necessary to successful manufactures. Does any one say, we lack capital? I answer, No, my friend, it was always so. It was so when we had capital. I have thought of these things a great deal. I have been placed where I was obliged to think of them, and I have reached this conclusion with perfect confidence of its correctness: Our provincialism, our want of literature, our lack of educational facilities, and our manufactures, like our lack of population, is all explained by one fact and one word—slavery. But for slavery, Georgia would be as densely peopled as Rhode Island. Wherefore, among many other reasons, I say again, I thank God that it is no more among us!

I mention, lastly, *some traits of character we should cultivate.*

First, the humble but all-prevailing virtues of industry and economy in business. There should be no non-producing classes among us—no wasting classes. The Northern people have more money than the Southern people, chiefly for the reason that they work more and save more.

Secondly, let us cultivate the sentiments and habits of political and social toleration. This is sorely needed among us. We need to feel that a man may vote against us and be our friend; we need to feel that we can be his friend although we vote against him.

Thirdly, let us cultivate respect for all law and authority as God's appointment. This is not a characteristic quality of our people. The educating influence of many generations have been unfavorable to the development of this sentiment as a mental habit, or, rather, as a mental characteristic. We must plant ourselves and bring up our children on the platform of St. Paul and St. Peter, as read and considered in the beginning of this discourse. Law, authority, we must reverence and obey as the ordinance of God.

Finally, let us cease from politics as a trust and a trade. Our duty of citizenship we must perform, but we should look no longer to political struggles as the means of deliverance from all our difficulties. If we succeed we would be disappointed. Political success may enrich a few place-hunters, who ride into office upon the tide of popular enthusiasm; but it will bring little reward to the masses of the people. There is no help for it; if we prosper, we must work for it. Our deliverance will come through millions of hard licks, and millions of acts of self-denial, through industry, economy, civil order, and the blessing of God upon obedience.

Secondly, let us look forward. Hitherto I have spoken before some of you of the South of the future. Again I say, Look forward! I do the heroic dead no injustice. But the only rational way in which we can emulate their virtues is to live for the country they died for. We are not called on to die for it, but to live for it; believe me, good friends, a much harder thing to do.

We should not forget what General Lee said to our General Gordon when it was all over: "We must go home and cultivate our virtues." Lee did that. He forthwith set himself to doing good. It is a good example. We are to do the work of today, looking forward and not backward. We have no divine call to stand eternal guard by the grave of dead issues. Here certainly we may say, "Let the dead bury their dead."

My friends, my neighbors, and my pupils, I declare to you today my hope is, that in twenty years from now, the words "the South" shall have only a geographical significance.

If any ask, "Why do you say such things here today?" I answer, [b]ecause I remember who are here, and I consider what they are to do and to be when we are gone hence.

I have spoken what I solemnly believe to be the truth. Moreover, the time has fully come when these truths should be spoken by somebody; and I try to do my part, persuaded that before many years there will happily be no longer any occasion or need for them to be spoken.

There is no reason why the South should be despondent. Let us cultivate industry and economy, observe law and order, practice virtue and justice, walk in truth and righteousness, and press on with strong hearts and good hopes. The true golden day of the South is yet to dawn. But the light is breaking, and presently the shadows will flee away. In fullness of splendor I may never see; but my children will see it, and I wish them to get ready for it while they may.

There is nothing weaker or more foolish than repining over an irrevocable past, except it be despairing of a future to which God invites us. Good friends, this is not 1860, it is 1880. Let us press forward, following the pillar of cloud and of fire always. With health and peace, with friends and homes, with civil liberty and social order, with national prosperity and domestic comfort, with bountiful harvests—with all these blessings, and good hope of heaven through Jesus Christ our Lord, let us all lift up our voices in the glad psalm of praise and thanksgiving: "Oh praise the Lord, all ye nations: praise him, all ye people. For his merciful kindness is great toward us: and the truth of the Lord endureth forever. Praise ye the Lord."

Bibliography

Primary Sources
Manuscripts and Record Collections

Consolidated Service Records of Confederate General and Staff Officers. Microfilm Records. Georgia Department of Archives and History, Morrow GA.

Deavenport, Thomas H. Diary. Tennessee State Library and Archives, Nashville TN.

Dobbs, Charles Holt. "Reminiscences of an Army Chaplain": Articles from The Presbyterian Christian Observer. *1874. U.S. Army Chaplain Museum Library, Fort Jackson SC.*

Girardeau, John L. "Address at the Reinterment Ceremony, Magnolia Cemetery in Charleston," Charleston *Daily Courier.* 11 May 1871. South Caroliniana Library. University of South Carolina, Columbia SC.

Kennedy, Francis Milton. Diary. Edited by Mrs. J. E. Hayes. vol. 5, Confederate Letters, Diaries and Reminiscences. Georgia Department of Archives and History, Morrow GA.

Oliver, Charles James. Journal. Special Collections Department. Robert W. Woodruff Library. Emory University, Atlanta GA.

Rice, Edmond Lee, ed. Civil War Letters of James McDonald Campbell. Undated typescript. Georgia Department of Archives and History, Morrow GA.

Smith, George G. Diary. Special Collections Department. Robert W. Woodruff Library. Emory University, Atlanta GA.

Tichenor, Isaac Taylor. Diary. Southern Baptist Historical Library and Archives, Nashville TN.

Books and Articles

Anthony, J. D. *Life and Times of Rev. J. D. Anthony. An Autobiography.* Atlanta GA: C. P. Byrd, Printer, 1896.

Betts, William A., ed. *Experience of a Confederate Chaplain 1861–1864*. Greenville, SC: privately printed, 1904.

Dabney, Robert L. *Life and Campaigns of Lieut. Gen. Thomas J. Jackson, (Stonewall Jackson)*. Harrisonburg VA: Sprinkle Publications, 1983.

Davis, Jefferson. *The Rise and Fall of the Confederate Government*. New York: Appleton and Co., 1881.

Doubleday, Abner. *Reminiscences of Forts Sumter and Moultrie in 1860–61*. Spartanburg SC: The Reprint Co., 1976.

Durkin, Joseph T., ed. *Confederate Chaplain: A War Journal of Rev. James B. Sheeran*. Milwaukee: The Bruce Publishing Co., 1960.

Evans, Clement A., ed. *Confederate Military History*. 13 vols. Secaucus NJ: Blue and Gray Press, 1975.

Haygood, Atticus G. "A Thanksgiving Sermon, Nov. 25, 1880." Edited by Judson C. Ward. *The New South*. Atlanta: Emory University Library, 1950.

Jones, J. William. *Christ in the Camp or Religion in the Confederate Army*. Harrisonburg VA: Sprinkle Publications, 1986.

Manarin, Louis H., ed. *Cumulative Index: The Confederate Veteran Magazine 1893–1932*. Wilmington NC: Broadfoot Publishing Co., 1986.

Minutes of the Annual Conferences of the Methodist Episcopal Church, South, 1888. Nashville: Publishing House M.E. Church, South, 1889.

Mullins, G.G., ed. *Caskey's Book: Lectures on Great Subjects*. St. Louis: John Burns Publishing Co., 1884.

Seddon, James A. *Regulations for the Army of the Confederate States, 1863*. Richmond: J. W. Randolph, 1863.

Sherman, William T. *Memoirs of General William T. Sherman*. New York: Da Capo Press, 1984.

Smith, George G. *The History of Georgia Methodism from 1786 to 1866*. Atlanta GA: A. B. Caldwell, 1913.

United States Government, Office of the Secretary of War. *The War of the Rebellion: A Compilation of the Official Records of the Union and Confederate Armies*. Ser. I, vol. 38. Washington, DC: Government Printing Office, 1891.

War Department. *Regulations for the Army of the Confederate States, 1863*. Richmond: J. W. Rudolph, 1863.

Secondary Materials

Ahlstrom, Sydney E. *A Religious History of the American People*. New Haven: Yale University Press, 1972.

Bettersworth, John K., ed. *Mississippi in the Confederacy: As They Saw It*. Baton Rouge: Louisiana State University Press, 1961.

Boatner, Mark M. *The Civil War Dictionary*. New York: David McKay Co., 1987.

Bradford, Ned, ed. *Battles and Leaders of the Civil War*. New York: Appleton-Century-Crofts, 1956.

Brinsfield, John W. "The Military Ethics of General William T. Sherman: A Reassessment," *Parameters* 12/2 (June 1982): 36-48.

Broadus, John A. *Memoir of James Petigru Boyce*. New York: A. C. Armstrong and Sons, 1893.

Cathcart, William, ed. *The Baptist Encyclopedia*. Philadelphia: Louis H. Everts, 1881.

Coulter, Ellis Merton. *The Confederate States of America 1861-1865*. Baton Rouge: Louisiana State University Press, 1950.

Davis, William C., et al. *Faith in the Fight: Civil War Chaplains*. Mechanicsburg PA: Stackpole Books, 2003.

Davis, Robert Scott, Jr., ed. *Requiem for a Lost City*. Macon GA: Mercer University Press, 1999.

Edgar, Walter. *South Carolina: A History*. Columbia: University of South Carolina Press, 1998.

Harwell, Richard B., ed. *The Confederate Reader: As the South Saw the War*. New York: David McKay Co., Inc., 1957.

Henderson, Lillian, ed. *Roster of the Confederate Soldiers of Georgia 1861–1865*. vol. 1. Hapeville GA: Logino and Porter, 1964.

Hewett, Janet B., ed. *The Roster of Confederate Soldiers 1861–1865*. vol. 7. Wilmington NC: Broadfoot Publishing Co., 1996.

Hieronymus, Frank L. "For Now and Forever: The Chaplains of the Confederate States Army." Ph.D. diss. University of California at Los Angeles, 1964.

Honeywell, Roy J. *Chaplains of the United States Army*. Washington DC: Office of the Chief of Chaplains, 1958.

Hubner, Charles W. "Some Recollections of Atlanta During 1864." *Atlanta Historical Bulletin* (1928): PAGE 2?

Lee, James W., et al. *The Illustrated History of Methodism*. St. Louis: The Methodist Magazine Publishing Co., 1900.

Lindsley, John B., ed. *The Military Annals of Tennessee: Confederate.*
    Nashville: J. M. Lindsley and Co., 1886.
McCallie, Elizabeth Hanleiter. *The Atlanta Campaign.* Atlanta GA: Atlanta
    Historical Society, 1939.
McPherson, Edward. *The Political History of the United States of America
    during the Great Rebellion.* Washington DC: Philp and Solomons, 1865.
Malone, Dumas, ed. *Dictionary of American Biography.* New York: Charles
    Scribner's Sons, 1946.
May, J. A. and J. R. Faunt. *South Carolina Secedes.* Columbia: University of
    South Carolina Press, 1960.
Miller, Francis T., ed. *The Armies and the Leaders: The Photographic History Of
    the Civil War.* New York: Castle Books, 1957.
Mitchell, Stephens. "Colonel L. P. Grant and the Defenses of Atlanta."
    Atlanta Historical Bulletin (1932):6.
Moore, John T. and Austin P. Foster. *Tennessee: The Volunteer State.* 4 vols.
    Nashville: S. J. Clarke Publishing Co., 1923.
Noll, Arthur Howard, ed. *Doctor Quintard, Chaplain C.S.A.* Sewanee TN:
    The University Press, 1905.
Norton, Herman A. "The Organization and Function of the Confederate
    Military Chaplaincy, 1861–1865." Ph.D. diss. Vanderbilt University,
    1956.
———. *Struggling for Recognition: The United States Army Chaplaincy,
    1791–1865.* Washington DC: Office of the Chief of Chaplains, 1977.
Pierce, Alfred M. *A History of Methodism in Georgia.* Atlanta: North Georgia
    Conference Historical Society, 1956.
Pitts, Charles. *Chaplains in Gray.* Nashville: Broadman Press, 1957.
Polk, William M. *Life of Leonidas Polk.* New York: Longsman, Green and
    Company, 1915.
Robertson, James I., Jr. *Stonewall Jackson: The Man, The Soldier, The Legend.*
    New York: MacMillan Publishing USA, 1997.
Romero, Sidney J. *Religion in the Rebel Ranks.* Lanham MD: University Press
    of America, 1983.
Scaife, William R. *Order of Battle: The Campaign for Atlanta.* Saline MI:
    McNaughton and Gunn, 1992.
Scott, E. C. *Ministerial Directory of the Presbyterian Church, US 1861–1941.*
    Austin TX: Von Boeckmann-Jones Co., 1942.
Shattuck, Gardiner H. Jr. *A Shield and Hiding Place: The Religious Life of the
    Civil War Armies.* Macon GA: Mercer University Press, 1987.

Smedlund, William S. *Campfires of Georgia's Troops, 1861–1865.* Lithonia GA: Kennesaw Mountain Press, 1994.

Sweet, William Warren. *The Methodist Episcopal Church and the Civil War.* Cincinnati: Methodist Book Concern Press, 1912.

Van Eldik, James. *From the Flame of Battle to the Fiery Cross.* Las Cruces NM: Yucca Tree Press, 2001.

Warner, Ezra J. *Generals in Blue.* Baton Rouge: Louisiana State University Press, 1964.

———. *Generals in Gray.* Baton Rouge: Louisiana State University Press, 1965.

Index